QUALITY AS AN ORGANIZATIONAL STRATEGY

QUALITY AS AN ORGANIZATIONAL STRATEGY

BUILDING A SYSTEM OF IMPROVEMENT

CLIFFORD L.
NORMAN

LLOYD P.
PROVOST

DAVID M.
WILLIAMS

PROVIDENT
HEIERMAN
PRESS

Austin, Texas

Quality as an Organizational Strategy
Building a System of Improvement

Clifford L. Norman
Lloyd P. Provost
David M. Williams

Published by Provident Heierman Press, Austin, Texas

Editor: Laura E. Pasquale, Ph.D.
Index: Russell Santana, e4editorial.com
Cover and interior book design: Yvonne Parks, pearcreative.ca
Publishing coordination: Janica Smith, publishingsmith.com

Library of Congress Control Number: 2024909257

Names: Norman, Clifford L., author. | Provost, Lloyd P., author. | Williams, David M. (David Michael), 1974- author.
Title: Quality as an organizational strategy : building a system of improvement / Clifford L. Norman, Lloyd P. Provost. David M. Williams.
Description: Austin, Texas : Provident Heierman Press, [2024] | Includes bibliographical references and index.
Identifiers: ISBN: 979-8-9904661-0-4 (paperback) | 979-8-9904661-3-5 (hardcover) | 979-8-9904661-1-1 (Kindle) | 979-8-9904661-2-8 (ePub) | LCCN: 2024909257
Subjects: LCSH: Total quality management. | Strategic planning. | Organizational change. | Leadership. | BISAC: BUSINESS & ECONOMICS / Total Quality Management. | BUSINESS & ECONOMICS / Leadership. | BUSINESS & ECONOMICS / Strategic Planning.
Classification: LCC: HD62.15 .N67 2024 | DDC: 658.4013--dc23

CONTENTS

FIGURES

TABLES

REFLECTIONS FROM LEADERS WITH QUALITY AS AN ORGANIZATIONAL STRATEGY

This book is about an approach to leadership of an organization based on the framework *Quality as a Business Strategy* (QBS) developed by Associates in Process Improvement in 1987. The title *Quality as an Organizational Strategy* (QOS) is updated to reflect the diverse organizations and industries that use the theory and methods presented. The material is detailed and comprehensive, but it only touches on the impact leaders and organizations experience when adopting QOS.

In the past 35 years, leaders of all types of organizations used the QOS framework to lead their organizations based on a quality philosophy. Many leaders have shared their eye-opening personal experiences of applying these methods in their organizations and the transformational nature of leading with quality as their strategy. Here are some of their reflections.

O. JOSEPH BALTHAZOR

President, CEO, and Founder of Hallmark Building Supplies Inc.

In the summer of 1994, I was exposed to QBS by a young entrepreneur who had just reviewed the strategy with several of his fellow distributors in Houston, Texas, sponsored by the DuPont Company. He shared the five activities (methods) associated with the "strategy." He then shared his purpose statement and systems view, which were very impressive. I knew he was a bright young man, but I also knew that he did not come up with this structure on his own, so I asked for the source of the strategy.

We contacted Cliff Norman at Associates in Process Improvement (API) and began with what he called an "Intent Day." He wanted to make sure that we were a fit for what API could contribute.

We had some knowledge of Deming quality from a five-day seminar I attended at Texas A&M University about quality applied to distributors. It was helpful, but it was not QBS. We were also taught, in detail, about Dr. Deming's Profound Knowledge. We invest a lot in leadership education for our senior leadership team and mid-level leaders, and profound knowledge represents 50% of that education.

The leadership team learned Dr. Deming's 14 Points from his book *Out of the Crisis*. The understanding of the 14 Points and profound knowledge resulted in many changes. For example, we recognized all associates for their contribution to the system. We do not have individual awards that make some associates feel good and some feel bad. We do not pay our salespeople on commission, creating conflicts when working with customers. We understand common and special cause variation, which helps us make better decisions.

We decided to introduce QBS to some of our key customers, which resulted in forming a formal partnership with them called the Partnership Resource Council (PRC). The intent was to introduce the customers, but it resulted in much more. These customers were competitors with each other, but their understanding of QBS allowed them to cooperate on solutions for common problems. They forged a "systems view" for their businesses and worked together on several improvement efforts. That kind of cooperation between competitors is rare, indeed. In effect, we enlarged our view of the system to include our customers and suppliers.

Our knowledge of QBS has been directly responsible for our growth as a company. We went from approximately $10 million in annual revenue with warehouses in Wisconsin and Minnesota to nearly $130 million with six warehouses serving twenty states. All six warehouses use the same processes for all functional areas of our system, regardless of the location.

We used our "systems view" and documented processes to plan and integrate new territorial expansions and acquisitions of other companies. Over less than thirty years, we replaced fifteen other DuPont distributors and bought the DuPont product lines from three of them.

I founded Hallmark Building Supplies Inc. in 1974. I can say, unconditionally, working with API and using QBS was the best decision I have made in my forty-eight years of leading the company. We leveraged their knowledge of QBS on and off from 1994. API continues to be an invaluable resource to our company and me. I am excited to get this new *Quality as an Organizational Strategy* book, and I will always be grateful for what I learned from QBS. The knowledge changed my life forever and made me a better father, husband, friend, and leader, and made us a very profitable company with a great culture.

ROGER B. QUAYLE

Senior Quality Manager at Brown & Root Inc., and Executive Vice President of Quality and Technology at Operations Management International Inc. (OMI)

We successfully implemented the five Quality As An Organizational Strategy (QOS) activities at Brown & Root (now part of KBR) and OMI (now part of Jacobs). I have also used the five activities in my work with not-for-profit and faith organizations.

The vector of measures (VOM) is hard work but fundamental. Quick wins for me in the engineering and construction business were financial and safety data, where data was plentiful. I spent several meetings with top financial executives at Brown & Root, developing control charts for financial reporting. They were very good managers, but this was extremely difficult for them to support. Reviewing the VOM monthly, quarterly, and annually with the leadership team for planning is fundamental to QOS and improvement.

Before QOS, my experience was that the "beautiful strategy" was finalized, communicated, and put on the shelf until the next year. QOS is the way to bring the strategy to life. Our most useful meeting of the year was always the strategic planning meeting (using the QOS methods) at Brown & Root and OMI. In addition, the VOM is an awesome way to monitor the strategy monthly and quarterly.

At OMI, we had a top-down approach to quality with QOS and a bottom-up strategy with our "Obsessed with Quality" training process. Every employee received quality training at least once a year, plus just-in-time training as needed. When I joined OMI, the bottom-up approach was in place and very good. We added QOS for the top-down leadership. In my view, an organization can't improve without both. In addition, you must budget for quality improvement each year. At OMI, the budget for quality and training was a percent of revenue. OMI was awarded the Malcolm Baldrige in the large business/service category in 2000.

The five activities bring Dr. Deming's philosophy to life. I can't thank Associates in Process Improvement enough for their training and support to my teams and me through the years.

BRUCE BOLES

Improvement Leader (retired), The Hewlett-Packard Company and Kaiser Permanente

I learned about Quality as an Organizational Strategy (QOS) in the mid-2000s at Hewlett-Packard as we worked with API (Cliff Norman and Lloyd Provost). Over the next fifteen-plus years at Hewlett-Packard and Kaiser Permanente, I taught its methods to leaders and quality improvement professionals and coached its application. As a result, the QOS framework became my core mental model, guiding teams to mature in their approach to leading quality.

In 2017, I was appointed the director of operations for Kaiser Permanente's Improvement Institute. I decided to apply QOS in my new role. The team learned about my leadership philosophy and the QOS framework and methods in the first few months. Next, we discussed and refreshed our purpose, focusing on who our customers are and their needs, our products, and services, and how we want to operate as a team. We shared our ideas for where we wanted to go and how to better contribute to Kaiser's Mission. We then identified our core processes and measures to build our first systems view of the organization. This helped the team focus on our system rather than each individual's work.

Since this initial work, the team continued to refine their processes and roles, created annual plans, and collaborated to improve their performance. This continued under the guidance of my successor, who is also aligned with Quality as an Organizational Strategy.

DR. MATS BOJESTIG

Director of Health and Medical Services, County Council, Jönköping County, Sweden

GÖRAN HENRIKS

Chief Executive of Learning and Innovation at Qulturum in Region, Jönköping County, Sweden

We were looking for models and methods to help us pursue quality. We used the Malcolm Baldrige framework when the Institute for Healthcare Improvement and the Robert Wood Johnson Foundation launched "Pursuing Perfection" to learn if and how healthcare organizations could improve performance, resulting in more efficient and effective healthcare systems.

"Pursuing Perfection" became an opportunity to show that system-wide quality improvement was possible and set a new benchmark for healthcare quality management. Associates in Process Improvement provided coaching and improvement expertise.

We worked together with a Dutch system and four English systems within the National Health Service. We were the only self-funded participant in the effort. During the planning phase, the Institute for Healthcare Improvement (IHI) faculty directed each organization to develop a portfolio of projects. We found it challenging to pick projects without appreciating the system. Cliff Norman and Jim Reinertsen served as our coaches. Cliff Norman helped us understand our organization as a system by developing a linkage of processes. Paul Batalden previously introduced this concept to us in an earlier exercise. This systems view helped us see where we needed to work. It was also the start of our use of the methods described here.

Jönköping County continues to use QBS twenty-plus years later. We use the parts of QBS to onboard and develop new leaders: our purpose, appreciating the system of processes and our work within it, and using the Science of Improvement to get better. We also expanded beyond healthcare into other areas of the county and municipalities. This is now who we are, and you can see examples anywhere you go.

DAVE HEARN

President, Metalforms Ltd.

While working for Brown & Root, I was first introduced to the Quality as a Business Strategy (QBS) methods and tools. This learning has stayed with me throughout my career. As a member of the continuous improvement staff, I learned the value and importance of teams and the criticality of senior management support. As I continued my career, I began teaching these methods and tools to others; the holistic approach of QBS is most beneficial to any organization, especially those who are faced with change and must adapt quickly.

Now that I am a business owner, I see that our company needs to make many changes quickly. These tools and methods have been critical to our business. As an owner and the president of our company, I insist that senior management support is a given. We trained our key personnel and expected them to be actively involved in improvements.

The COVID years slowed our progress but did not stop it. As part of onboarding new employees, I sit down with each one and discuss our purpose and practical values. I invite everyone to observe our behavior, and a follow-up meeting is held in ninety days when I ask them for examples of where we are living up to values and discuss areas where we are weak.

My learning will never be complete, and QBS provides the framework for this learning.

PETER MARGOLIS, MD, PHD

Co-Director, James M. Anderson Center for Health Systems Excellence, Cincinnati Children's Research Foundation Chair in Improvement Science, Professor of Pediatrics, Cincinnati Children's Hospital Medical Center

Quality as a Business Strategy (QBS) provided a framework that enabled me to build on what I had learned about quality improvement and apply it to the complex work of leading and managing an entire organization as a system. It was extremely useful as a means to think about building a new organizational form called a Learning Health Network. It has been the foundation for developing the ImproveCareNow (ICN)

Network for children and youth living with Crohn's disease and ulcerative colitis. I credit the learning from QBS for ICN's receipt of the Drucker Award for Nonprofit Innovation.

QBS has been useful for several reasons:

- It is integrative. Organizations tend to separate activities like strategy, operations, and support functions (e.g., HR, finance) without explicit ways to bring them together. QBS provides a way to organize leadership activities so that the implied connections become more explicit.
- QBS helped me, as a leader, understand leadership as a process that could be developed to improve the organization's performance. Previous leadership training focused on topics such as personal development, attributes of the leader as a person, communication, structure, and value. QBS enabled me to learn to view leadership as a set of processes and activities that could be optimized over time, and that might be independent of personal attributes.
- It has a developmental lens. It recognizes that building a quality focus into an organization is a journey. As leaders, it's common to aspire to achieve transformative performance levels. QBS provides a data-driven approach to understanding work as a process and then applying methods to systematically identify and improve key processes. Pursued relentlessly, one can begin to understand its potential.
- It was modular and practical. The book's format identifies a set of activities that take place in organizations. The chapters provide practical guidance that is clear enough to be adapted to an organization's specific needs (e.g., a system for planning) and priority setting.

I have found using it immensely helpful over a twenty-year experience.

DIANNE K. IRBY

Vice President and Managing Director (retired), Brown & Root/KBR. Past Executive Director, City of Mobile, Alabama

I was first introduced to Quality as a Business/Organizational Strategy in the mid-1980s while serving as Vice President of Quality Management for a large, diverse global engineering and construction company. The conceptual framework of quality from the

Deming principles provided me with substantial knowledge and tools that I used and benefited from the balance of my forty-year career.

API was the consulting group I worked with early on, and the body of information they brought to our organization provided a structure for learning and improving at a time of fast-paced change in the industry. The focus was on improving business processes and services to better meet our customers' Needs. In addition, their approach helped us enhance the flow of information from management to employees—where the work gets done, and from employees to management—full circle, resulting in better communication and performance.

It profoundly impacted me as I used this framework and moved from staff roles to operations in the engineering/construction world. I went on to leadership roles with nonprofits and executive management of private and public institutions. I spent the last five years of my career as Executive Director of Engineering, Planning, and Development for the City of Mobile, Alabama. QBS was essential to my ability to lead change and improvement in these diverse environments because the QBS platform is so portable—so transferrable to these different organizations. The vocabulary it provided made the concepts teachable and applicable.

I'm indebted to API and its focus on the teachings of Dr. Deming, along with countless resources, reading and study guides, colleagues, and mentors along the way.

JOSEF PENNER

Executive Director (retired), Mecklenburg Emergency Medical
Services Agency, Charlotte, North Carolina

For me, the pursuit of Quality as a Business Strategy (QBS) came by chance. I participated in the Improvement Advisor program at the Institute for Healthcare Improvement when the faculty—Sandy Murray and Lloyd Provost—presented an overview of the five QBS activities.

QBS is an operating system, a coherent symbiotic method to lead an organization. I wish I'd learned it in business school or earlier in my years of executive leadership.

We felt we were doing well at MEDIC, and our industry benchmarks reflected it. However, when we started working with Dave Williams and assessed our purpose, we quickly learned that we had a lot to understand about our business and how to do it.

We had used Shewhart charts for years but were weak in understanding the interconnectedness of actions and processes within the business and with results. When we began developing a system map of the organization, we realized we had much work to do and could now see where to work. Processes were not defined; people were not clear about what the work was or what the next person's requirements of their work included. All work is accomplished in processes. Now, we know what the work is, the processes involved and performance, who is responsible for what, and the system's interdependence toward our outcomes.

In addition to the traditional planning process inputs, we can now prioritize and anticipate the impact of improvement. And when coupled with expected volume changes, the planning process results in strategic objectives, improvement projects, operating plans, and financial plans all aligned to drive performance—planning to improve and planning to operate changed how we deploy our strategy. Results are better: measurable, public, and reflecting the improvement achieved.

Finally, two important surprises: culture and momentum are two outcomes I did not anticipate, yet they are two of the most important results of implementing this system! If I had appreciated how QBS provided the ability to manage culture, see employees thrive, and build robust momentum earlier, our implementation would have been different. It isn't easy to quantify the impact on momentum and team member trust/trustworthiness year after year.

These are real-life experiences of the robust effect of using the Quality as an Organizational Strategy (QOS) method to build a system of improvement across various sectors and organization types. This book presents those methods.

PREFACE

Throughout the 1980s, W. Edwards Deming reached thousands of people with his message to transform their organizations based on his concepts of quality. He envisioned an organization that works as a system with the aim for all stakeholders to win. This focus would set off a **Chain Reaction:**[1]

> **Improve quality > Decrease costs through less rework > Improve productivity > Capture market with better quality and lower price > Stay in business > Provide jobs and more jobs**

The transformation to ignite this chain reaction requires a new style of management and new philosophies, knowledge, and methods.

Organizations that understood the importance of Deming's message sent others to his seminars for education and began to work to accomplish the transformation. But most were overwhelmed by the magnitude of this transformation. They struggled with as many failures to move ahead as successes. In his last book, Deming acknowledged this lack of progress, saying, "These concepts had not yet penetrated company-wide systems and the overall business strategy and planning of organizations."[2]

Many organizations had a difficult time connecting their activities in quality improvement to the strategic and day-to-day management of their organizations. What was missing was a framework to get started. The framework needed to:

- Be applicable to all types and sizes of organizations.
- Give guidance, but not be too prescriptive.
- Lead to quick wins as well as long-term performance.
- Incorporate useful systems already in place to make improvements.
- Be robust relative to the speed of implementation, order of focus, and setbacks.
- Self-correct and self-improve as progress is made.

In 1985, the Associates in Process Improvement (API) members began work on a framework to help organizations incorporate the philosophy and concepts taught by Deming into the way they led their organizations. Jerry Langley, Ron Moen, Tom Nolan, and Lloyd Provost of API worked with Deming at his four-day seminars throughout the 1980s. In addition, they were working and consulting with different types of organizations, trying to incorporate Deming's ideas.

The framework that API developed in 1987 was called "Quality as a Business Strategy" (QBS). The strategy elements evolved from Deming's "Production as System," which he first presented in 1950.[3] The three basic elements of this strategy were:

1. A foundation of continuous matching of products and services to a Need through design and redesign of processes, products, and services.
2. An organization that performs as a system to achieve this, focusing on matching the Need.
3. A set of methods to ensure that changes result in real improvements to the organization.

The QBS framework cannot simply be installed or implemented in an organization like a new computer operating system. There is a need for knowledgeable leadership to carry out the strategy, make it successful, and continually improve its application. Five activities for the organization's leaders provide the structure to begin working on making quality a business strategy. These activities are centered on:

1. Purpose.
2. Viewing the organization as a system.
3. Obtaining information to improve.
4. Planning.
5. Managing improvement.

These five activities form a system for the leaders of an organization to focus their learning, planning, and actions.

During the late 1980s, QBS developed into a comprehensive strategy with methods centered on the five leadership activities. Organizations began to use this framework in 1987. Cliff Norman and Kevin Nolan joined the API team and helped add more description, detail, and examples around each method. Feedback, experience, and examples from large and small organizations in a variety of industries, government, and education have provided the material for a workbook first produced by the API team in 1995.[4] In addition, some of API's clients used this framework to win the Malcolm Baldrige National Quality Award.[5]

QBS is not the same as a quality management system that focuses on day-to-day operations, quality control, and quality assurance activities. And it does not separate "quality activities" from running the organization. Instead, those operational activities are assumed to be present; when they are lacking, QBS will lead to their development and enhancement just as it would address any other weakness in the organization.

Our experience with QBS is that it accelerates the pace at which organizations improve and reduces the chance that improvement will be a short-lived experience. The structure of the strategy, centered on the five leadership activities, provides enough guidance to begin the process of building improvement into the organization's fabric. The structure is flexible enough to incorporate many components of a quality-focused organization that have already been developed in many companies. The QBS framework can incorporate new methods as they are developed. QBS can be used to focus an organization on new directions as its marketplace or competitive situation changes.

Another observation from organizations using QBS is that employees can better connect their work (both operations and improvement) to their organization's mission. This provides both motivation and pride in their work. This outcome has been recognized in several industries.[6]

This book is our attempt to organize what we have learned in the past twenty-five years about incorporating Deming's management philosophies and concept of profound knowledge into the fabric of organizations. We have renamed this approach "Quality as an Organizational Strategy" (QOS) to acknowledge that many organizations do not have a business focus. Education, health care, and nonprofits, for example, have the same need for an organizational strategy as corporations, but they do not usually have a strong business orientation.[7] Many of these organizations are exploring the concept of becoming a "learning organization,"[8] and QOS brings the methods to do this.

We have created this book as an introduction to the theories, concepts, and methods for building improvement into the fabric of an organization. The chapters of this book contain examples from our clients and other organizations to help appreciate the methods and vignettes we have created to help bring the concepts in the chapters to life. The vignettes are shaded in each chapter to differentiate them from real examples. We also developed a companion field guide with additional examples, templates, tools, and stories about using QOS. While the chapters here illustrate examples of applications of the QOS methods, our publication *The QOS Field Guide* contains some cases to illustrate applications of all the methods in organizations.

Is it time to get the chain reaction working in your organization? The first step in the chain reaction is to "improve quality," so a review, understanding, and consolidation of current projects designed to improve processes or products is the high-leverage place to start. If formal improvement activity does not exist, then initiate a few projects to create the opportunity for leaders to learn about improvement in their organization. Then quickly read Chapter 11, "Getting Started." After that, begin exploring the other chapters in this book. We hope you have many rewarding experiences with *Quality as an Organizational Strategy*!

NOTES

1. W. Edwards Deming, *Out of Crisis* (Cambridge: Massachusetts Institute of Technology, Center for Advanced Engineering Study, 1986), 3. (Learn more about Deming in Chapter 2.)

2. W. Edwards Deming, *The New Economics: For Industry, Government, Education*, 2nd ed. (Cambridge: Massachusetts Institute of Technology, Center for Advanced Engineering Study, 1994), 37.

3. "The 1950 Lecture to Japanese Top Management," Cecelia S. Killian, *The World of W. Edwards Deming*, 2nd ed. (Knoxville: SPC Press, 1992), 61–71.

4. Associates in Process Improvement, *Quality as a Business Strategy: Building a System of Improvement* (Austin: Associates in Process Improvement, 2007).

5. See "Using Quality Awards to Evaluate Progress," in *The QOS Field Guide*.

6. John R. Drew and Meghana Pandit, "Why Healthcare Leadership Should Embrace Quality Improvement," *BMJ* 368 (March 31, 2020): m872, https://doi.org/10.1136/bmj.m872.

7. Stephanie Mercado, "Quality As A Business Strategy To Address National Healthcare Crisis," *Chief Executive* (February 10, 2023): https://chiefexecutive.net/quality-as-a-business-strategy-to-address-national-healthcare-crisis/. Stephanie Mercado, CEO of the National Association for Healthcare Quality, advocates adopting quality as a business strategy to address the current healthcare crisis.

8. David A. Garvin, "Building a Learning Organization," *Harvard Business Review* (July 1, 1993): https://hbr.org/1993/07/building-a-learning-organization.

ACKNOWLEDGMENTS

Goethe observed, "Knowing is not enough; we must apply. Willing is not enough; we must do." The authors are privileged that many leaders with deep experience in a wide range of businesses follow this dictum by integrating Quality as an Organizational Strategy (QOS) into their organizations, like the people below who reviewed this book. One remarked, "Once you use QOS, you can't return to traditional approaches." We are profoundly grateful for their insights and guidance in our learning journey.

Don Berwick – Don was instrumental in helping Associates in Process Improvement (API) integrate the Deming Philosophy and Science of Improvement into healthcare globally. Since 1995, he has provided guidance and contributed to our knowledge of improvement through his leadership at the Institute for Healthcare Improvement (IHI).

Mats Bojestig – Mats is a physician and the director of health and medical services in Jönköping, Sweden. For over 20 years, he has led his colleagues to develop their community's health system with patients at the center and quality as their strategy. He uses QOS's five activities to develop leaders who contribute to improving the community.

Bruce Boles – Bruce led several efforts within Hewlett Packard to use QOS ideas and concepts, enabling many HP organizations to make improvements. Bruce more recently worked with Kaiser Permanente to advise on QOS and the Science of Improvement.

David Hearn – David worked as a manager at Brown and Root during the early phases of developing QOS. More recently, as CEO of Metalforms Inc., David was instrumental in introducing QOS to his leadership team.

Göran Henriks – Göran is the former chief executive of learning and innovation at Qulturum in Region Jönköping County, Sweden. He has convened and led improvement initiatives locally and worldwide. Göran's work at Qulturum has expanded the application of the Science of Improvement and helped leaders learn how to pursue QOS.

Kevin Little – Kevin is an improvement advisor for IHI worldwide. In this role, he has offered guidance in the development of QOS.

Byron Murray – Byron has worked with QOS from its early development and has advised clients on the application and use of its methods. The work has contributed to our knowledge of QOS.

Kevin Nolan – Kevin is a partner in API and was instrumental in the early development of the ideas associated with QOS and the Science of Improvement. He is also a senior fellow at IHI and has assisted clients globally.

Jane Norman – Jane was an early adopter of QOS as a vice president at ConAgra Poultry; this learning contributed greatly to its initial development. She later applied QOS as a vice president of operations at the Conrad Company (DuPont distributor) and as COO of OCHIN, a software developer for medical records. As a consultant, she advised clients on applying QOS methods at Eklund's Custom Elevator Cabs and Jönköping Healthcare in Sweden.

Josef Penner – Joe is the former executive director of the ambulance system serving Mecklenburg County in Charlotte, North Carolina. A constant learner, he trained as an improvement advisor while he was chief executive and led his leadership team through developing and using QOS in the organization.

Roger Quayle – Roger began helping the leadership team at Brown & Root as a manager within the quality improvement department during our efforts in the early development of QOS. Roger became a vice president of OMI Inc., where he led the effort to develop QOS, which resulted in OMI winning the Malcolm Baldrige National Quality Award.

Mike Taigman – Mike is a former paramedic and improvement advisor. He helps paramedics and ambulance leaders understand the Science of Improvement and how to incorporate QOS ideas in the emergency service sector.

FOUNDATIONS

CHAPTER 1

INTRODUCTION TO QUALITY AS AN ORGANIZATIONAL STRATEGY

Monique just accepted the position of chief executive at a successful health care informatics company:

> I take great pride in breaking through the glass ceiling and stretching to meet the challenge of a new role leading an organization. My previous five-year stint was a rewarding experience as Chief Quality Officer. My focus was on using improvement methods to develop innovative solutions for the company's growth opportunities.
>
> I wonder if I can apply the concepts and tools of quality improvement to develop the strategies in my new organization. Can I build the organization's strategy around the concepts of quality? I am eager to discuss this with my leadership team on my first day of work next week. I will start by asking the team to reflect on the current strategies that drive the organization.

During the past fifty years, many significant changes have occurred throughout the world relative to the concepts of quality and improvement. These changes include:

- More focus on quality and customer satisfaction.
- Higher customer expectations of quality and reliability.
- Increased numbers of people involved in the improvement of quality.

- Increased access to data and information and computing power.
- Embracing the Science of Improvement by health and education.
- Recognition that many organizations operate in complex environments that require increased cooperation and more use of teams, starting with the leadership team.
- Increased use of statistical methods for improvement programs that get results.
- Greater coverage of quality issues in newspapers and magazines.
- The maturity of "quality awards" for nations, states, and communities.

Organizations trying to build quality into their core and make the **Science of Improvement**[1] serve as their theory of management, and their methods to get results require a roadmap. This chapter will introduce W. Edwards Deming's charge that leaders need a new theory of management and an organizational strategy built on quality. Then, the chapter will define quality as a strategy and describe a theoretical framework that leads to a set of five activities for leaders that can generate both immediate results and improved long-term performance.

DEMING AND QUALITY AS AN ORGANIZATIONAL STRATEGY

In *The New Economics*, Deming challenged the progress in incorporating the concepts of quality in organizations.[2] He acknowledged the implementation of quality principles and methods to improve individual processes but said that these concepts had "not yet penetrated company-wide systems and the overall **business strategy** and planning." Deming described "a flow diagram" that "was the spark that in 1950 and onward turned Japan around."[3] Figure 1.1 shows an adaptation[4] of that diagram that "directed their knowledge and efforts into a system of production...." Deming's challenge was to think about the organization as a system and to drive the concepts of quality at the strategic level.

Appreciating organizations as systems designed to fulfill a fundamental Need was, and still is, a radical shift from the prevailing management style, which focused on the organizational chart and on merely meeting customer requirements. Deming[5] argued this required transformation and framed the **System of Profound Knowledge**—an appreciation for a system, understanding variation, a theory of knowledge, and psychology—as a theory providing leaders with an outside view or lens to look at and understand the organization. Readers might recognize these lenses as the foundation of what is today known as the Science of Improvement (it is the focus of Chapter 2).

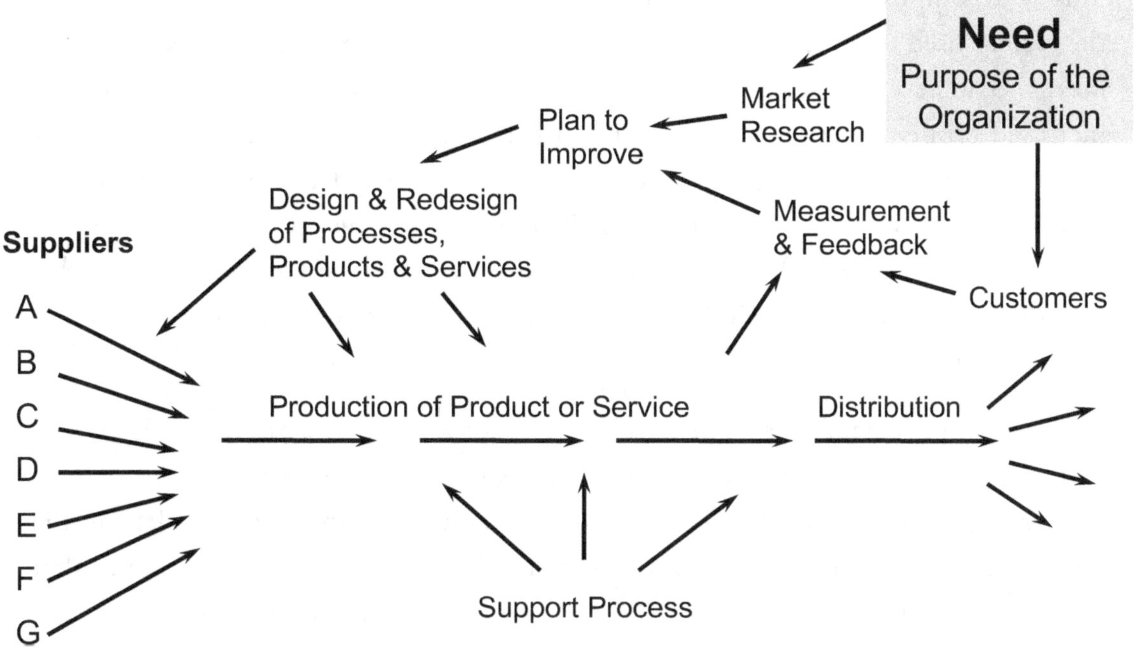

Figure 1.1. An organization viewed as a system.

Building on this foundational science, leaders and staff integrate their specific subject matter expertise with improvement theories and methods to develop, test, implement, and spread changes that result in improvement. QOS provides the methods (through the five leadership activities) for leaders to apply the theories of the Science of Improvement as their key organizational strategy.

An organizational strategy drives an organization's actions and decisions to accomplish its purpose. The strategy can lead to quick wins as well as long-term success. Adopting quality as an organizational strategy requires learning and focus from the organization's leadership team in order to benefit from the concept of quality at the organizational level. This strategy can be applied to all types of organizations, including manufacturing and service companies, schools, hospitals, and government agencies. The strategy directly aligns with the concept of a learning organization.[6]

> **Quality as an Organizational Strategy (QOS) enables the organization to produce products and services that will be in demand and provide a place where people can take pride in their contributions to the organization's purpose.**

This is accomplished by focusing on understanding, challenging, and improving the system used to get results for customers. Concentrating on quality becomes the means to achieve the goals and objectives of the organization, whether that means increased profits or share of the market, growth, better-educated citizens, a cleaner environment, lower costs, higher productivity, or increased return on investment. Deming refers to this as the quality chain reaction.[7] If quality is to become their organizational strategy, the leaders of the organization must understand how this chain reaction applies to their organization and then provide leadership for carrying out the strategy.

Before Deming, managers viewed the concept of quality as a tradeoff, one where higher quality means increases in costs for people, time, or inspection to control or assure quality. Staff in quality control and quality assurance would calculate the "cost of quality"[8] to ensure that not too much was spent on inspection and other detection activities. This perception is still present in many organizations today. Figure 1.2 contrasts the view of quality based on inspection with Deming's view of quality improvement. Deming would often ask leaders, "Why is it that productivity increases as quality improves? Anyone who has ever worked for a living can tell you in just two words: less rework."[9]

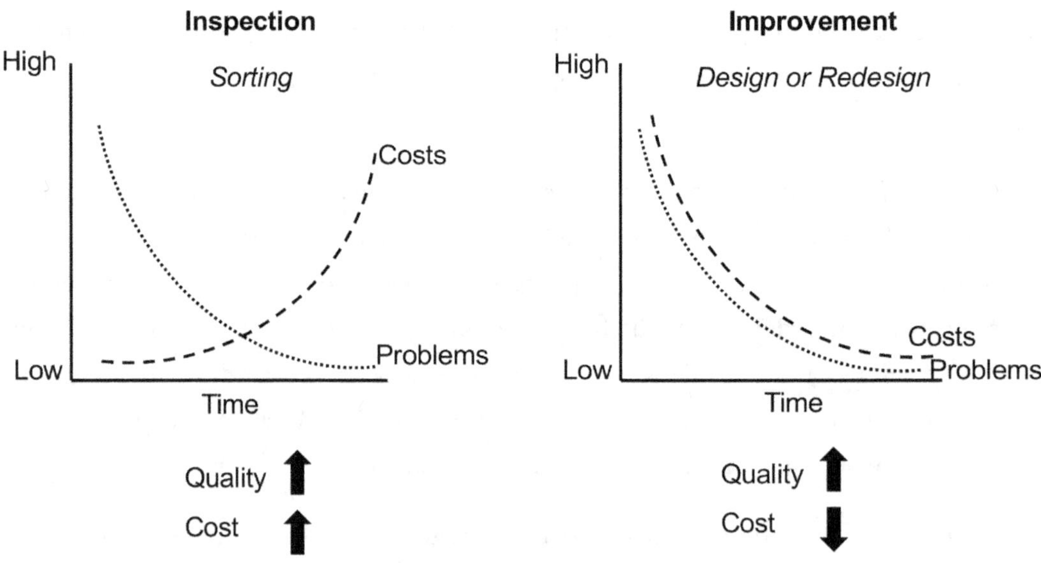

Figure 1.2. Two paths to achieve quality in products and services.

What are some attributes of an effective organizational strategy?

- Provides methods to reach the goals of the organization
- Can deliver short-term wins as well as long-term success
- Encourages and recognizes the importance of innovation to stay in business
- Can be sustained over the long term while addressing short-term needs
- Balances internal and external focus
- Compatible with different divisions and functions in the organization
- Remains useful despite changes in the marketplace
- Can be understood and practiced by all members of the organization

Over time, organizations have adapted and adopted a variety of business strategies. Table 1.1 shows nine common business strategies used as organizational strategies. The chosen strategy defines how leaders intend to develop (or grow) the organization.[10,11] Choosing to focus the organization on a particular strategy does not imply that other strategies are not also important to success.

Quality as an organizational strategy provides an alternative to these traditional choices. QOS can incorporate many aspects of conventional strategies. While strategy must be dynamic and react to the realities of the marketplace, QOS provides a consistent approach to leading the organization through both steady times and periods of change.

THEORETICAL FRAMEWORK FOR QUALITY AS AN ORGANIZATIONAL STRATEGY (QOS)

To set quality in the framework of an organizational strategy, we explore three foundational areas:

1. The foundation of the strategy
2. The transformation from the mental model of the organizational chart to viewing the organization as a system
3. Methods to ensure that the changes made result in improvement

Table 1.1. Examples of business strategies that organizations have adopted

Strategy	Typical characteristics of strategy	Example
Product (Service)	New products (or services) evolve from existing products. Quality of product or service and reputation key to success.	Automotive industry, Apple, Mayo Clinic, Harvard University
Customer (Market)	Understand the desires of a specific group of customers. Develop products to meet these desires. Customer satisfaction and loyalty determine success.	Luxury hotels, health insurance plans
Pricing	Including "low cost" and exclusivity "high price." Offer prices to the marketplace aimed at specific market segments.	Retail (Walmart, Neiman Marcus), airlines
Technology	Derive new products from core technologies. Look for new applications of technology.	Laser systems, Google
Platform	Build products and services around a scalable platform.	Smartphones, Uber, Facebook
Production (operational excellence)	Keep production running at full capacity. Expand capacities and increase productivity. Often commodity products where low price determines success.	Oil refineries, agriculture
Raw material	Take advantage of position/control of raw materials.	De Beers, mining, Exxon
Distribution	Focus on effective logistical methods. Products and services offered are designed to leverage the delivery system.	Amazon, UPS
Financial	Buy and sell companies, divisions, product lines, etc., to maximize the organization's financial objectives.	Holding companies, PNC Financial Services Group Inc.

The Foundation of Quality as a Strategy

How do organizations make improvements that can show immediate and sustained results? There are five essential ways for this to happen:

1. Design of a new product (or service)
2. Redesign of an existing product (or service)
3. Design of a new process
4. Redesign of an existing process
5. Improvement of the system as a whole (e.g., a new software platform for the company)

The concepts of a **change** and an **improvement** are closely linked. **All improvement requires a change, but not all change will lead to improvement.** Figure 1.3 (using Shewhart chart[12]) provides an **operational definition of an improvement**:

A change that alters how work is done, or the makeup of a product, that produces visible, positive differences (relative to historical norms) in relevant measures, sustained into the future.[13]

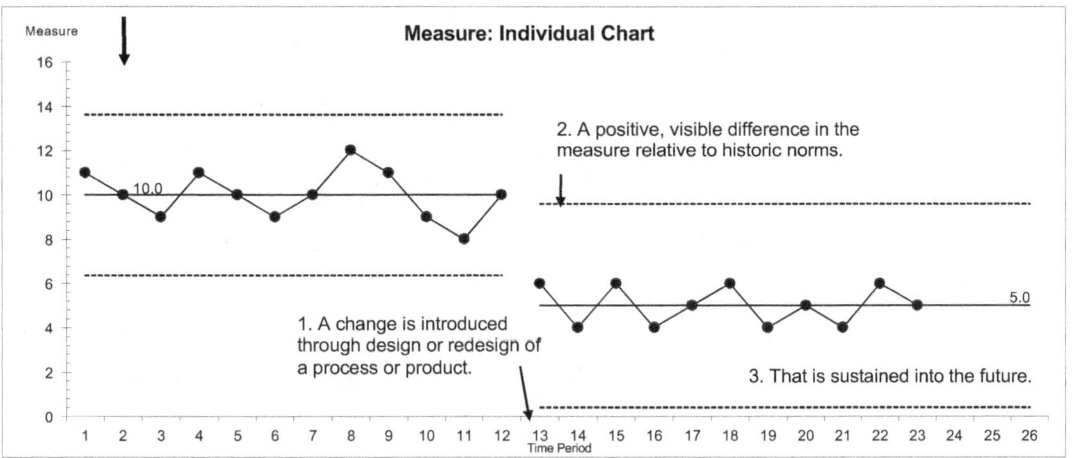

Figure 1.3. Operational definition of an improvement.

It is a challenge to know where improvements should be focused in an organization. Should we design a new product, or should we simply redesign the process that produces the product? Should we make some improvements to the system as a whole? The five approaches to making changes listed earlier in this section may be carried out within various parts of the organization. The efforts to improve will include innovation and creativity. These efforts must be coordinated and focused on a common purpose to succeed.

The **foundation of quality as an organizational strategy** that provides the focus for these five approaches to change is **the ongoing matching of products and services to a Need.**

Two essential ideas underlying this concept are **Need** and **matching**. The following two sections discuss these two ideas.

UNDERSTANDING THE NEED

The Need[14] in the marketplace, or society, that the organization intends to fulfill provides the focus for matching and the permanence of the QOS strategy. Focusing on this Need helps organizations understand why customers have come to them in the past and why they will continue to be customers in the future. For example, a Need may be for personal transportation, food, shelter, garbage disposal, a pleasant environment in the workplace, or transfer of knowledge. If the strategy is to sustain an organization over the long term, then the Need should be expected to persist over a long period.

If working or living in a city, people require personal transportation. A century ago, walking, riding horseback, or using a carriage met that Need. Over time, many other services have become available, such as bicycles, cars, streetcars, taxis, buses, light rail, and subways. More recently, ridesharing (cars and electric scooters) has become popular. How will you get to work today? You will pick the service that best **matches** the Need for personal transportation. (Maybe walking is still the best match!)

In today's world, there are usually several products or services in the marketplace at the same time aimed at the same Need. Table 1.2 provides a list of Needs and examples of products or services intended to fulfill each Need. As you review this table, think about additional products or services that match the Needs in this table.

Table 1.2. Need as a target for products and services

Need	Possible products or services
Personal transportation	Automobile, bicycle, bus system, rideshare, train
Transfer of knowledge	Blogs, books, school, social media, television programs
Health care	Health club, hospital, nursing home, telehealth
Information about current affairs	Internet, newspaper, podcast, radio programs, TV news
Food	Farmers market, garden, grocery store, restaurant
Getting bills paid	Checking account, credit card, mobile payment applications
Shelter	Apartment, hotel, house, short-term rental
Computation (handheld)	Abacus, calculator, slide rule, smartphone

After focusing on the need, the concept of a customer follows. Customers include anyone who possesses the need. Needs do not come from customers; an organization's customers come from the Need in society that the organization is attempting to meet. Customers include those who currently purchase or use the organization's products and services, those who use products similar to their competitors' products, those who choose different products and services to satisfy the need, and those whose Need goes unfulfilled.

It is usually much easier for an organization to list its present products and services than to define the Needs these products and services are intended to match. For example, a school superintendent could quickly describe classrooms, qualified teachers, curricula, books, materials, and staff development as the assets of their schools, but what is the Need their school district is attempting to match with these products and services? Is it to prepare young people to be effective learners and responsible, productive citizens? The statement of purpose of an organization (the focus of Chapter 4) should articulate the Need the organization plans to fulfill. This allows the organization to look beyond its current products and services and provides a vision for innovation.

The five questions in table 1.3 help define the need of your organization.

Table 1.3. Questions to discover the need

Q1	What are your current products and services?
Q2	Who are your current customers?
Q3	How do these customers use your products or benefit from your services?
Q4	Why are these products and services vital to your customers?
Q5	What different products or services could be used instead of yours (not just the same products or services offered by your competitors)?

There should be a balance between a definition of a Need that is so abstract that it is not useful and a description that is so specific that organizational leaders believe the Need is for **their** current products and services alone. The answers to questions 3, 4, and 5 should begin to describe that need.

Monique began exploring the application of QOS to her new organization:

This concept of Need was completely new to me. My historic review of our business showed that our products and services had evolved over time. The medical records of ancient Greeks were narratives written to describe cures and outcomes and teach others who provided medical care. Up until the 1960s, data management was a manual pencil-and-paper task. I worked with the leadership team to try to answer the five questions in table 1.3:

Q1: What are our current products and services?
<u>Products:</u> databases, data management software, standard protocols
<u>Services:</u> cleaning and validating data, collecting data, data analysis and statistical modeling, data warehousing, training, integration and aggregation of data, programming

Q2. Who are our current customers? Government agencies, health care sites and networks, health insurance companies, hospitals, research projects,

Q3. How do these customers use our products or benefit from our services? Billing, conducting research, learning and improving, operations

Q4. Why are these products and services vital to our customers? Documentation for financial services and regulation, decision-making at all levels of the organization leading to enhanced patient experience, improved outcomes and cost-effective care.

Q5. What different products or services could be used instead of ours (not just the same products or services offered by our competitors)? Customers could move these activities inside their organizations, and artificial intelligence software could complete many of our current tasks.

There was a lot of back-and-forth dialogue on the team as we worked on these questions. In the end we concluded there was a Need in health care organizations for managing data for regulatory, operational, and improvement purposes. This was the Need that provided the focus for our company's products and services.

DEFINING QUALITY

If we improve quality by better matching products and services to a Need, then quality must be defined relative to the specific Need. This definition of quality[15] consists of measurable characteristics, sometimes called quality characteristics or measures of quality. For example, some quality characteristics relative to the Need for transportation would be safety, timeliness, and comfort. It is essential to make a distinction between quality characteristics of a Need versus a specification for a specific product or service. For example, usability is an important dimension of the Need for communication while the specification for a smartphone might be the size that would allow the user to hold it in one hand.

Many have defined characteristics or dimensions of quality. Feigenbaum[16] discussed the different characteristics (such as reliability, serviceability, maintainability, and attractability) that form the composite concept of quality. Garvin[17] proposed eight dimensions of quality to help people define the quality of products and services. One of his aims in developing the list was to broaden people's perspective when listing characteristics related to quality. The Institute of Medicine[18] defined six dimensions of quality for health care systems: safe, effective, patient-centered, timely, efficient, and equitable. Table 1.4 describes fourteen dimensions that build on these sources.

Some additions to the list in table 1.4 are merely subheadings under the various dimensions used by others. For example, time could be a subheading under performance. We listed them separately for emphasis and ease of using the list. Note that the list encompasses all attributes of a product or service except **price**. We have not found it useful to consider the concept of price (or total cost to purchase) a direct component of the concept of quality (see next section on the concept of **value**).

To define quality relative to a need, one should develop a list of quality characteristics and then check the list against the dimensions to test for comprehensiveness. A list of quality characteristics for a specific Need does not have to contain all dimensions. Two completely different versions of a product can be considered high-quality because different dimensions of quality are considered essential for the two products. For example, different users could describe both a stripped-down compact car and a fully-loaded luxury car as high-quality.

Table 1.4. Dimensions of quality

Dimension	Meaning of dimension
1. Performance	Primary operating characteristics
2. Features	Secondary operating characteristics, such as added options or touches (not included in other dimensions)
3. Time	Cycle time, time to complete a service, time waiting
4. Reliability	Extent of failure-free operation over time
5. Durability	Amount of use before replacement is preferable to repair
6. Uniformity	Low variation among repeated outcomes of a process
7. Consistency	Match with documentation, forecasts, or standards
8. Serviceability	Resolution of problems and complaints
9. Aesthetics	Relating to the senses such as color, fragrance, fit, or finish
10. Personal Interface	Punctuality, courtesy, and professionalism
11. Flexibility	Willingness to adapt, customize, or accommodate change
12. Harmlessness	Relating to environment, health, or safety
13. Perceived quality	Inferences about other dimensions; reputation
14. Usability	Ergonomics; relating to logical and natural use

Garvin[19] points out that to compete on quality, an organization must determine what dimensions are essential to the group of customers (segment of the market) on which the organization is focusing. (This topic is explored in Chapter 7.) All quality-characteristics are not equal, especially in the way they influence customers. Kano[20] has developed a useful model that describes three types of quality characteristics (the example in parentheses is for a hotel room):

1. **One-dimensional:** a characteristic that gives satisfaction when fulfilled and results in dissatisfaction when not fulfilled (size of the hotel room).

2. **Attractive quality:** a characteristic that gives satisfaction when fulfilled but is acceptable even when not fulfilled (having a warm cookie waiting on check-in).

3. **Must-be quality:** a characteristic that is taken for granted but results in dissatisfaction when not fulfilled (having a clean bed in the room).

Figure 1.4 illustrates how each of these types of characteristics impacts customer satisfaction. In a later section of this chapter, we connect these types of quality characteristics to three categories of improvement.

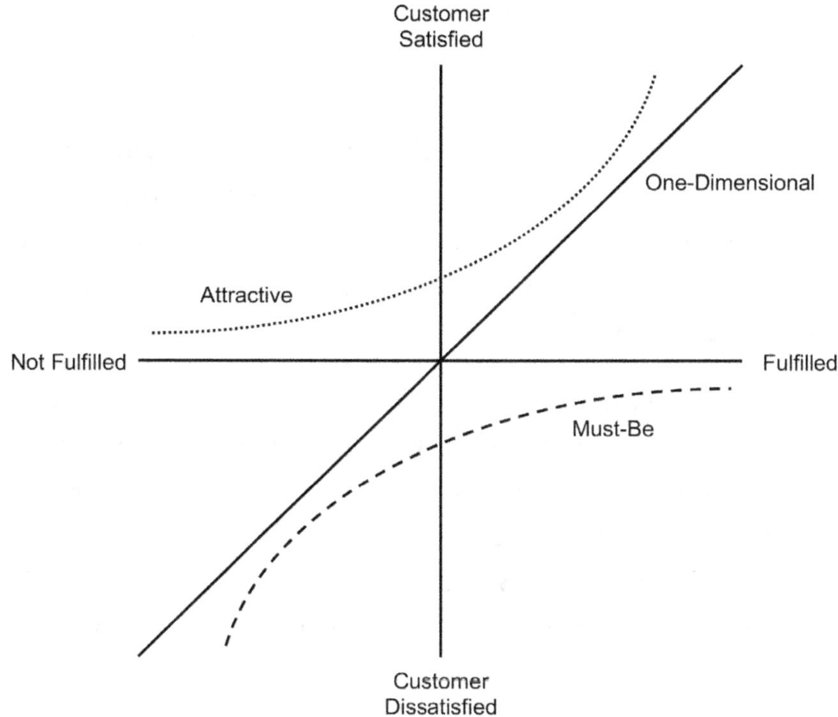

Figure 1.4. Kano two-dimensional model for quality characteristics.

We improve quality by improving the matching between products and services and the Need. The degree of matching is determined using the definition of quality.

Market research must seek to understand how customers define quality and how this definition differs among different groups of customers. Focusing on attractive quality-characteristics offers potential innovation and growth to an organization. When considering "matching" the Need, address the following issues:

- Definitions of quality will differ among individual customers.
- Definitions of quality will change over time.
- An important part of matching is selecting a price for the product or service that the customer is willing to pay (see the concept of value in the next section).
- In the dynamic environment in which we live, the matching must be **ongoing**.

VALUE

Customers make purchasing decisions and other judgments by considering quality and price combined in a concept called **value** (or, more specifically, economic value). The concept of value means the benefits received for the burdens endured.[21] Whether the provider is a contractor, a manufacturer, a distributor, or a bank, customers judge products and services by their quality **and** price. Decisions about quality and price are fundamental to success in business.

Quality describes how well a product or service matches a Need. The concept of quality includes all of the dimensions in table 1.4. **Price** refers to what the customer has to pay for a product or service (usually in terms of money) and the nonmonetary costs or the "cost to use" for the product or service. This combination is often called the "total cost." For example, if a product must be repaired or adjusted before use, the price includes the purchase price and the cost to repair or modify. The time and cost to purchase (physical and mental effort, shipping charges, travel expenses, etc.) might also be considered part of the price component.

For a business, establishing the sales prices for its products and services is fundamental to the company's success. The marketplace (customers, competitors, and community) sets a narrow price range for many products and services (e.g., commodity items like gasoline). For others, the producer or seller has flexibility in setting the price. Many organizations have a well-defined pricing process that includes considerations such as the cost to produce and service different customers, customer price sensitivity and perceptions, the pricing structure of the company's other products and services, expected reactions of competitors to price changes, and emotional responses of customers.

Value is the relative worth, utility, or importance of something. The concept of value combines quality, price, and cost to use. Therefore, the definition (not a mathematical equation) of value is:

Value = Quality/Total Cost (where total cost = price plus cost to use)

This emphasizes the direct influence of quality and the inverse effect of price, but the precise relationship is usually more complex. From this relationship, it is easy to see that higher quality does not necessarily mean higher value; we must also consider the total cost. Also, the price must be easy to understand and linked to the customer's perceptions of value. The cost to use may not be as apparent as the initial price tag. Pricing strategies are essential for successfully making quality an effective organizational strategy.

What does the value equation mean for organizations where the user is not a direct purchaser, for example, a homeowner who relies on the local fire service, or a parent with a child in public school? These services are present to meet a Need, and there is a desire and expectation for quality. Community leaders and elected officials serve as customers on behalf of citizens. The taxes citizens pay for these services reflect the price. The users' choice in who serves them comes through elections and various budget approval processes. Elected officials are responsible for matching the quality expected of the citizens and being accountable for their tax contributions. For example, many cities have a standard for fire engines of a four-minute response to emergency incidences. Often citizens reject government-proposed expenditures that they do not perceive as a good value.

Monique dedicated one of her leadership team meetings to explore the QOS concept of matching:

> I quickly learned that there was a lot of disagreement about the important dimensions of quality for our products and services. And no one had data to back up their anecdotes and opinions. Our Marketing VP agreed to organize data from our customer help desks and some other existing sources of customer feedback using the fourteen dimensions of quality and share that analysis at a future meeting. We explored quality-characteristics of our products and services for each of the Kano-types:
>
> **One-dimensional:** completeness, timeliness of reports
>
> **Attractive quality:** flexibility, innovative statistical analysis, personal interface with data analysts
>
> **Must-be quality:** data errors, regulatory compliance
>
> I noted that this topic is a big opportunity for future work as we try to differentiate our products and services from our competitors.

The foundation of quality as an organizational strategy is the ongoing matching of products and services to a Need. Once the organization determines the Need it intends to match and quality is defined relative to that Need, then matching of products and services to that Need can begin. Again, the value, including quality and total cost to the customer, determines the degree of matching for different customers or users. To successfully perform this ongoing matching, a second key element of the strategy is the organization must operate as a **system**.

The Organization as a System

Most of us work in an organization with multiple departments (marketing, administration, production, purchasing, etc.), in various locations (regions, offices, schools, etc.), and sometimes with different business teams (Automotive, Chemicals, Energy). Companies use organizational charts to manage this complexity and describe where everyone fits in and to whom they report. Figure 1.5 shows a typical organizational chart (upper portion). Unfortunately, an organizational chart can promote something called "silo thinking" and suboptimization. For example, typical charts depict the organization as a group of independent departments rather than the organization as a system of linked processes. In addition, the organizational chart suggests accountability and promotes the view that the boss is the customer.

Contrast this with the lower portion, which depicts an organization as a system (from figure 1.1). This diagram is an adaption of Deming's "Production Viewed as a System."[22] The system diagram communicates how the various departments work together to accomplish the organization's purpose. When we learn to view the organization as a system, we identify more crucial internal customer-supplier relationships.

In 1950, Deming began using this depiction in Japan.[23] At that time, Japanese leadership's approach to quality centered on inspection. Deming introduced several emerging ideas, such as statistical techniques, market research, and an early iteration of the Plan, Do, Study, Act Cycle to make a case for quality as an organizational strategy. He also drew an early draft of the organization as a system diagram on the blackboard behind him to explain this new thinking.[24]

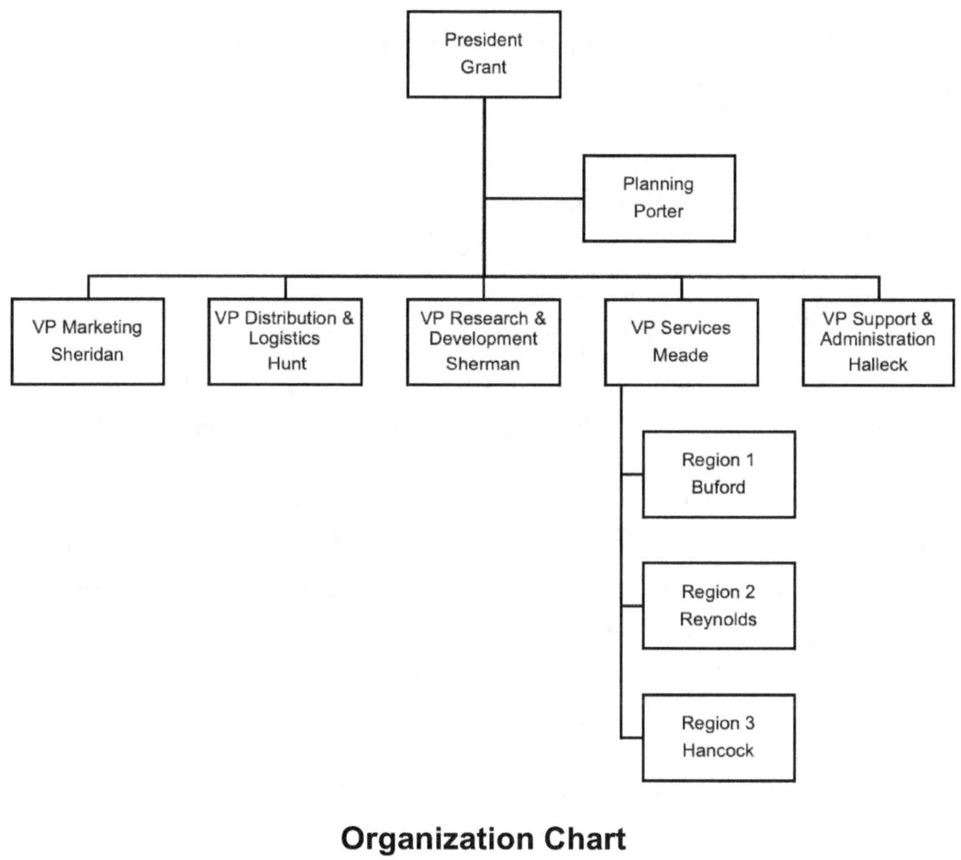

Organization Chart

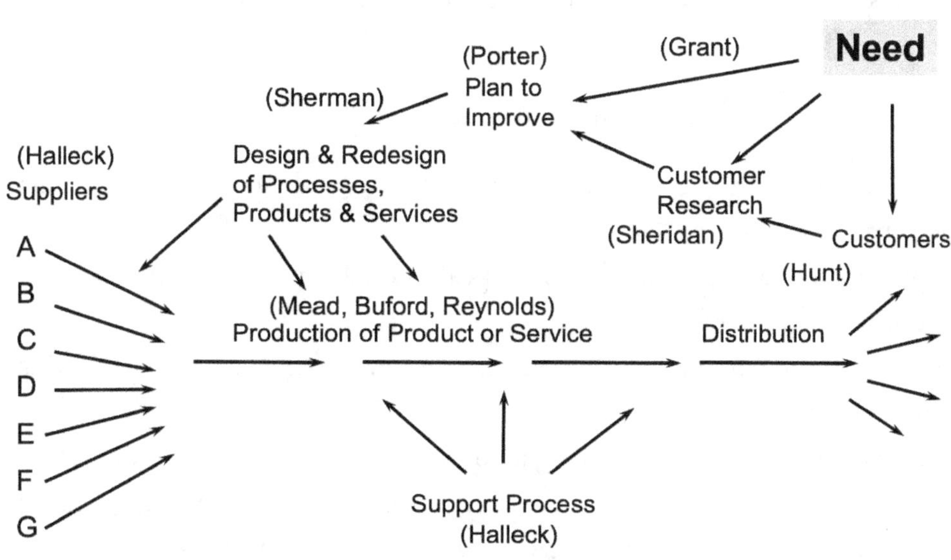

Concept of Organization Viewed as a System

Figure 1.5. Organization chart versus concept of organization viewed as a system.

A system is an interdependent group of items, people, or processes working together toward a common purpose. Some crucial aspects of quality as an organizational strategy included in figure 1.5 are:

- The **Need** is the primary focus for efforts to improve.
- Matching products and services to the Need is ongoing.
- The close connection of suppliers and customers to the system.
- Customer research and planning are prerequisites for improvement.
- Improvement results from the design or redesign of some aspect of the system.
- Everyone in the organization should contribute to improvement.

It is essential for leaders to understand and manage the organization as a system to make quality an organizational strategy. There are usually fundamental changes required in an organization before it can function as an integrated system. For example, communication processes must help everyone understand how they contribute to the system. Everyone should develop, test, and implement changes, but unless leaders coordinate this work, the changes may not improve the organization's performance.

Many forces promote suboptimization of the organization, such that parts of the organization function without regard for what is best for the entire organization. For example, in many organizations, budgeting processes cause people to focus on how their time is spent instead of how they are contributing to the overall purpose of the organization, or the immediate match required by customers.

Some other causes of suboptimization include:

- People do not know the organization's purpose and how their work relates to the purpose.
- People focus on guidance from professional specialties rather than the organization's purpose.
- Well-intentioned management systems that promote short-term thinking or a narrow point of view.
- Fads that come and go encouraging managers to turn their department into a profit center or new ways to create competition between people in the same organization.
- Internal competition overemphasizes allegiance to one's workgroup.
- Technical or functional shortsightedness.
- Optimizing a single measure of success (such as sales) rather than simultaneously optimizing multiple measures of success.

DEFINING APPROPRIATE "SYSTEMS"

As introduced in the previous section, the idea of viewing the organization as a system composed of processes derives from Deming's "Production Viewed as a System." The various components of the system must work with suppliers and customers to deliver products and services of value to the customers. Deming pointed out that this diagram applied to all organizations: manufacturing, service, administrative, etc.

Applying the idea of **the organization as a system** (presented earlier in figure 1.1) offers many choices for applying boundaries and defining the system in an organization. Ideally, it would be desirable to view the entire organization as one system and to focus on optimizing that system. This is the view that the chief executive of an organization must have. However, for many organizations, this approach leads to levels of complexity that can overwhelm any type of learning and understanding.

Often there are ways to divide the organization into parts that result in less complexity. The focus is then on optimizing the smaller systems created by the boundaries. Some examples of obvious divisions of an organization are business teams that operate in different markets and regions that operate in different geographic areas. Of course, suboptimization can still occur in these smaller systems, so leaders must remain vigilant.

Improving the organization's ability to function as a system provides another way to increase value besides designing or redesigning products and processes. Changes that affect the entire system, such as establishing constancy of purpose, can be high-leverage opportunities.

> Monique wondered about the importance of applying systems thinking to her company:
>
> > All my experience has included using organizational charts and departmental budgets to control the functioning of a company. It's a scary proposition to think about giving up these management tools. I have a lot of learning to do, but I can really relate to that list of causes of suboptimization. In my previous jobs, I felt the destructive power of internal competition. I have a meeting coming up with the marketing department to review next year's budget. I will pay particular attention to these suboptimization issues during the meeting.

To review, thus far we have introduced two ideas to describe quality as an organizational strategy:

1. The strategy is based on the ongoing **matching** of products and services to a **Need**, and
2. This matching is achieved by viewing and operating the **organization as a system** with the **Need** that the organization intends to fulfill as the focus of its purpose.

A third element to make the strategy viable is a **set of activities** to carry out the improvements. These improvements are designed to increase customer value by improving the match of products and services to the Need they possess.

Activities to Make Quality an Organizational Strategy

Three aspects of the system depicted earlier in figure 1.1 that relate to methods for improvement are:

- Market research
- Planning for improvement
- The design and redesign of products, services, and processes

These three aspects provide the link between the day-to-day operation of the system and the improvement of the system. In organizations where quality is a strategy, they are well developed. In organizations where quality is not yet at the strategic level:

- Market research is nonexistent, anecdotal, or composed of negative feedback such as complaints or warranty claims.
- Planning for improvement is nonexistent or separated from business planning.
- Emphasis is on solving problems or resolving crises rather than making lasting improvements to products and processes.

MARKET RESEARCH

Most organizations have a variety of methods to gather information about consumers' Needs and preferences, such as online feedback ratings, surveys, interviews, and complaint lines. Using QOS, this market research should focus on the Need that the organization intends to fulfill. It should provide a method to identify, segment, and learn from customers while enhancing relationships. Obtaining feedback and market research are active activities using mixed methods, including surveying, focus groups, and observation. Relying on negative feedback, such as complaints or warranty claims, is insufficient. Present customers of existing products and services will be an essential source of information; however, they should not be the limit of the research. Anyone possessing the Need the organization intends to fulfill is a potential customer and a source of information.

PLANNING FOR IMPROVEMENT

When quality is an organizational strategy, strategic planning and business planning include methods for planning to improve. The broad aim of improving the value of products and services to customers falls into the following three major categories:[25]

- **Eliminating problems** due to failing to meet the expectations of customers (this is the focus of Deming's Chain Reaction, as discussed earlier)
- Making significant **cost reductions** while maintaining or improving quality (often associated with what is termed "lean thinking")
- **Innovation** or changing customers' expectations by providing products and services that customers perceive as unusually high-value

These categories are related to Kano's types of quality-characteristics described earlier. **One-dimensional Quality and Must-be Quality** characteristics are usually associated with projects focused on eliminating problems. Cost reductions are designed to maintain these characteristics while reducing costs (e.g., reducing waste). And projects targeting **Attractive Quality** characteristics are usually connected with innovation and projects targeting increases in revenue.

An organization focused on improving value will often have activities in each of the three categories (see Chapter 8 for categories considered in the planning process). In **eliminating problems**, we make changes that significantly reduce the occurrence of problems such as defects in a product, errors in shipments, or long waiting times. Doing a good job of eliminating problems does not guarantee a business's success if the demand for the organization's products and services disappears. However, reducing problems often has the side effect of reducing the costs associated with resolving the problems, thus improving value. The changes typically developed include simplification and standardization of processes, training, mistake proofing, and preventive maintenance.

Cost reduction focuses on making changes that reduce operating expenses. Anyone can reduce costs if they are willing to sacrifice quality buying cheaper materials, cutting resources, or postponing maintenance. It takes substantial skill and knowledge to reduce costs while maintaining or improving quality. Cost reductions allow the producer to offer products and services to customers at lower prices. In addition, if the quality is maintained, value is improved. In a labor-intensive industry, essential changes in this category removes work that does not add value or contribute to the desired outcomes (for example, doing unnecessary procedures during a medical visit). Other types of changes include smoothing the workflow, substituting less expensive materials or supplies that serve the purpose, cross-training, and reducing inventory.

Innovation involves changing customers' expectations and is about developing products and services that attract customers to the organization with unusually high value. The increases in quality gained from new products or services must be balanced with any price increases to maintain a high value. Note that some customers will be willing to pay higher prices for particularly attractive products and services.

Consider problems that customers might not complain about. For example, customers will often not be aware that existing products and services are not great matches to their needs. So, asking them, or waiting for them to complain, is not a productive way to gain the information necessary to develop new products and services.

Planning for improvement helps decide the category on which to focus the organization's resources. Many times, the focus is obvious. For example, an organization with customer complaints and returns, excessive rework, high warranty costs, late deliveries, and lawsuits should usually concentrate its resources on improvements that solve these problems. Organizations that cannot compete in the marketplace because of the prices they have to charge to cover their production costs should focus on changes that can reduce these costs. Finally, an organization that wants to grow or increase market share should include improvements in their initiatives that are likely to change the expectations of their customers. Typically, an organization will have some activities in all three categories.

One process for planning for improvement consists of the following steps:

1. Develop strategic objectives.
2. Relate these to new and existing products and processes.

3. Set priorities for improvement, identifying what categories of improvement are being addressed by the organization.
4. Match resources to the priorities.
5. Develop improvement briefs for design or redesign of products, services, or processes.

The outcomes of the plan are:

- Strategic objectives for the organization (Ends)
- Defined improvement efforts and appropriate changes to operations (Ways)
- Allocation of resources (Means) [26]

The development of an improvement plan must be fully integrated with the entire planning system of the organization.[27] Chapter 8 focuses on planning for improvement and integrating with existing planning processes in the organization.

METHODS FOR THE DESIGN AND REDESIGN OF PRODUCTS AND PROCESSES

Planning leads to **choices** about which processes, services, and products to design or redesign. These improvement efforts should not be confused with just solving problems or firefighting, but instead on work that leads quickly to better results in important measures of the organization's performance. Although necessary for most organizations, solving problems usually just maintains the status quo. Instead, lasting improvements come from the design or redesign of processes or products or changes to the system.

Although improvements result from change, all change does not result in improvement.[28] Changes that result in improvement come from people with increased knowledge of the system. The Model for Improvement[29] shown in figure 1.6 provides a framework for learning, developing changes, testing changes, and implementing changes.[30] The three fundamental questions and the **PDSA cycle** (plan, do, study, act) guide individuals and teams to make improvements. Tools and methods such as Shewhart control charts, scatterplots, and planned experiments are useful to support the effort guided by the Model for Improvement.

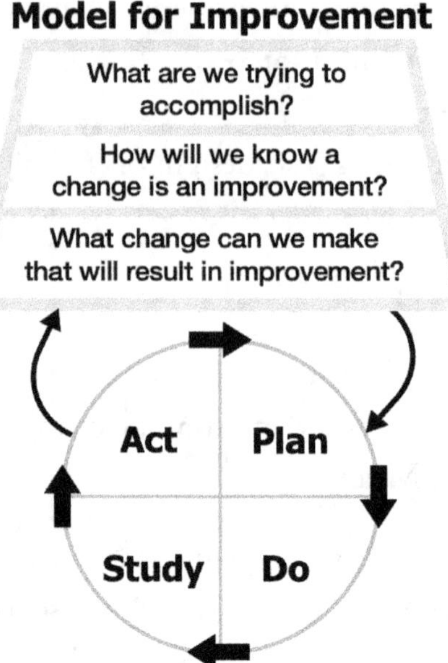

Figure 1.6. Model for improvement.

Because of the interdependencies and complexity in a system, many strategic improvements will come from the efforts of cross-functional teams. Therefore, staff require basic skills related to conducting meetings, obtaining balanced participation in teams, resolving conflicts, and team-based decisions. Chapter 9 focuses on the methods to facilitate improvement efforts that lead to accomplishing the organization's strategic objectives.

Monique reflected on the organization's current approaches to market research, planning, and improvement:

We have some form of each of these activities in place in the organization. That said, I will learn how we must improve our current approaches to make quality the focus of these methods. Marketing is already working on the dimensions of quality, and we are scheduled to run a strategic planning session next month, which will give me a great opportunity to understand the deficiencies in our current approaches. I will also attend some meetings of our existing improvement teams to better understand how we currently approach improvement.

QUALITY AS AN ORGANIZATIONAL STRATEGY (QOS)

The theoretical framework described in this chapter provides the foundation of this book. Quality as an organizational strategy (QOS) is a transformative system of five activities for leaders:

1. **Purpose Activity**: Establish and communicate the purpose of the organization.
2. **System Activity:** View, operate, and improve the organization as a system.
3. **Information Activity**: Establish a system for obtaining information relevant to the Need the organization is fulfilling.
4. **Planning Activity**: Plan for improvement of the system.
5. **Managing Improvement Activity**: Managing individual and team improvement efforts.

Figure 1.7 overlays these five activities on the Organization Viewed as a System framework (from figure 1.1). These five activities form a system for leading improvement in an organization. Each activity includes methods for pursuing quality as an organizational strategy, and the activities are linked and interdependent. As a result, they lead to both short-term wins in organizational performance and long-term accomplishment of the mission.

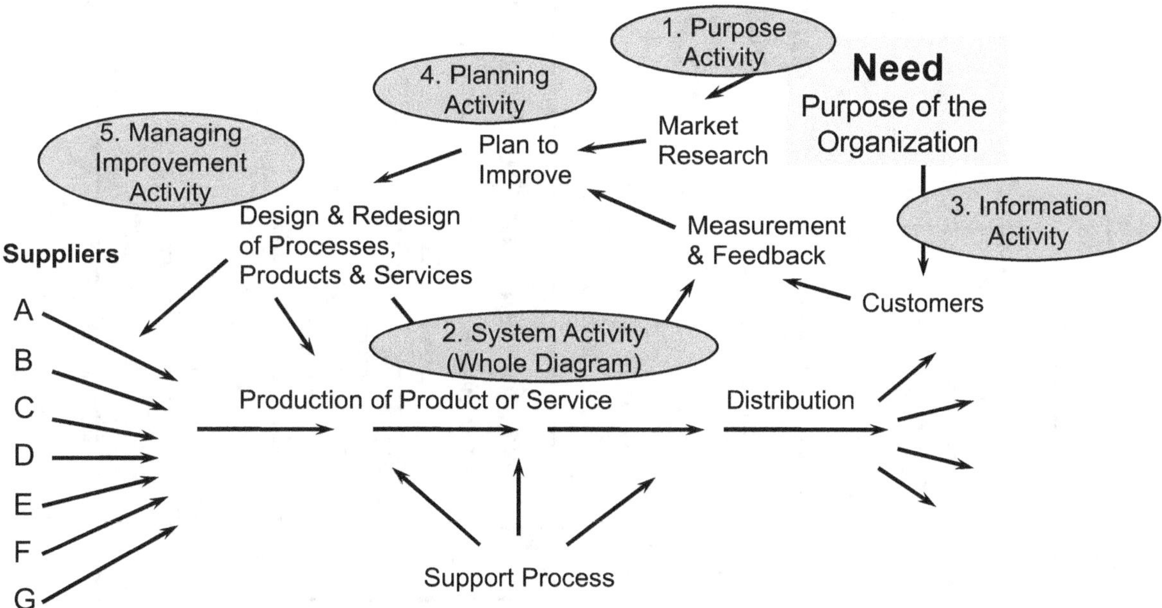

Figure 1.7. Organization as a system with the five leadership activities.

Figure 1.8 shows these five activities as a system with their linkages. This system of activities supports leaders in adopting quality as an organizational strategy.

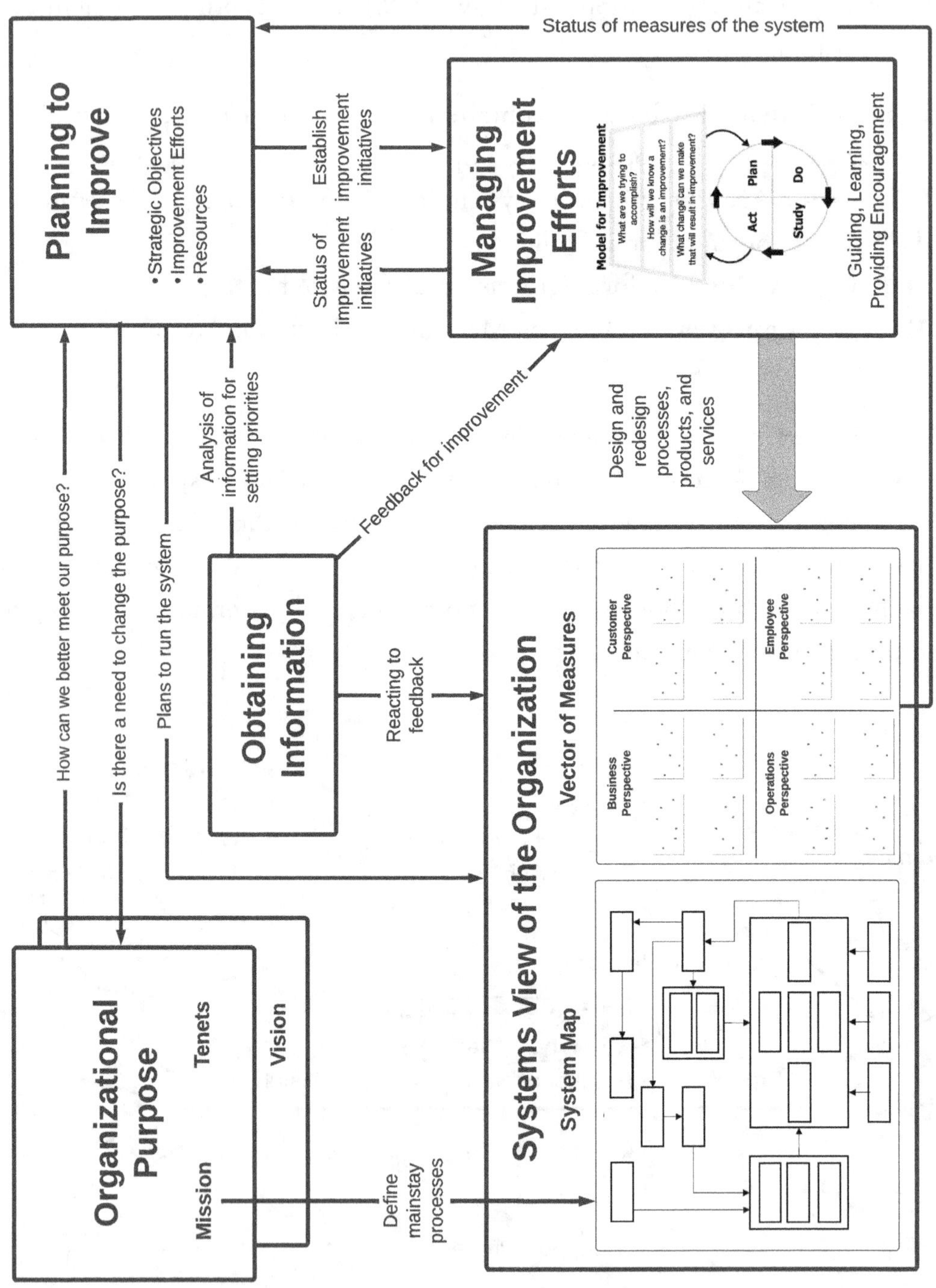

Figure 1.8. Activities for leaders to build a system of improvement.

ATTRIBUTES OF AN ORGANIZATION TO SUCCESSFULLY PURSUE QOS

Organizations differ dramatically in their cultures, often with differences between departments.[31] Organizations try to define their culture in statements of beliefs or principles (see Chapter 4), but the *actual* culture is observed in the behaviors of the members of the organization, especially the leaders. The culture may be one in which most decisions are made at the top or one in which decisions are primarily made by consensus. The culture may encourage improvement or may expect everyone to follow strict protocols and rules. The application of QOS is not limited to any particular culture, however. The framework can be adapted to the strengths and weaknesses of different cultures.

Regardless of the culture, some fundamentals should be in place if an organization is to be successful with the QOS framework:

- The desire for continuous learning and improvement
- An environment that nurtures mutual respect among people
- A culture of encouragement
- An expectation of cooperation among all members of the organization.

Creating the Habit of Continuous Learning and Improvement

The QOS foundation is the ongoing matching of products and services to a need. This requires a culture where members are motivated to improve the system, its products, and its services. This motivation comes from:

- A belief that the purpose of the organization is worthwhile.
- An organization that attracts employees that are curious and have a desire to learn.
- An environment that harnesses peoples' intrinsic desire to improve.
- A system that allows people to enjoy their work and to take pride in its outcomes.
- An environment that formally provides time for people to participate in improvement.
- Recognition and appreciation of efforts to improve.

People naturally enjoy and are motivated by improving what they do. As leaders learn to rely on these intrinsic motivators, they will learn to rely less on outside, or extrinsic, motivators such as bonuses, awards, competition, and the trappings of success which can divert attention and energy from the purpose of the organization.

Creating an Environment That Enables Mutual Respect Among Members

Leaders should recognize that not everyone is equal in experience or competence, but all have equal worth as human beings. All members, but especially leaders, should pay attention to behaviors that show respect:

- Let employees know that you do not have all the answers and are in a learning mode. Everyone should both teach and learn from one another to be successful.
- Listen and respond with empathy.
- Minimize negative talk unless it is for learning.
- When trying to persuade others, talk in a firm but friendly way.
- Drive out both excessive fear and/or complacency in the organization.
- Show sincere interest in the opinions of others and the reasons behind them.

Providing Encouragement

Both encouragement and discouragement come from the systems in which people work and from the interactions they have with others in the system. People can be very discouraged when beset with problems occurring from bad systems, especially if there is no time or resources to solve problems or address the overall system issues. A leader can provide significant encouragement simply by improving the systems in which people work and by giving them opportunities to make improvements in their daily work. Ideally, everyone in the organization should be able to describe the changes they are currently testing and what they are learning.

Before communicating with someone, leaders should ask, "What can I communicate that will make this person more willing to make improvements?"

Promoting Cooperation

Focusing on the organization as a system makes it easy to see that there are substantial dependencies among employees and departments within an organization. There are important internal customer and supplier relationships where the work of one group (supplier) is used by another (customer). Understanding these ideas keeps the focus of the system on the customer and helps people avoid suboptimization. Since systems are made up of interrelated people and processes, changes to one part of a system impacts other parts. The insistence of cooperation among people and organizational entities is one of the biggest contributions a leader can make to an organization's ability to improve. Focusing on the common purpose is the starting point for cooperation, while an environment of mutual respect and encouragement (discussed earlier) helps makes it happen.

The Leader's Role

The organization's leaders must both establish and maintain the culture of the organization. They will also be the focus of building the system of improvement based on QOS. These complex roles are described in Chapter 3. Regardless of their best intention, the organization may not be successful on a sustainable basis. Deming[32] described what he called the "Deadly Diseases," serious barriers leaders will face when working to establish a system of improvement. They are deadly in the sense they can completely derail the best intentions of leaders to build a system. The diseases are:[33]

1. Lack of constancy of purpose
2. Emphasis on short-term profits
3. Annual rating of performance
4. Mobility of management[34]
5. Use of visible figures only
6. Excessive medical costs
7. Excessive costs of warranty, fueled by lawyers' work for contingency fees

THE JOURNEY AHEAD

Many things must happen if quality is to become the strategy of any organization. This strategy cannot simply be installed or implemented like a new IT system. It is important for knowledgeable leadership to carry out the strategy and make it successful. Deming accurately emphasized: "The job of a leader is to accomplish the transformation" of the organization.[35] This book will serve as a roadmap to start the journey.

Looking ahead, Chapter 2 summarizes the Science of Improvement. Based on the four lenses of Deming's system of profound knowledge, this science is defined and presented in the context of leading quality across an organization.

Chapter 3 focuses on the role of the leadership team. Leaders must make this transformation and learn to lead differently. Leading differently requires new ideas, new methods, and constant focus to lead this work and create the conditions for success.

Chapters 4 through 9 establish a system of five activities for continuous study and learning by the organization's leadership team as the first priority. In addition, these chapters describe the five activities that this leadership team must lead.

Chapter 4 begins with understanding the Need the organization aims to fill. How do you define the organization's purpose, communicate it, and use it?

Chapter 5 explores understanding organizations as a system of interdependent, linked processes working in concert to meet the Need.

Chapter 6 continues the systems focus with developing and using a system of measures for the organization.

Chapter 7 introduces a system for gathering and learning from information to aid in understanding the Need and planning for improvement.

Chapter 8 uses information from diverse sources through a method to decide where to focus the design or redesign the organization's products and services.

Chapter 9 frames how to manage the improvement efforts across the organization to get quick results on current issues and long-term performance and growth.

Chapter 10 focuses on the role of workers at all levels of the organization in making quality an organizational strategy.

Chapter 11 outlines the steps to begin making quality your organizational strategy. It includes a section on "Why Change?" for those who are realizing how significant the work of QOS is. Those anxious to get started on this work might do a quick read of Chapter 11.

BEFORE READING FURTHER

How does your organization currently stack up to the methods QOS? First, fill out the assessment grid[36] in table 1.5 based on your current understanding; then, as you study each of the following chapters, update the assessment to reflect your learning.

Table 1.5. Assessment of progress in making Quality an Organizational Strategy (QOS)

Activities	Operational definition and scoring					
	Just Beginning (Score = 0)	Aware (Score = 2)	Informed (Score = 4)	Integrating (Score = 6)	Understanding (Score = 8)	Successful and renewing (Score = 10)
Purpose	No written statements	Statement exists	Mission and tenets defined and visible	Communicated and understood by employees	Used to align and guide the organization	Fully integrated into the structure
Organization as a system	Work as a process is not understood	Major processes are documented	Relationships between processes are documented	Systems thinking and language are common	Systems diagrams are used in the organization	Management systems have integrated the systems view
System measures	Financial data are used for management reports	Financial and other operational measures are used	Family of measures is assembled and reported regularly	Balanced set of measures, each presented as a time series	Set of measures aligned; both variation and interrelationships are understood	Set of balanced measures fully integrated into all management systems
Information	Information is gathered on an ad hoc, reactive basis	System is based on passive information	System is well documented and includes active sources	Information is documented and communicated	Comprehensive system with analysis and synthesis for decision-making	Marketing leads and integrates information system
Planning for improvement	No formal long-term planning, reactive culture	Planning for improvement is done on an informal basis	A formal, documented process exists for planning improvement	Integrated process identifies objectives, efforts, and resources	All other planning processes are defined and linked with planning to improve	Planning system is regularly improved and integrated in all areas
Managing improvement efforts	No system exists to manage improvement efforts	Improvements recognized on an as-needed basis and resources assigned	Leaders provide formal guidance for individuals and teams	Improvements are guided by planning; leaders learn from all improvements	The impact of improvement is understood and actively managed to achieve benefits	Improvement system is integrated and continuously improved
Model for Improvement	No standard approach to improvement efforts	Various approaches are used for improvement	Training on the model and expectation of its use	Theory behind the model is understood	Improvements are managed as PDSA cycles	Model for improvement is routinely used by all
Leadership system	Structure does not exist to make improvement a focus of the organization	The importance of improvement is recognized, and responsibility assigned	A formal system for improvement is defined	Leadership team assumes responsibility for integrating improvement	Improvement is linked to planning and other key business activities	Improvement is completely integrated into all aspects of operating and developing the business

SUMMARY

Quality was described as a strategy for an organization to achieve both short-term results and long-term goals. This strategy consists of three essential elements:

1. The foundation is the ongoing matching of products and services to a need.
2. The organization performs as a system with the Need as the target.
3. A set of methods assures that changes and innovations result in improvement.

Figure 1.9 is a modified version of Deming's Chain Reaction[37] introduced in the Preface. This figure summarizes the intent of making quality an organizational strategy.

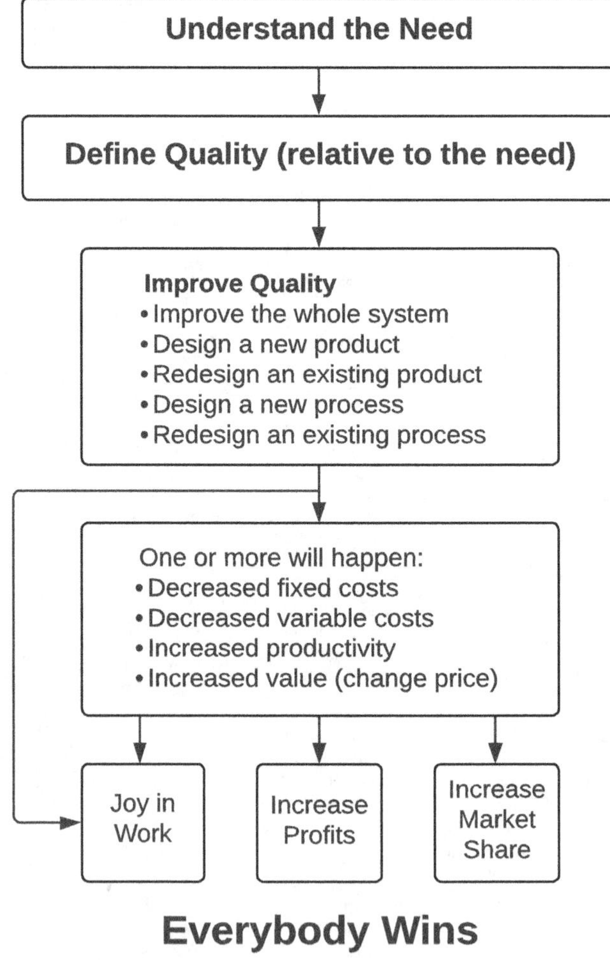

Figure 1.9. Why quality as an organizational strategy?

Monique reflected on learning about quality as an organizational strategy during the past month:

I summarized my learning relative to the attributes described in an effective organizational strategy [see the beginning of this chapter] to share with my leadership team:

- **Provides methods to reach the goals of the organization.** The organization's long-range goals are a crucial input to the plan for improvement. An outcome of the plan is guidance on products and processes to be designed or redesigned that can lead to immediate results and accomplish long-term goals. The use of the Model for Improvement (figure 1.6) will aid these improvement efforts.

- **Can be sustained over the long term.** The Need that the organization intends to fulfill provides permanence to the strategy. If quality is to be a long-term strategy, the Need must be one that will exist for a long time. Constancy of purpose is the essential element that focuses the organization on that persistent Need and sustains long-term improvement efforts.

- **Balances an internal and external focus.** The Need the organization intends to fulfill and the definition of quality for different customer segments provide the external focus. Improvements are made so that products and services produced by the organization better match that Need. Understanding the organization as a system of linked processes provides an internal focus. Improvement of these processes is the primary means of ensuring that people in the organization can take pride in their work.

- **Compatible with different businesses in the organization.** The primary distinction in the strategy among different businesses is that the Needs that the businesses intend to fulfill may differ. However, the three elements of the strategy remain the same.

- **Remains useful despite changes in the market.** The fact that the marketplace is dynamic is one reason that static strategies and those that do not build in organizational learning are difficult to sustain. QOS is based on people learning. Although the marketplace is continually changing, an aim or purpose must provide direction and maintain stability. The Need the organization intends to fulfill serves this function. By using a definition of quality relative to the Need, designers of products and processes are aided in looking past present products and services to those in demand in the future.

- **It can be understood and practiced by all members of the organization.** As part of the strategy, leaders communicate the Need the organization intends to fulfill to everyone in the organization. All understand how their work helps provide products and services that meet that need. Everyone in the organization works within one or more processes, and everyone is given a chance to improve these processes and satisfy their customers better. The Model for Improvement (figure 1.6) and the tools associated with it are applicable to the design and redesign of products and processes and improvements to the system.

I filled out the assessment in table 1.5 and scored each item from "1" to "4." I wasn't used to scoring less than 50% of the scale on any assessment, but I was encouraged to expect opportunities for learning in each of the upcoming chapters. Before I begin that study, I am going to describe precisely how the chain reaction (figure 1.9) should play out in the organization. Next, I am going to get involved with the two improvement projects that are currently active to better understand how the organization is using the Model for Improvement. Then I will begin to learn more about the leadership activities required to build my organization's system of improvement.

NOTES

1. "API Definition of the Science of Improvement," Associates in Process Improvement, accessed May 27, 2022, https://apiweb.org/. "The Science of Improvement includes the interaction of systems thinking, understanding variation, psychology of change, and the theory of knowledge that are applied to improve the performance of processes, products, services, organizations, and communities. The proper application of this science requires integration of a set of improvement methods and tools with knowledge of subject matter to develop, test, implement, and spread changes."

2. Deming, *The New Economics*, 1994, 37.

3. W. Edwards Deming, "On the Use of Theory," *Industrial Quality Control* 13, no. 1 (July 1, 1956): 1–3.

4. Associates in Process Improvement, *Quality as a Business Strategy: Building a System of Improvement*, 2–11.

5. Deming, *The New Economics*, 1994, 92–93.

6. Garvin, "Building a Learning Organization." "A learning organization is an organization skilled at creating, acquiring, and transferring knowledge, and at modifying its behavior to reflect new knowledge and insights."

7. Deming, *Out of Crisis*, 3. An expansion of the chain reaction for QOS is presented at the end of this chapter.

8. Frank M. Gryna, "Quality and Costs," in Juran's *Quality Handbook*, 5th ed. (New York: McGraw-Hill, 1999), 8.5 (Figure 8.2 "Cost of Quality and Quality Improvement") The original source of the figure was AT&T, "AT&T Cost of Quality Guidelines (Document 500-746)" (AT&T Customer Information Center, Indianapolis, IN, 1990), 16. These costs could be ten to thirty percent of sales or twenty-five to forty percent of operating expenses. These calculations were then used to motivate management to improve quality.

9. Deming, *Out of Crisis*, 1.

10. Michael E. Porter, "What Is Strategy?," *Harvard Business Review* (November 1, 1996): https://hbr.org/1996/11/what-is-strategy.

11. Michel Robert, *Strategy Pure and Simple* (New York: McGraw-Hill, 1993).

12. Figure 1.3 is an example of an Individuals Shewhart chart. Shewhart's method is discussed in Chapter 2, and more information can be found in Lloyd P. Provost and Sandy K. Murray, *The Health Care Data Guide: Learning from Data for Improvement*, 2nd ed. (San Francisco: Jossey-Bass, 2022).

13. Gerald J. Langley et al., *The Improvement Guide: A Practical Approach to Enhancing Organizational Performance*, 2nd ed. (San Francisco: Jossey-Bass, 2009), 16. Note: this definition is appropriate when the change is designed to impact a specific measure for a process. It can be adapted to other situations including new products, services, and processes and situations where the focus is on qualitative data or multiple system measures.

14. Kelsey Miller, "3 Methods for Identifying Customer Needs | HBS Online," *Business Insights Blog* (blog), August 6, 2020, https://online.hbs.edu/blog/post/methods-for-identifying-customer-needs. The term "Need" is used commonly in organizations to describe client or customer expectations, requests, or requirements. In the context presented here, "a **need** is a fundamental function or opportunity which people seek a product or service to fulfill."

15. "Quality" has been defined in different ways by authors and leaders in quality improvement. Our definition builds on these sources. An expanded discussion of these alternative definitions is included in the Chapter 1 of *The QOS Field Guide*.

16. A.V. Feigenbaum, *Total Quality Control*, 4rd, rev. ed. (New York: McGraw-Hill, 1991), 253.

17. David A. Garvin, "Competing on the Eight Dimensions of Quality," *Harvard Business Review*, November 1, 1987, https://hbr.org/1987/11/competing-on-the-eight-dimensions-of-quality.

18. Institute of Medicine Committee on Quality of Health Care in America, "Crossing the Quality Chasm: A New Health System for the 21st Century," *Crossing the Quality Chasm: A New Health System for the 21st Century* (Washington, D.C.: National Academies Press, 2001), https://www.ncbi.nlm.nih.gov/books/NBK222273/.

19. Garvin, "Competing on the Eight Dimensions of Quality."

20. C Berger et al., "Kano's Methods for Understanding Customer-Defined Quality," *Center for Quality Management Journal* 2, no. 4 (1993): 3–36; Noriaki Kano, "Quality in the Year 2000: Downsizing Through Re-Engineering and Upsizing Through Attractive Quality Creation" (ASQC Quality Conference, Las Vegas, NV, May 24, 1994).

21. Leonard L. Berry and Manjit S. Yadav, "Capture and Communicate Value in the Pricing of Services," *MIT Sloan Management Review*, July 15, 1996, 41–51, https://sloanreview.mit.edu/article/capture-and-communicate-value-in-the-pricing-of-services/.

22. Deming, *The New Economics*, 1994, 4.

23. W. Edwards Deming, *Elementary Principles of the Statistical Control of Quality - Series of Lectures.* (Tokyo: Nippon Kagaku Gijutsu Remmei, 1951).

24. Killian, *The World of W. Edwards Deming*, 61–71.

25. "Integrating Methods for Improvement of Value," Chapter 10 in G.L. Langley et al., *The Improvement Guide*, 217.

26. Arthur F. Lykke Jr., "Military Strategy," *Military Review*, January-February (1997): 183. These ideas go back to von Clausewitz, first published in 1831, translated in 1874. See "Ends and Means," Chapter 2 in Carl von Clausewitz, *On War*, trans. J.J. Graham, 1874, https://www.gutenberg.org/files/1946/1946-h/1946-h.htm. "During a visit to the US Army War College in 1981, General Maxwell D. Taylor characterized strategy as consisting of objectives, ways and means…Strategy equals ends (objectives toward which one strives) plus ways (courses of action) plus means (instruments by which some end can be achieved). This general concept can be used as a basis for the formulation of any type of strategy-military, political, economic, and so forth, depending upon the element of national power employed."

27. Josef Penner, former Executive Director of Mecklenburg Emergency Medical Services Agency, reflected on the impact of planning for improvement on his organization. "Previously, we squandered time/money and were not accountable. This planning activity and arbitration of what was funded came from a myriad of known/unknown thought. With this set of collaborative processes, we committed to solid plans and secured widespread support to implement. Results were better—measurable, public, and the improvement achieved. And [it was] difficult to measure the impact on momentum and team member trust/trustworthiness year after year."

28. Langley et al., *The Improvement Guide*, 2.

29. Langley et al., 23; Ronald D. Moen, Thomas W. Nolan, and Lloyd P. Provost, *Quality Improvement Through Planned Experimentation*, 3rd ed. (McGraw-Hill Education, 2012), 9; Provost and Murray, *The Health Care Data Guide*, 4.

30. Langley et al., *The Improvement Guide*, 23.

31. Adapted from Gerald J. Langley et al., *The Improvement Guide: A Practical Approach to Enhancing Organizational Performance*, 1st ed. (San Francisco: Jossey-Bass, 1996), 256–60.

32. *Management's Five Deadly Diseases: A Conversation with Dr. W. Edwards Deming* (Encyclopaedia Britannica, 1984), https://youtu.be/KgoSuVcHWpg.

33. See Chapter 2 in *The QOS Field Guide* for further discussion of Deming's "deadly diseases."

34. Roger Quayle described his experience with this "disease": "A change in senior leadership can stall or even stop QOS. This happened at Florida Power & Light after they won the Deming prize. It also happened at OMI when Don Evans, President, was promoted. At Brown & Root, when Ber Pieper, President, retired, the next leader declared victory for quality and eliminated the quality department and budget. That was in 1995 when I left Brown & Root and went to work at OMI. I'm not sure what the remedy might be, but it is a serious concern that I experienced firsthand multiple times."

35. Deming, *The New Economics*, 1994, 119.

36. A more detailed version of the QOS Assessment, including definitions, is in *The QOS Field Guide*.

37. Deming, *Out of Crisis*, 3. A multi-city healthcare system demonstrated inpatient harm reduction is associated with reduced inpatient LOS, mortality, and readmission rates, which benefits patients. Harm reduction is also associated with lower costs and higher contribution margin for hospitals. Adler et al. "Impact of Inpatient Harms on Hospital Finances and Patient Clinical Outcomes." *Journal of Patient Safety* 14, no. 2 (June 2018): 67-73. Chapter 1 of *The QOS Field Guide* further discusses the Chain Reaction.

CHAPTER 2

THE SCIENCE OF IMPROVEMENT

Gwen is the Chief Nursing Officer of a large academic health system. She started her career as a critical care nurse in the intensive care unit. As she furthered her education with her MBA and a doctorate in nursing practice, she gained experience climbing the ladder in progressively more senior leadership roles within her organization. Joining the C-suite should be the pinnacle of her career, but after all her studies and years of experience, she felt there was more she could do to lead quality across her organization.

Gwen reflected, "I have been reading and studying examples of health systems that are achieving better results. I am learning these results are achieved by applying something called the Science of Improvement. We have much more learning to do in health care, and there is much work to be done to discover how to apply this science."

Gwen is not alone as a leader. As she sipped her coffee, Gwen thought, "I have very good experience and have become very knowledgeable in the work I do. I went to good schools and have acquired the core skills and abilities to be an effective manager and leader. I am fortunate to have real-world clinical experience combined with management and leadership experience. With all of that, I still feel like more can be done to serve patients and to identify opportunities to improve our health system. Maybe the Science of Improvement will give us the theory and methods to do it."

Gwen's dilemma is a common one for leaders. She learned her craft and the traditional approaches to management and business. She has a broad awareness of topics in finance, human resources, and marketing that reflect the current thinking of management practices. What is missing is how this all fits together—a theoretical foundation that is focused on the Science of Improvement to make sense of it all and apply it consistently across the organization.

INTRODUCTION TO SCIENCE OF IMPROVEMENT

W. Edwards Deming[1] proposed a framework he called a system of profound knowledge (figure 2.1) which is the interplay of the theories of systems, variation, knowledge, and psychology. Knowledge is based on **theory**.[2] Theory enables us to predict. The word "Profound" denotes the deep insight this knowledge provides into how to make changes that we can predict will result in improvement in a variety of settings.

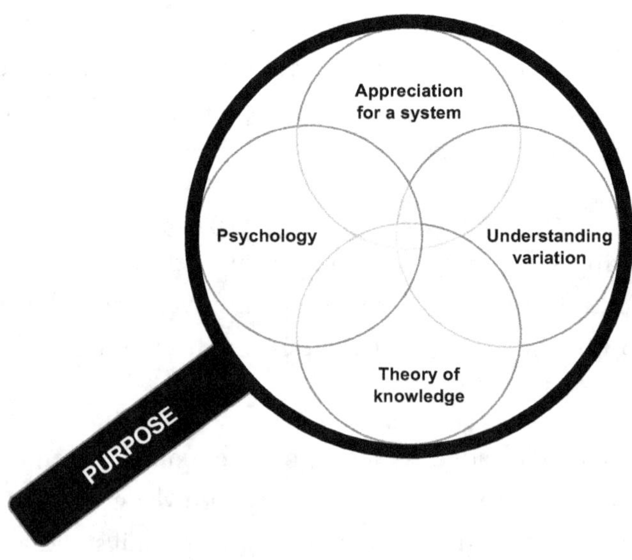

Figure 2.1. Deming's System of Profound Knowledge.

Deming observed: "The aim is…to provide an outside view—a lens—that I call a System of Profound Knowledge. It provides a map of theory by which to understand the organizations that we work in." He added, "One need not be eminent in any part nor in all four parts in order to understand it and to apply it…The various segments of the system of profound knowledge…cannot be separated. They interact with each other. Thus, knowledge about psychology is incomplete without knowledge of variation."[3]

Deming's journey to framing profound knowledge evolved over a half-century of work and study.[4] It began by translating statistical thinking in Japan to improve quality, to generating a theory of management as he continued his work in the U.S. and culminated with the framing of the system of profound knowledge (figure 2.1).[5]

Deming's framework has formed the foundation of the Science of Improvement:[6]

> The Science of Improvement includes the interaction of systems thinking, understanding variation, psychology of change, and the theory of knowledge that are applied to improve the performance of processes, products, services, organizations, and communities. The proper application of this science requires integration of a set of improvement methods and tools with knowledge of subject matter to develop, test, implement, and spread changes.[7]

Gwen was approached by her boss to attend a workshop.

"Gwen, we have thought about your desire to ensure we create internal capability to learn and improve. Would you be available to attend this workshop? Check it out to see if it applies to our organization."

Gwen quickly looked over the brochure and spotted the Science of Improvement. She immediately replied, "Yes!"

While at the workshop, she reflected on the importance of the concept. "This has been missing in our efforts. We focused on tools and techniques without the guidance of theory. Understanding the four theories and their interactions should give our leadership team a shared meaning of what is to be done and, even more important, of why."

What knowledge will enable us to develop, test, and implement changes that result in improvement? Consider the concepts of subject matter knowledge and knowledge required to make improvements:

- **Subject Matter Knowledge:** knowledge basic to the things we do in life; professional knowledge and experience.
- **Improvement Knowledge:** the interaction of the theories of systems, variation, knowledge, and psychology.
- **Improvement**: learning to combine subject matter knowledge and improvement knowledge in creative ways to develop effective changes for improvement.

Figure 2.2 describes the combining of these two types of knowledge to increase the capability to make improvements.[8]

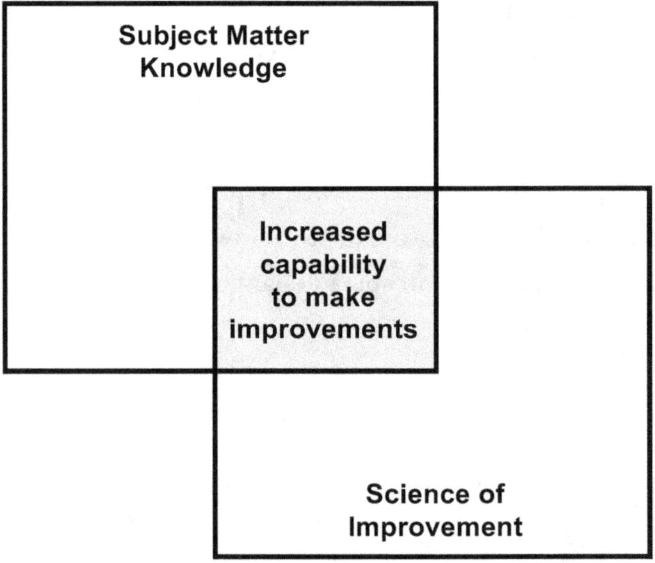

Figure 2.2. Interplay of subject matter knowledge and the science of improvement.

SCIENCE OF IMPROVEMENT: UNDERSTANDING THE FOUR PARTS

Deming's framing of profound knowledge builds on the contributions of many scholars and practitioners from many disciplines, including systems, psychology, statistics, design, sociology, and many management and organizational theories. Table 2.1 highlights a sample of the important contributions to the Science of Improvement.[9]

Table 2.1. Milestones for System of Profound Knowledge

Decade	FOUR COMPONENTS			
	Psychology	**Knowledge**	**Systems**	**Variation**
1900	1890: *Principles of Psychology,* William James	1870–1905: *Pragmatism,* C Pierce, W James, J. Dewey		
1910			1910: *Scientific Management,* F. Taylor; Frank & Lillian Gilbreth	
1920	1920: *B=(PE),* Kurt Lewin 1923: *ID, ego, Superego,* Sigmund Freud 1925: *Participatory Management,* Mary Parker Follet 1927: *Hawthorne Experiment,* Elton Mayo	1929: *Mind and the World Order,* C.I. Lewis		1924: *Control Chart,* Shewhart 1925: *Design of Experiments,* Sir Ronald Fisher
1930	*Anthropology experts apply psychology theory to business*	1933: *How We Think,* John Dewey		1931, 1939: *Books on Quality Control,* Shewhart 1938: *Shewhart lectures at USDA* organized by Deming
1940	1947: *Man For Himself: Psychology of Ethics,* H.L. Harlow 1949: *Intrinsic Motivation & Incentives (How Incentives destroy performance in monkeys),* H.L. Harlow		1949: *General Systems Theory,* Ludwig Von Bertalanffy	1941–1945: *Sampling Methods Statistical Methods to Support War Efforts,* H.F. Dodge 1945: *Control Chart for Determining Tool,* Wear. J. Manuele
1950	1951: *Socio-Technical System,* Eric Trist; *Organizational Development,* M. McGregor (Tavistock Institute) 1957: *Cognitive Dissonance,* Leon Fistinger		1951: *Organization Viewed as a System,* Deming 1959: *Holistic Management* Stafford Beer	1950: *Publishes paper on I (Individuals) Chart* L. H. C. Tippett 1959: Publishes paper on CuSum Chart G.A. Bernard
1960	1960: *Human Side of Enterprise,* McGregor 1962: *Hierarchy of Needs,* Maslow 1968: *Motivation Theory,* Herzberg	1968: *Experiential Learning Theory,* Carl Rogers	1968: *Principles of Systems,* Jay Forrester	1960: *Enumerative Versus Analytic Studies,* Deming
1970	1977: *Attribution Error,* Lee Ross	1973: *Adult Learning Theory,* Malcolm Knowles 1977: *Double Loop Learning In Organizations,* Chris Argyris 1978: *Bounded Rationality,* Herbert Simon		
1980	1988: *Why Work?,* M. Maccoby *(Maslow's Theory Reconsidered)*	1986: *Shewhart Learning Cycle,* Deming 1987: Model for Improvement (Three Questions) Associates in Process Improvement (API)	1981: *Creating the Corporate Future,* R. Ackoff *Open Systems,* Fred Emery 1984: *The Goal,* E. Goldratt 1989: *Linkage of Processes,* API	
1990	1998: *Dunning-Kruger Effect,* Dunning and Kruger	1993: *PDSA Cycle,* Deming 1994: *Improvement Model,* API *(Three Questions plus PDSA)*	1990: *Fifth Discipline,* Peter Senge *Theory of Constraints,* E. Goldratt	
2000	2003: *Narcissistic Leaders: Who Succeeds & Who Fails,* M. Maccoby	2005: *Descriptive & Normative Model For Theory Building,* Carlile & Christianson	2006: *Idealized Design,* Russell Ackoff 2007: *Strategic Intelligence,* M. Maccoby	

Deming described these four bodies of knowledge as an interdependent system that "cannot be separated." We will explore each component of the Science of Improvement to learn about the distinct contributions and bring the components back together in order to appreciate their interconnectedness.

Appreciation for a System

The word "system" appears all around us: our children go to school in school systems, we get our power from an electrical system, our computer connects to an IT system, and we commute home on a transportation system. So, what do we mean by that term?

Russell Ackoff defines a system as "a whole that cannot be divided into interdependent parts."[10] One of the best examples is the human body. A body possesses organs, including the brain, heart, lungs, liver, and kidneys. Each organ has its function. For example, the lungs oxygenate the blood, but our organs are also interdependent. Remove the heart from the body, and it cannot function independently. The body cannot continue to operate without the heart.

Organizations can be defined as systems: A **system** is an **interdependent** group of components (items, people, or processes) working together toward a common **purpose**.[11] Organizations have a purpose to meet specific Needs of customers. The organization includes functions like marketing, sales, operations, finance, etc., with specific functions. Each of those functional areas must be interdependent for the organization to be successful. For example, marketing must help understand the market so that production can produce products that match the need, and the sales team leverages market knowledge to sell the products and services.

WHY IS SYSTEMS THINKING CHALLENGING?

Systems thinking is a departure from what we have learned since we were children. When we give children toys, the first thing that many do is to pull them apart to see how they work. Later we learned that this is called analysis. The terms analysis and synthesis are derived from the Greek language;[12] analysis means to "loosen up." Systems thinking is very different from analysis, and it begins and ends in synthesis.

Synthesis in our context means "to put together." Ackoff observed the difference between the two learning journeys:

> These two approaches should not (but often do) yield contradictory or conflicting results: they are complementary. Development of this complementarity is a major task of systems thinking. Analysis focuses on *structure;* it reveals *how things work.* Synthesis focuses on *function;* it reveals *why things operate as they do.* Therefore, analysis yields *knowledge;* synthesis yields *understanding.* The former enables us to describe and the latter to explain.[13]

Table 2.2 summarizes the two journeys of analysis and systems thinking (synthesis).

Table 2.2. Analysis and synthesis (systems thinking)

Stages	Method of inquiry	
	Analysis	**Synthesis (systems thinking)**
First stage	Break into parts the whole which is to be explained	Identify and see the whole system to be explained
Second stage	Explanations are made for each part separately	Explain the behavior or properties of the whole system
Third stage	Explanations are then taken together to explain the whole	Explain the behavior or the properties of the system and subsystems in terms of their role or function within the whole system
Outcomes		
Focus	Structure	Function
Question answered	How things work?	Why do things operate as they do?
Result	Knowledge (describe)	Understanding (explain)

After considering the differences between analysis and synthesis (systems thinking) consider the following definition of systems thinking:

> Systems thinking is a way of making sense of the complexity of the world by looking at it in terms of wholes and relationships rather than by splitting it down into its parts. It has been used as a way of exploring and developing effective action in complex contexts, enabling

systems change. Systems thinking draws on and contributes to systems theory and the system sciences.[14]

Note the focus on the whole, relationships, patterns, and the changes that may be required in our perceptions.

PRINCIPLES FOR APPRECIATING THE ORGANIZATION AS A SYSTEM

Appreciating organizations as systems is foundational for designing an organization to serve the Need of customers, operating it predictably, and improving it over time. This appreciation involves these underlying principles:

- Every social system has an aim or purpose, explicit or implicit.
- A system is a collection of interdependent parts or processes that each have a function and also work in concert with each other. All work can be described as a process.
- Leaders are responsible for the design and redesign of the system.
- Improving outcomes requires changes to the system.
- Complexity is in the system, not just linear cause-and-effect actions.

Ackoff describes organizations as **social systems**. A social system is one where both the parts and the whole are purposeful (e.g., organizations such as universities, corporations, and hospitals). Consider the definition of organization viewed as a system presented earlier: a **system** is an **interdependent** group of components (items, people, or processes) working together toward a common **purpose**.

When considering an **aim or purpose**, the purpose aligns the parts of the system toward a common aim, while interdependence considers relationships and interactions among the parts. Optimization of a system is the process of orchestrating the efforts of all components toward the achievement of the stated purpose.

Deming described a system as "a network of interdependent components that work together to try to accomplish the aim of the system."[15] People participate in interconnected and interdependent work (process) in service of the organizational purpose. Ackoff put forth a vital system principle: **"If each part of a system, considered separately, is made to operate as efficiently as possible, the system as a whole will *not* operate as effectively as possible."**[16]

The leadership team is responsible for ensuring that the system is designed and redesigned to achieve its mission. From an improvement perspective, the system must be changed to affect the desired improvement. What do we mean by improvement? Figure 1.3 (in Chapter 1) described the following operational definition of an improvement: **a change that alters how work is done, or the makeup of a product, that produces visible, positive differences (relative to historical norms) in relevant measures, sustained into the future.**

When considering a change that results in an improvement to the system, it is essential to distinguish between two basic types of change:[17]

1. **Reactive** (first-order change): a change that occurs within a given system. The system remains the same, for example, reacting to and solving a problem that returns performance to a prior condition, such as rebooting a personal computer when a program is acting buggy.
2. **Fundamental** (second-order change): a change which changes the system. For example, changing a process that results in a new level of performance or moving to a new operating system on the personal computer.

The methods associated with QOS primarily focus on fundamental change resulting from the design or redesign of processes, products, services, or the whole system. Leaders focus on this type of change with improvement projects.

APPRECIATING SYSTEM COMPLEXITY

Too often, techniques and approaches framed in books or journals assume immediate cause and effect are understood, and that if you change X, then Y will happen. In reality, organizational systems include two types of complexity: detail and dynamic.[18]

- **Detail complexity** deals with the many variables in a system. Processes with many steps and moving parts require tracking and analysis to maintain function.
- **Dynamic complexity** is present when the same action has dramatically different effects in the short run and the long run. Delays, feedback loops, and interactions between variables drive the performance of the system. There is dynamic complexity when an action has one set of consequences locally and a different set of consequences in another part of the system. When obvious interventions produce nonobvious consequences, there is dynamic complexity. For example, the

power goes off and comes back on, resetting the sprinkler system. Next month, the water bill is sky-high! The technician called out to diagnose the problem had discovered the power failure and reset the programmed watering schedule from the programmed two days to the default setting of four days, doubling water use.

Related to understanding the system complexities just described is the reality of **unintended consequences.**[19] Organizations are multilayered with dynamic complexity. Changes upstream in the system are often seen much further downstream in a delayed time frame. Siloed support processes may lack urgency without understanding the consequences. A systems view of the organization helps us see how work travels through the system processes, using arrows showing relationships between processes.

ADVANTAGES TO THE LEADERSHIP TEAM IN VIEWING THE ORGANIZATION AS A SYSTEM

When a leadership team switches to viewing the organization as a system, the mental model shift facilitates several advantages:

- The focus is on the organization's purpose and customers.
- Significant relationships are understood in the system relative to meeting the purpose.
- The importance of cooperation and collaboration throughout the organization becomes clear.
- When things go wrong, the focus is on the system, and the "blame game" is minimized.
- Various improvement efforts noted on the system map can be better coordinated.

Chapter 5 describes how to view the organization as a system and introduces the concept of work as a process and a method to develop and use an organizational system map. These methods allow leaders to appreciate how work is linked and interdependent to achieve the system's purpose. Such recognition of a system demands collaboration as a practical value.

While Gwen was at the workshop, she had a discussion with one of the other attendees. At end of the presentation on systems, she asked, "How long has your organization been using QOS?"

Sue took a sip of her coffee, "About three years; I am in the fourth group of managers to attend this workshop."

Gwen continued, "Have you had experience using a system map?"

"Oh, yes," Sue replied. "The first group of managers developed our original map of our organization as a system. As a leadership group we continue to update the map documenting our learning and improvement. I noticed that using the map eliminated the blame game, finding fault before we understand the system. We have learned the system is typically getting the results that we deserve given our design or lack of design."

Laughing, they finished their coffee and returned to the workshop.

Appreciating organizations as systems designed to meet their purposes is a major shift and opportunity for leaders to pursue quality as their strategy. Understanding the system empowers leaders to see it as both a whole and in parts, to locate opportunities to design or redesign processes to enhance performance, and to manage the interdependencies of the people and parts.

Knowledge About Variation

Variation is a natural part of the life, and we must interpret variation in data in a way to make appropriate decisions. For example, are the children in my class on track? Does this month's change in sales mean we are losing market share? Do the two medication errors this month in our hospital indicate an undesirable trend? Was this week's improved performance the result of the change we made or just random luck? The ability to answer these questions and others like them is inseparable from making improvements.

In the early days of the telephone, managers at Western Electric Hawthorne in Cicero, Illinois—a factory that made telephone equipment—received reports every month on performance in their area and were expected to improve quality.[20] But, like all of us, they struggled to determine what issues required fixing from the noise of the random variation built into the process.

Walter A. Shewhart was then a member of the Bell Labs Inspection Engineering Department staff. Plant superintendent R.L. Jones contacted Shewhart and shared his challenge and that he needed "an acceptable form of inspection report which might be modified from time to time, in order to give, at a glance, the greatest amount of accurate information."[21] Shewhart developed a novel solution, and figure 2.3 is his letter responding to Jones. He attached his first chart and described the meaning and use of the chart. He says, "I have already started the preparation of a series of memoranda covering these points in detail."[22]

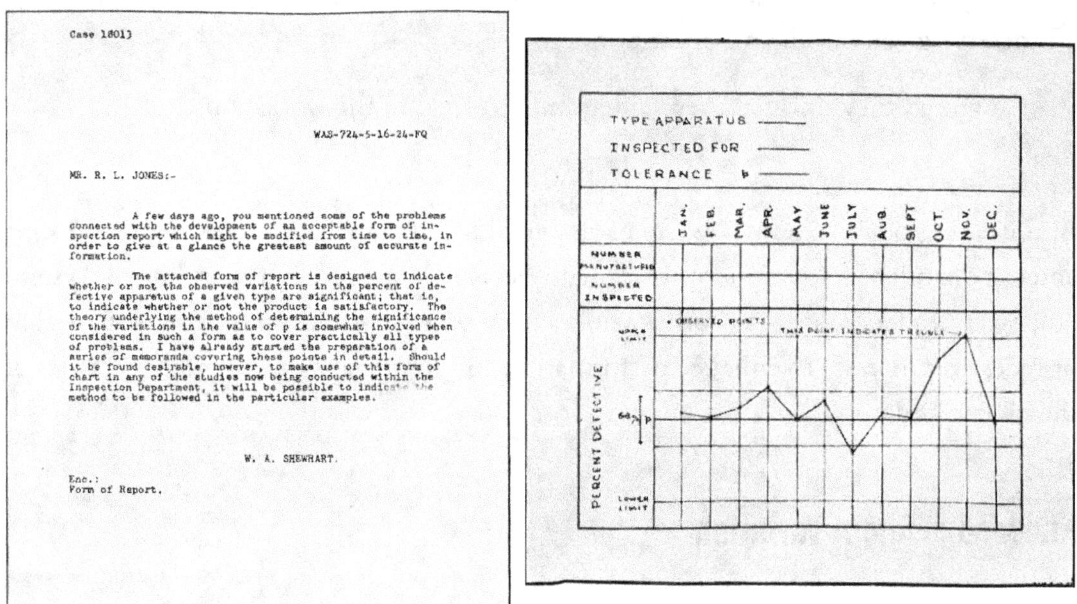

Figure 2.3. Letter and original Shewhart chart (courtesy of the American Society of Quality).

Shewhart made several discoveries that inform our understanding of variation based on his first control chart application:

1. Plotting data over time in a visual display on control charts helps us see patterns of variation.
2. Variation of data is from both common and special causes inherent in the system.
3. How one takes an action to improve is based on the type of variation present.

TWO TYPES OF VARIATION IN DATA

Shewhart observed two situations when plotting data over time. In some cases, the patterns in the data were predictable and appeared random, as if they happened by chance. In other cases, however, they seemed to show unpredictable data. These data appeared not to be random, as if they were from some attributable cause.

These observations led Shewhart to use statistical theory and develop a means of understanding variation in systems based on patterns of variation over time. His theory of variation made a distinction between two causes of the variation[23] of data:

- **Common Causes**: those causes inherent in the system (process or product) over time affect everyone working in the system and affect all outcomes of the system.
- **Special Causes**: those causes are ***not*** always part of the system (process or product) all the time or do not affect everyone but arise because of specific circumstances.

What does Shewhart's theory look like in practice? Consider the monthly sales for a distribution company. The leadership is concerned about last month's below-average sales performance. Figure 2.4 visually displays the organization's monthly sales data over time on a Shewhart control chart.

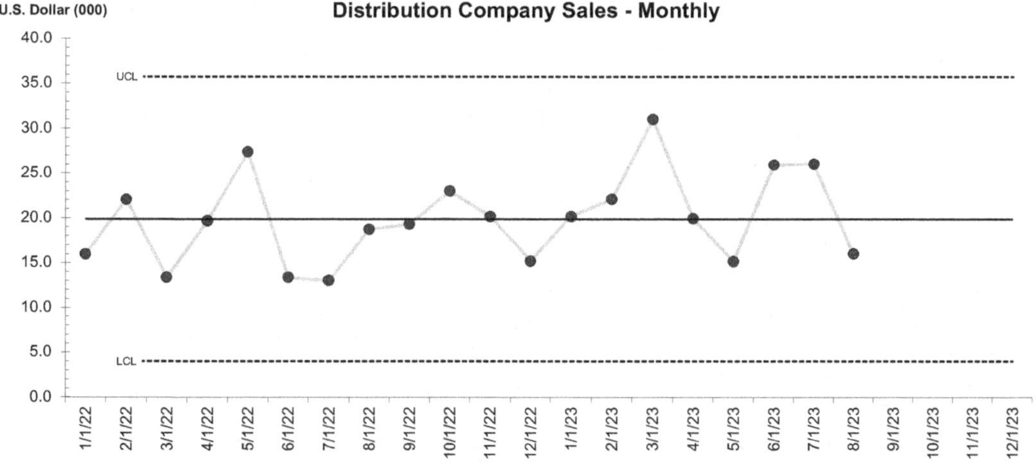

Figure 2.4. Shewhart chart for sales.

What are we to conclude from this data? Was the past month that bad compared to the sales history in the months before? Does the variation in sales look random from month to month? What actions should we take to improve sales? How does this compare with a traditional approach of comparing this month's sales number to the same month last year, such as May 2022 to May 2023? Would we arrive at different conclusions?

A process with only common causes affecting the outcomes is a **stable** process; in other words, it is in a state of **statistical control**. The Shewhart chart in figure 2.4 of the sales data is an example of a variation in the outcomes of the process, meeting the definition of a stable process; sales are predictable within the limits established in the chart. This does not mean that sales are meeting requirements. It only implies that the variation is predictable within statistically established limits. In practice, this indicates that improvement in sales requires a fundamental change (redesign) to the system to achieve a different result.

A process whose outcomes are affected by special causes of variation is called an **unstable** process. An unstable process is not necessarily one with considerable variation. Instead, the variation from one period to the next is unpredictable.

Five rules (figure 2.5) for identifying special causes are recommended for general use with Shewhart charts. These rules are consistent in that the chance of occurrence in a stable process of Rule 2 through Rule 5 is close to the chance of Rule 1 occurring.[24]

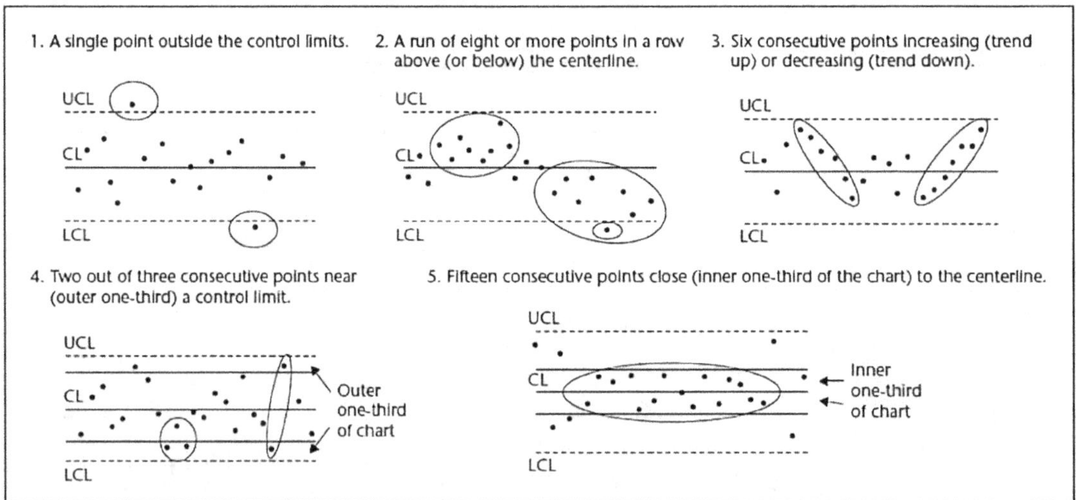

Figure 2.5. Special cause patterns.

The occurrence of a special cause does not mean something is bad or wrong. A shift (Rule 2) or a trend (Rule 3) may result from changes made to the process to improve it. A special cause tells us something is happening, and we want to understand it. If it is not desirable, such as a failure or a defect, we want to figure out how to remove it. If it is positive—perhaps a staff person did the process differently and got a better outcome—we may want to figure out how to make it the standard for the process.

If unwanted special causes can be identified and removed, the process becomes stable. Its performance becomes predictable, with only random variation, that is, common cause variation. In practical terms, improvement can occur by identifying the special causes and taking appropriate action. Once making a change, plotting data over time, and observing the patterns helps determine whether the change is an improvement.

USING SHEWHART CHARTS TO GUIDE ACTION

Using Shewhart charts to see and learn from variation is just the start. So how do we use this learning to support making decisions about how to act on organizational systems in order to improve?

Shewhart observed that people typically can make two mistakes[25] when acting based on data:

- **Mistake One**: Reacting to an outcome as if it came from a special cause when it actually came from common causes of variation (overreaction). We see a point move in a direction we do not like, or the data point shows performance that is not where we want it, so we react as if it's unique and not like the other data points.
- **Mistake Two**: Treating an outcome as if it came from common causes of variation when in fact it came from a special cause (underreaction). This is a lack of reaction when something unusual is going on, and we assume it's typical and do not learn about it or act on it.

Shewhart observed that the Shewhart chart helps minimize the total cost when people stop over- or underreacting to their data (see table 2.3). When the actual situation of the system is that a special-cause change occurred, the proper action of people in the organization is to take action to learn and work with the special cause (Correct Decision A). If there is no special cause and the results are not desirable, the proper action is to improve the system (Correct Decision B). Reacting with correct decisions to the variation results in learning, improvement, and saving money and time. The opposite is true when making one of the mistakes.

Table 2.3. Balancing the mistakes made in attempts to improve

Action	Actual situation	
	No special cause is occurring in the system	A special cause is occurring in system
Act on the individual outcome; treat as a special cause	-$ (Mistake One)	+$ (Correct Decision A)
Treat outcome as part of the system and work on changing the system; treat as common cause variation	+$ (Correct Decision B)	-$ (Mistake Two)

WHAT IS NEEDED TO DEVELOP A SHEWHART CHART?

The development and effective use of the Shewhart Chart requires five steps:

1. Selection of a measure and a statistic to be plotted
2. Method of data collection: measurement, observation, and sampling procedures
3. Strategy for determining subgroups of measurements (including subgroup size and frequency)
4. Selection of the appropriate Shewhart chart[26]
5. Criteria for identifying a signal of a special cause (see figure 2.5)[27]

Shewhart called the limits on the chart **three-sigma limits** and gave a general formula to calculate the limits for any statistic. The rationale for the use of Shewhart's three-sigma limits are:

- The limits have a basis in statistical theory.
- The limits have proven in practice to distinguish between special and common causes of variation (see figure 2.5).
- In most cases, the use of the limits will approximately minimize the total cost due to overreaction and underreaction to variation in the process (see table 2.2).
- The limits protect the morale of people in the process by defining the magnitude of the variation built into the process.[28]

This last item is a particular gift from Deming, who observed the problem of not being able to distinguish between special and common cause variation:

> A fault in the interpretation of observations, seen everywhere, is to suppose that every event (defect, mistake, accident) is attributable to someone (usually the one nearest at hand), or is related to some special event. The fact is that most troubles with service and production lie in the system. Sometimes the fault is indeed local, attributable to someone on the job or not on the job when he should be. We shall speak of faults of the system as common causes of trouble, and faults from fleeting events as special causes.[29]

Gwen and Sue decided to go to dinner after the workshop. Gwen was eager to learn more from Sue about the variation component of profound knowledge. Gwen opened the conversation, "Sue, this was a rough day as we discussed the theory of variation and the Shewhart charts. I am afraid that many times I have reacted and blamed people, when in fact, we were suffering from common cause variation."

Sue replied, "I know what you mean. I have had people written up for mistakes, and now I am wondering if this was the correct action. I wish I had this knowledge years ago. But as we learned from Deming's teachings, we must let the guilt go and focus on helping others now that we understand the difference between special and common cause variation."

Psychology

Organizations are filled with diverse people of different ages and backgrounds, from different places and cultures, who each have their own lived experience. This is one of the greatest gifts of working with colleagues in the organization and often one of the most challenging aspects.

Psychology in the context of organizational systems includes many considerations:

- People are different, and they interact differently.
- People are born with a desire to learn, and they learn in different ways and at different speeds.

- People are intrinsically motivated to serve a meaningful purpose and to do work they are proud of and have control over.
- People will embrace that change when they can be part of it.

Psychology is the science of mind and behavior, which helps us understand ourselves and others and shapes our leadership style. As leaders, it helps us understand and embrace the challenge to lead and help people change while focusing on QOS. These ideas, methods, and tools help leaders understand themselves and those they lead and deliver changes.

Dealing with the people side of change in many organizations is a challenge. There are continually new methods, products, tools, and sometimes a clash of vastly different cultures as our world becomes smaller. So how can we deal with these changes successfully? Now more and more people agree that managing the people aspect of change is an important task. However, much remains misunderstood about how people and organizations face challenges and undergo change.

One common mistake is to think of change as only a technical issue. This view would confine us to consider only the new methods and equipment to ensure that they function as planned. As Juran noted, "There is no such thing as a technical change without a social effect. Any proposed technical change automatically is proposing some social change as well." [30] These changes must be planned and managed to implementation if we are to gain the predicted benefits of the change. Therefore, we must learn how to change more effectively. Creating structures such that we **make it easy for people to do the right thing and hard to do the wrong thing** is a high-leverage approach to helping people adapt to a change.

PEOPLE AS LEARNERS

People begin the learning journey from childhood. They learn in different ways and have different interests. Some are very curious about the world; others are more reserved and cautious. Many people believe they can learn from experience alone. Deming observed:

> Experience without theory teaches nothing. In fact, experience cannot even be recorded unless there is some theory, however crude, that leads to a hypothesis and a system by which to catalog observations. Sometimes only a hunch, right or wrong, is sufficient theory to lead to useful observation. [31]

With children, a parent may advise, "Don't touch the stove; it is hot." Some of us needed to test that theory. We soon learned what "hot" meant.[32]

Leaders who understand personality theory understand themselves better and are better positioned to avoid unnecessary conflict over personality differences. More importantly, personality theory guides the leader in how to better communicate with those who are differently motivated.[33]

ALIGN AND MOTIVATE OTHERS TOWARD THE ORGANIZATION'S PURPOSE

A leader who motivates without alignment to the organization's purpose can hurt their credibility and be labeled a cheerleader, potentially impairing another part of the organization. Chapter 4 describes leadership's use of the purpose statement, an essential method for aligning people's roles and the purpose of the system to enable engagement.

When we understand why a change is necessary and align it to the organization's vision, we are helping the organization and others understand why change is needed and their role in it. But can we motivate others to do something different? Maccoby[34] learned that people tend to embrace and work on things they care about, the things that make them feel good about themselves and generate genuine interest for them. He demonstrated that people **could** be motivated when using what he framed as the Five Rs of motivation, allowing the leader to align their motives with the organization and the individual's role in the change. Addressing all five is required for success:

1. **Reasons:** Why should we change? How does this change align with the purpose of the organization and my role? How will this help us?
2. **Relationships:** How will this change impact other parts of the system and help them and our customers? What are the important relationships to enlist for this change?
3. **Responsibilities**: What are my responsibilities? Are they clear enough for me to contribute to the purpose for which we are working?
4. **Recognition**: How will we be recognized and appreciated for our personal contributions? How will this change affect my worth and dignity?
5. **Rewards:** Am I being paid fairly for my level of expertise and skill?

Recognition and rewards specifically address intrinsic and extrinsic motivation. Recognition creates satisfaction (intrinsic motivation) from fulfilling social and personal needs. For example, working with a team to improve one's job where ideas are considered and used. In comparison, rewards focus on extrinsic motivation and fair compensation.

However, general practice often uses only one R to motivate: rewards. This has mixed results. Why?[35] Daniel Pink[36] recovered research from the 1940s showing that extrinsic rewards are highly effective in transactional work, such as paying handlers per package. However, extrinsic motivation can lead to worse performance for knowledge workers where ideas and creativity are required. This finding counters the widely accepted notion that everyone is motivated by extrinsic rewards.

> Gwen reflected on engagement and motivation:
>
> > We are typically entertaining the question of what to do to engage people in their work within the leadership team. I can't wait to share the roadmap of the Five Rs and more importantly how our purpose relates to the work of all of our employees. I can now see a path forward. I'll make a note to learn more from Sue on how they define jobs better to align people to the purpose of the organization!

Theory of Knowledge

Deming[37] described prediction as a key role of management. Leaders are responsible for planning or designing an organization to produce the outcomes or results desired. The organization of the company, the people hired, the practices followed, and the behaviors promoted are all based on theory. Consider, for example, a theory that people with specific credentials (such as certifications or degrees) make good staff or that following standard work practice reduces variation in performance. This theory means that these attributes or activities will deliver the desired results wanted. How can we develop those theories and build knowledge about what works and does not work? How do we grow knowledge and learn? This is the basis of the theory of knowledge.

Philosophers and scientists have been addressing the theory of knowledge for centuries. The theory of knowledge component of the Science of Improvement is focused on several key ideas:

- PDSA: Iterative Nature of Learning through Deduction and Induction

- Enumerative and Analytic Studies
- Hierarchy of Knowledge: Data-Information-Knowledge-Understanding-Wisdom[38]
- Operational Definitions and True Value
- Biases and Judgment Heuristics: Avoiding the Traps in Thinking & Decisions

PDSA AND THE ITERATIVE NATURE OF LEARNING THROUGH DEDUCTION AND INDUCTION

The PDSA cycle appears to be very simple.[39] In fact, the theories of deductive and inductive learning are built into the method. Many users are not aware of the underlying theory that drives learning while using the PDSA cycle. Figure 2.6 describes the role of PDSA cycles in carrying out the learning journeys of deduction and induction. In each arrow, note the deductive and inductive journey labeled. The authors Box, Hunter, and Hunter provide a picture that describes the iterative nature of theory building described above:

> Learning is advanced by…iteration. An initial hypothesis leads by a process of deduction to certain necessary consequences that may be compared with data. When consequences and data fail to agree, the discrepancy can lead, by a process called induction, to modification of the hypothesis. A second cycle in the iteration is thus initiated. The consequences of the modified hypothesis are worked out and again compared with data…that in turn can lead to further modification and gain of knowledge.[40]

Properly prepared PDSA cycles are built with deductive and inductive learning. From Plan to Do is the **deductive** approach. We test theory or hunch with the aid of a prediction. In Do, we make observations and note departures from the prediction. From Do to Study, the **inductive** learning process takes place. We study gaps (anomalies) to the prediction, and update the hypothesis, conjecture, model, or theory accordingly. We act on the new learning. When dealing with complex situations, it is difficult to define the problem adequately initially; therefore, we refine both the problem and the solution through learning.

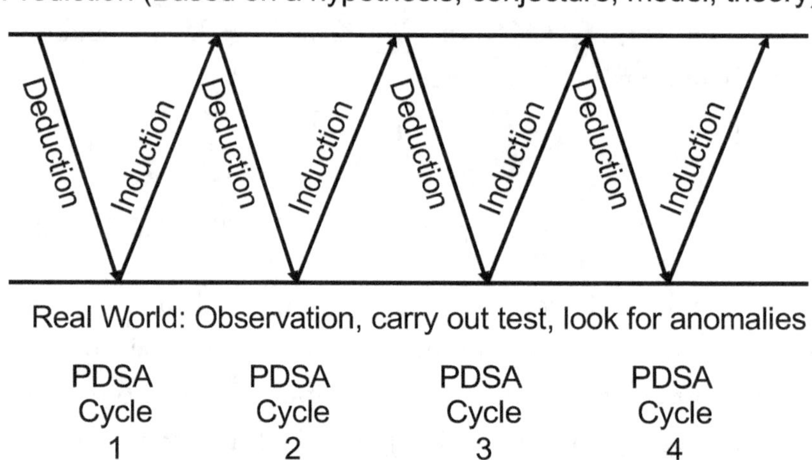

Figure 2.6. The iterative nature of learning: deduction and induction.

The use of PDSA cycles documents our iterative learning and improvement process to increase our degree of belief in our theory and changes. Figure 2.7 describes this learning and improvement journey, with PDSA cycles[41] moving us from our current knowledge to predictive knowledge. Typical PDSA cycles move from developing changes, testing changes, implementing changes, and finally spreading the changes to other parts of the organization.

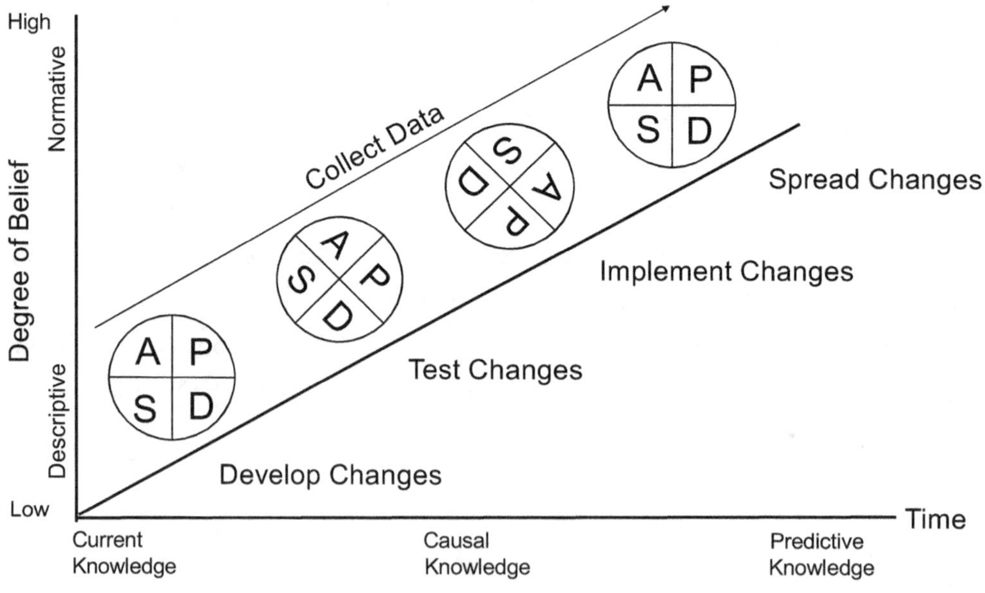

Figure 2.7. The iterative process of learning and improvement with PDSA cycles.

PREDICTION IS THE PROBLEM: TWO TYPES OF STUDIES

Figure 2.8 depicts the difference between the **enumerative** and **analytic** approaches to designing studies for learning.[42] The objective of the experiment (or study) will

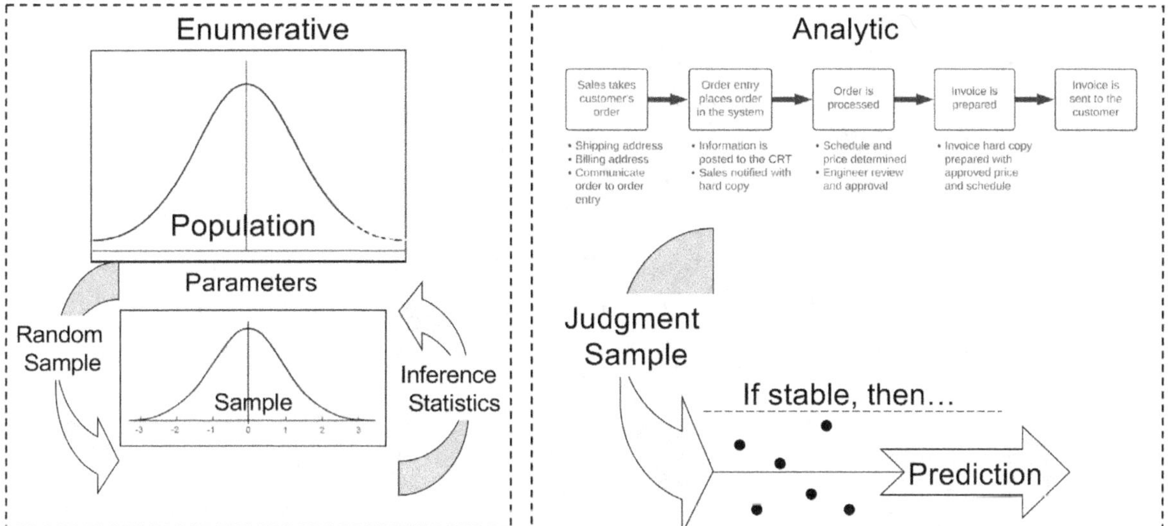

Figure 2.8. Difference in approaches to enumerative and analytic studies.

In an **enumerative study**, we take a random sample[43] from a population to make a judgment about the population. Given this sample, we calculate some statistics (e.g., average, standard deviation, etc.) and then infer our confidence that the samples taken represent the population. We then decide to accept or reject what we learned. On the analytic side, we take judgment samples[44] from a process and plot those on a Shewhart Chart to learn about stability. If stable, this allows us to predict; to understand the quality, cost, and productivity in the future.

An **analytic study** emphasizes **prediction.** Deming observed the importance of prediction for managers and leaders:

> Prediction is the problem, whether we are talking about applied science, research and development, engineering, or management in industry, education, or government. The question is, what do the data tell us? How do they help us to predict?[45]

As leaders involved in making QOS, we are making changes today to transform the organization in the future.

HIERARCHY OF KNOWLEDGE

> *An ounce of information is worth a pound of data.*
> *An ounce of knowledge is worth a pound of information.*
> *An ounce of understanding is worth a pound of knowledge.*
> Russell Ackoff[46]

Many authors touch on the components of what constitutes the Hierarchy Of Knowledge in the twentieth century. Ackoff[47] was the first to write specifically about the hierarchy of knowledge. Figure 2.9 describes this process.[48]

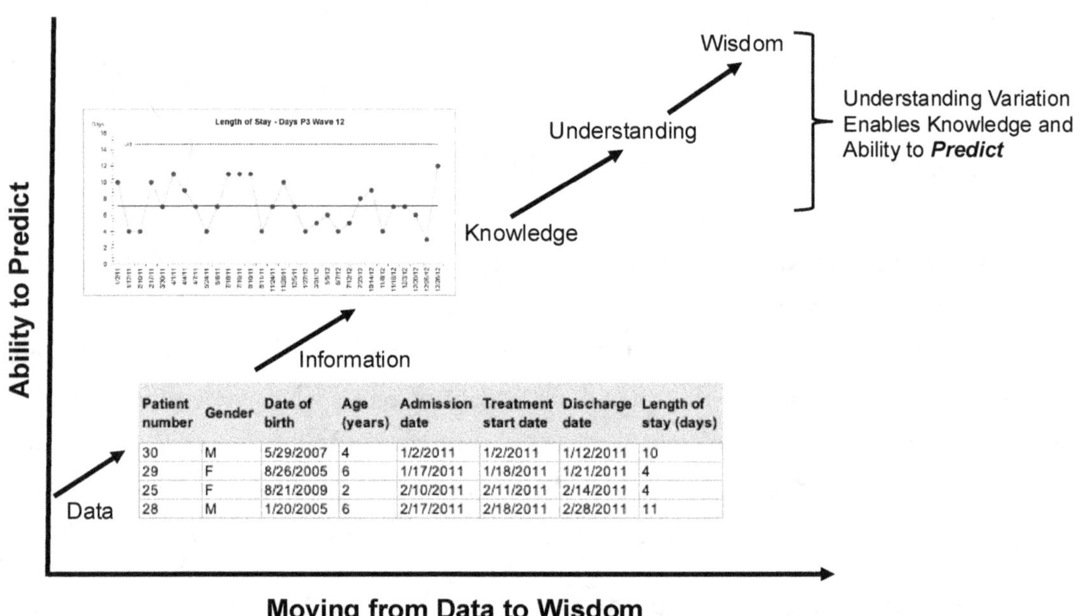

Patient number	Gender	Date of birth	Age (years)	Admission date	Treatment start date	Discharge date	Length of stay (days)
30	M	5/29/2007	4	1/2/2011	1/2/2011	1/12/2011	10
29	F	8/26/2005	6	1/17/2011	1/18/2011	1/21/2011	4
25	F	8/21/2009	2	2/10/2011	2/11/2011	2/14/2011	4
28	M	1/20/2005	6	2/17/2011	2/18/2011	2/28/2011	11

Figure 2.9. Graphical depiction of the hierarchy of knowledge.

Ackoff defined the various componants as follows:

- **Data**: documented observations and measurements
- **Information**: data that are processed to be useful; provides answers to "who," "what," "where," and "when" questions
- **Knowledge**: application of data and information; answers "how" questions

- **Understanding**: appreciation of "why"
- **Wisdom**: evaluated understanding

A well-defined PDSA cycle emphasizes a plan for collecting **data,** and placing this data in a table helps us describe some relationships and provide **information.** Placing data on a Shewhart chart enables **knowledge** and **understanding** of the variation present in our process. Knowledge and understanding of the variation relative to special and common cause variation allow us to predict and yields **wisdom** in the present for decisions to impact the future.

People often complain that their data are flawed or incomplete. Various reasons could be in play for poor data. Often data are collected without regard to the question being answered. This almost always results in the data being meaningless and much frustration for those collecting the data. A well-defined PDSA cycle can often prevent this chronic time waste. Table 2.4 summarizes the phases of the PDSA cycle and the role of the hierarchy of knowledge.

Table 2.4. PDSA and the hierarchy of knowledge

PDSA cycle phases	Role of the Hierarchy of Knowledge
Plan	Learning objectives, questions and predictions drive plan for **data** collection and tests of change
Do	Collect **data**, plot data to create **information** and early analysis, **knowledge** based on observation and learning
Study	Compare **data** to predictions and update **knowledge**
Act	Act based on **knowledge**, create **wisdom** over time.

OPERATIONAL DEFINITIONS

The lack of operational definitions in industry, business, education, and government can lead to unnecessary misunderstandings and conflict. Poorly defined terms in contracts often end up in court and then defined with increased costs. Deming noted:

> In the opinion of many people in industry, there is nothing more important for transaction of business than use of operational definitions. It could also be said that no requirement of industry is so much neglected. One learns about operational definitions in colleges

of liberal arts, in courses in philosophy and theory of knowledge, but hardly ever in schools of business or engineering in the United States.[49]

To develop an operational definition,[50] consideration needs to be given to:

- A method of measurement or test.
- A set of criteria for judgment.

The first step to obtaining an operational definition of a concept is to define a test or measurement related to the concept. For physical characteristics, such as fat percentage, hardness, or viscosity, experts such as analytic chemists or metallurgists may be needed to define the tests. For a concept such as delivery time, the measurement may be defined simply by determining when the clock starts and stops and providing a procedure for recording the start and stop times. For a concept such as completeness, a measurement relating to the degree of completeness could be use of a checklist of items to be included or tasks to be performed.

Operational definitions are critical to having shared meaning on anything measured. Deming observed:

> There is no true value of any characteristic, state, or condition that is defined in terms of measurement or observation. Change of procedure for measurement (change in operational definition) or observation produces a new number. [51]

BIASES AND JUDGMENT HEURISTICS: AVOIDING THE TRAPS IN THINKING AND DECISIONS

Learning and decision-making are key to a leader's success. Yet, decision-making is impacted by bias and judgment heuristics.[52] Awareness of these thinking traps has been known for many years, and Kahneman popularized these ideas in *Thinking, Fast and Slow*.[53] The biases include the hindsight bias and the confirmation trap. The judgement heuristics include anchoring, availability, representativeness, the conjunction fallacy, and insensitivity to sample size. Quality improvement tools and methods are designed to protect learning and decision-making from these biases and traps.[54]

Leaders should be aware of three more thinking blocks that impair decision-making that can derail our best intentions:

- Dunning-Kruger Effect: Tendencies to over- or underestimate our own abilities. Research has shown that the more people know about a subject, the less they think they know, and the less they know, the more the overestimate their knowledge.
- Bounded Rationality: We may never have enough time or data to make the perfect decisions. These constraints typically cause us to fall back on rote procedures, habits, rules of thumb, and simple mental models.
- Cognitive Dissonance and Self-Justification: When dealing with a conflict of ideas and the results of our decisions, we justify our actions.[55]

Leaders who develop strategies and plans to make improvements are far more effective when they avoid these thinking traps.

SCIENCE OF IMPROVEMENT AND MODEL FOR IMPROVEMENT

The Model for Improvement (MFI) was created with Deming's profound knowledge as a guide. The design of the MFI has a holistic and effective impact on guiding changes in the organization. The theory of knowledge is the foundation that defines the PDSA cycle, the cycle by which we learn and improve. Figure 2.10 depicts the use of all four interconnected parts of the Science of Improvement in the design of the MFI. Included is a table which relates the three questions of the MFI with the four parts of Deming's profound knowledge.

All organizations require a common road map for improvement. The Model for Improvement, used throughout this book, can serve this function.

After the close of the workshop, Gwen discussed some reflections with Sue relative to the Model for Improvement.

"Sue, this seems so easy—just three questions and run some tests! However, I can now appreciate how important the underlying theory is to properly use the PDSA cycle. When this was introduced in my MBA program, this seemed rather simple and not memorable. I can now see the power in it."

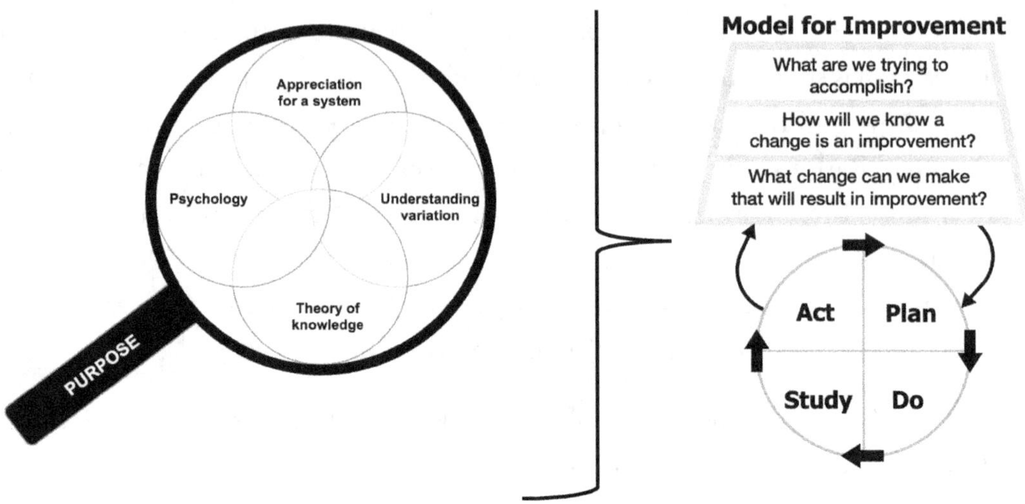

Science of Improvement and Relationship to the Model for Improvement

Science of Improvement	Model for Improvement
Systems	**1st Question:** What are we trying to accomplish? It gives a common aim and defines the system targeted for improvement. In developing changes (3rd question), there is an appreciation for reactive vs. fundamental changes.
Variation	**2nd Question:** How will we know a change is an improvement? Measures for improvement efforts are analyzed using Shewhart charts to minimize over- and underreaction to changes.
Psychology	**3rd Question:** What changes can we make that will result in improvement? Many of the change concepts have their basis in psychology. All employees can be part of developing, testing, and implementing changes, and people tend to support what they help to create.
Knowledge	The three questions provide an operational definition of improvement. PDSA cycles are based on the Scientific Method with deductive and inductive learning as the underlying theory.

Figure 2.10. Science of Improvement: interconnected components and design of Model for Improvement projects.

Sue replied, "Gwen, I think you have made it. Methods and tools guided by theory are far more effective than chasing problems with tools. I have had the advantage of using the Model for Improvement in our organization for several years, and it was great to see the power of the theory underlying the methodology."

Both exchanged contact information and agreed to stay in touch during their learning journey.

SUMMARY

Once an individual or leader understands the Science of Improvement, applying its principles should become second nature if they work in an organization that reinforces this thinking. For example, in organizations, leaders will use QOS as a basis for judging their own decisions as well as transforming their organizations.

Deming often challenged us to consider all four parts of profound knowledge as we approach issues. An essential use of the Shewhart chart is helping leaders to avoid assigning blame to individual people's actions and focusing attention on changing the system to help people do a better job. The systems, psychology, and variation all play a part in these actions.

Leaders who learn how to integrate subject matter expertise with the Science of Improvement are equipped to understand the impact of changes to the system, measures, people, and learning. Using the four parts of the Science of Improvement and their interactions creates a unique lens to view the organization today and in the future.

As leaders, we appreciate differences in people and match our system processes with their skills and education. And we understand people work within defined processes. Their success or failure is our responsibility. The interaction of the system with people can be reflected in the measures. We can use those measures to understand special causes, which might then be eliminated or duplicated; or we can identify opportunities from common cause variation where the processes must be redesigned, or perhaps new processes designed to meet our organization's or customers' goals.

Knowledge is built on theory through a systematic revision and extension of our beliefs based on comparing predictions and observations: deductive and inductive learning. The PDSA cycle helps facilitate this process. In addition, employing people to share their knowledge to develop, test, and implement solutions builds teamwork and motivational aspects of the system while integrating the social aspect of any change.

Changes with a significant long-term positive impact occur only if someone takes the initiative. Someone must stand up and say, "Let's make this better." But there are risks involved any time we make a change. The Science of Improvement helps us mitigate these risks and make better decisions for our organization and our customers. While the Model for Improvement is useful when used alone, it becomes very powerful in developing, testing, and implementing changes when guided by the Science of Improvement.

NOTES

1. Deming, *The New Economics*, 1994, 92. *The QOS Field Guide*, Chapter 2 adds more on Deming and his contributions.

2. "Theory (n)," in *Oxford Dictionaries*, March 8, 2023, https://www.oxfordlearnersdictionaries.com/us/definition/english/theory.

3. Deming, *The New Economics*, 1994, 92–93.

4. Ronald D. Moen and Clifford L. Norman, "Always Applicable. Deming's System of Profound Knowledge Remains Relevant for Management and Quality Professionals Today," *Quality Progress*, June 2016, 47–53. Deming's journey of learning and how the system of profound knowledge was developed has been documented in this article.

5. Adapted from figure 4.2 "Deming's system of profound knowledge," in Langley et al., *The Improvement Guide*, 77. Chapter 2 of The *QOS Field Guide* includes more on Deming's background and contributions including his development of the system of profound knowledge.

6. Rocco J. Perla, Lloyd P. Provost, and Gareth J. Parry, "Seven Propositions of the Science of Improvement: Exploring Foundations," *Quality Management in Health Care* 22, no. 3 (2013): 170–86, https://doi.org/10.1097/QMH.0b013e31829a6a15.

7. Associates in Process Improvement, "API Definition of the Science of Improvement."

8. Adapted from figure 4.1 "Increasing Capability to Make Improvements," in Langley et al., *The Improvement Guide*, 76.

9. Adapted from table 4.1, "Important Milestones for Profound Knowledge Components," in Langley et al., 86–87.

10. Russell L. Ackoff, *Ackoff's Best. His Classic Writings on Management.* (New York: John Wiley & Sons, Inc, 1999), 16.

11. Langley et al., *The Improvement Guide*, 37. Definition adapted from "A system is an interdependent group of items, people, or processes working together toward a common purpose."

12. Adapted from Tom Ritchey, "Analysis and Synthesis: On Scientific Method-Based on a Study by Bernhard Riemann," *Systems Research* 8, no. 4 (December 1991): 21–41.

13. Russell L. Ackoff, *Creating the Corporate Culture* (New York: John Wiley & Sons, Inc, 1981), 17.

14. "Systems Thinking," in *Wikipedia*, July 11, 2023, https://en.wikipedia.org/wiki/Systems_thinking. The term "systems thinking" is used in many texts but without a proper definition. The definition in Wikipedia merges several ideas from various sources and forms a useful definition.

15. Deming, *The New Economics*, 95. This definition was presented in Chapter 1 of this book.

16. Ackoff, *Ackoff's Best. His Classic Writings on Management.*, 18.

17. Langley et al., *The Improvement Guide*, 111–16.

18. Peter M. Senge, *The Fifth Discipline: The Art and Practice of the Learning Organization* (New York: Currency Doubleday, 1990), 71.

19. D. M. Berwick, "Controlling Variation in Health Care: A Consultation from Walter Shewhart," *Medical Care* 29, no. 12 (December 1991): 1212–25.

20. Joseph M. Juran, *Architect of Quality. The Autobiography of Dr. Joseph M. Juran* (New York: McGraw-Hill, 2004), 108–9.

21. Walter A. Shewhart, "The First Shewhart Control Chart," *Industrial Quality Control*, 24, no. 2 (August 1967): 72. Shewhart's letter and first chart were published in an issue of Industrial Quality Control at the opening of a special issue dedicated by the Board of Directors of the American Society of Quality Control in recognition of his outstanding professional accomplishments.

22. The "detail" Shewhart describes became the foundation for his landmark book: Walter A. Shewhart, *Economic Control of Quality of Manufactured Product*. (New York: D. Van Nostrand, 1931). Permission to use figure granted by American Society of Quality.

23. Provost and Murray, *The Health Care Data Guide*, 124.

24. Adapted from figure 4.4, "Rules for Detecting Special Cause," from Provost and Murray, 135.

25. Adapted from table 4.1, "Balancing the Mistakes Made in Attempts to Improve," in Provost and Murray, 134.

26. Description of the seven basic types of Shewhart charts are found in Chapter 5, "Understanding Variation Using Shewhart Charts," in Provost and Murray, 159.

27. Provost and Murray, 132.

28. Provost and Murray, 135.

29. Deming, *Out of Crisis*, 314.

30. Joseph M. Juran, *Managerial Breakthrough – The Classic Book on Improving Management Performance*, 30th Anniversary (New York: McGraw-Hill, 1995), 155–56.

31. Deming, *Out of Crisis*, 317.

32. This is an example of the concept of heuristics or "simple rules of thumb." As we experience the world, we develop thinking patterns which allow us to make judgments and decisions. These simple rules of thumb, while efficient for many challenges, also result in biases and create thinking traps. More detail follows later in Chapter 2.

33. Michael Maccoby, *Narcissistic Leaders: Who Succeeds and Who Fails* (Boston: Harvard Business Review Press, 2007) This work presents more on personality types and leaders.

34. Michael Maccoby et al., *Transforming Health Care Leadership: A Systems Guide to Improve Patient Care, Decrease Costs, and Improve Population Health*. (San Francisco: Jossey-Bass, 2013), 155–60.

35. Frederick Herzberg, "One More Time: How Do You Motivate Employees?," *Harvard Business Review*, January 1, 2003, https://hbr.org/2003/01/one-more-time-how-do-you-motivate-employees. And Alfie Kohn, *Punished by Rewards* (New York: Houghton Mifflin Company, 1993).

36. Daniel Pink, "The Puzzle of Motivation" (TEDGlobal2009, July 2009), https://www.ted.com/talks/dan_pink_the_puzzle_of_motivation.

37. Deming, *The New Economics*, 1994, 101.

38. Russell L. Ackoff, "From Data to Wisdom," *Journal of Applied Systems Analysis* 16 (1989): 3–9.

39. Julie E Reed and Alan J Card, "The Problem with Plan-Do-Study-Act Cycles," *BMJ Quality & Safety 25*, no. 3 (March 1, 2016): 147, https://doi.org/10.1136/bmjqs-2015-005076. Julie Reed and Alan Card have observed, "the PDSA method is conceptually simple, simple does not mean easy."

40. George E.P. Box, J. Stuart Hunter, and William G. Hunter, *Statistics for Experimenters: Design, Innovation, and Discovery*, 2nd ed. (New York: Wiley, 2005).

41. Figure 2.7 is adapted from figure 7.2, "Sequential Building of Knowledge with Multiple PDSA Test Cycles," in Langley et al., *The Improvement Guide*, 146.

42. W. Edwards Deming, "On a Classification of the Problems of Statistical Inference," *Journal of the American Statistical Association* 37, no. 218 (1942): 173–85, https://doi.org/10.2307/2279212; W. Edwards Deming, "On Probability as a Basis for Action," *The American Statistician* 29, no. 4 (1975): 146–52; Lloyd P. Provost, "Analytical Studies: A Framework for Quality Improvement Design and Analysis," *BMJ Quality & Safety* 20, no. Suppl 1 (April 1, 2011): 92–96, https://doi.org/10.1136/bmjqs.2011.051557.

43. Random sampling can be simple or systematic. A simple random sample is the selection of data from a frame by use of a random process such as a mechanical device or random numbers. A systematic random sample is created by choosing a starting point from a frame and then selecting data at specific intervals. Provost and Murray, *The Health Care Data Guide*, 55.

44. Judgement sampling is the most common sampling strategy used in improvement work. In judgment sampling, we rely on those with process knowledge to select useful samples for learning about process performance and the impact of our changes. Provost and Murray, 56.

45. This quote is from the Foreword written by W. Edwards Deming in Moen, Nolan, and Provost, *Quality Improvement Through Planned Experimentation*, xiii.

46. Ackoff, "From Data to Wisdom."

47. Ackoff, 3–9.

48. The figure is adapted from Gene Bellinger, Durval Castro, and Anthony Mills, "Data, Information, Knowledge, & Wisdom," *Mental Model Musings* (blog), 2004, http://www.systems-thinking.org/dikw/dikw.htm.

49. Deming, *Out of Crisis*, 276.

50. "The Importance of Operational Definitions," Provost and Murray, *The Health Care Data Guide*, 47–50.

51. Deming, *The New Economics*, 1994, 104.

52. Daniel Kahneman, Paul Slovic, and Amos Tversky, eds., *Judgment under Uncertainty: Heuristics and Biases* (Cambridge: Cambridge University, 1982), https://doi.org/10.1017/CBO9780511809477.

53. Daniel Kahneman, *Thinking, Fast and Slow* (New York: Farrar, Straus and Giroux, 2011).

54. Additional information on these traps is discussed in Chapter 2, "The Science of Improvement," in *The QOS Field Guide*.

55. This idea is covered in more detail in Ch. 10, including **Figure 10.5**. Culture can change attitudes in individuals.

LEADING WITH QUALITY AS AN ORGANIZATIONAL STRATEGY

Celeste works for a global technology company. She recently accepted a promotion from director in one division to vice president in another division. In her former position, the top management understood the benefits of focusing on *quality as an organizational strategy*. Several projects demonstrated evidence of the chain reaction of improvement of quality. As a result, Celeste improved quality, reduced costs, increased productivity, and engaged the staff.

In her previous job as a director, Celeste led a project to redesign a power supply unit plagued with customer complaints and warranty returns. Her project team solved the returns and complaint issues, and when the team calculated the global savings, their work projected a savings of $12 million annually! What surprised Celeste was the impact on her project team. The team members took pride in their contribution. They were engaged and eager to work on new challenges.

Now in her promoted role, Celeste reflected on her new division:

I am not seeing a focus on improving quality. My new colleagues seem to view quality improvement as a trade-off with cost and scheduling. I hear too often, "If you want to improve, it may cost more or take longer to receive the product or service." Then I hear the old refrain, "You can spend too much on quality, and you will take precious time away from the day's work!" People appear disengaged and tell me their work feels routine and like something they must get done.

Celeste recently read a published report on a Gallup Survey[1] that found only thirty-six percent of U.S. employees are engaged in their work and workplace. She knew the former team was far more engaged and worries the new division likely falls below the Gallup national average.

Celeste shared her experiences from her prior assignment with her new boss, Hugh. At first, he appeared to dismiss her experience. "Well, we are different here; the culture is different." Celeste persisted, "From what I see, we have specific opportunities to apply the methods of *quality as an organizational strategy* to the division, adapting the culture, and enabling our people to contribute to making improvements. More importantly, we can improve quality at the same time we reduce costs."

The economic impact of the power supply project Celeste led with her previous team intrigued Hugh, and he was curious to learn more about the ideas Celeste had for bringing these methods to the division. "Okay, Celeste, let's give it a try."

"This provides the benefit of getting tangible improvements and creating an environment where people are engaged and take pride in their work." Celeste added, "Thanks, Hugh, for your support!"

This chapter focuses on the leadership team's role in building the structure and methods that enable quality as an organizational strategy. The following sections discuss:

- Attributes of leaders who appreciate the Science of Improvement (Chapter 2).
- Types of leaders and differences between leaders and managers.
- Importance of strategic intelligence to position the organization for future success.
- How QOS provides methods to ensure a roadmap for this success.

ATTRIBUTES OF LEADERS APPLYING THE SCIENCE OF IMPROVEMENT

Chapter 2 discusses the Science of Improvement, which is the foundation for the thinking and work of leaders. Let's consider the attributes that we would expect to see from leaders who have knowledge of the Science of Improvement in four key areas.

1. **Variation**: Leaders understand and explain variation in the results they see in terms of common causes and special causes. They use graphical methods to learn from data and expect others to consider variation in their decisions and actions. They understand the concept of predictable and unpredictable processes and the potential losses due to tampering. Leaders understand the current capability of a process or system before attempting changes.

2. **Systems**: Leaders study and manage the organization as a system. They emphasize the importance of common purpose and interdependencies among organizational groups. They understand that the organization's performance depends more on the interaction of the various parts than how the parts perform individually. They understand both detail and dynamic complexity in a system. They consider fundamental systems concepts such as boundaries, feedback loops, constraints, and leverage points. They deeply understand the concept of **all work as a process**. They use these concepts to develop, test, and implement changes to optimize the system.

3. **Knowledge**: Leaders understand that management is prediction that comes from knowledge, and knowledge is built on theory. They know that people learn in different ways, and they are aware of the importance of judgment heuristics[2] and recognizing blind spots. They use the Plan-Do-Study-Act cycle to learn, run tests before implementation, make better decisions, and improve. To enhance learning, they make predictions before making changes. They understand paradigms, mental models, the use of paradox, and reframing to create a collaborative environment where "failures" are learning opportunities.

4. **Psychology**: Leaders appreciate differences in people and cultures and communication styles. They avoid making the fundamental attribution error.[3] They understand the value of teams and search out subject matter experts for improvement. They know how to motivate others by creating an intrinsically motivational environment for learning. They appreciate the challenge that change brings to the human system. They plan for the social impact of technical change and make people part of the solution. Resistance to change in their organizations is minimal as they routinely engage others to solicit ideas to test, learn from mistakes, and share successes. People who work with these leaders feel valued and appreciated.

The Science of Improvement provides a theory for leaders as they adopt and use the five activities of QOS. The lens of the Science of Improvement helps leaders to engage complexity and move from what seems a mess to more effective decision-making and actions. When the Science of Improvement combines with the five leadership activities as an organizational strategy, more effective alignment with strategy and results are enabled.

Celeste decided she should talk to an influencer in her new division. Tom is Vice President of Engineering and holds 108 patents. Nothing happens in a division without Tom being on board. Celeste made a visit to his office. Knocking on his open door, she started, "Tom, can I have a few moments to discuss a challenge I have taken on?

"Come on in," Tom replied back as he swung his chair around to face the door. "And welcome to the team!"

Celeste shared with Tom the conversation she had with Hugh. Tom listened and thought about Celeste's assessment and the results her previous team was able to accomplish. "Celeste, I'm skeptical, not having had the experience you're describing, but I'm curious. When I first started here twenty-five years ago, the company got excited about quality and started Quality Circles. That fizzled out after two years. We committed to quality and started a Zero Defects program. We all had to sign pledges committing to no defects and had a few events. That too fizzled out. You can understand my experience with quality programs in the company hasn't led to improvement like you describe. How is this different?"

"Great question," Celeste responded. "I can see why past attempts have you skeptical! Thanks for your candor. This effort is different because it's aimed at getting the business results the company is already committed to, and our improvement efforts are guided by the Science of Improvement: a body of knowledge based on broad evidence."

Celeste explained the four streams of the Science of Improvement. The combination of understanding variation, systems thinking, knowledge, and psychology grabbed Tom's attention and resonated with his engineering experience. "Celeste, I am excited to hear that methods and tools will be driven by theory. A complaint I always have is that everyone is using quality tools, but they are not getting results."

"I call that an activity trap," Celeste added. "To prevent it, we will use a methodology called the Model for Improvement. It guides us to develop, test, and implement necessary and useful changes. To be effective, the changes we choose to work on will be driven by our strategic plan to help us better meet our purpose."

"When will you be sharing this with our leadership team?" Tom asked.

"Hugh asked me to report at the next meeting," confirmed Celeste.

Tom leaned forward in his chair, "I am eager to learn more and look forward to our next meeting."

TYPES OF LEADERS, MANAGERS AND FUNCTIONAL RESPONSIBILITIES

Organizations include people who serve different roles, including leaders, managers, and subject matter experts. Each is necessary and adds value to the organization. What is a leader? **Leaders are people others want to follow**. Deming[4] described a leader's three sources of power:

1. Authority of office
2. Knowledge
3. Personality and persuasive power; tact

If you have people who ask your opinion about specific topics, search you out, and listen to you, they are followers, and you are a subject matter leader with knowledge. The leader creates a **relationship** with their followers, who respect and trust the leader's perspectives, and these **leaders can be found in any role within the organization**. Effective leaders create an environment that transforms followers into collaborators. Within the leadership team, effective leadership means people follow those who work to further the purpose and the well-being of all people associated with the organization.

In contrast, management requires skills that enable the manager to plan, organize, staff, direct, and control.[5] Both leadership and management are essential for the success of an organization. Ideally, all managers should be leaders, and many can be developed for leadership roles. Unfortunately, not all leaders are managers. We have worked with many leaders who have a great following but are aware of their weaknesses as managers. For example, a leader may articulate an innovative idea for change but not be skilled at designing and executing the idea in practice. Leaders typically surround themselves with others who can manage the areas where they are weak. Together, they make an effective leadership team.

Integrating QOS into the organizational system assumes the managers possess the skills to **plan, organize, staff, direct, and control**[6] the work necessary to accomplish the organization's mission. Managers who find it challenging to carry out improvement efforts often lack one or more of these basic skills.

The QOS framework assumes managers can apply these five principles and requisite skills. Table 3.1[7] describes these five principles and the corresponding strategic and tactical skills for each principal function of management.

Another distinction between managers and leaders is in delegation. Managers can delegate authority, but leaders cannot delegate the relationships and environment they have created with their followers.[8] Business history is full of examples where a charismatic leader leaves an organization and creates a vacuum that is next to impossible to fulfill.[9]

Organizations need leaders throughout. High-performing knowledge-based organizations require an **interdependent leadership system** with four different leadership perspectives represented on the team. An individual leader can possess one or more of these talents, but it is rare for an individual leader to have all four of the following perspectives:

- **Strategic leaders**: Strategic leaders use foresight to ensure the organization's vision is developed and communicated. Articulating a vision engages people to help close the gap to attain the ideal design of the organizational system.
- **Operational leaders**: Operational leaders ensure that the organization viewed as a system operates effectively and efficiently with effective managers in place. They ensure execution of the match to the Need that brought customers to the organization, and the result is customers who brag about the organization.
- **Network leaders**: Network leaders are essential to ensure the execution of communication within and outside the organizational system. In addition, they are effective at building trust and creating collaboration.

- **Subject matter expert leaders**: Subject matter expert leaders are sought out by others in the system in order to leverage their knowledge to solve problems, make improvements, or mitigate other challenges to the organization.[10]

Table 3.1. Principle functions for managers and corresponding skills

Five principal functions of management	Strategic and tactical skills
Plan	Forecast: Where will the present course lead? Set objectives Develop strategies Establish priorities and timing of steps Budget: develop and manage the budget, allocate resources Set procedures and standards Develop policies: standing decisions on recurring matters
Organize	Establish an organizational structure Define relationships to facilitate coordination Create position descriptions (role statements) Establish position qualifications
Staff	Select employees: recruit qualified people for each position Orientate employees Train and educate Development: ongoing improvement of knowledge and skills
Direct	Delegate: assign responsibility and exact accountability for results Motivate Coordinate: relate efforts relative to purpose and system Manage differences in people: encourage independent thought and resolve conflict Manage change: stimulate creativity and innovation in achieving goals
Control	Establishing a reporting system Developing performance standards such that key duties are well done Measuring results: deviation from goals and standards Taking corrective action: adjust plans, counsel, replanning, and repeating Rewarding: praising, remunerating, or administering discipline

A leadership team needs all four types of leaders. For example, when Southwest Airlines started in the early 1970s, competing airlines kept founder and lawyer Herb Kelleher in court with lawsuits. Kelleher was a strategic leader. He had a vision for Southwest Airlines to be a new kind of company in the airline business, and the competition tried to prevent Southwest from operating in Texas.

As Southwest got underway, they had four aircraft. The startup was also losing money ($1.6 million in the first year). To stay in business, Southwest had to sell one of the aircraft. How could the airline maintain its schedule with only three planes? This problem fell to Bill Franklin, Vice President of Ground Operations, and an operational and network leader. Franklin observed that airlines only make money when airplanes are in the air. He proposed a new strategy known as the "10-Minute Turn." People involved were challenging the industry perception that it took sixty minutes to turn the plane around. To achieve this fifty-minute reduction, the strategy required a collaborative effort with ground crews, pilots, and flight attendants working together. The plan worked, saving Southwest Airlines.[11]

In this scenario, Herb Kelleher was the strategic leader, and Bill Franklin was the operational leader. Kelleher established a compelling vision, and Franklin served as a pragmatic leader networking with subject matter experts to improve the system to achieve the vision.

Successful organizations share a mixture of individual leaders with strength in one or two types. As a team, they complement each other and create a leadership system (figure 3.1).[12] They act as integrated, interactive forces to ensure the leadership team makes strategic choices, addresses significant operational concerns, and leads the organization's internal and external networking.

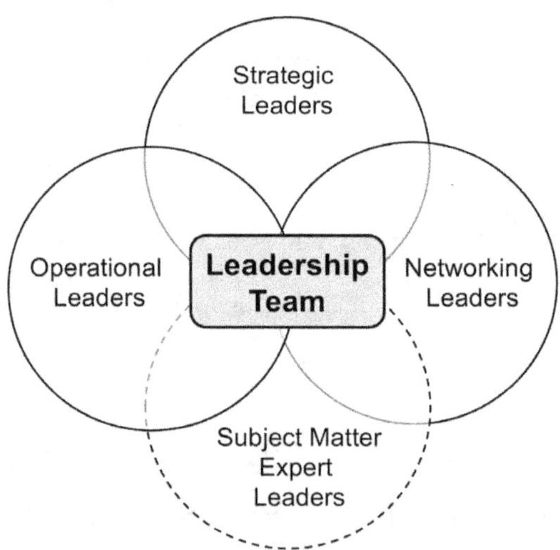

Figure 3.1. Leadership team with four integrated leadership types.

Steve Jobs, when CEO of Apple, observed the benefit of diverse talent comprising an effective leadership team. Jobs was an admirer of the Beatles and the combined talent of its four musical leaders. Here is how he described his observations of his favorite musical group:

> My model for business is The Beatles. They were four guys who kept each other's kind of negative tendencies in check. They balanced each other, and the total was greater than the sum of the parts. That's how I see business: Great things in business are never done by one person; they're done by a team of people. [13]

It is essential that a leadership team includes the four types of leaders described earlier. It is rare that one leader possesses all the skills and talents of all four types. It is also essential that effective managers are in place that can **plan, organize, staff, direct, and control**. An effective leadership team with effective managers are essential to making quality as an organizational strategy effective.

Celeste finished making her presentation on *QOS* to the Division's leadership team. The aim of the meeting was to discuss and ask questions. Sam, from Sales and Marketing, started with, "Haven't we tried these quality programs before?"

Celeste leaned forward to answer, but Tom beat her to it: "Celeste, may I respond to Sam's question?" Celeste nodded and thought, "This might be very helpful."

"Sam," Tom continued, "you are correct, we have tried various quality programs in the past. What is different here is that this effort is driven by the Science of Improvement, and the application of the improvement is connected to our strategy. These past efforts let the leadership team off the hook and made improvement the job of others. What Celeste has shared is that the makeup of our leadership team is essential to making improvements on purpose. We all have roles as strategic, operational, network, and subject matter leaders."

Celeste's meeting with Tom paid off. His comment completely swayed the room.

Hugh turned to Celeste, "Thanks for a great presentation. Looks like we are ready to learn more and get started."

STRATEGIC INTELLIGENCE FOR THE LEADERSHIP TEAM

QOS requires collaboration among leaders throughout the organization with a focus on learning and adaptation to an ever-changing world. This can be accomplished by an interrelated system of concepts and skills that helps leaders to learn from inside and outside the organization and articulate changes needed in the future while providing a collaborative environment that engages all roles.

Figure 3.2 depicts a set of interrelated skills known as strategic intelligence.[14]

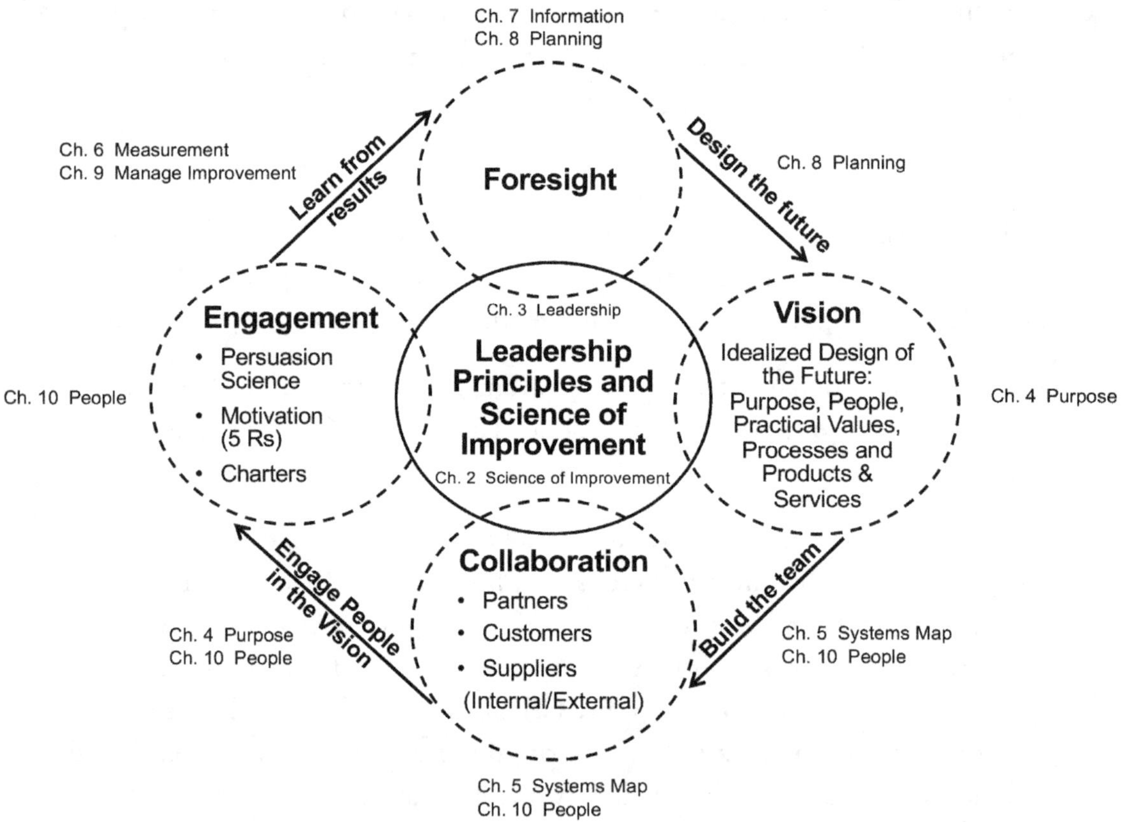

Figure 3.2. Interrelated skills of strategic intelligence.

Note that figure 3.2 has a dual meaning. The circles describe the qualities of heart and mind that interact with each other to strengthen the ability of the leadership team to continually adapt and learn as they shape and direct an organization. The arrows describe typical paths of the leadership team action that employ these qualities. While some leadership teams collaborate in designing an ideal future, other organizations might develop the vision before forming a team.

The essential components of strategic intelligence are:

- **Foresight**: Predict the future direction of the organization based on internal and external subject matter expertise, experience, research, dynamic trends, threats, and opportunities. This may be reflected in the requirement for new or revised products or services or other changes to ensure the organization's future.[15]
- **Vision**: Assess the impact of the foresight prediction on the organization. Ensure the alignment of the organization's strategy to achieve the vision. Create the idealized design[16] of this future by addressing how these changes will impact the organizational system and services.[17]
- **Collaboration**: Ensure teams include subject matter expertise to establish productive relationships both internally and externally, based on mutual trust, a shared philosophy, and shared risks and rewards. Communicate progress and recognize contributions of all stakeholders.
- **Engagement**:[18] Communicate, align, and motivate people toward the future by sharing predictions and the idealized design to provide reasons ("why") the changes are needed and the predicted results. Share where the changes will occur, including needs for new skills, roles, and responsibilities, with changes in compensation to reward those skills, if needed. Utilize charters to create teams, encourage innovation, and develop ownership for the changes.

LEADERSHIP AND QOS METHODS

The transformation from viewing the organization as an organizational chart to viewing the organization as a system[19] creates the need for collaboration and engagement with everyone in the organization, beginning with the leadership group. QOS demands the active participation of everyone. In a system, everyone matters. Table 3.2 describes the roles of the leadership team, management, and the individual employees in the organization focused on QOS.

Transformation of an organization takes time and demands alignment of beliefs of the leadership team and on individuals for achieving the vision or ideal design of the future.

Table 3.2. QOS and role of the leadership team, management, and employees

QOS methods	Leadership team role	Management role	Individual employee's role
Establish purpose	Create purpose, tenets, and vision.	Use the purpose, tenets, and vision in all aspects of running the business. Develop role statements for all employees.	Use role statements to understand how they support overall purpose and contribute to the success of the organization.
Systems view	Create a conceptual view and a detailed view of the whole system.	Use views of the organization as a system to communicate changes, processes, and roles while running the business. Use systems maps to discuss challenges. Develop more detailed systems maps for subsystems. Contribute to assessing specific processes.	Role statement connects all employees to the system by describing what processes they work in and who are their internal customers and suppliers. Appreciate how their job connects with others in the organization.
Measurement of the system	Establish a vector of measures (VOM) for the organization.	VOM drilled down to the department or unit level for regular review and learning by all managers.	Understand how one's job impacts key measures in the VOM.
Gathering information	Create a system to gather, organize and analyze information from key stakeholders of the organization.	Use an information system to react to current challenges and opportunities to serve customers better. Contribute feedback and observations for use in planning.	Contribute to organizational learning by being the "eyes and ears" from the perspective of their role in the system (a listening post). Post feedback and observations.
Planning for improvement	Create a strategic plan and communicate priorities. Run the annual planning for improvement activity and connect to other operational planning.	Participate in developing, providing, and presenting inputs for the planning process. Supply necessary subject matter expertise as required for making choices and setting priorities. Connect strategic plan to planning activities in their units.	Provide subject matter expertise for the planning process. Be aware of the strategic objectives of the organization and how their role can contribute.
Managing individual and team efforts	Ensure accomplishment of prioritized improvement efforts. Learn about the system from improvement projects.	Support strategic improvement projects with employees with knowledge on improvement teams. Help to remove roadblocks.	Participate in improvement projects as team leaders and team members. Contribute subject matter knowledge and ideas to improve the system.

Common purpose, tenets, and vision help to define the culture; changes introduced must align with these to be accepted. Fundamentally two interdependent transformations are underway as an organization pursues QOS:

- Transformation of the organization
- Transformation of the individuals on the leadership team[20]

Deming discussed why the transformation journey in the organization begins with the individual leader:

> The first step is transformation of the individual. This transformation is discontinuous. It comes from understanding the system of profound knowledge. The individual, transformed, will perceive new meaning to his life, to events, to numbers, to interactions between people.[21]

Once one understands the System of Profound Knowledge, that individual will apply its principles in every kind of relationship with other people. They will have a basis for judgment of their own decisions and for transformation of the organizations that he belongs to. The individual, once transformed, will:

- Set an example.
- Be a good listener, but will not compromise.
- Continually teach other people.
- Help people to pull away from their current practice and beliefs and move into the new philosophy without a feeling of guilt about the past. [22]

These two interdependent transformation journeys require some detailed work by the leadership team. How should they begin?

First, a transformation from viewing the organization as an organizational chart to viewing the organization as a system creates a **structure** that reinforces collaboration internally and externally.[23] As with any structural change, there is usually a social impact. Consider some of the expected changes:

- People performing work in the system understand their roles in meeting the organization's purpose.
- The defined role of people in the system enables them to carry out actions to ensure that their part of the system is aligned to meet the purpose. This could entail a change in operations or improvements to ensure alignment.

- The defined roles of people act as an organizational passport to communicate and act as defined by the role statement. This could be a challenge to historical norms in a hierarchically-driven organization.
- For people who have had personal success and promotions within the old organizational structure, some dissonance is expected. They may feel threatened and unable to control others as they have in the past. As a result, it is not unusual for some to leave rather than transform their leadership style.
- Others may feel more comfortable being told what to do and how to do it rather than engaging. These people may also decide to find other employment.

Second, the leaders move from being a group to becoming a team. This transformation brings about the need for cooperation.

- Leaders understand their respective roles relative to their contributions to the leadership team.
- Trust and collaboration to meet the purpose and act at the system level rather than suboptimizing for the good of their departments in a siloed manner of operating.
- As people carry out their roles and less often seek permission, more time is available for leaders to engage in thinking about the future and focusing on improving the system.

Quality as an organizational strategy creates a structure that impacts everyone in the organization and how their roles interact with the system's purpose. Safety engineers teach us much about introducing change and getting commitment. In most organizations, safety is a tenet, and structure has been created to ensure it is practiced. There is no tolerance for unsafe acts.

When safety engineers introduce changes, they put forth the change **structure**: "Wear your safety glasses, earplugs, and back brace." Safety as an accepted tenet accompanies this structure. If change is introduced and explained as contributing to safety, the change is usually greeted with enthusiasm. Providing the structure and reason for change provides the necessary conditions for people to want to make the change.

Figure 3.3 depicts a relationship between change (new structure or methods) and culture, attitudes, and behaviors.[24] The large arrows in the model moving counterclockwise demonstrate the power of a change that requires new behaviors. That then impacts attitudes and, eventually, the culture of the organization. If the change is not aligned with culture, leadership must explain why the culture needs to change or adapt to work in the new structure successfully. The smaller arrows moving clockwise show the impact of culture on new people coming into the organization. New people learn the importance of the organization's culture (tenets and beliefs)[25] and the corresponding work methods that exist to help them be successful. As people conform to the organization's culture, their attitudes adapt, and their behavior matches the expected behaviors in the organization.

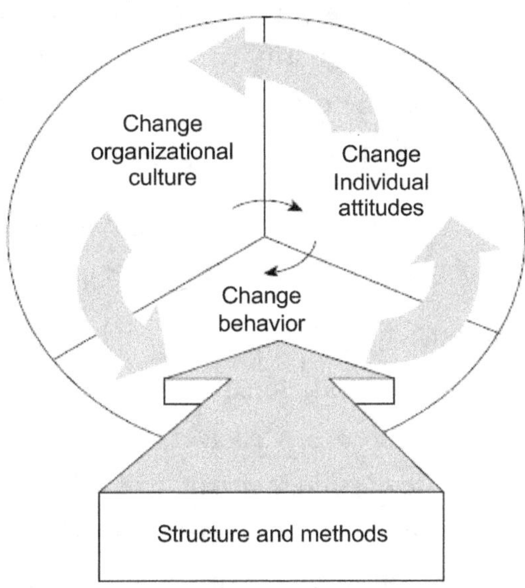

Figure 3.3. Effect of structure on culture, individual attitudes, and behaviors.

BECOMING A LEADERSHIP TEAM

When introducing change to the organization, the leaders who share their identity by consistently aligning decisions and expected conduct to the organization's purpose validate their commitment and dedication to everyone in the larger organizational system. Two principles from the **science of persuasion** reinforce these ideas to focus conversation and actions on the larger system:[26]

- **Commitment and Consistency Principle:** The desire to be seen by others as consistent with prior actions, statements, and commitments.
- **Unity Principle – Moving to "We":** When we focus on the larger system, we move the conversation to "we"; this can result in more agreement, trust, help, liking,

cooperation, emotional support, and forgiveness. The result: leaders are even judged as being more creative, moral, and humane.

Utilizing the organization's mission and tenets, the leadership team creates a shared identity, destroying the "us-versus-them" hierarchical perceptions. "We" make decisions consistent with all roles in the organization, aligned to the purpose and tenets, creating aligned leaders and followers. Vision, strategy, or change initiative explanations include how these efforts will benefit the larger system or the common good of the organization. Each leader represents their areas of responsibility and their multiple aligned individual roles. Contributions at all levels of the organization are visible to leadership to ensure that individuals and groups of individuals are recognized holistically.

Within his three levels of ethical and moral reasoning, Kohlberg[27] would describe the shared identity as a Level 3 focus, as applicable to leaders on a leadership team:

- **Level 1 (Me):** Looks out for Number One.
- **Level 2 (My Group):** What an individual considers good for family, group, or department within the organization as well as themselves, without concern for the effect of their actions on those outside their circle of influence.
- **Level 3 (Larger System):** Focused on what benefits the larger system or organization; invoking the commitment, consistency, and unity principles. Leaders may be challenged to make tough decisions that don't directly benefit themselves or their departments but decisions that benefit the larger organization.

Figure 3.4 depicts the nesting of these three levels of ethical and moral reasoning.

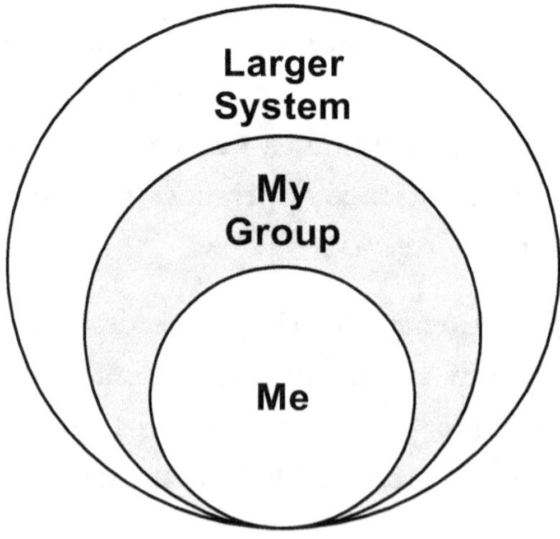

Figure 3.4. Three levels of ethical and moral reasoning.

Three months later, Celeste's boss Hugh called her to a meeting. "Celeste, I am astonished at our progress," started Hugh. "People are engaged in their work as I have never seen them before. They have pride in the contributions they are making to improve our organization. We have moved from focusing on departmental silos to understanding how we work as a system to meet our purpose better and serve our customers. It is obvious we have a lot to learn ourselves in applying these concepts and methods."

"Thanks, Hugh," replied Celeste. "We have just begun. Up to now, we have been identifying projects based on obvious problems, many of which were pointed out by our customers. We must integrate improvement into our strategic planning process to take full advantage of QOS. We must begin to make intentional improvements proactively and not just react to problems. You are correct, though. This is a good start, and I believe leadership is ready for the next steps."[28]

SUMMARY

Pfeffer[29] observed the ineffective state of training and education regarding leadership and poor engagement. We agree. Deming often shouted, "By what method?"[30] He was also a champion of good theory. We take the advice to heart and provide:

1. Leadership **methods** from QOS that enable strategic intelligence for the leadership team.
2. The foundation of the Science for Improvement.
3. The importance of moving the **leadership group** to a **leadership team** through the structure provided by the QOS methods and recognizing the contributions of the four types of leaders on the team.

When taken together, we can create a positive environment for people to be engaged and contribute to QOS. Making improvements intentionally means focusing on the Need by which customers come to our organization and how we match that Need. In the next chapter, we will discuss the components of an effective purpose statement and how this purpose helps communicate why our organization exists, what we do, and how we will conduct ourselves in carrying out the purpose.

NOTES

1. Jim Harter, "U.S. Employee Engagement Data Hold Steady in First Half of 2021," *Gallup. Com* (blog), July 29, 2021, https://www.gallup.com/workplace/352949/employee-engagement-holds-steady-first-half-2021.aspx.

2. Heuristics can be thought of as "simple rules of thumb." People naturally develop thinking patterns that allow them to make judgments and decisions. These simple rules of thumb, while efficient for many challenges, can also result in biases which result in thinking traps. These thinking traps were introduced in Chapter 2 and are discussed in detail in Chapter 2, "The Science of Improvement," in *The QOS Field Guide*.

3. Langley et al., *The Improvement Guide*, 2009, 84. Fundamental attribution error: We make this error when we explain our behaviors in terms of the situation or environment while holding other people personally accountable for their behavior.

4. Adapted from Deming, *The New Economics*, 1994, 126.

5. R. Alec Mackenzie, "The Management Process in 3-D," *Harvard Business Review*, November 1, 1969, https://hbr.org/1969/11/the-management-process-in-3-d. These skills are essential for executing improvement projects.

6. Henri Fayol, *General and Industrial Management* (London: Sir Issac Pitman & Sons, 1949); first published in French as "Administration Industrielle et Generale-Prevoyance, Organisation, Commandment, Co-ordination, Controle," Bulletin de la Societe de I'lndustrie Minerale, 1916.

7. Table 3.1 adapted from Mackenzie, "The Management Process in 3-D."

8. Much of the work in this chapter has been influenced by, and integrates ideas from, W. Edwards Deming, Russell Ackoff, and Michael Maccoby. The chapter applies methods to these ideas to help leaders make actionable changes.

9. David Halberstam, *The Reckoning*, 1st ed. (New York: William Morrow & Co, 1986), 565. When Lee Iacocca left Ford and came to Chrysler, he infused Chrysler with a winning spirit. He also brought over a Hal Sperlich, the driving force behind the Ford Mustang and the Mini Maxx at Ford. Sperlich and Iacocca failed to convince Ford to produce the Mini Maxx, which became the Dodge Caravan in 1983 at Chrysler. The Mini Maxx set off twenty-five years of success for Chrysler. Iacocca retired from Chrysler in 1992. Unfortunately, Chrysler filed for bankruptcy in 2009. In 2014, Chrysler was integrated with Fiat.

10. Adapted from F. John Reh, "What Is a Subject Matter Expert? Definition & Examples of Subject Matter Experts," The Balance Careers, *Management & Leadership* (blog), April 8, 2024, https://www.liveabout.com/subject-matter-expert-2275099.

11. "The Man Who Saved Southwest Airlines With A '10-Minute' Idea," *All Things Considered* (NPR, June 28, 2015), https://www.npr.org/2015/06/28/418147961/the-man-who-saved-southwest-airlines-with-a-10-minute-idea.

12. Adapted from figure in 3.1 in Maccoby et al., *Transforming Health Care Leadership*, 39.

13. Steve Jobs, interview by Dan Rather, *60 Minutes Overtime: Steve Jobs*, 2003, https://www.cbsnews.com/news/steve-jobs-1955-2011/.

14. Adapted from figure 5.1 "Strategic Intelligence, Leadership Philosophy, and Profound Knowledge," in Maccoby et al., *Transforming Health Care Leadership*, 62.

15. In this book, Chapter 6 on "Measures of the System" and Chapter 7 on "A System of Obtaining Information" are critical to giving insight to enable the thinking required for foresight.

16. Russell L. Ackoff, Jason Magidson, and Herbert Addison, *Idealized Design: Creating an Organization's Future* (Upper Saddle River: Wharton School Publishing, 2006).

17. Vision and the method of Idealized Design are discussed in Chapter 4, "Establishing and Communicating a Purpose of the Organization."

18. Engagement related to quality as an organizational strategy is covered in more detail in Chapter 10, "Engaging People with QOS."

19. Transformation from Viewing the Organization as an organizational chart to the organization viewed as a system was introduced in Chapter 1, figure 1.5.

20. In figure 3.1, "Leadership Team with Four Integrated Leadership Types," although subject matter experts are depicted as contributing part of the leadership team by supplying knowledge, they may or may not be on the actual leadership team.

21. Deming, *The New Economics*, 1994, 92.

22. Deming, 92–93.

23. Transformation from viewing the organization as an organizational chart to the organization viewed as a system was introduced in Chapter 1, figure 1.5.

24. This figure was developed by the Associates in Process Improvement (API) based on work on Antecedent, Behavior and Consequences (ABC) used by safety engineers (see Thomas R. Krause, John H. Hidley, and Stanley J. Hobson, *The Behavior-Based Safety Process,* New York: Von Nostrand Reinhold, 1990). The figure originally appears in Chapter 13, "Making the Improvement of Value a Business Strategy," in Langley et al., *The Improvement Guide,* 2009, 316. The framework is discussed further in Chapter 4 on "Establish and Communicate the Purpose of the Organization" and Chapter 10 on "Engaging People with QOS."

25. See Chapter 4, "Establish and Communicate a Purpose of the Organization" for a detailed discussion of tenets and beliefs.

26. Adapted from Robert B. Cialdini, *Influence, New and Expanded: The Psychology of Persuasion,* New and Expanded (New York: Harper Business, 2021). See Commitment and Consistency Principle, Chapter 7, and Unity Principle, Chapter 8 in this book.

27. Lawrence Kohlberg, "The Claim to Moral Adequacy of a Highest Stage of Moral Judgment," *The Journal of Philosophy* 70, no. 18 (October 1973): 630–46. Kohlberg's theory was based on Jean Piaget's earlier theory of cognitive development in children.

28. See Chapter 8, Planning to Improve, for the process to integrate improvement into planning.

29. "Preface" in Jeffrey Pfeffer, *Leadership BS: Fixing Workplaces and Careers One Truth at a Time* (New York: Harper Business, 2015).

30. W. Edwards Deming, unpublished personal communication, n.d. (Authors Norman and Provost recall Deming frequently using the phrase "By what method?" in his four-day seminars.)

PART II
BUILDING A SYSTEM OF IMPROVEMENT

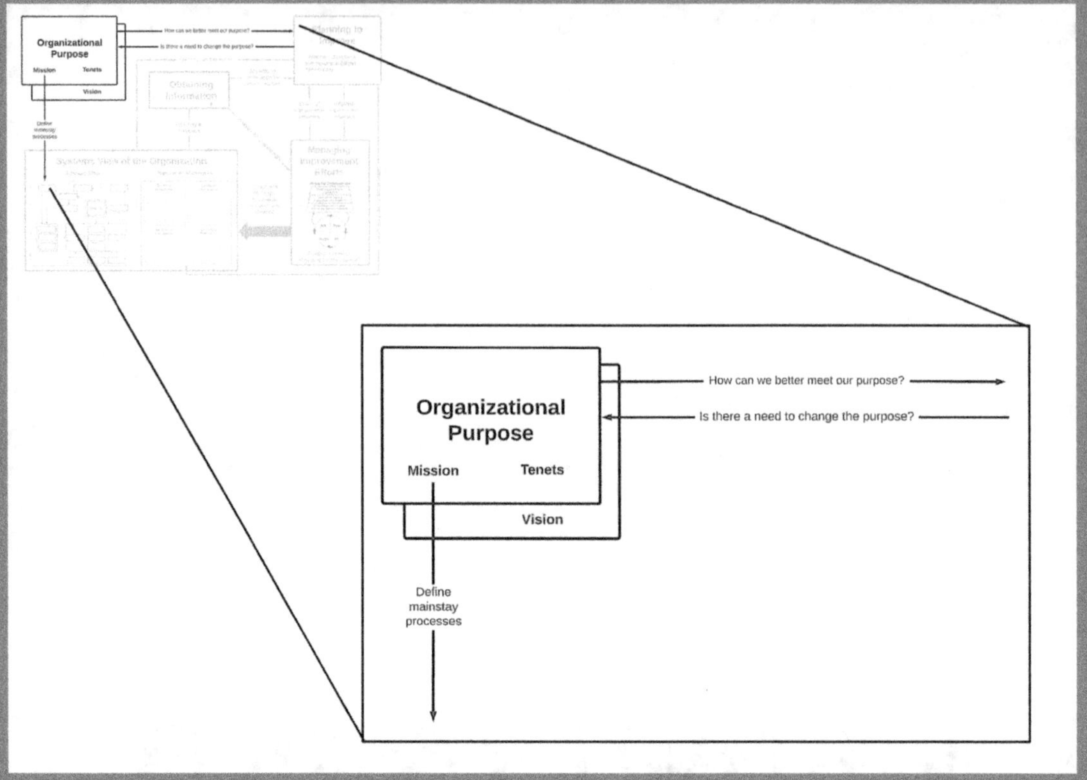

ACTIONS FOR LEADERSHIP TEAM

- Develop a written statement of purpose for the organization, including the mission, tenets, and vision.
- Communicate this purpose to the organization by relating the work of different parts of the organization to the purpose.
- Document connection of purpose with the role statements for departments and all employees.
- Use this purpose to guide and focus the organization as it conducts business, makes decisions, and manages improvement.

CHAPTER 4

ESTABLISH AND COMMUNICATE THE PURPOSE OF THE ORGANIZATION

Stan spent afternoons shooting hoops just outside the warehouse. His dad's roofing business was all he and his brothers knew growing up. After studying business at the state university, he returned to join the company for his first job.

"I started in the back office, then I moved to sales, and eventually moved up to operations."

Stan's dad, Lawrence, started as a roofer, installing industrial roofs on business and office buildings. As he learned his trade, project after project, he watched how hard it was to purchase and gather the materials at the worksite to complete a job.

"My dad had an idea, a new technology, a system to design, package, and deliver everything needed to do a roofing job right to the worksite. His approach eliminated dealing with different suppliers, varied delivery and pick-up schedules, and multiple invoices. No longer would the roofers have to sort everything and get it organized; they could just get to work."

Lawrence started his own company. His method slashed the roofers' time, effort, and total cost and helped them get to work and complete their projects.

"His experience as a master roofer earned him credibility with his customers and his family-style approach to running a business built trust," said Stan.

Over several decades, Lawrence grew the business nationwide and is now ready to step back from leading the company. He looked to Stan to take his place.

"I joined the leadership team and prepared to follow in my dad's place."

Not long after Stan stepped into leadership, though, he felt something was off.

"My dad built a team of dedicated and hardworking people, but my early conversations with staff left a sense that the team wasn't clear about the company's purpose."

While his dad was a values-based leader, Stan began to see that those values were not hardwired into the culture.

Walk into most organizations today or go to their websites, and there is a good chance that somewhere there is documentation describing what the organization is about and the tenets they believe are important to operate their business and contribute to the community. Most organizations take the time to develop their versions of a statement of purpose. However, **how** organizations use that statement varies significantly.

There was a time that people believed the only purpose of a corporation was to generate value for the owners or shareholders. There is a famous story of two brothers who owned a ten-percent share of the Ford Motor Company. The brothers—John and Horace Dodge—sued Henry Ford because he was investing the company's profits in growing the business and, at the same time, improving the workers' wages instead of passing the profits onto the stakeholders. The Michigan Supreme Court ruled at the time that the primary purpose of the organization was to shareholder value,[1] and Ford had to pay the Dodge brothers an extra dividend. The money helped the brothers expand their competing company, the Dodge Brothers Company.

Leaders have begun to learn the importance of considering their key stakeholders, including staff working in the organization and people in their communities, and how the organization approached work as systems of people.[2]

In the 1980s, W. Edwards Deming[3] emphasized to leaders that we were in a "new economic age." Global markets have made change the rule, rather than the exception. Effective change requires direction, and direction requires leaders. It is the job of the leadership to establish this direction by communicating the organization's purpose.

The organization's purpose is the reason it exists, the Need that it fulfills in society. Unless the organization's purpose fulfills a worthwhile and long-term need, it may not be around in the future. Instead, another company may find a better way to match the need.[4]

Peter Drucker[5] also wrote extensively about management theory and practice and observed that the word "organization" is a new phenomenon, a tool that started post–World War II during what has been called the "Management Revolution." The attribute that made it distinct was people coming together to perform a given task. The task is the reason the organization exists.

At the end of his career, like Deming, Drucker saw this changing world and argued that the clearer the members of the organization are on what they are trying to accomplish, the greater their capacity. He also saw a common understanding of the purpose was required to prevent suboptimization:

> Because the organization is composed of specialists, each with his or her own narrow knowledge area, its mission must be crystal clear. The organization must be single-minded; otherwise, its members become confused. They will follow their specialty rather than applying it to the common purpose. They will each define "results" in terms of that specialty, imposing their own values on the organization. Only a clear, focused mission can hold the organization together and enable it to produce results. Without such a focused mission, the organization soon loses credibility.[6]

Deming[7] advocated a transformation of industry must occur and outlined 14 Points for Management. Point One—Create constancy of purpose for improvement of product and service—is the most important:

> Your customers, your suppliers, your employees need your statement of constancy of purpose— your intention to stay in business by providing product and service that will help [people] to live better and which will have a market.

Figure 4.1 depicts the relationship between the ongoing Need in society and the organization's work.[8]

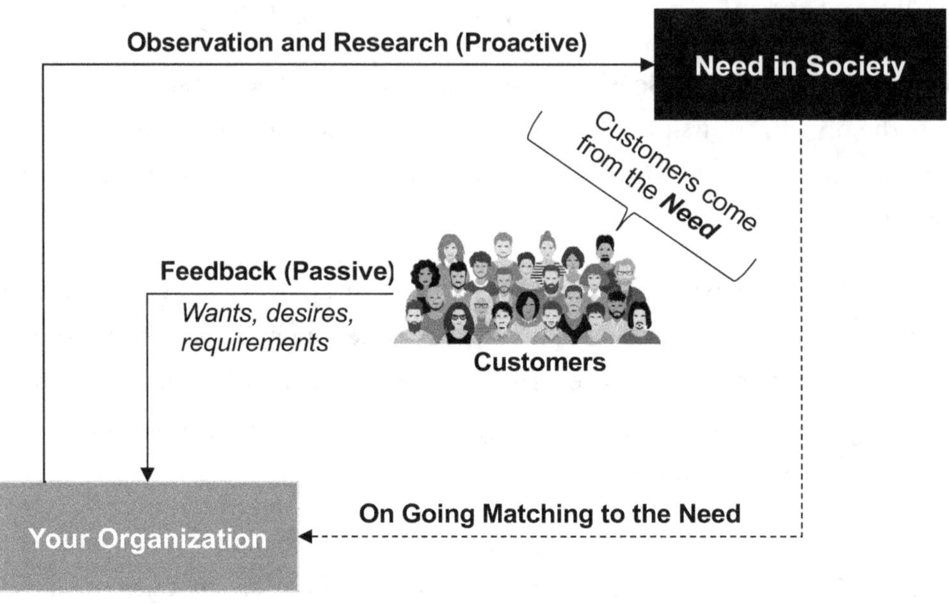

Figure 4.1. Quality as a strategic relationship to the Need.

Whole Foods Market's[9] mission statement is: "to nourish people and the planet. We're a purpose-driven company that aims to set the standards of excellence for food retailers. Quality is a state of mind at Whole Foods Market." The statement begins by describing the **Need** ("to nourish people and the planet") and then follows with the focus of the **business to contribute** ("to set the standards for excellence for food retailers"). Finally, it states the **competencies** it brings ("Quality is a state of mind….").

In a mature organization focusing on QOS, the leaders understand the reasons to have a statement of purpose and have developed the organization's mission, tenets, and vision. The purpose is communicated to all employees by relating the work of different parts of the organization to the purpose. Departments, projects, and other groups have developed role statements that relate their specific work to the organization's purpose. The statement guides and focuses the business and is used by all employees in work, such as decision-making, recruiting, new employee orientation, company websites and reports, and communications outside the organization. Each employee knows how their individual role contributes and supports the purpose of the organization.[10] The purpose is a key input to planning for the organization, and key measures are related to the purpose. The statement is incorporated into job descriptions, used to communicate, and explain organizational changes, and regularly referred to in decision-making, especially in times of crisis.[11]

This chapter frames the format for a statement of purpose and defines each key component. Then we consider how to assess the current version of an organization's purpose. An organization without a purpose should develop one. Organizations with an existing purpose will evaluate it and improve it as necessary. This evaluation will include guidance on being clear and communicating the purpose throughout the organization. Finally, we describe strategies for using the purpose in the organization.

WHY DOES PURPOSE MATTER?

Why is it so crucial for leaders to be clear about the purpose of an organization? Why does a successful company need to pause to clarify or communicate the organization's purpose?

It is difficult for an organization to have constancy of purpose unless everyone knows why the organization exists;[12] what Need in society is the organization serving? Even in small organizations, people often have different ideas about the organization's purpose. One way for top leadership to communicate the purpose is to develop a statement that explains the organization's mission, tenets (e.g., values, beliefs, guiding principles), and vision. The leadership team should then publish this statement and share it with all organization stakeholders. A statement of purpose is essential in the early stages of transforming the organization's focus to improvement.

For some organizations, even though not all members fully understand the implications of the purpose, the fact that the statement exists provides a sense of belonging, which is an excellent motivator for many people.[13] Understanding this human need, the leadership of an organization has an opportunity to create an environment that provides a sense of belonging for people. This is accomplished by explaining **why** the organization's work is vital to society and **why** the individual should take pride in belonging.

Explaining why requires leaders to communicate the organization's purpose. Investing time communicating to staff sometimes appears unnecessary to leadership, who might wonder, "Doesn't everyone already know why we are in business and what we do for customers?" Publishing and communicating a statement of purpose can appear redundant to what is assumed is "already known by everyone in the organization." However, does everyone really understand the purpose of our organization and how their role contributes to achieving it?

Deming[14] asserted that, "People must be able to take pride in their work." Therefore, an organization's statement of purpose should be positive and inspiring. The leadership's job is to explain, through the statement, how everyone's work contributes to the purpose of the organization and how the organization contributes to the greater good of society. These statements should come from a positive intent.

FORMAT FOR AN ORGANIZATION'S PURPOSE

Organizations produce products and deliver services to best **match** the Need that drives customers to their company. The way that customers define their desired match to the Need is through quality characteristics, grouped into dimensions of quality. These ideas are inputs to developing or enhancing the organization's purpose.

What should an organization's purpose include? Reviewing the purpose from a sample of organizations illustrates various approaches. There is no standard format. A useful organizational purpose contains one or more of the following components: mission, tenets, vision, role statements, and themes or slogans (see table 4.1). We will review each of these components.

Mission

The mission includes a description of the contribution and the Need the organization intends to fulfill. It answers the questions: "Why do we exist (the Need)?" and "How do we match the Need?" The mission may also include the organization's core competencies (table 4.2). The mission should be stated concisely, often in one to four sentences.

Table 4.1. Components of an organizational purpose

Component	Definitions	Key questions
Mission	A description of the *contribution* of the organization and the *Need* the organization intends to fulfill now and in the future; defines the business we are in and our competencies to match the Need.	**What** Need are we fulfilling in society? **Why** do customers come to us? By what business do we match this need? What is our unique **contribution**?
Tenets	How we conduct ourselves in carrying out the mission; defines the organization's culture.	**How** do we expect leaders and employees act in the organization?
Vision	A plan of how we will change in the future to better match the need; plays a key role in planning.	**Where** are we going as an organization? How will we be different as an organization in the future? Do we need to change the mission or our tenets to match this future state?
Role statement	Defines how a department, other groups, or an individual supports the organization's overall purpose.	**What** is the role of a department and its staff members in supporting the organization's larger mission? What is the role of each employee?
Themes and slogans	Tagline used to remind people of the purpose and align the organization.	How can we describe our contribution in ten words or less that are easy to remember? Often connected to the organization's history and sometimes used in marketing.

Table 4.2. Components in a mission

Need	The Need in the marketplace, or society, that the organization intends to fulfill provides the target for the matching and constancy of purpose for the organization.
Contribution	The targeted industry, service, or marketplace in which the Need will be matched; defines the mainstay processes of the organization.
Core competencies	Special abilities or leverage points possessed within an organization that provide access to markets, enhance value to the customer, and are difficult to imitate.

NEED

The Need in the market or society provides the target for organizations to fulfill. The Need should be defined in a way that it remains constant over time. The organization's customers are those who have that Need. Organizations with quality as their strategy develop their products and services to best match the Need of their targeted customers. The concept of Need is frequently confused with customer desires or wants.[15] The Need is a constant, but customers' expectations relative to the need will change over time. Thus, organizations bring their talent and knowledge to continue to find new or better ways to match the Need with their products and services.

Many organizational mission statements only include the products or services the organization presently offers and do not make explicit the Need(s) they fulfill. While this is acceptable for a product-focused organization, there may be different ways to satisfy a Need than the products or services that are currently available.[16] For example, publishing a book and delivering a workshop both fulfill the Need of sharing knowledge.

CONTRIBUTION

Regardless of the organization's chosen strategy,[17] the business focus and contribution should be explicit in the organization's mission. Table 4.3 presents excerpts from mission statements highlighting the potential business foci introduced in table 1.1.

Table 4.3. Focus of alternative strategies and mission statements

Business focus	Organization example	Excerpt from the mission statement
QOS (need)	Mecklenburg EMS Agency	*To save a life, hold a hand, and be prepared to respond in our community when and where our patients need us.*
Product (service)	YETI Coolers	*Build the cooler we'd use every day if it existed.*
Customer (market)	Southwest Airlines	*Connect people to what's important in their lives through friendly, reliable, and low-cost air travel.*
Pricing	Walmart	*Everyday low prices on a broad assortment—anytime, anywhere.*
Technology	Dell	*We create technologies that advance human progress.*
Production (operational excellence)	Greater Baltimore Medical Center[18]	*To provide medical care and service of the highest quality to each patient and to educate the next generation of clinicians, leading to health, healing, and hope for the community.*
Raw material	ONE Gas	*To deliver natural gas for a better tomorrow.*
Distribution	uShip	*To revolutionize the shipping and transportation industry through the power of technology.*
Financial	Goldman Sachs	*We aspire to be the world's most exceptional financial institution... we mobilize our people, culture, technologies, and ideas to advance the success of our clients, broaden individual prosperity, and accelerate economic progress for all.*

CORE COMPETENCIES

Within the mission statement, it may be helpful to include the organization's core competencies. **A core competency is an ability, or abilities, possessed within an organization that provides access to markets, enhances value to the customer, and is difficult to imitate.**[19] The Michael Hsu Office of Architecture[20] provides an example of an organization that has recognized its core competencies in its mission statement:

> We re-imagine materials to create essential experiences. We believe in the active collaboration of designer, client, and artisan. Our work connects us with nature and manifests a sense of wellbeing. We design spaces that engage our local, regional, and global communities.

These competencies define what is unique about this practice of architects and what is vital to their ability to design new projects for future customers. Including these competencies in the statement communicates to all stakeholders what is essential to their approach and how they will continue to serve their customers in the future.

Tenets

Various words describe the second component of a purpose statement: **beliefs, values, guiding principles, or tenets** of the organization. **Tenet** may be the most descriptive word for what is to be accomplished by these statements. The definition of tenet is "a principle, belief, or doctrine generally held to be true; [especially] one held in common by members of an organization, group, movement, or profession."[21]

Tenets describe **how the organization conducts itself while accomplishing its mission.** The tenets create the basis for the intended culture of an organization. The culture of any organization or society includes language, beliefs, values, ideas, rituals, and myths. Leaders should develop tenets to describe their intended organizational culture. Figure 4.2 illustrates the relationship between the tenets of the purpose statement and an organization's culture.[22]

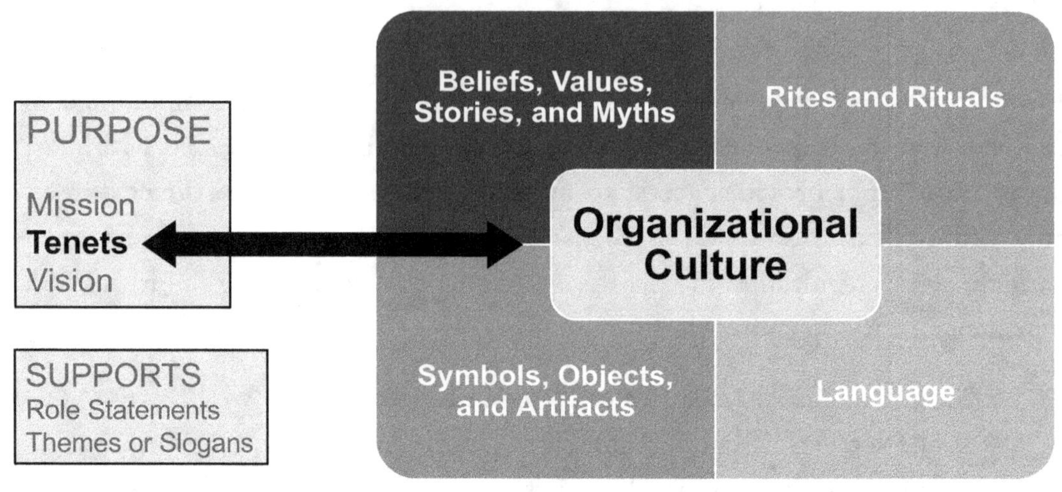

Figure 4.2. Tenets, beliefs, and defining culture.

The leadership in Jönköping County Council in Sweden[23] wanted to humanize their vision of creating a system where people worked together to provide high-quality care for patients and lived their belief in patient-centered practice. They created a persona— named Esther—to represent the elderly population they served and to help them concentrate on their patient experience. Improvement efforts used Esther to ground teams in thinking with the patient at the center and improve their journey through the process. Any changes, along with the related structures and methods chosen (that is, to design or redesign the organization to achieve the purpose), should be introduced and explained within the context of the organization's tenets. If change is introduced that contradicts the tenets and culture, leadership must pause and reflect on whether the change is appropriate or consider updating the tenets.[24] The tenets stated in the organizational purpose are those we want to retain in the culture.

Booz Allen and the Aspen Institute[25] conducted a global study in thirty countries across five regions and discovered that eighty-nine percent reported having written statements of values. While this is positive, many organizations publish the same set of values and include things every organization should do simply to be in business, like being ethical or customer-oriented.[26]

Former IBM CEO Lou Gerstner also noted this but affirmed that values are really important to organizational culture. He said, "The question is, do you create a culture of behavior and action that really demonstrate those values…?"[27] How do the espoused values translate into behaviors that guide leaders and create the desired culture?

To be accepted and shared throughout the organization, the development and ratification of the organization's tenets require reaching some type of agreement. Leadership must take the time to select the vital few tenets that reflect the culture, clearly define each, and address critical issues related to understanding and accepting those stated tenets.

If the tenets are vague or general and poorly defined, they provide no practical guidance. For example, if leaders publish that the clinic desires to deliver "evidence-based care," what does this look like when a new study comes out indicating a change in protocol is required? If we declare we believe in "teamwork," what does this look like in practice when the sales team collaborates with staff from fulfillment to improve the link (for example, a sales order) between their work?

Thomas Stewart states, "[Values] have to be compatible with the culture that's already there; pretty words won't bloom in the wrong soil."[28] For example, transparency and learning are difficult to practice if competition and individual accountability are the practices in use. This culture can change when staff collaborate on an improvement project and learn and practice quality improvement methods that foster discovery and learning. Cox describes that effective value statements exist "when people hear good, previously unexpressed words that ring true, they say with recognition and pride, 'Sure enough, that's the way we do things around here.' That is tapping into the organizational soul." [29]

Table 4.4 are guidelines for U.S. emergency medical technicians and paramedics to carry out their mission. The STARCARE[30] guidelines were developed by a field supervisor to help leaders quickly onboard staff for a new contract to provide ambulance service to an urban region. Drawing from principles most medics share, the guidelines were drafted to support decision-making in complex environments like delivering care on the street corner and helping a patient who called 9-1-1. Medics were assured that if they can answer these questions with a "Yes," their decisions will align with the company's expectations.[31]

Table 4.4. STARCARE Guidelines

Principle	Operational definition
Safe	Were my actions safe—for me, for my colleagues, for other professionals, and the public?
Team-based	Were my actions taken with due regard for the opinions and feelings of my co-workers, including those from other agencies?
Attentive to human needs	Did I treat my patient as a person? Did I keep him/her warm? Was I gentle? Did I use his/her name throughout the call? Did I tell him/her what to expect in advance? Did I treat his/her family and/or relatives with similar respect?
Respectful	Did I act toward my patient, my colleagues, my first responders, the hospital staff, and the public with the kind of respect that I would have wanted to receive myself?
Customer Accountable	If I were face-to-face right now with the customers I dealt with on this response, could I look them in the eye and say, "I did my very best for you."
Appropriate	Was my care appropriate—medically, professionally, legally, and practically considering the circumstances I faced?
Reasonable	Did my actions make sense? Would a reasonable colleague of my experience have acted similarly, under the same circumstances?
Ethical	Were my actions fair and honest in every way? Are my answers to these questions?

The Baldrige Performance Excellence Program describes "core values and concepts"[32] that underpin the beliefs and behaviors of high-performance organizations (table 4.5). Latham[33] studied Baldrige award–winning organizations and identified five shared values: valued employees, trust, teamwork, excellence, and customer focus.

Table 4.5. Baldridge core values and concepts

Values and concepts
Systems perspective
Visionary leadership
Customer-focused excellence
Valuing people
Agility and resilience
Organizational learning
Focus on success and innovation
Management by fact
Societal contributions
Ethics and transparency
Delivering value and results

Finally, many organizations issue policies on such concepts as safety, environment, and quality, sometimes as a part of certification or licensing. The tenets component of the purpose provides the opportunity to include these critical issues in the company's purpose rather than be perceived as an additional policy or an afterthought. It demonstrates their importance and keeps them in front of the organization's stakeholders.

Vision

In the 1950s, Ronald Lippitt[34] began taping planning meetings. When he played them back, he noticed people initially feeling anxious when they described problems that needed to be fixed. The energy shifted as those same people started to focus on their future in rich detail and work backward.[35] Lippitt and colleagues continued to learn, and their work became the foundation for visioning or futuring methods.[36] Visioning defines a desired future state we wish to evolve toward.

At its root, the vision statement should answer the question, "Where do we want to go in the future? What do we want to accomplish regarding our organization's products and services, our customers, markets, and competitive position in the future?" A vision statement can act as a guide to help organizations focus on strategy and their day-to-day efforts and choices.[37] The work we do today creates the vision of tomorrow. For example, Eklund's, an elevator company, operates with this vision:

> By creating a skilled, trained workforce who believes in and reinforces constant improvement, Eklund's will address all market sectors relative to the need for architectural products for elevator cabs, entrances, and escalator cladding. Eklund's will be recognized for its delivery of quality, integrity, communication, and integration of current technology to meet customer needs.[38]

These statements may not be fulfilled today for Eklund's, but they establish direction. Some organizations find developing visions for five, ten, twenty, and even fifty years helpful. Vision statements express the leadership's view of the organization's **future structure, image, and actions** to accomplish its purpose. For example, Southwest Airlines'[39] mission is: "Connect people to what's important in their lives through friendly, reliable, and low-cost air travel." Currently, their vision is "To be the world's most loved, most efficient, and most profitable airline."

Consider creating a vision statement when the organization is planning changes in direction or operating philosophy or when changes in the external environment dictate the change in direction. There are many methods leadership teams may use to look into the future and formulate compelling visions.[40] The result of a visioning exercise will serve as an important input to the planning activity (see Chapter 8).

EXAMPLES OF DESCRIBING AN ORGANIZATION'S STATEMENT OF PURPOSE

The two examples below show how organizations are using mission, vision, and tenets to describe the organization's purpose. The first is a healthcare example from the Mayo Clinic Health System.[41]

Mayo Clinic Health System	
Vision	Mayo Clinic will provide an unparalleled experience as the most trusted partner for health care.
Mission	To inspire hope and contribute to health and well-being by providing the best care to every patient through integrated clinical practice, education, and research.
Value	The needs of the patient come first.

Next is an education example from the Charter School of San Diego[42] in California, a 2015 and 2021 recipient of the Malcolm Baldrige National Quality Award.

Charter School of San Diego	
Vision	The educational community known as The Charter School of San Diego is committed to the development of a personalized instructional program with intensive parental involvement that demonstrates positive outcomes for each student. The Charter School of San Diego is dedicated to the creation of instructional, service, organizational, and governance models that can serve as prototypes for educational reform. The Charter School of San Diego is committed to collaborative efforts to improve the quality of life for students, their families, its employees, and the community at large.
Mission	The Charter School of San Diego will implement personalized educational programs to facilitate student achievement. These educational programs will demonstrate that standards-based educational reform can provide a prototype for changing the way teachers teach and students learn in the future.

	Charter School of San Diego (*continued*)
Tenets	<ul><li>Kids come first.</li><li>Education at CSSD is personalized, individualized, and high quality.</li><li>CSSD is made up of a community of highly professional people. These committed individuals are independent, self-motivated, high-energy people who speak for themselves. They work to create a positive, challenging environment that is centered on teaching and learning.</li><li>CSSD is committed to the creation of educational reform models centered on how effective educational organizations run, how teachers teach, and how students learn.</li><li>CSSD employees are accountable for their work.</li><li>People-centered teams focus on supporting quality teaching and learning. Performance is measured on a variety of indicators that include productivity, credit ratio, auditability, quality, performances, and commitment to the vision of CSSD.</li><li>CSSD is committed to improving the quality of life for students, their families, and the community at large.</li><li>CSSD uses business principles in managing the school.</li></ul>

While Stan was away at school, Lawrence had worked with a consultant to develop the company's first mission, vision, and tenets with the leadership team. The event was productive.

"I can still remember seeing the rolled-up flip chart paper covered in sticky notes living on a side table in my dad's assistant's office for several weeks. The assistant eventually typed it up, and the final product was produced into a framed poster for display."

Stan remembered seeing the poster in the building back then—where was it now?

"I asked one of the leaders who was around back then if she knew where it was. She recalled it was hung on the wall in the conference room, but it was not there when they went to look for it. Then it hit us: the conference room we use now was part of the recent renovation, and the old conference room had long been converted to office space. As the company grew, it needed more space. The addition we were in now was added on, and older areas were made into more offices."

"We went to the old conference room location, and behind a projector screen that dropped from the ceiling, we found the framed poster of the organization's purpose." He took down the poster and carried it back to his office.

Star Roofing Systems

Statement of Purpose

Vision: Star Roofing Systems will be the North American pioneer in the industrial roofing industry.

Mission: Industry needs buildings to produce their products and services and keep their roofs on with quality products, exceptional service, and technical expertise.

Tenets: Experienced crews, quality products, customer service, safe work, and a family atmosphere.

Clearly, the product of the previous work to develop a mission, vision, and tenets was not in use in the organization today. It was physically hidden. Stan knew, however, that people central to the company contributed to it, and it was a place to start. Gathering the artifacts of their purpose provides Stan and his team a place to reflect and build from.

Useful Ways to Leverage the Purpose

The purpose includes the organization's mission, tenets, and vision. After the hard work of developing a purpose, leaders may find it useful to help people understand how their role and work contribute to the organization's overall purpose. It can also be useful to develop themes or slogans that ease communication of the overall purpose across the organization.

Role statements

To operate as a system, everyone in the organization must understand how their work contributes to the overall purpose. Managers may find it helpful to explain how their department's work supports the purpose of the whole organization in a written statement. These statements are called **role statements** and should reference the purpose of the larger organization.

Table 4.6 summarizes the difference between role statements and mission statements. Role statements are also different from a typical job description. A job description includes compensation, reporting structure, skills, and responsibilities, usually with reference to the department or manager the job reports to. A **role statement**[43] defines the intent of the job, including the information from a job description, and it also includes responsibility for processes, measures, expected conduct in relation to tenets, responsibilities for learning, and system improvement, all in support of achieving the organizational purpose.

Table 4.6. Mission and role statements

	Mission statement	Role statement
Objective	Defines Need(s) and how the organization contributes to match the Need(s)	Defines work and relationships as they relate to specific tasks or functions
Focus	Broad	Narrow
Degree of independence	Independent; can accomplish purpose	Interdependent
Customers	External (to the system)	Internal (could be some external)

When should parts of an organization have role statements? It depends on how the organization is divided. For each part that is its own system, like a stand-alone business unit, a nested **mission** statement is useful to define the Need or business focus that the subsystem intends to match for customers and the processes (mainstay) of the system by which we contribute (see also Chapter 5). Parts of the organization, like a division, department, or project group within the larger system, needs to understand their **role** in the system or how they contribute to the overall system. Thus, if a part of the organization is considered a separate system, it should have a nested mission statement. All other parts of these systems should use a role statement to describe how their function relates to the purpose of the total system.

How we think about customers is different for mission and role statements. The mission statement focuses the organization on the Need from which customers seek out the organization's products or services. This focus helps people within the system understand for whom they are working, in order to better match the Need...a primary reason for the organization's existence. Departments and organizations within the larger organizational system communicate with internal and external customers. When defining their role, the primary concern of the roles statement is to define the work of the group or department and how it contributes directly to the mission. The sales department within a company is an example of a part of the organization with a specific role. That role provides information to both external and internal customers. For example, a salesperson can be invaluable to a customer in understanding how the company's products or services are the best match, and internally they may provide insight into customer expectations and demand.

Themes and slogans

After the hard work of thinking about and defining the purpose of an organization, leaders may find it useful to develop a **theme or slogan** that simplifies the purpose and makes the organization's focus more concrete or use a tagline with historical significance to the organization (e.g., Ford's "Quality is Job 1"). Sometimes these already exist in organizations and should be formalized as part of the purpose. A theme is a statement that can be remembered and communicated by all organizational stakeholders. For example, many law enforcement organizations use the theme "protect and serve," which speaks to all business units involved in some stage of the organization's work, from 9-1-1 call center employees to administrative staff to patrol officers. The use of the theme allows the everyday actions of people and the improvement efforts to be more easily directed toward a common goal. Table 4.7 lists themes for different organizations.

Campbell and Nash[44] described the attributes of a successful theme:

1. It represents the core of both the organization's purpose and value system.
2. It is easy to translate into behavior standards.
3. It has strong value associations that are attractive to large sections of management and employees.
4. It is noncontroversial and enables all the power bases in the company to submerge their differences and support it.

For the theme or slogan to be effective, base it on the ideas essential to the leadership. Their actions must be consistent with these ideas. If this is not the case, then the actions of the leaders and the theme or slogan will lose credibility.

Table 4.7. Example of organizational themes

Organization	Theme
Dunkin' Donuts	*America runs on Dunkin'.*
Apple	*Think different.*
Police department	*To serve and protect*
Airbnb	*Belong anywhere.*
Verizon	*Can you hear me now?*
Energizer	*It keeps going, and going, and going…*
Avis	*We're number two; we try harder!*
De Beers	*A diamond is forever.*
Southwest Airlines	*You are now free to move around the country*
Nike	*Just do it!*
Uber	*Move the way you want.*
Capital One	*What's in your wallet?*
United Parcel Service	*What can brown do for you?*

Summary: Components of an Organization's Purpose

Taken together, the organization's purpose includes a mission, tenets, and vision. Role statements and themes, and slogans support the purpose. Table 4.1 summarized the components and includes questions each component should answer. These questions are useful for leaders as they evaluate your organization's present purpose and improve it or consider it when developing an initial purpose.

DEVELOPING A STATEMENT OF PURPOSE

If no other document exists, organizations should consider the following questions[45] to prepare the leadership to develop a purpose for the organization:

- Why should we develop a purpose for the organization?
- Can we afford the time and effort required to develop and communicate the purpose? Are we willing to lead this effort? How much time is needed?

- Are we willing to discuss and examine the vision of our direction as an organization? In what areas are we sensitive about discussion?
- Are we willing to discuss and examine management practices and organizational relationships? What are the sensitive issues?
- Are we willing to use and make the purpose our tool to manage, lead, work, and communicate as an organization?

If the leadership team can give positive answers to the questions above, then the time required to develop a purpose will add value to the organization. If there are one or more "no" answers to these questions, the effort to develop an organizational purpose could result in a meaningless exercise and wasted time for the team. Before the team proceeds, explore and thoroughly understand the varying views.

Assessment of the Organization's Purpose

The purpose invites the question, "Does this statement reflect who we are?" The following questions have proved useful in this critical task:

1. Does the purpose explicitly contain the Need (or other business focus) that the organization intends to fulfill? What is this Need (or focus)?
2. Is this Need (or focus) worthwhile and inspiring? How does it reinforce the organization as something one should identify with and deserves admiration inside and outside the organization?
3. Does the purpose define the core system of delivery to the customer?
4. Does the purpose describe the core competencies, capabilities, or other unique strategies for developing the business and contributing as an organization? What are they?
5. How does it view committing the organization to develop new products and services for the future? Will resources be allocated to market research, training and education, research, and development to support this view?
6. Does the purpose account for all those concerned with the organization's survival (stakeholders), such as suppliers, customers, owners, and communities? How does it describe the relationship between these stakeholders and the organization?
7. As established in the mission statement, will the purpose remain constant despite leadership changes? What could cause it to change?

8. Are there other aspects of the purpose that should change? Does the purpose reflect who we are? What are some inconsistencies between our current culture and the words in this purpose?

9. Is the purpose inspiring? Is it easy to read and understand? If not, how could it be improved?

When using the previous questions to assess the purpose, encourage people to go beyond simple yes or no answers. Instead, get them to ask, "Why?" This exercise will create much-needed feedback for fine-tuning the organization's purpose.

Developing an organization's purpose is not an easy process, but it is necessary work. Leaders often discover they were not conscious of how much opportunity there is for the organization to enhance its alignment and clarify its shared understanding of what it is trying to accomplish. The hard work of crafting and refining a purpose is challenging and valuable. In the remaining section of the chapter, we will learn how to build on this work, share it with the organization, further clarify it with input, and begin to use it in our work.

SHARING THE ORGANIZATION'S PURPOSE

The leadership of an organization spends considerable time and effort reaching a common understanding of the organization's purpose and expressing it concisely in writing. However, it is difficult to recreate and transfer the learning process of developing the purpose to the rest of the organization. Therefore, the leadership team must champion the effort to communicate the purpose to the organization's stakeholders to express the word and the spirit of the document.

Once leadership puts forth the purpose and direction of the organization, they must communicate and make it a shared purpose. This development of a purpose begins with a small group of leaders, but it becomes a shared purpose after gathering the support of others. **People tend to support what they understand and help create.** Therefore, the leadership of an organization should create the opportunity for people to contribute to the purpose and direction of their future. Creating this opportunity helps ensure that the purpose becomes shared by the organization members. Farnham[46] offers guidelines for establishing a meaningful and shared purpose, including:

- Involve everyone.
- Allow customization.
- Expect and accept resistance.
- Keep it short.
- Challenge it.
- Live 'em.

Just sharing through a process of cascading communication throughout the organization does not ensure the purpose is shared and meaningful to the organization. Leaders require methods of communicating the purpose that helps us act on Farnham's guidelines. Developing a plan ensures that the hard work of creating the purpose transitions to its use. Leadership should address the following questions:

1. Are there words selected by the leadership team that carry special significance? Why are these significant and important to understand the business? Do any words in the purpose require operational definitions?
2. Will the purpose be tested with a small group of people? If so, how will the testing be done?
3. What is the plan to communicate the purpose to the rest of the organization?
4. What is the process to address questions or request clarification from organization members?

Operational Definitions for Key Words

Developing the wording of the components of the purpose and documenting operational definitions of keywords is essential. Operational definitions put a "communicable meaning into a concept."[47] Wordsmithing starts with a small, select group. Emphasize selecting keywords that communicate the most information and guide with the fewest words. The words should also be accessible and meaningful to people throughout the organization. As this process evolves, the words take on more meaning and power for the organization.

Develop operational definitions for keywords in the statement of purpose. Operational definitions are exactly what the term sounds like: shared definitions of words or phrases so everyone understands what they mean in context. Earlier, we shared operational definitions for the values in the STARCARE Guidelines. A tenet like "team-based" may mean each team member is considered and included in decisions. Operational definitions must be documented and distributed to those who must communicate the meaning of the words. More importantly, document and distribute these definitions to those who must understand their more profound meaning and put them into action.

Operational definitions[48] are essential in various settings. They bring meaning to ideas and thus avoid conflict due to misunderstanding terms. If the purpose is to have the same meaning for all in the organization, then some concepts in the purpose most likely will need to be operationally defined. These operational definitions can be part of the purpose if made brief, or part of the supporting documentation.

Looking at the examples presented in this chapter, several organizational purposes contain terms needing an operational definition. Table 4.8 is an example from Whole Foods Market.[49] The organization's mission is to "nourish people and the planet." Core values are included in the organization's purpose, and an operational definition accompanies each.

Table 4.8. Defining words in the purpose (from Whole Foods Market Statement of Purpose)

Core values	Examples of definitions
We sell the highest quality natural and organic foods.	"Responsibly farmed and sustainable wild-caught seafood…" "…if it doesn't meet our standards, we don't sell it."
We satisfy and delight our customers.	"Meet or exceed their expectations on every shopping experience…" "Continually experiment and innovate to offer a better customer experience…"
We promote team member growth and happiness.	"Design and provide safe and empowering environments …" "Earn trust through transparent communication, open door policies, and inclusive people practices…"
We practice win-win partnerships with our suppliers.	"View our trade partners as allies in serving our stakeholders…" "We always seek win-win relationships with everyone we do business with…"
We create profits and prosperity.	"[Profits] are the "seed corn" for next year's crop and creator of sustained prosperity…" "We will grow at such a pace that our customer satisfaction, team member happiness, and financial health continue to flourish together."
We care about our community and the environment.	"We serve and support a local experience, and practice and advance environmental stewardship."

As Stan's staff worked through the questions to assess their purpose, several terms stood out and needed clear meaning. Did they have the same understanding of what "quality" means? What did "exceptional service" look like in practice? Many words in the purpose felt familiar and probably right, but the team agreed it made sense to develop an operational definition they all shared.

"Technical expertise" was very important to staff who knew what it was like to be on a roof doing an installation. Understanding the job of roofers and the requirements of a good installation made the company distinct and was often noted by new and returning customers for why they worked with the company.

Technical expertise was defined as "practical and technical experience with the planning and installation of flat roofs."

Test with a Small Group

Often, it is helpful for leadership to introduce a small group of people to the purpose before communicating it to the entire organization. This pilot test helps identify parts of the purpose that need clarification or concerns people have about the written purpose. The selection of people for this initial group varies by organization. Some organizations test the purpose with the next layer of the organizational hierarchy. Others decide to involve people from all levels of the organization.

Planning to Communicate to the Organization

Communicating the purpose to the entire organization is accomplished by various means. There are often two basic groupings of people to consider: those inside and those outside the organization. Internally, the groups could be determined by geographic region (local, domestic, international), organizational unit (headquarters, division, plant, department), or organizational hierarchy (management, supervisor, operator, office, etc.). In addition, several stakeholders outside the organization may need to understand the organization's purpose. These include categories of people like customers, suppliers, members of the community, and stockholders or investors.

There are various means of communicating the organization's purpose to these groups. For example, in a small organization, the leadership can share the purpose personally or in an informal meeting. In larger organizations, managers at various levels need to help executive management communicate the organization's purpose to the rest of the organization. These managers may need resources to aid them, such as a video message from a board chair or chief executive or talking points containing key ideas provided by leadership.

Communication of the organization's purpose is not a one-time event. The organization's purpose should be used ongoingly in company reports and internal communications to explain new ventures, programs, and changes. Talks by organizational leaders should incorporate language from the purpose statement. Opportunities to better communicate using the organization's purpose present themselves daily.

Addressing Questions and Clarifying

People will have questions about the purpose statement and the details within the different components. Develop a process for staff to easily submit their questions or requests for clarification to the leadership team. Allow all submissions to reach the leaders responsible for reviewing staff input.

Record each entry and the responses for the leadership team to review. Input may include changes required to improve the purpose statement. Any questions or requests for clarification should be addressed, and feedback returned to the individuals. Share a summary of common questions and answers to share with all staff.

USING THE ORGANIZATION'S PURPOSE

The organization's purpose must be communicated, used continually, and clarified as needed to be used effectively. If not used continually, the statement has no long-term impact, or it possibly negatively impacts the organization. Individual behaviors of the leaders will become more important than the stated purpose. As Drucker[50] observed: "[that the] … business purpose and business mission are so rarely given adequate thought is perhaps the most important cause of business frustration and failure."

Survey any organization and ask, "What are the biggest problems?," and a top response is likely to be "Inadequate communication." The annual cumulative cost of lost productivity per worker resulting from communications barriers was estimated at $26,041 in 2009; in 2024, that would equate to $38,441.[51] Using the purpose to communicate is a first step toward reducing the failure to communicate. The organization's leadership should be conscious of how the purpose statement is appropriately used and when the purpose statement is not helpful.

The following is a list of some instances when the use of the organization's purpose may be useful in practice:

- Whenever a significant change occurs in an organization, explain the change in terms of its purpose.
- Input to decisions at all levels of the organization (e.g., business development).
- Used to align department and individual roles within the organization.
- The basis for feedback in the organization.
- Input to planning, aligning the organization's goals, objectives, and plans with the purpose (see Chapter 8 on "Planning").
- An aid to innovation by reminding those in the organization of the Need that their products and services fulfill.
- A focus on organizational learning in all education and training.
- A tool to communicate with people outside the organization: customers, suppliers, potential employees, government, and the community.
- Input to develop a view of the organization as a system (see Chapter 5 on "Systems").
- Input to develop a vector of measures for an organization (see Chapter 6 on "Measures of the System").

Implementing Change in an Organization

The concept depicted in figure 4.3[52] was first introduced in Chapter 3 to describe the relationship between changes represented by new structures and methods, behavior, attitudes, and culture. Earlier in this chapter, "tenets" described how the organization conducts itself while accomplishing its mission. The tenets create the basis for the intended culture of an organization. In established organizations, the culture defines the espoused tenets (depicted in the arrow at the top of figure 4.3 from culture to tenets).

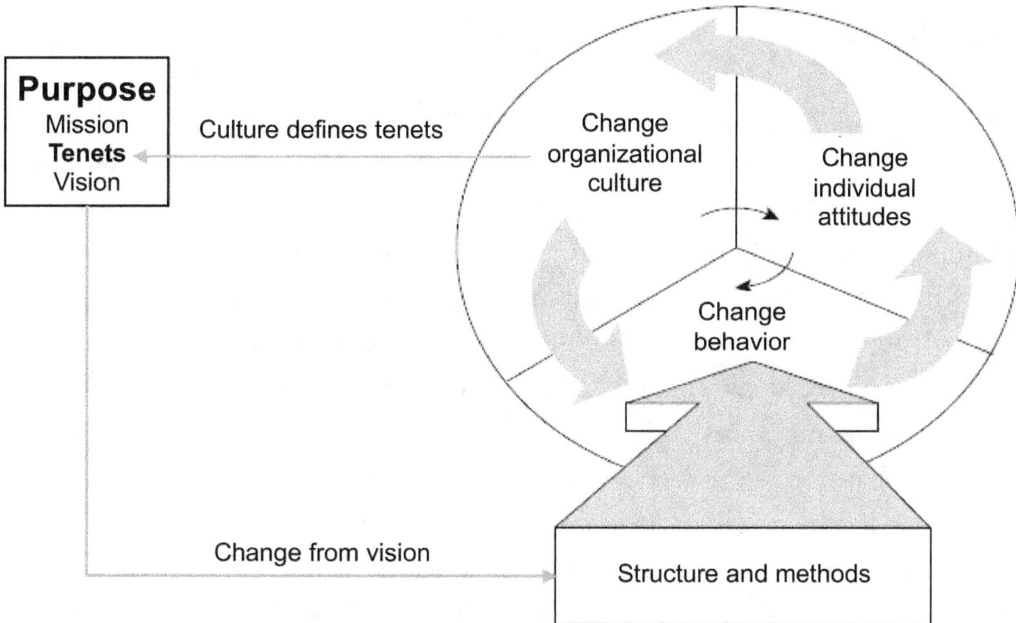

Figure 4.3. The organization's purpose and change.

There is a common belief that no one likes to change. It is more accurate to say no one likes to be changed or to have change applied to them. However, people do accept change more easily when it is familiar, and they have some part in the change process. When a leadership team can explain **why** a change is necessary by explaining it in alignment with the organization's stated purpose, the change can have greater acceptance; people appreciate it in the context of why the organization exists and know that the change is happening through the tenets. If the change is rooted in the organization's purpose, it better fits the culture.

When an organization creates a new vision, we can expect that a number of changes will take place to make the vision a reality. Explicitly connecting new structures (e.g., a reorganization of departments) to the vision can clarify why new behaviors are expected (as shown in the arrow in figure 4.3 coming down from the Purpose and connecting to structure and methods). When the leadership can communicate this way, their actions appear consistent with the stated purpose and are more likely to gain support. This will, in turn, impact individual attitudes. If the new behaviors align with the culture, integrating the change should be easier than if no explanation were given.

Input to Decisions

A clear organizational purpose, with tenets defined that describe how people should conduct themselves in the organization, allows people at all levels to respond to situations with flexibility while staying in alignment with the organization's purpose. For example, most of us have been customers when something did not go right. When these situations were resolved well, often the staff were empowered to settle the issue immediately to our satisfaction. An additional supervisor or approval was not necessary because the employee knew what needed to be done and had the authority to act in the most common circumstances. This ability to make decisions on the spot saved time and hassle and probably made us feel better about doing business with the establishment. Organizations led by a leadership team that communicates the desired relationship with customers through their tenets routinely operate this way. This ability to serve customers is one benefit to an organization that has established "constancy of purpose": a clear, ongoing alignment with purpose.

How does this look in practice? Joe Balthazor, CEO of Hallmark Building Supplies,[53] received a phone call from the Vice President of Operations in the middle of a snowstorm. He asked if the business should continue to make deliveries. Mr. Balthazor asked his colleague to consider the organization's tenets in consideration of his question. One of the tenets is: "We share a personal and professional commitment to ensure the safety and well-being of all stakeholders." Continuing to deliver through a snowstorm could put staff, the public, and property at risk. They agreed the proper thing to do was to call customers and let them know the shipments would be delayed until it was safe to deliver.

Senge[54] described a picture of alignment versus that of not being aligned with the aid of arrows, as shown in figure 4.4. The top figure illustrates the disjointed efforts of everyone going their own way, reacting to problems, and acting in isolation. The bottom of the figure shows arrows that represent the harmony found in an organization where people are aligned on purpose and are all operating in service of shared mission and tenets.

Management sometimes calls on an organization's purpose in a crisis. One such noted example occurred in 1982 with Johnson & Johnson. Tylenol capsules laced with cyanide caused the deaths of seven people in Chicago.[55] "The Credo,"[56] developed by Johnson & Johnson's founder forty years earlier, was called on for guidance by all levels of the Johnson & Johnson organization. Within "The Credo," the message is clear:

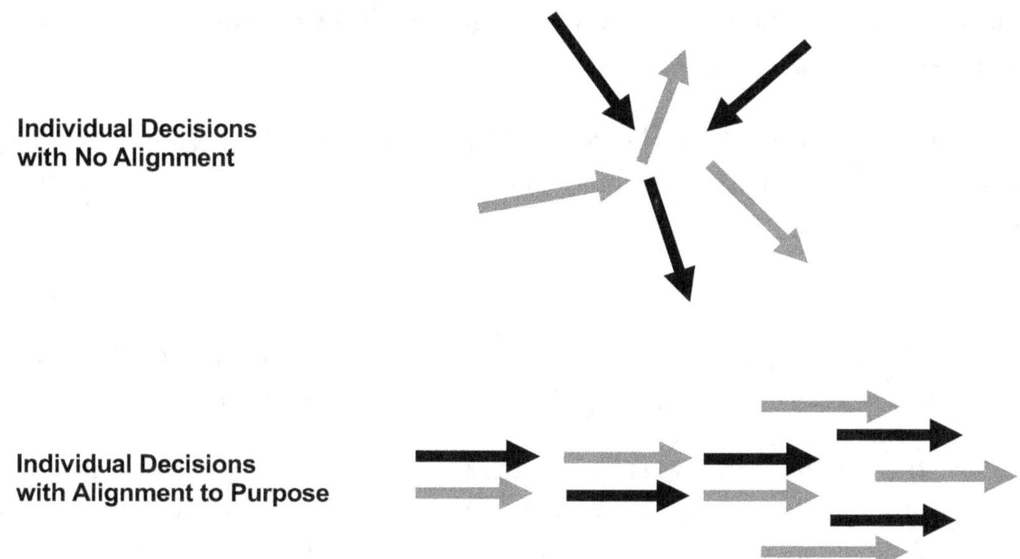

Figure 4.4. Individual, unaligned decisions versus alignment with purpose.

> We believe our first responsibility is to the doctors, nurses, and patients,
> to mothers and all others who use our products and services.

With this direction, Mr. James Burke, Chief Executive Officer at the time, was ready to respond to press inquiries. Throughout the U.S., Johnson & Johnson employees began removing Tylenol from store shelves[57] at the cost of $100 million. In addition, they designed a new safety seal package at the time of the recall. In just three months, Tylenol was back on store shelves and had recovered most of its market share. This was possible because Johnson & Johnson was purpose-driven and ready to make decisions based on "The Credo." Others, not so driven, would have spent their time with attorneys and developing strategies to "stonewall the press."[58]

Feedback Approaches

The organization's purpose is most useful when someone becomes misguided and begins to act at cross-purposes with the organization. For example, a manager makes a local decision that changes an accepted business practice. The change results in some clients not receiving service as expected, or work must be redone to get the expected output. The leadership team reviews the change with the manager using the organization's purpose.

They all recognize that the change is not aligned with the organization's purpose or the manager's role, and the change is reversed.

Everyone in an organization should feel empowered to use the organization's purpose in this way. Often this leads to a better understanding of what the purpose really means to the organization.

> Stan was eager to try using the organization's purpose in practice. The leadership team agreed to use the purpose when making decisions. He shared:
>
> > It took less than a week before the team faced our first opportunity. The warehouse received a shipment of rolls of PVC membrane from their primary supplier. An order was being prepared for a customer to go out before the end of the business day. When staff inspected the membrane, they noticed some imperfections in the rolls. Imperfections like this are rare but do occur, and the company normally doesn't pass them on to the customer.
> >
> > We had to decide whether to send the product with the imperfection and meet the order deadline or order new product and overnight it to the client and absorb the additional cost. We used the tenets to reflect on the choices. They did not like delaying delivery, and they knew they were committed to delivering quality products.
> >
> > Shannon, the fulfillment manager, called the client, and we all listened as she described the circumstances and explained our plan. They would receive two shipments the next day: an incomplete order from the warehouse that would arrive as scheduled and, shortly after, PVC membrane free of imperfections. In the end, the client was thankful for the personal call and how we, as a company, worked to deliver a quality product with limited delay.

Input to Planning

The organization's purpose is a significant input into the planning process (see Chapter 8 on "Planning"). The mission statement guides the planning activity by focusing on the Needs that the organization fulfills in society. This focus guides those who must develop solutions to today's problems while preparing for tomorrow's problems and solutions. Deming indicates that the constancy of purpose means thinking about products and services that the customer has not even thought about yet:

> The customer is not in a good position to prescribe a product or service that will help him in the future. The producer is in a far better position than the consumer to invent new designs and new services. Would anyone that owned an automobile in 1905 express a desire for pneumatic tires, had you asked him what he needed? Would I, carrying a precise pocket watch, have suggested a tiny calculator and quartz timepiece?[59]

The producer used knowledge of the Need to provide a better match.

The vision component of the purpose acts as a beacon for the planning process. The vision statement guides what the organization wishes to become in the future, five, ten, or even twenty years ahead.[60] For example, suppose the company wants to have offices in the international marketplace in five years. In that case, develop one- or two-year strategic objectives to achieve this vision. What human resource skills and education will be required to staff these offices? What is necessary to identify these resources and their respective development? What processes need development and improvement to support this vision? The answers to these questions, combined with customer feedback, help focus the planning process on those improvement efforts that support the organization's business strategy.

The vision statement is sometimes a detailed document. While an essential statement and part of the overall purpose, the vision statement is better presented separately from the mission and tenet sections of the purpose. Separating the documents allows frequent—often five-year—updates to the vision as needed without changing the organizational purpose's more permanent mission and tenets components.

Communication to Stakeholders

The organization's purpose provides an understanding of what the organization does, who it is, and what is expected in the future. Community members may want to know the company's beliefs about corporate responsibility concerning environmental safety. Current employees and people interested in joining the organization may wish to understand the company's stand on employee development and career growth. The purpose can provide information to those inside and outside the organization on various topics. For example, a leader may routinely use the organization's purpose in communications with prospective staff or hires to aid them in understanding their new positions. The use of the purpose and the role statement provides clarity in the onboarding period and eases the efforts of the staff to reach a stage where they can work independently.

More organizations have included the organization's purpose in their annual report to stockholders in recent years. The purpose helps describe how the **company's new actions** fit the established purpose. This communication can help stockholders understand management's actions regarding new market ventures, product and service offerings, and acquisitions for the company.

Aid to Innovation

The organization's purpose should encourage innovation by emphasizing the Need the organization intends to fulfill rather than the current products and services. For example, Tesla Motors began with the mission: "To accelerate the advent of sustainable transport by bringing compelling mass-market cars to market as quickly as possible."[61] Initially, it was primarily an electronic car company, and it developed high-end electric sports cars to develop its technology. Over time, Tesla expanded its mission "to accelerate the world's transition to sustainable energy" to reflect better a shift from a transportation company to developing products that fulfilled the Need for sustainable energy. As a result, Tesla has expanded its original transportation product lineup and developed scalable clean energy generation and storage products, including solar panels and battery technology.[62] So what can be done to cause innovation through the contribution of products, services, and knowledge to help customers be more successful?

Focus for Organizational Learning

To help staff develop awareness, organizational leaders use awareness sessions to introduce the concepts of quality, the organization's purpose, what making improvements looks like, and the respective roles of people and departments in QOS.

Use the organizational purpose as the framing to teach the employee's role in this shift. Leadership-delivered awareness sessions should begin as soon as QOS implementation is begun, and the curriculum should be built around the purpose.

Resources slated for education and training can enhance the defined competencies, skills, and tenets described in the organization's purpose. In what areas do we need to invest in the further development of people? What do we need today? What about the future? The purpose should give guidance to the leadership in answering these questions.

Many healthcare organizations want to improve the patient experience while they improve outcomes and reduce costs. Including patients in their care planning and decision-making is central to that aim. Some organizations have also started asking, "What matters to you?"[63] which may include requests outside traditional care.

NHS Greater Glasgow and Clyde (NHSGGC) is a large health board in the U.K. Its mission is to "deliver effective and high-quality health services, to act to improve the health of our population and to do everything we can to address the wider social determinants of health which cause health inequalities."[64] To achieve this purpose, the organization has a strategy[65] that includes several aims. One aim is to deliver "person-centered care." One method to achieve this aim is asking patients, "What matters to you?" and acting on what patients say to their care providers.[66] This focus requires new or adapted skills for doctors and nurses to learn how to do this well, blend it into existing work processes, and be prepared to act on their patients' requests.

For these organizations, education and training resources were directed toward the new behaviors and practices they needed today. It also shifted the practice and culture of who the organization wanted to be going forward. The roles of people should be reviewed with the purpose in mind. These roles should be redefined and updated with changes to the purpose.

Inputs to Other QOS Activities

In addition to the ongoing uses previously described, the organization's purpose serves as a direct input to three other QOS leadership activities:

- Developing a view of the organization as a system (see Chapter 5).
- Developing a vector of measures for an organization (see Chapter 6).
- Planning (see Chapter 8).

WHAT IS THE "BOTTOM LINE" FOR AN ORGANIZATION'S PURPOSE?

The Economist encouraged readers to consider the relationship between an organization's purpose and results:

> Do such expressions of corporate philosophy and mission motivate employees and make a firm more competitive—or are they, as cynics claim, just motherhood and apple PR? To find out, Messrs. Collins and Porras asked about 170 American bosses to identify the 20 companies they thought were the most visionary. A dollar was then "invested" in shares of each of the firms in the mid-1920s. If any of the companies did not exist at that time, the dollar was left in an interest-bearing account until the firm was born; it was then invested. On average, over the period, the visionary firms outperformed Wall Street by a factor of 50. Fascinating—but not conclusive. "Visionary" may simply remain a synonym for successful, not an identifiable cause of success.[67]

What would be the payoff for the leader running the organization driven by purpose? Jim Collins said, "The most visionary leaders, if you will, are those who don't make every decision; rather, the leader builds an organization that endures beyond himself or herself, that embodies certain principles, precepts, etc."[68] Everyone benefits when a constancy of purpose is clearly stated, communicated, and supported by action.

SUMMARY

This chapter discussed the development, communication, and use of the organization's purpose. An organization's purpose may include a mission statement, tenets, and vision. Role statements, themes, and slogans can be used to support the organization's purpose.

For an organization implementing QOS, the mission statement should include a description of the contribution and the Need the organization intends to fulfill now and in the future. It may also define any strategic competencies. The tenets are stated from the viewpoint of "who we are" today and how we will conduct ourselves in carrying out the purpose. The tenets define the organization's culture. The vision paints a picture of "where" we would like to be and "how" we would like to act in the future. Vision statements play a crucial role in planning. Role statements can be useful in defining how a department, another group, or individual employee supports the organization's overall mission. Finally, meaningful themes and slogans can be used to focus attention on the organization, remind people of the actual purpose, and align organizational marketing with the theme.

In establishing Quality as an Organizational Strategy, developing the organization's purpose is the "cornerstone" activity of the leadership team. The organization's purpose is used throughout the other activities to build a system of improvement and provide leadership. The organizational leadership's regular use of the components of the purpose leads to "constancy of purpose."

When Stan first shared the poster with the company's purpose with the team and suggested they work to update it and use it, some didn't see the benefit, and a few felt it would be a soft exercise:

> It didn't take us long to review the vision, mission, and tenets and see both new and old employees valued and share what it said. We agreed to test it in our daily work, and stories began to surface of how it helped clarify our direction, reach agreement on what to do, and generally provided a benchmark to ping against. It also served as a catalyst for pausing to check assumptions and to confirm our choices, actions, and behaviors aligned with the company we were striving to become.

NOTES

1. Harwell Wells, "The Purpose of a Corporation: A Brief History," *The Temple 10-Q*, January 16, 2014, https://www2.law.temple.edu/10q/purpose-corporation-brief-history/.

2. Marvin R Weisbord, *Productive Workplaces: Dignity, Meaning, and Community in the 21st Century*, 3rd ed. (San Francisco: Jossey-Bass, 2012). Marvin Weisbord provides an accessible survey of the shift of organizational and management thinking including the focus on the human side.

3. Deming, *Out of Crisis*, 23.

4. Pursuit of QOS enables the leadership team to focus on the long-term helping to ensure what Deming called "Constancy of Purpose." The primary fiduciary responsibility of corporate officers is to act in the best interests of investors, apply their best business judgment, act in good faith, and promote the best interests of the corporation. The long-term focus on matching the Need in society to ensure a future is very much in line with this fiduciary responsibility and will benefit those stakeholders who are aligned with the organization.

5. Peter F. Drucker, "The New Society of Organizations," *Harvard Business Review*, September 1, 1992, https://hbr.org/1992/09/the-new-society-of-organizations.

6. Peter Drucker, *Post-Capitalist Society* (New York: Harper-Collins Publishers Inc., 1993).

7. Deming, *Out of Crisis*, 26.

8. Chapter 1 defined the purpose of an organization. Pursuing QOS directly influences how leaders design the organization as a system built to produce products and services that fulfill their targeted Need. The mission is directly linked to the "core business" or mainstay (see Chapter 5) processes of the organization. It provides focus on the Need the organization is designed to fulfill and how the organization will match the need; the key process that directly serves customers. It also serves as a point of direction to planning. In Chapter 7, developing a system for gathering information will add customer research in support of continually learning about consumer expectations, the competition, and shifts in technologies or materials that may require adapting existing products and services to continue to match the need.

9. "Mission and Values" Whole Foods Market, accessed October 14, 2021, https://www.wholefoodsmarket.com/mission-values.

10. See Chapter 10, "Engaging People Using a Structured Role Statement" to learn how individual role statements support connecting each staff member to the organization's purpose.

11. In Chapter 1, Table 1.5 is a tool for leaders to assess the organization's progress in making quality an organizational strategy. This paragraph is the operational definition for the top score for "Understanding the purpose of the organization." *The QOS Field Guide* contains a more comprehensive version of the assessment tool.

12. Bruce Boles served as a quality leader at Hewlett Packer and Kaiser Permanente. Each of these organizations provided additional context to the organization's "why." Included was context on the organization's history and how the purpose was consistent over time (Boles, personal communication, October 2022).

13. Robert Kreitner and Angelo Kinicki, *Organizational Behavior*, 2nd ed. (Homewood: Irwin, 1992).

14. Deming, *Out of Crisis*, 225.

15. It is common to hear people describe "Need" in the context of something their customer is asking for or an expectation they have in how a product or service is delivered. Chapter 1 and table 4.2 clarify the concept of Need as always present. Organizations adopting *quality as an organizational strategy* are aiming to deliver products and services that best match that Need. They learn what quality characteristics are important to the customer segments who possess this Need and that they intend to service. This is very different from reacting to customer asks or requests without understanding the basic Need behind why and how they are using the product or service. For example, the customer requires a table to be clean. A clean table might be okay for eating or playing cards, but not clean enough for surgery. We can't possibly serve a customer until we understand the "why" and "how" of their intended use of our product or service. Chapter 7 includes more about developing a system for gathering information to support the organization's knowledge of the customer's Needs and how our products and services are presently matching.

16. See in Chapter 1, table 1.2 for examples of the differences between the concept of Need and products or services that can match that need.

17. See Chapter 1, table 1.1, "Examples of business strategies that organizations have adopted." Included are variations of business strategies, typical characteristics of the strategy, and examples.

18. Greater Baltimore Medical Center was a 2020 award recipient of the Malcolm Baldrige Quality Award.

19. C. K. Prahalad and Gary Hamel, "The Core Competence of the Corporation," *Harvard Business Review*, May 1, 1990, https://hbr.org/1990/05/the-core-competence-of-the-corporation.

20. "Michael Hsu Office of Architecture | About," Michael Hsu Office of Architecture, accessed October 24, 2021, https://hsuoffice.com/about/.

21. "TENET," Merriam-Webster, accessed October 24, 2021, https://www.merriam-webster.com/dictionary/tenet. Many organizations use the word "values" in the purpose. Values are defined as "something (such as a principle or quality) intrinsically valuable or desirable." Tenet is used here because the definition more clearly describes that these are shared beliefs, held to be true and held in common by members of the organization.

22. Krause, Hidley, and Hobson, *The Behavior-Based Safety Process.*

23. Maccoby et al., *Transforming Health Care Leadership*, 202.

24. Chapter 10, "Engaging People in QOS," includes further discussion on cognitive dissonance and the conflict between a change and tenets.

25. Maggie Van Lee, Lisa Fabish, and Nancy McGraw, "The Value of Corporate Values," *Strategy+business*, May 23, 2005, https://www.strategy-business.com/article/05206.

26. Denise Lee Yohn, "Ban These 5 Words From Your Corporate Values Statement," *Harvard Business Review*, February 5, 2018, https://hbr.org/2018/02/ban-these-5-words-from-your-corporate-values-statement.

27. "Lou Gerstner on corporate reinvention and values," *McKinsey Quarterly*, accessed October 28, 2021, https://www.mckinsey.com/featured-insights/leadership/lou-gerstner-on-corporate-reinvention-and-values.

28. Thomas A. Stewart, "Why Value Statements Don't Work," *Fortune*, June 10, 1996.

29. Allan Cox, "Linking Purpose and People," *Training & Development*, March 1996.

30. Mike Taigman and Thom Dick, "STARCARE: Guidelines for Customer Sense," *JEMS*, September 1991.

31. "EMTs and paramedics work in remote, unsupervised settings, with autonomy and great responsibility. Tenets are especially valuable in employee conversations and help staff connect to the organization better when understood. Use of the tenets shifts culture and creates better performance and less friction." Josef Penner, Executive Director (retired), Mecklenburg EMS Agency, Charlotte, NC, personal communication, November 2022.

32. Baldrige Performance Excellence Program, "Core Values and Concepts," NIST, September 24, 2019, https://www.nist.gov/baldrige/core-values-and-concepts. The Baldrige Excellence Program describes these values and concepts as "embedded in high performance organizations." No other source is provided.

33. John R. Latham, *[Re]Create the Organization You Really Want! Leadership and Design for Sustainable Excellence.* (Colorado Springs: Organization Design Studio, 2016), 295.

34. Weisbord, *Productive Workplaces*, 275–77.

35. Working backward is a useful approach. Examples of methods for working backwards are described in *The QOS Field Guide.*

36. Wendell L. French and Cecil H. Bell, *Organization Development: Behavioral Science Interventions for Organization Improvement*, 6th ed. (Hoboken, NJ: Prentice Hall, 1999), 173–74.

37. Mark Lipton, "Demystifying the Development of an Organizational Vision," MIT Sloan Management Review, accessed May 22, 2021, https://sloanreview.mit.edu/article/demystifying-the-development-of-an-organizational-vision/.

38. "Beliefs/Vision," Eklund's, accessed February 10, 2023, from https://eklunds.com/company.

39. "Purpose, Vision, and The Southwest Way," Southwest Airlines, accessed June 7, 2023, https://www.southwestairlinesinvestorrelations.com/our-company/purpose-vision-and-the-southwest-way.

40. Examples of approaches for facilitating strategic visioning are presented in *The QOS Field Guide.* Included are: Idealized Design, Design Thinking, Future Search, and the Appreciative Inquiry Four-D Cycle.

41. "Learn about Mayo Clinic Health System," Mayo Clinic Health System, accessed April 14, 2023, https://www.mayoclinichealthsystem.org/about-us.

42. The Charter School of San Diego, "Vision, Mission, Values," CSSD, accessed April 14, 2023, https://charterschool-sandiego.net/about/.

43. Maccoby et al., *Transforming Health Care Leadership*, 264. See Chapter 10 for more on use of role statements including examples.

44. Adapted from Andrew Campbell and Laura L. Nash, *A Sense of Mission: Defining Direction for the Large Corporation* (Reading, MA: Addison-Wesley Publishing Company, 1992).

45. Perry Pascarella and Mark A. Froham, *The Purpose-Driven Organization* (San Francisco: Jossey-Bass Publishers, 1989), 40.

46. Alan Farnham, "State Your Values, Hold the Hot Air," *Fortune*, April 19, 1993.

47. Deming, *Out of Crisis*, 276. Operational definitions are not just words and their definitions, but agreement on the quality characteristics used and how you will know, how you will measure.

Consider adjectives including "good, reliable, uniform, round, tired, safe…" A detailed description from Shewhart cited. Walter A. Shewhart, *Statistical Method from the Viewpoint of Quality Control.* Washington, D.C.: Graduate School, Department of Agriculture, 1939), 130–37.

48. Deming, *Out of Crisis.*

49. "Our Core Values," Whole Foods, accessed November 6, 2021, from https://www. wholefoodsmarket.com/mission-values/core-values.

50. Peter Drucker, *Management: Tasks, Responsibilities, Practices* (New York: Harper & Row, 1973), 78.

51. S. I. S. International, "SMB Communications Pain Study White Paper," March 11, 2009, https://www.sisinternational.com/smb-communications-pain-study-white-paper-uncovering-the-hidden-cost-of-communications-barriers-and-latency/.

52. Based on Krause, Hidley, and Hobson, *The Behavior-Based Safety Process.* Chapter 10, "Engaging People with QOS," discusses this model further.

53. Hallmark Building Supplies was a client. API supported Hallmark through their journey to build a system of improvement and adopt quality as their organizational strategy.

54. Adapted from Senge, *The Fifth Discipline*, 234; and Baldrige Performance Excellence Program, "2019–2020 Baldrige Excellence Framework: Proven Leadership and Management Practices for High Performance." (U.S. Department of Commerce, National Institute of Standards and Technology, 2019), https://www.nist.gov/baldrige.

55. "Chicago Tylenol Murders," in Wikipedia, accessed June 1, 2021, https://en.wikipedia. org/w/index.php?title=Chicago_Tylenol_murders&oldid=1026380509.

56. Johnson & Johnson, "Our Credo," Johnson & Johnson, accessed June 3, 2021, https:// www.jnj.com/credo/.

57. Howard Markel, "How the Tylenol Murders of 1982 Changed the Way We Consume Medication," PBS NewsHour, September 29, 2014, https://www.pbs.org/newshour/health/ tylenol-murders-1982.

58. In 2019, Johnson & Johnson's leadership did not mirror this approach when the federal Food and Drug Administration found a sample of the company's iconic baby powder tested positive for asbestos. As of 2024, more than 50,000 lawsuits had been filed, an $8.9 billion settlement had been announced, and the company was exploring bankruptcy. Kate Gibson, "Johnson & Johnson Reaches Tentative Deal to Resolve Talc Baby Powder Litigation," *CBS*

News, January 23, 2024, https://www.cbsnews.com/news/johnson-johnson-talc-baby-powder-cancer-j-j-lawsuit/.

59. Deming, *Out of Crisis*, 167.

60. Andrew Griffiths, "Where Will Your Business Be in 100 Years?," *Inc.Com*, June 5, 2018, https://www.inc.com/andrew-griffiths/where-will-your-business-be-in-100-years.html.

61. Elon Musk, "The Mission of Tesla," November 18, 2013, https://www.tesla.com/blog/mission-tesla.

62. "About Tesla," Tesla, accessed December 16, 2021, https://www.tesla.com/about.

63. Michael J. Barry and Susan Edgman-Levitan, "Shared Decision Making — The Pinnacle of Patient-Centered Care," *New England Journal of Medicine* 366, no. 9 (March 1, 2012): 780–81, https://doi.org/10.1056/NEJMp1109283; Sosena Kebede, "Ask Patients 'What Matters to You?' Rather than 'What's the Matter?,'" *BMJ* 354 (July 22, 2016): i4045, https://doi.org/10.1136/bmj.i4045.

64. "Mission Statement," NHSGGC, accessed December 16, 2021, https://www.nhsggc.org.uk/our-performance/quality/our-quality-commitment/mission-statement/.

65. NHS Greater Glasgow and Clyde, "The Pursuit of Healthcare Excellence: NHS Greater Glasgow and Clyde Healthcare Quality Strategy," accessed December 16, 2021, https://www.nhsggc.org.uk/media/253754/190219-the-pursuit-of-healthcare-excellence-paper_low-res.pdf.

66. "What Matters to You?," NHSGGC, accessed December 16, 2021, https://www.nhsggc.org.uk/patients-and-visitors/information-for-patients/what-matters-to-you/.

67. James C. Collins and James I. Porras, "Organizational Vision and Visionary Organizations," *California Management Review* 50, no. 1 (1991): 117–37. Cited in "The Vision Thing," *Economist*, November 9, 1991.

68. Tom Brown, "On the Edge with Jim Collins," *Industry Week*, October 5, 1992.

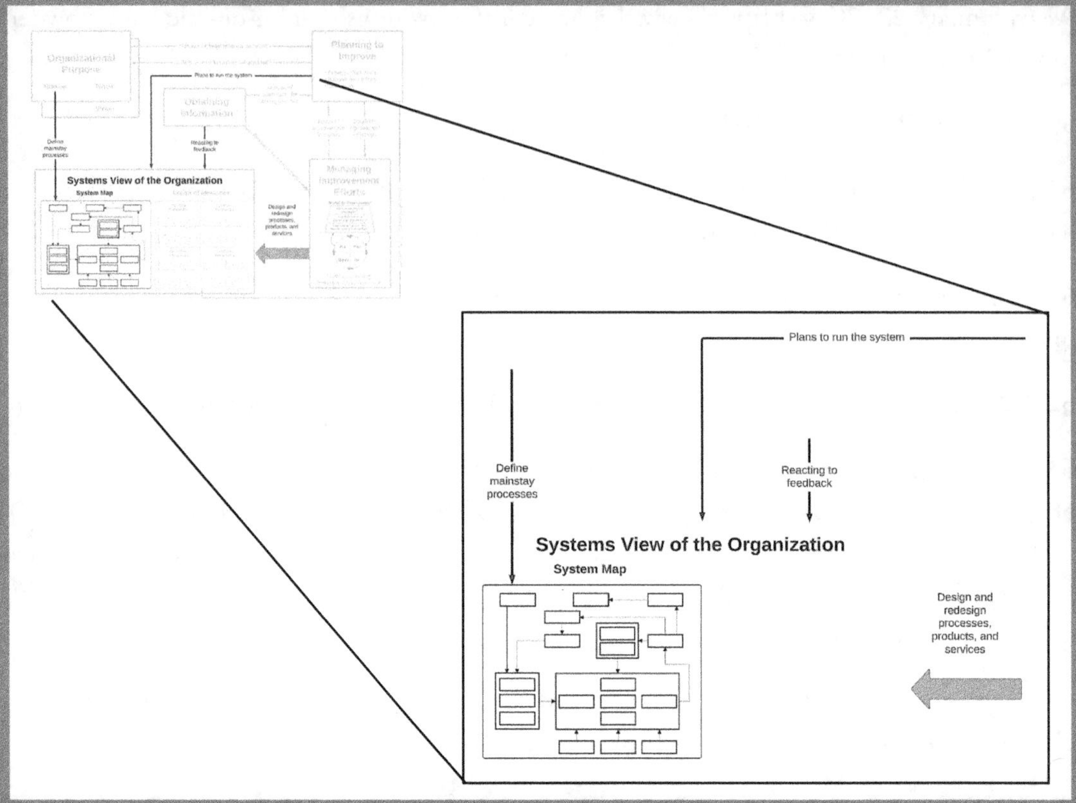

ACTIONS FOR LEADERSHIP TEAM

- Understand the major processes and products/services in the organization.
- Document how these processes link together to form a system.
- Use the system map of the organization to understand the work and focus of improvement efforts.

CHAPTER 5

VIEWING THE ORGANIZATION AS A SYSTEM

Chief Allan was promoted to lead the department at the start of the year. Her vision to adopt *quality as an organizational strategy* was key to the city council's decision to select her as the top candidate. In the first quarter, she engaged an external advisor and worked with the project team to understand the Need the department intended to fulfill and to update its purpose to include a shared vision, a mission directed toward the Need, and tenets important to public safety. It was time to shift the team to view the organization as a system. Allan stated:

The fire service is built on a lot of tradition. There was no example of QOS in our industry to look to. Updating our purpose to be practical and relevant built more will than I expected. When the leadership team began communicating our purpose to the frontline, we were all surprised by the engagement that started.

A fire department is the definition of command and control. Its structure is paramilitary, with very clear lines of accountability. It's also where people believe in "getting it right" and doing good work. People know that standard protocols and procedures save lives and reduce mistakes. I'm eager to build on their process orientation and sense of teamwork to develop a systems view of the department to help us understand and improve.

The word **system** has become exceedingly popular in recent years. A **system** is an **interdependent** group of components (items, people, or processes) working together toward a common **purpose**.[1]

Why do we need to operate and improve our organization using knowledge about systems? First, depicting the organization as an interactive system provides insight into how the organization works interdependently, defines its gaps, and helps determine how to redesign it to achieve strategic goals. And a systems view allows leaders to focus on the big picture and enables others on a team to focus on details that make coordination possible.

In a mature organization that fully adopts systems thinking[2] and the method of viewing the organization as a system, behaviors are evident:

- Major management systems, such as reporting, accounting, budgeting, data management, and marketing, consistently integrate the view of the organization as a system.
- System maps are updated as organizational learning occurs.
- All improvement activities are related to specific processes in the system or to new processes that leaders will integrate into the system.
- Systems dynamic[3] models are used in planning, analysis, and decision-making.[4]

To accomplish this ideal state an organization requires these facets:

- People throughout the organization understand work as a process. Relationships and linkages between the key processes are documented. System maps (also known as linkages of processes) are developed for the organization.
- The language of systems thinking is used in the organization. The organization's leaders understand the concept of optimizing the system versus the individual components.
- Different parts of the organization (organization structures such as business groups, regions, and divisions) are understood as subsystems or parts of the larger system. Leverage points are identified and exploited. Improvement activities are connected to the system.
- Systems diagrams that include processes and process descriptions are an integral part of the QOS. Documents describing the organization as a system are used in reports, analysis, etc., to understand and communicate how the organization works as a system. Attempts are underway to align the various management systems with this systems view.

TYPES OF SYSTEMS

Ludwig von Bertalanffy[5] pioneered the concept of a general system theory in the 1930s and called for a broader view of understanding complex systems across fields, including the traditional sciences, technology, and society. Other contributors brought more definitions and an understanding of the types of systems.

Russell Ackoff[6] defines three types of systems. Table 5.1 shows each system type relative to the purposefulness of the whole and parts (an ability to make choices).

Table 5.1. Three types of systems and relationships relative to purposefulness

System types	Parts	Whole	Examples
Deterministic	Not Purposeful	Not Purposeful	Braking system on a car
Animated	Not Purposeful	Purposeful	Animals, people
Social	Purposeful	Purposeful	Corporations, hospitals, universities

QOS focuses on the **social** type of systems, where both the parts and whole of the system are purposeful, making choices. The alignment of groups of items, people, or processes (the parts) in a social system with overall organization (whole system) requires leadership. The concept of the social system will use the definition introduced at the beginning of this chapter: A **system** is an **interdependent** group of components (items, people, or processes) working together toward a common **purpose**.

SYSTEM THINKING APPLIED TO ORGANIZATIONS

Forrester,[7] Ackoff,[8] Senge,[9] Drucker,[10] and others contributed to bringing the idea of systems thinking into the mainstream of organizational thought. So how do we understand organizations as a system of interdependent parts working toward a purpose? Ackoff describes this challenge in the context of leaders:

> Managers are not confronted with problems that are independent of each other, but with the dynamic situations that consist of complex systems of changing problems that interact with each other. I call such situations messes…Managers do not solve problems; they manage the mess.[11]

Deming integrates "appreciation of a system" into his theory of transformation or profound knowledge (Chapter 2). He defines a system as a "network of interdependent components that work together to try to accomplish the aim of the system."[12] He defines management's job as leading the efforts of all the parts of the organization to achieve the organizational purpose. Deming created a diagram he called "production viewed as a system" in 1950 during a presentation to the Japanese Union of Scientists and Engineers. Note the photo with Deming giving his lecture (figure 5.1) on the concept of the organization viewed as a system.[13] Adjacent is the diagram adapted from Deming's original concept.

Deming Introducing Production Viewed as a System in Japan

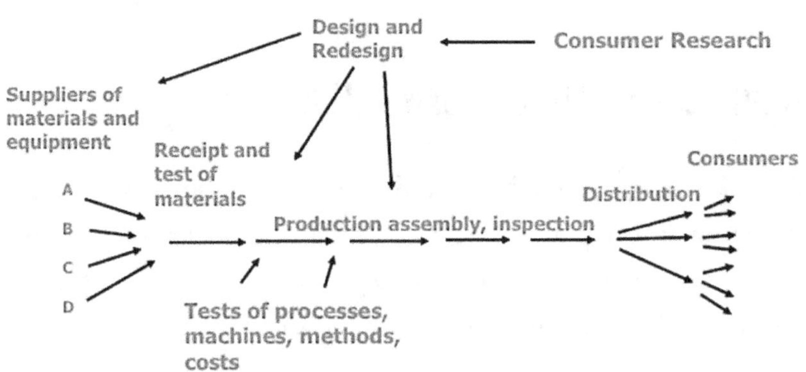

Early Diagram of Production Viewed as a System

Figure 5.1. Deming introduces the organization viewed as a system in Japan (1950).

Deming stated his thinking for introducing production viewed as a system to Japanese management:

> Mere talk about quality accomplishes little. It was necessary to go into action. The flow diagram…provided a start. Materials and equipment come in at the left. It would be necessary, I explained, to improve incoming materials. Work with your vendor as a partner on a long-term relationship of loyalty and trust to improve the quality of incoming materials and to decrease costs. The consumer is the most important part of the production line. Quality should be aimed at the needs of the consumer, present and future.[14]

Deming was making the case to Japanese leaders that suppliers and customers are an integral part of the production system and must be embraced as partners to ensure the achievement of quality throughout the production and delivery system. Therefore, quality was not just the "Quality Department's responsibility" but must be built-in from beginning to end.[15]

A systems view is an important way to think about making changes and improvements. This means depicting a changing organization over time to better match the customer's Needs. The study of systems requires a new vocabulary and set of thought processes. Many methods derived from systems theory are just the opposite of our analytical approaches to understanding things. When applying systems thinking to organizations, the attention is to the entire organization o segmented parts of the organization that forms distinct subsystems like a region or business unit.

Ackoff describes the following system principle as fundamental:

> If each part of a system, considered separately, is made to operate as efficiently as possible, then the system as a whole will not operate as effectively as possible.[16]

In other words, the performance of a system depends more on how its parts interact than how they act independently of each other. We can begin to understand the behavior of a system when we can view it as a whole.

Ackoff[17] used specific examples to explain this principle. Adapting one of his examples, consider all the available cars on the market (Tesla Model 3, Toyota Camry, Ford F-150, etc.). Imagine asking the top automotive engineers to find the best quality parts across those vehicles. Which one has the best battery or the best transmission or the best brakes? Once the best of each part is identified, remove them from the cars and lay them out together on the floor. Now, assemble all these best parts into a single supercar.

What do you think will happen? Would it not be the best quality car? No, it would be impossible to assemble these parts together into a single car. Each part was designed for a different car and was not made to fit and work together with the others. Mashing together the best individual parts does not add up to the best car.

Now think about this in the context of organizations. A popular move by many organizations is to recruit executive talent from successful organizations that get great press. The executive arrives on the scene and starts making changes which often result in failure.[18] Why did they fail? The system where the executive was successful was not in the new organization to support their efforts. The job of the leadership team is to ensure that the various components are **integrated** into an interdependent system.

To create a high-performing organization, leaders must optimize the system by orchestrating the efforts of all system components toward achieving the stated purpose. The organization must manage the components and the interactions in service of the aim. Management of the system must include adaptation to changes outside the system (the environment within which the system operates) and encourage cooperation among the parts of the system. Any competition within a system can be destructive. The people who work in a system must operate their portion of the system together toward the purpose of the organization.

Earlier, we defined systems thinking as including three things: purpose, components (items, people, or processes), and interconnection or interdependence. What do these things look like in the context of the organizational systems we work in?

The organization's **purpose** is the reason it exists and the Need that it fulfills in society. The purpose includes the organization's mission, vision, and tenets. Chapter 4 presented the importance of an organization clearly defining its purpose, described methods for developing a purpose statement, and explained how to use it in practice. A well-written mission should define the system by which the organization meets the Need in society with its products and services.

Peter Drucker discussed the importance of a documented purpose:

> Every enterprise requires commitment to common goals and shared values. Without such commitment there is no enterprise; there is only a mob. The enterprise must have simple, clear, and unifying objectives. The mission of the organization has to be clear enough and big enough to provide a common vision. The goals that embody it must be clear, public, and constantly reaffirmed. Management's first job is to think through, set, and exemplify those objectives, values, and goals.[19]

Each part of the organization should be arranged to support the overall purpose. Activities in the organization that do not contribute to its purpose are a source of extra expense, waste, and poor quality. Changing and eliminating such activities are important sources of improvement.

Organizations are comprised of many components or parts. This includes very tangible components like buildings, desks, computers, and people needed to do the work. It also includes how work gets done, the processes followed to achieve the desired results. Deming said it is the leader's job "to direct the efforts of all components toward the aim of the system."[20] This requires understanding the components within the organization and how they interact to accomplish the purpose. The concept of **interdependence** (or **interaction**) recognizes that components of a system do not work with complete independence. To understand the organization and develop more effective change, we need to understand the interdependent nature of the relationships between the parts, people, and processes within the organization. In an organizational system, not only the parts but also the relationships between the parts become opportunities for improvement.

An example of these ideas is to consider the difference between a bowling team and a symphony.[21] On a bowling team, each team member strives to perform their best and produce the highest individual score possible. They calculate the team score by adding together the individual member scores. While the team members wear the same shirts and encourage each other, there is little relationship between their individual contributions and the key result (total team score).

Now consider a symphony orchestra, with nearly one hundred musicians playing string, woodwind, brass, and percussion instruments (elements or parts). The conductor (the leader) leads the symphony (system), and the musicians use the same sheet music (process) to perform beautiful music for the audience (purpose). When the symphony begins to play, each musician has an individual role and awareness of their interdependence with their fellow musicians. At any time, a musician may need to adjust their individual tempo or volume to synchronize with their colleagues in service of their shared aim to produce beautiful music.

Failure of leaders to understand the relationships or interdependencies between parts prevents the results of improvement efforts from adding together in a straightforward way. This could cause changes that are improvements at the local level to result in no improvement or even have a negative impact on the organization.

Consider a common example. A local newspaper includes a story that the local school system has seen a reduction in tax revenue and must reduce its overall budget. The superintendent proposes to the school board a strategy to cut each school campus's budget by five percent next year. The proposal is presented as fair because every school will be affected by the burden. But will this strategy create an equitable result? The likely answer is no.

A superintendent viewing the school district as a system understands the system's success depends on more than the success of each part. Those parts, in this case school campuses, may have different current requirements to meet the demands of the neighborhoods they serve. Therefore, the school district should be aware of the school system and adjust funding, resources, and improvements to continually improve the system as a whole.

A fundamental step in developing a systems view of an organization is recognizing that organizations are composed of individuals, groups, departments, and processes whose performance is dependent upon and affects other individuals, groups, and departments. The greater the interdependence, the greater the need for cooperation within the system. The obligation of every component of a system should be to contribute its best to the system, not maximize its own performance. The basis for negotiation in a system should be on optimizing the entire system.[22]

"It's funny," reflected Chief Allan. "The fire service is built on a tenet of teamwork. We know we must work together to get the job done and be safe. When one crew goes out on an emergency call, another unit moves into position to cover their neighborhood and be ready for the next call."

Despite this deep tenet, the leadership always managed people, not systems.

Chief Allan continued, "We assess firefighter or paramedic performance, not the performance of the system they are working in. We coach or ding people for mistakes but only ask about the system if a big issue gets scrutiny in the press or by the city council."

But she emphasized, "Our employees are the best people, and I believe they will embrace thinking about our organization as a system. As a system we are continuing to improve, and that is dependent on us working together as a team."

SYSTEMS AND PROCESSES

What is the difference between a process and a system? Since both terms are conceptual, it is useful to differentiate them with operational definitions and how we depict them in improvement work.

A *process* is a set of causes and conditions that repeatedly come together in a sequence of steps to transform inputs into outcomes. A process includes decisions we make, equipment, forms, and so on that we use to transform the inputs. Figure 5.2 depicts the concept of a process.[23]

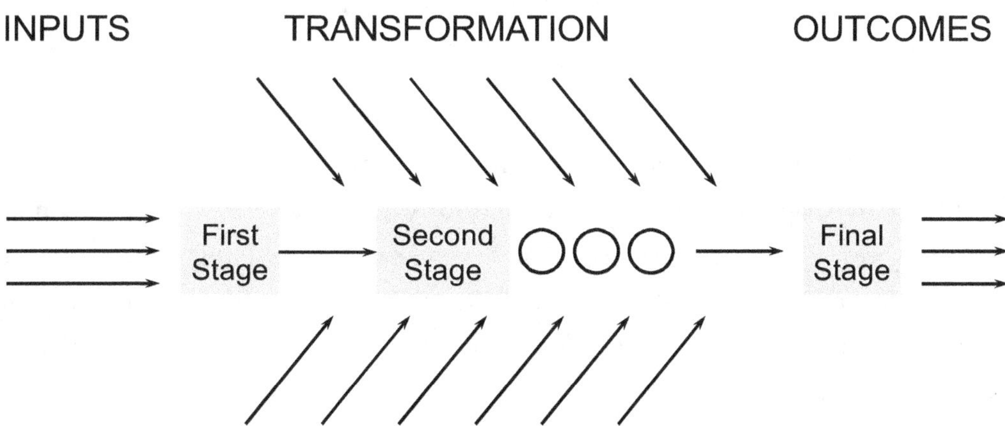

Figure 5.2. Concept of a process.

All work within any organization can be viewed as a process or a group of processes. A **flow diagram** is a graphic representation of the series of activities that define a process. A process has a beginning and an end. Using a flow diagram, one can follow the steps and decisions of a process as inputs are transformed into outcomes. Decision-making stages are shown on a flow diagram with diamonds. Figure 5.3 depicts a simple version of an invoice process that goes from taking an order to sending an invoice to a customer. Some detailed steps are included with the various stages.

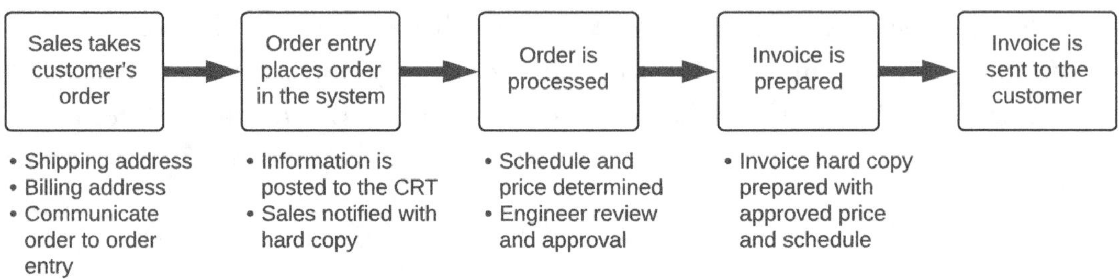

Figure 5.3. Invoice process: flow diagram from sales to invoice.

The idea of a **process** is a useful artificial construct to understand a work activity. Everything is connected. Processes in the real world have feedback and lead to other processes. Everything is a system or subsystem in the real world. For example, when turning on the dining room light by flipping the wall switch, there is no light. This leads to the process of changing the light bulb. Still no light. This leads to a process of working through the breaker switches. We attempt to make things simple by creating simple flow diagrams. Teaching a child how to turn on the dining room light would be restricted to two or three steps—simple. The other related processes will come with time and experience.

The authors have observed a phenomenon with flow diagrams that may result in an activity trap. Flow diagrams are typically straightforward to create. People often confuse this activity with making progress in understanding systems thinking. Flow diagrams, like any other tool, should only be used when needed to document and improve processes. Adapting a slogan from the wine industry, "We will prepare no flow diagram before its time."[24]

Criteria for Evaluating the Condition of Processes

As you begin to understand your organization's processes, it is useful to rate their condition. The criteria in table 5.2 are a useful method to do this.

Table 5.2. Rating definitions of process conditions

Rating	Operational definition of rating
6	Process is not defined. This is a new process that needs to be designed and documented.
5	There is a general understanding about the process by those who work in it. No documentation or process standards exist. No formal work to improve the process has been done in recent history.
4	Process has been defined for all stakeholders (managers, workers, suppliers, and customers). The intent of the process is understood. Documentation of the process exists, such as process flow diagrams, standards, policies, procedures, job descriptions, training manuals, or other supporting documents.
3	Process is well-defined, and measures of process performance and quality of outcomes are used to monitor the process. Graphical methods, such as run charts, control charts, and Pareto charts, are used to evaluate and learn from the measures.
2	Process has been formally improved during the past year. Ongoing measures exist for the process, including supplier input and customer feedback. Standards and process documentation are kept up-to-date as the process is improved.
1	Key measures of the process and the process outcomes are predictable. The products and services from the process consistently meet the Needs and expectations of the customers.

Note: The criteria for the ratings are cumulative. For example, to obtain a rating of "2," all requirements for "3" and "4" should be satisfied. Select the most descriptive definition of the current process; all criteria do not have to be satisfied.

DEFINING THE ORGANIZATION AS A SYSTEM USING A SYSTEM MAP

A system map is a method used to visually depict how processes within an organization fit and link together as a system to plan, support, and provide services and products to our customers. The connecting arrows show the interdependent nature of these processes. A system map has also been called a "linkage of processes." Preparing meals to order, teaching workshops, paying bills, and producing reports are all processes we may perform in our daily work lives. An essential step to understanding the organization viewed as a system is to **consider all work in the organization as a process.**

An organizational system also includes the equipment, materials, and people that are part of processes; they are included when we focus on processes. Figure 5.4 is an example of the key processes for a cleaning and maintenance[25] subsystem for a trucking company.

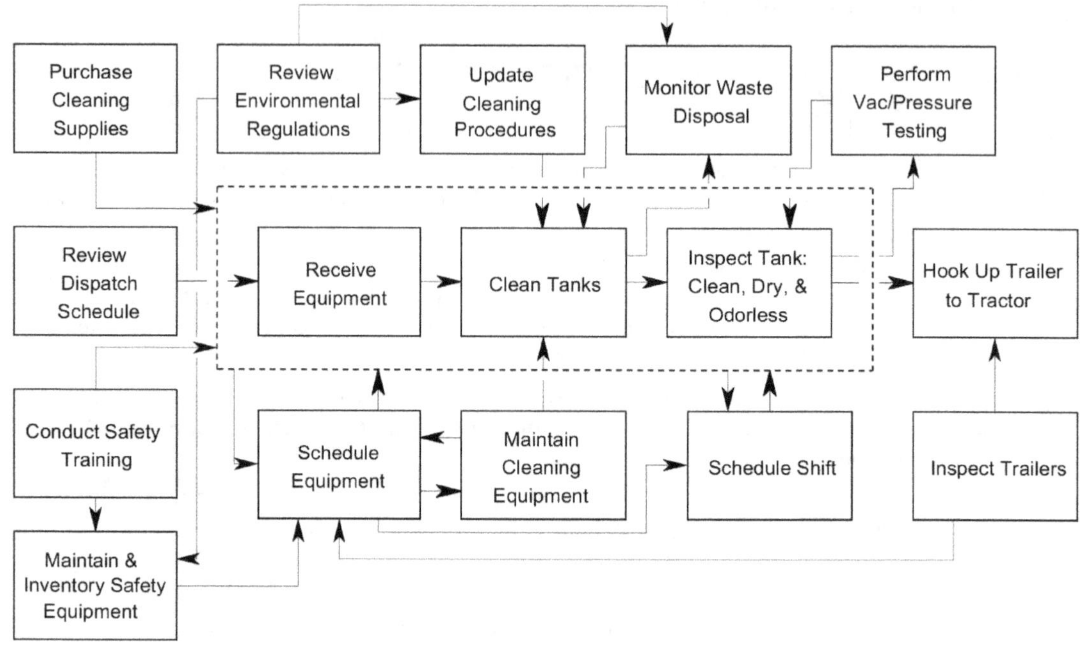

Figure 5.4. System map of cleaning and maintenance subsystem.

Getting a useful level of detail for these processes is important to creating a useful systems map. This idea appears simple to grasp but is challenging in practice. Figure 5.5 aids us in thinking of the level of detail in a system map, much as an atlas does. Depending on our focus, we can choose an appropriate map to look at the whole world, a continent (North America), a country (United States), a state or province (Texas), a city (Austin), or even a neighborhood.

How the map will be used dictates the useful level of detail. The detail is always present, but, at the solar system's low level of detail, Austin is not visible. Progressing to a more detailed view, Austin, with the system of highways, blocks of housing, etc., is more visible.

More detail may be required within a hierarchy of system levels; for example, seeing Austin at the street level and understanding what may be causing traffic jams or accidents. Within an organization, it may be possible to answer questions with a low level of detail (solar system level). However, this may not be enough; focus on the more detailed elements **and** how or if links are defined may be necessary. Understanding how processes link or perhaps dead-end gives new insight for improvement and helps eliminate silos of knowledge within organizations.

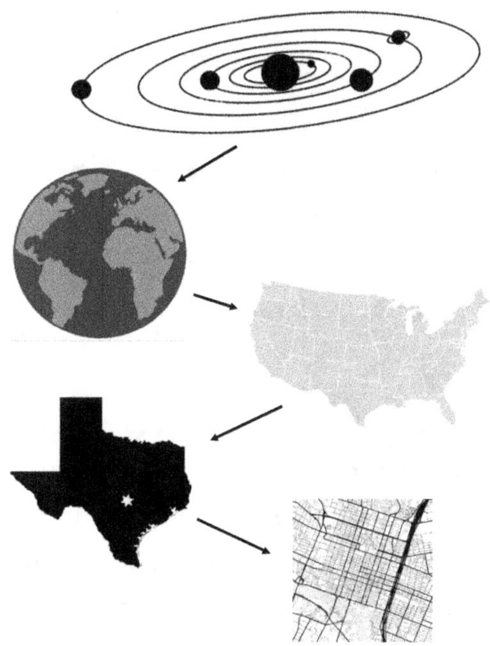

Figure 5.5. Hierarchy of system levels.

Figure 5.6 illustrates this idea of a hierarchical view in the context of an organizational system. The concept described here is the same as presented in figure 5.5, each level contains more detail as presented earlier, moving from the solar system to finally defining Austin.

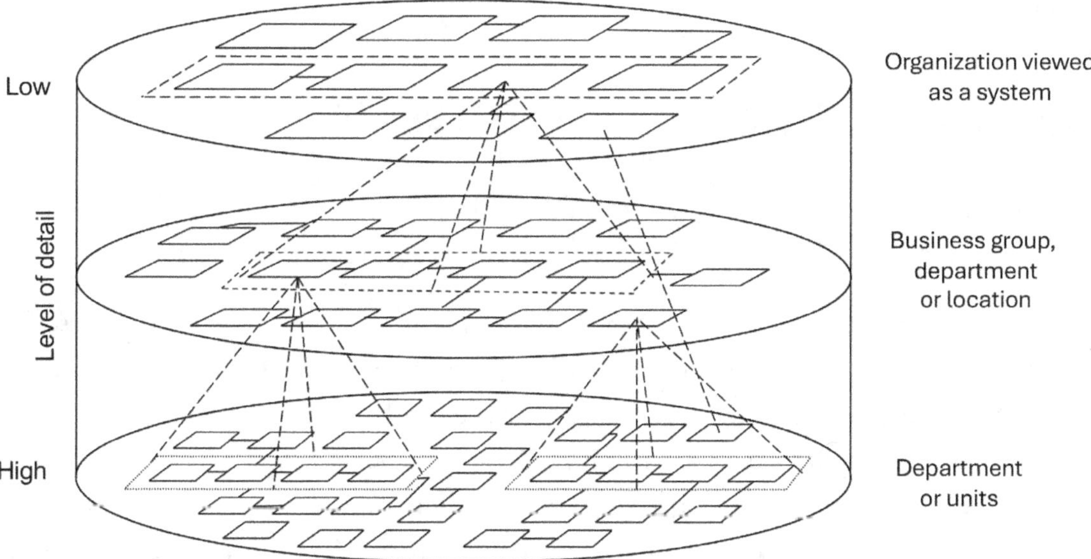

Figure 5.6. Concept of a key process and level of detail.

At the lowest level of detail, we see the whole system of interest. We might show more detail for specific departments or functions. At the next level, we can see the processes for specific workgroups in our organization.

System maps create a picture of how the organization uses processes to plan, support, and provide products and services to the customer aligned with the organization's purpose. More detailed nested system maps also offer insight into the alignment of people to the purpose. The more complex the organization, the more layers of detail are useful.

Creating a useful system map for an organization can be expected to remain a work in progress for quite a while. Leaders often wonder when the map will be finished. An initial system map provides an understanding of how the organization works today. We may decide to add new processes not yet defined or developed on this map. The map evolves as we learn and improve our theory of how the organization works.

To develop a system map of any organization, people must first have a common understanding of the purpose of the organization and their collaborative role in accomplishing it (see Chapter 4). Leaders design, integrate, and align these diverse components so that they serve the purpose. Ultimately, the success of any organization depends on this interaction and collaboration rather than the performance of the individual components. A system map supports the organization's transformation to a learning organization, one that is focused on designing a system to match the Need stated in the purpose.

CLASSIFICATIONS OF PROCESSES ON A SYSTEMS MAP

When constructing a system map, it is useful to think about three different classifications of processes.[26]

1. **Mainstay processes**: The first group, *"mainstay"* or delivery processes, represents the organization's primary business. Those processes relate to the organization's purpose and add value to the customers or clients. These are the delivery processes that create the products or services for customers or clients.

2. **Driver processes**: These processes "drive" the organization's mainstay. Examples of driver processes are customer feedback, planning, research, development, budgeting, etc. These processes prepare the organization to **match the Need** (the

Need as defined in the purpose) when performing its mainstay processes. Many driver processes are similar regardless of the type of organization.

3. **Support processes**: These processes are necessary to support and run the organization, especially the mainstay processes. Examples include accounting, maintenance, hiring, traveling, handling communications, etc. Many support processes are similar regardless of the type of organization.

Deming's production viewed as a system (depicted in figure 5.7) provides a generic, conceptual model of a system map for any organization.[27] Overlayed are the classification terms mainstay, driver, and support process. Some leaders find it useful to adapt Deming's diagram to develop a conceptual model of their own organization before adding more detail based on processes. This is particularly true for a large organization with multiple business units, regions, and locations. For example, departments (such as Research and Development or Human Resources) or locations (a production facility, a retail space) within an organization may benefit by developing a more specific conceptual view of how its area fits into the rest of the organization.

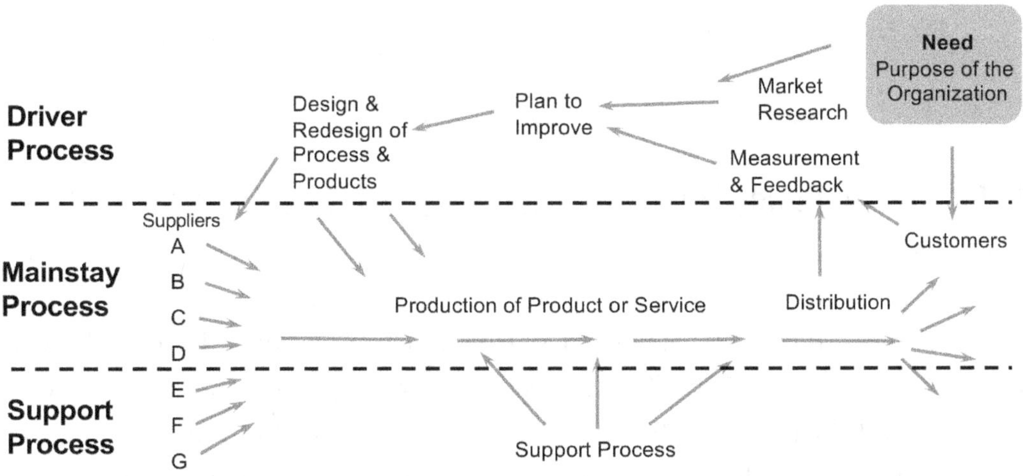

Figure 5.7. Driver, mainstay, and support, described for production viewed as a system model.

To build a system map based on processes, begin by identifying the mainstay processes from the statement of purpose. (As a point of interest: the word "mainstay" is a nautical term referring to the support rope connecting a sailing ship's mainmast to the foremast.[28]) These are the processes that directly define how the organization achieves its mission. The mainstay of an organization denotes what we do in the system that **directly** adds value to the system's customers or clients. This is the core business. Describing the processes that form the organization's mainstay is typically a good first step in building a system map.

Chief Allan drew the conceptual map of Deming's "Production Viewed as a System" on the large whiteboard in the conference room. Everyone had a printout copy of the department's organizational chart. She then instructed her leadership team to try to depict their department's version of Deming's model. Each person had a pack of stickie notes and a permanent mark. She observed:

> I think it helped that one person just jumped up and started putting up notes. As people placed stickies in different areas, it was interesting to see them realize they had roles in various places, not a single silo or clump. Many of us shared roles in areas like "planning to improve" or "designing or redesigning our services." Little conversations broke out at the whiteboard around different parts. The way they talked about the department was so different from our norm. It was engaging. Everyone was ready to go deeper.

MOVING FROM ORGANIZATIONAL CHARTS TO ORGANIZATIONS VIEWED AS A SYSTEM

The organizational chart in figure 5.8 illustrates a banking organization's functional or administrative groupings. This is typically how organizations depict how they have organized their work. When people describe "silos" within the organization, the organizational chart is their picture or mental model. But an organizational chart does not include the customer or help us understand how people accomplish the work in service of the organization's purpose. This view can lead managers to focus on people versus process as the source of improvement.

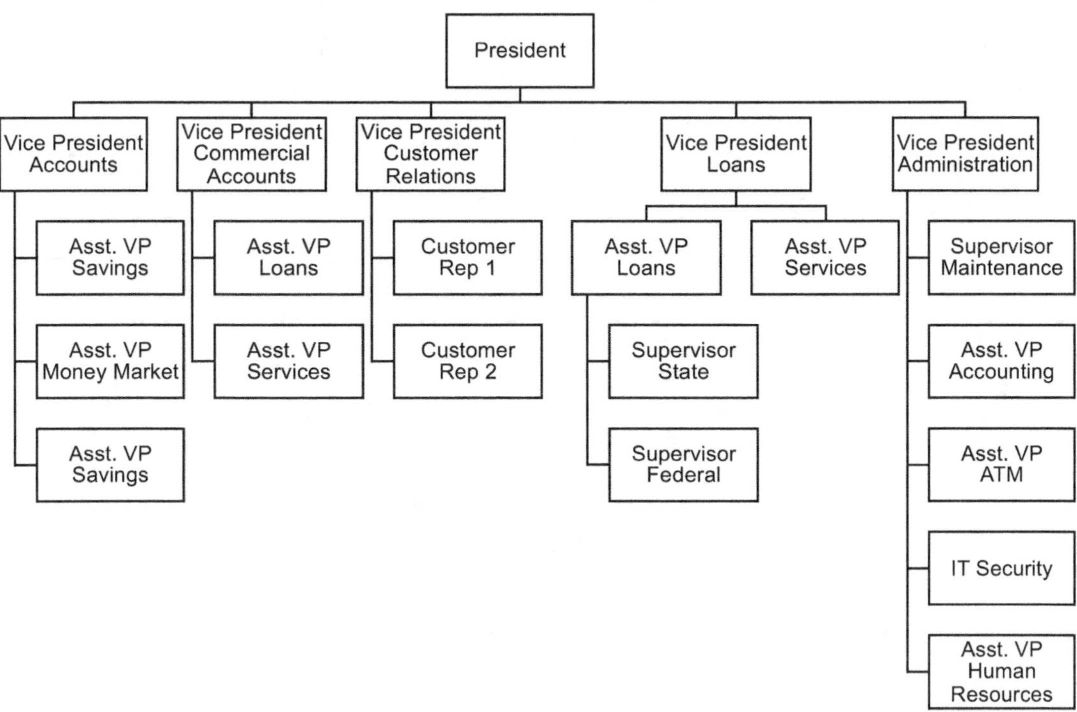

Figure 5.8. Organization chart for a banking organization.

Figure 5.9 shows the same banking organization reflected as a system map. The system map includes boxes for each process and depicts links between processes, reflecting the interdependence. Each process box **names** the process by describing the **action** being taken. Notice that each process starts with action words or verbs. For example, instead of describing a unit of work as "paperwork," a clear action is described, such as "enter and schedule the order" or "audit the order." A critical component in a system map is the naming the protocol, which requires action-oriented and unambiguous terms.

In the diagram, try to identify the unclear processes. How about "Work with?" Does that mean audit, partner, or debug IT software? Remember, the descriptions need to be useful to everyone in the organization to learn more about this process and its impact on other people and processes. System maps are vital to sharing knowledge about what people are doing and how their actions impact other processes and people within a key process or downstream. With a system map, we can start an inquiry anywhere on the diagram. In a sense, there is no beginning, and there is no end.

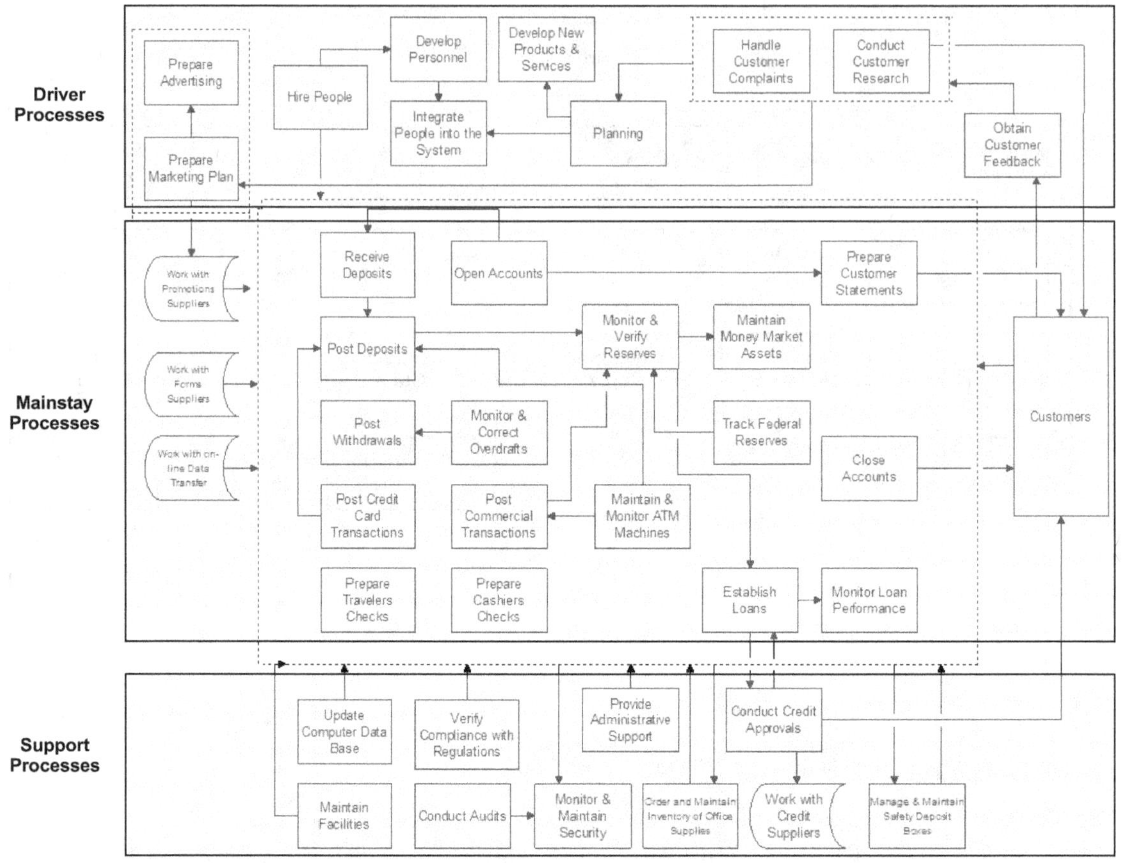

Figure 5.9. System map for a banking organization.

IDENTIFYING KEY PROCESSES IN THE ORGANIZATION

A useful technique within a system map is to show subsystems. **A subsystem is reflected by drawing a box around areas with multiple processes and naming the boxed grouping.** For example, two key subsystems are in the bank example: focus on customer and plan marketing. Both grouped subsystems included multiple defined processes.

At first, using a system map feels complex and conceptual, but once we appreciate its utility, it becomes very practical and useful. Think of it this way: imagine owning an apartment house with three apartments like figure 5.10. On the top is a schematic of the apartment building with three units.[29] Each apartment is a subsystem containing multiple sinks (circled), toilets, and showers. Thankfully, all the plumbing is connected!

The plumbing links them together. How all the plumbing links together shows a relationship between each toilet or shower within the building. If someone flushes a toilet, the shower might either lose pressure or changes temperature. This is a perfect example of interdependent processes and the impact of their interdependence.

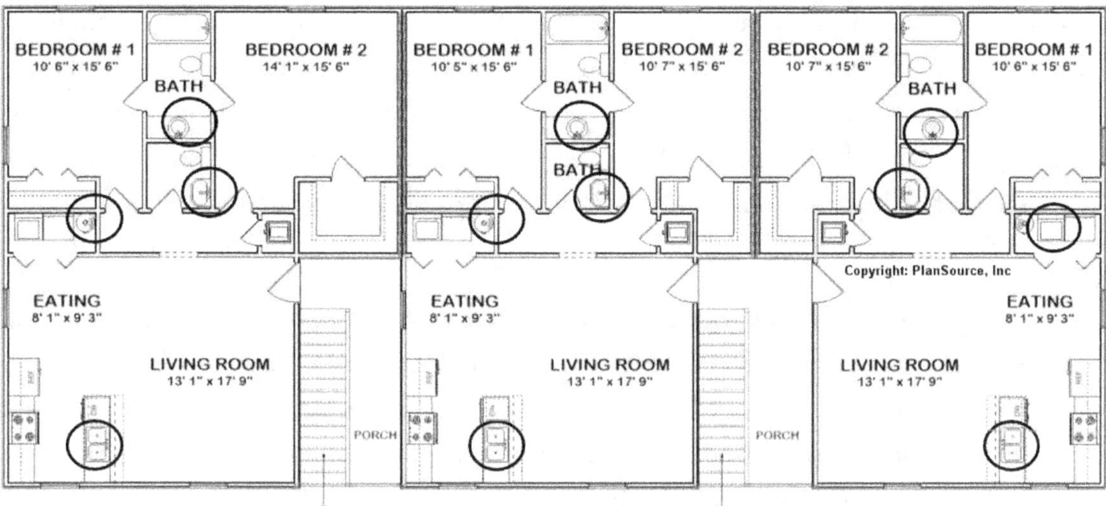

Apartment building with three apartments

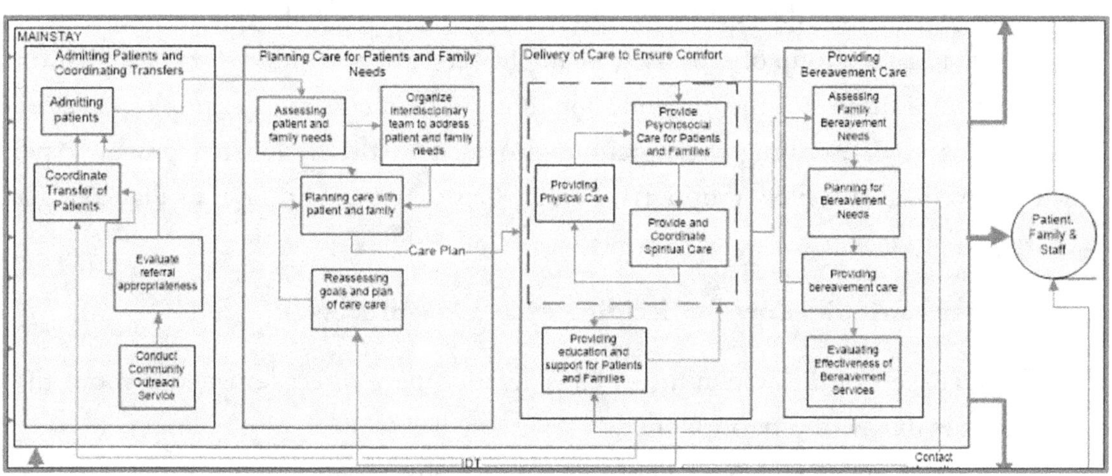

Hospice viewed as a system with four subsystems (processes identified)

Figure 5.10. Apartment buildings as analogy for a system map.

Instead of our imaginary "apartment units," consider the bottom figure, which is a system map for the mainstay processes of delivering care for hospice patients.[30] It contains four subsystems represented by four boxes (apartments): admitting patients and coordinating transfers, planning care for patients and family need, delivery of care to ensure comfort, and providing bereavement care.

Within each of the four subsystems (boxes), processes are identified as essential to carrying out the work. Each process can be defined using a Process Boundary Form and a Process Flow Diagram. Also, as with the apartments, the individual processes link together, like the plumbing of the toilets and showers. In the third subsystem box, "Delivery of Care to Ensure Comfort," three processes are organized in subgroups; this is a useful technique to reduce the complexity of system maps and additional links.

Some organizations find it useful to denote the names of the people who run that process or the "role title" in each process block. This helps in understanding and learning how one person who is seemingly "in charge" of "Managing Inventory" relies on others to run the group of processes effectively. A department color-coded legend can also support depicting who runs each process.[31]

In a system map, we generally do not use department names (Accounting, Engineering, IT) in the process descriptions. When using a legend to color code "who" is responsible for an individual or group of processes, we might detect opportunities for consolidation and communication to the organization and individuals. For example, describe "Accounting" by describing the functions provided in the designated process type, such as Oversee Cash Flow (Support), Invoice Customers (Mainstay), or Plan Budget (Driver).

The following are **guidelines for deciding what a key process** is:

- The managers of the system under consideration have direct knowledge about the processes, plans, and performance.
- Collectively include the work of ninety to ninety-five percent of the people working in the organization.
- Any single process that encompasses the work of more than one percent of the people in the organization.
- For small and medium-sized organizations, there may only be one view, which identifies the key processes and subprocesses in sufficient detail as to be useful.

Figure 5.11 compares the use of the system map at three levels (nested views) versus an organizational chart when targeting a specific process for improvement.

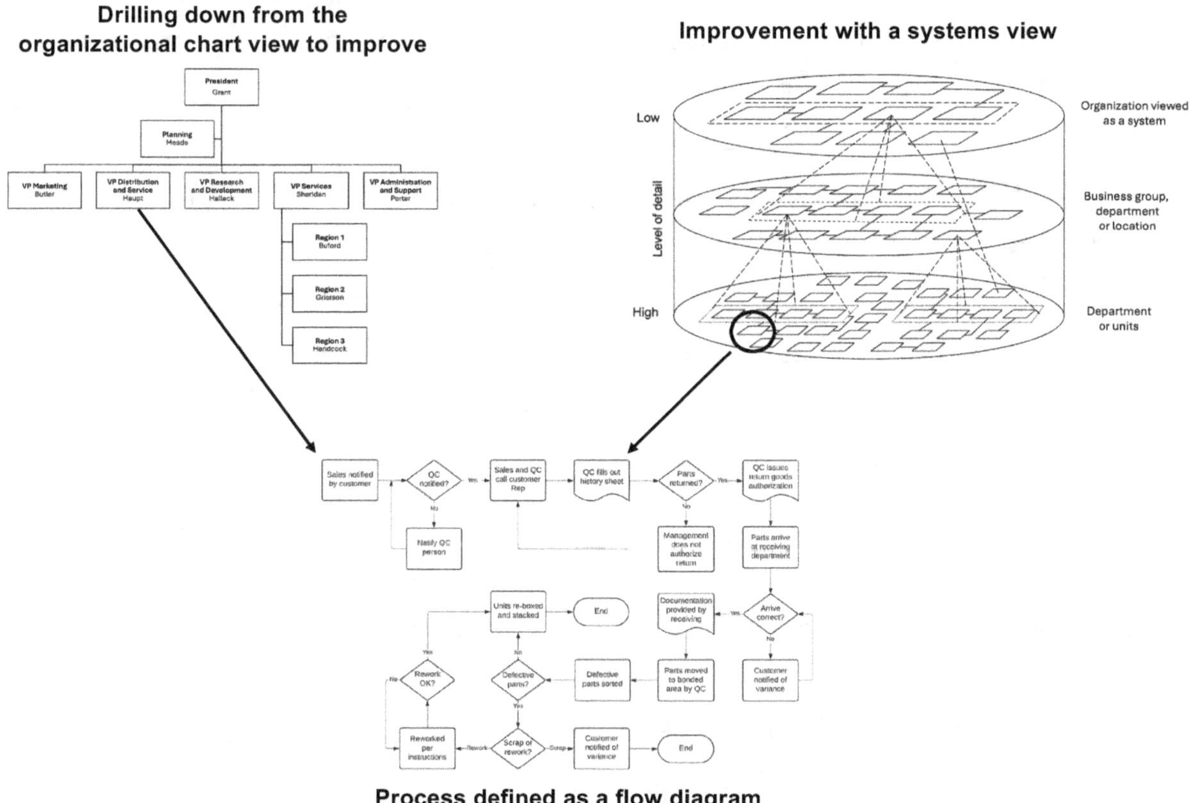

Figure 5.11. Using the systems view to ensure coordinated improvement.

With the system map views, it is easy to appreciate the other key processes that could be impacted by the improvement. The circle indicates the process on the detailed subsystem-level map. The flow diagram is useful to describe the details of that process. Without this view, many embark on changes at that level only to discover later that these changes were not integrated into higher levels of the system causing new problems. For some organizations, these new problems are typically greeted with a pronouncement of the need for another improvement project. The systems view helps to prevent the activity of suboptimizing the system.

STEPS FOR BUILDING THE SYSTEM MAP

How does one create a system map for an organization to support leading with systems thinking? To facilitate this process, we can use traditional methods like whiteboards and sticky notes or electronic tools like diagramming software or virtual whiteboards. Ease of use and the unrestricted ability to add, subtract, and move information around is essential. Starting with traditional methods and transitioning to electronic tools is common as the system map is developed. Figure 5.12 shows an approach for organizing a whiteboard for the exercise.

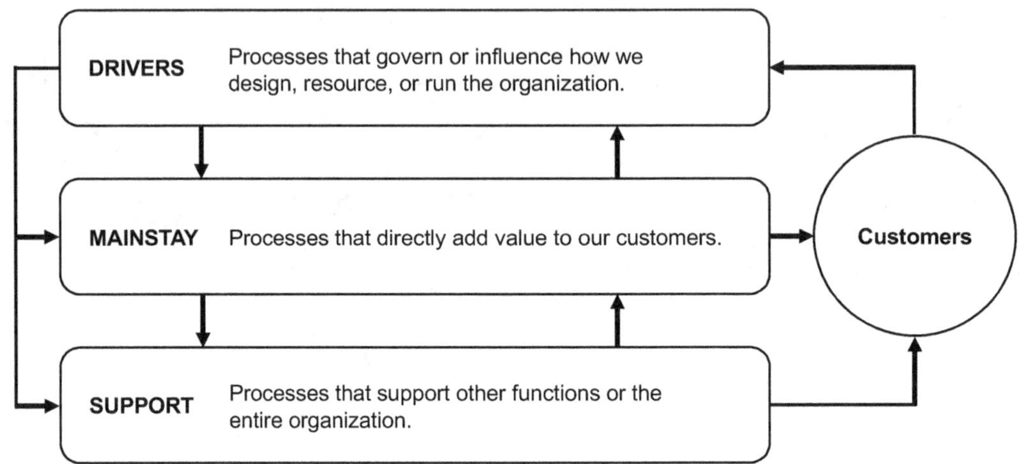

Figure 5.12. Developing a system map with mainstay, driver, and support processes.

The following steps describe a method to guide leaders to produce a first draft system map.

1. Obtain the mission statement for the organization. Post it on the working space in a visible place near where the team will draft the system map. The mission statement is vital to maintain clarity on the boundaries of the organization (system) of study and to understand the organization's primary work (mainstay).

2. List the primary products and services the organization provides. Post these under the mission.

3. Create three large rectangles, each approximately one-third of the height of the workspace, stacked above each other. Link each diagram as shown with arrows. Label the rectangles "Drivers," "Mainstay," and "Support," moving from top to bottom. It is useful to include the operational definition to help categorize processes into their respective "box." For example, note the definitions for Mainstay (Step 4), Driver (Step 5), and Support (Step 6).

4. Within each rectangle (Mainstay, Driver, and Support processes), create boxes for the major groupings of processes (see the Hallmark example in figure 5.13). These larger boxes are the "apartments" described earlier, where individual processes will be detailed later.

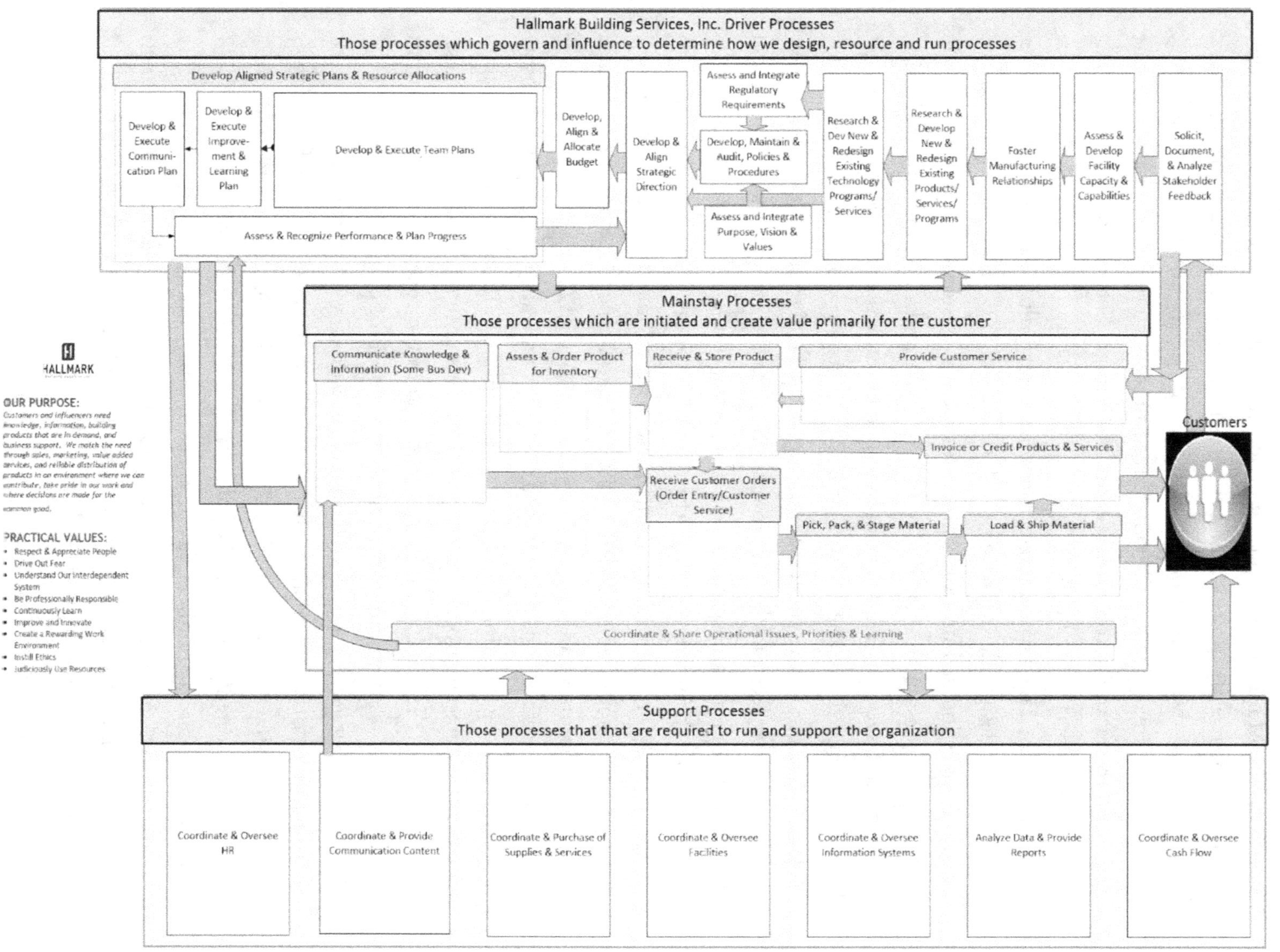

Figure 5.13. Hallmark Building Supplies: major groupings (conceptual view of apartments) of processes with the Driver, Mainstay, and Support sections of the systems view of the organization.

5. Start with the **Mainstay**. Using the mission statement, list the primary activities required to deliver the products and services identified to the customer or client. For businesses, these tend to start with sales processes and end with customer deliveries and invoices. Include outsourced processes critical to and part of the mainstay. To get an appropriate level of detail, target between ten and thirty key processes to describe the mainstay(s) of an organization.

6. Next, define the **Driver** processes. These processes influence or drive how other processes are designed, improved, and resourced and relate to the Need the organization is focused on. Such processes include customer feedback, strategic planning, business planning, budgeting, research and development, marketing products and services, and developing policies and procedures. Again, target between ten and thirty key "driver" processes to get a reasonable level of detail.

7. Next, arrange the Driver processes starting at the far right (For example, process "to use customer feedback") and move to the left. The voice of the customer and stakeholders and research will influence processes to the left.

8. Finally, define between ten and thirty key **Support** processes necessary to "support" and run the organization. These tend to match department names; however, each should be preceded by a verb (e.g., Manage Accounting, Manage Personnel, Coordinate IT).

9. Support processes are logically arranged since they typically impact most Mainstay processes. The organization of the processes is optional. If there is a strong link to a particular Mainstay process, position the process under or close to the process. For example, if "Invoice Customer" is the Mainstay process, "Manage Account Receivables" is a related Support process and is positioned just below.

10. Show links between processes. Connect processes with **important** flow or coordinating efforts with an arrow indicating the primary direction. If the flow is bidirectional, draw two separate lines, one in each direction. Rearrange and "box" key processes to reduce the number of links that must be drawn.

11. Give each process a number. The process numbers will be useful when using the system map in customer feedback (Chapter 7) and planning (Chapter 8) activities. Numbering should follow a meaningful sequence (from left to right, using meaningful groupings, etc.).[32]

After completing these steps, the systems view should resemble the Hallmark Building Supplies[33] example in figure 5.15 (see page 164). Conceptual boundaries from figure 5.13 now have detailed processes contained for each. This is apparent in the Driver and Mainstay sections of the systems view. Many organizations find they have the same basic Support processes, such as legal, IT, and supporting employees; additional conceptual boundaries were not used in the support section. These are only guidelines and should be used when they produce a useful view.

12. Finally, add the process condition rating (see table 5.2). These process condition ratings are used in the planning process to prioritize processes for improvement to achieve the strategic objectives. Figure 5.14 shows where to add the process condition rating to each numbered process in the system map.[34]

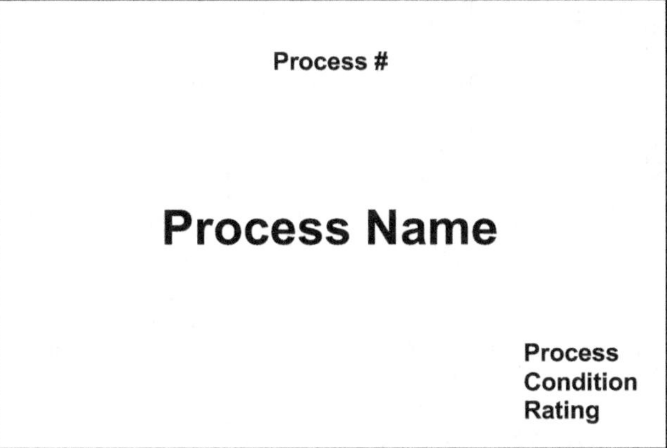

Figure 5.14. Code for each process.

Following these steps gives leaders a first look at the organization as a system of key processes. Leaders can further refine the system map to make it useful for running, expanding, and defining improvement efforts. Sometimes a system map becomes too complex to fit on one page (or to be viewed on one screen.) Work to reduce the level of detail of the key processes and ensure all processes are consistent in the level of detail. More detailed views are created by mapping subsystems (service lines, departments, regions) of the overall system map.

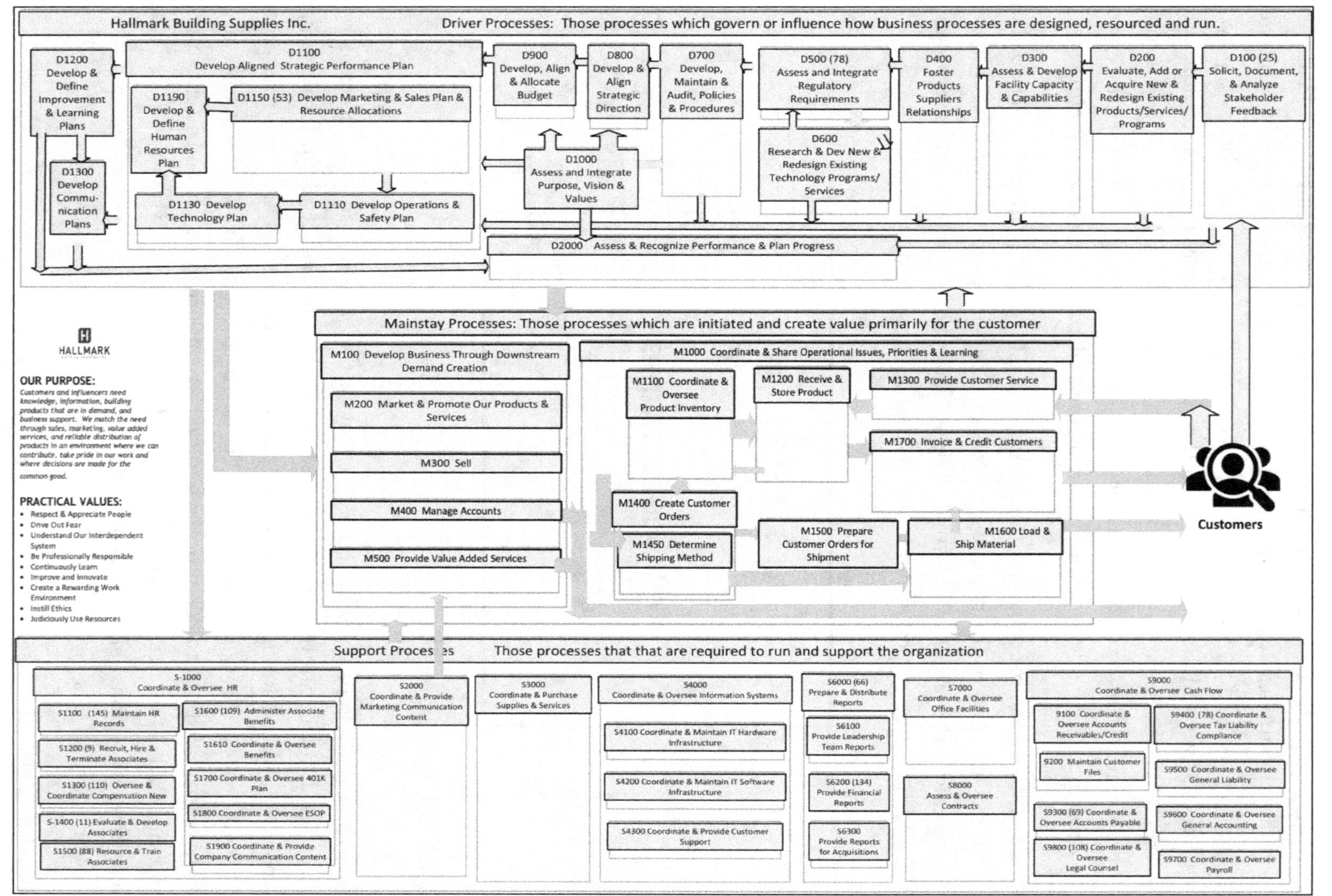

Figure 5.15. System map for Hallmark Building Supplies.

Building on the momentum from the leadership team's work to develop a conceptual view, Chief Allan blocked a day to work on developing a first draft system map. Her advisor provided a set of building steps for the team to work through and encouraged them to take their time. Chief Allan set the tone by encouraging everyone to focus on learning and discussion and not just try to complete the task.

"Every step was challenging but rich in learning," she said. "When we started listing key processes, they just flowed. There were so many. It was interesting how we struggled by just calling out things instead of using action words to describe a process. "Training" became "Developing or Conducting Training Programs.""

She asked each leader to post the processes they own on the whiteboard. "It was interesting to watch how hard it was for them when a process they felt was important was a support process," she remembered. "We finished posting all the processes, moved them around to reflect the flow, and captured major linkages." She sat back while the team studied what they had just created.

"Part of me felt like a novice realizing how much I still didn't understand about the Department and needed to learn," she admitted. "At the same time, I had a new confidence. I was looking at the first real picture of what we thought the work of the organization was. I couldn't help but think this would change how we improved and managed going forward."

USING AND IMPROVING THE SYSTEM MAP

Having the organization's first draft of a system map in place, the next step is to test it to improve its accuracy and usefulness.[35] One practical approach for improving a draft system map is to run some tests using scenarios. Begin by developing between three and five typical scenarios of issues in the organization. For example, consider a problem that cropped up last week that required a meeting to be resolved. Identify what processes are involved and how they connect to other processes. This testing helps identify missing gaps and supports familiarizing people with the systems view. If you identify missing processes and links, add them using dotted lines until each is verified.

When using the system map to understand a problem, consider the following steps and questions in order:[36]

1. Where was the problem detected?
2. What process(es) contributed to the problem? Trace these on the system map.
3. What drivers or influencing processes are related to the problem process(es)?
4. What support processes are related to the problem process(es)?
5. Would it be easy for this problem to happen again?
6. How much does the system design contribute to this problem versus the individuals who work in and own the process under investigation (process flow diagrams may be useful).
7. Investigate these processes to see other contributing factors (use of a cause-and-effect diagram or force field analysis might be used).
8. Look for patterns on Shewhart charts for key measures of the affected processes. Is the variation special or common cause variation?
9. Identify processes to design or redesign to prevent these problems in the future.

We may add or modify processes as we use the initial system map and get deeper insights into how the organization works as a system. The system map will change and evolve over time with our learning. It is dynamic and will reflect the understanding of how work is done and the interdependencies in that time frame. It is not unusual to update the system map annually or more frequently.

With the draft system map complete, it was recreated using software to make it readable and available in the Cloud. Each leader identified the processes for which they were currently responsible, met with their teams, and assigned the proper rating to each process based on the operational definitions.

Chief Allan began, "Talk about eye-opening! There were mainstay processes around our emergency operations that we could rate "4." I was surprised how few we could agree met the definition of "4." Mostly because the measurement was light or nonexistent or we know from our Process Boundary Form experience, we must better define the quality characteristics of the inputs and outputs."

Allan then pointed out different processes across her system map. "Seeing so many processes were rated "5" or "6" was a wake-up call. We had a vague definition or none. No wonder we burn so much time and energy just trying to do the day-to-day."

Seeing the map with all the process ratings was initially disturbing, and then she realized that they finally had a method to help figure out how to improve the department. After the leadership team developed the first draft system map, they tested it under different scenarios. When a leader started an agenda item in meetings, they directed the team to the related process on the map. If a complaint came in or a staff member raised a problem to fix, they would start by locating the process on the map. Each test helped the team learn about the system and continue to improve the system map. They also began to see the value of integrating it into their daily management of the organization.

"I was surprised how many places I found our system map useful," said Chief Allan. "It's common practice for leaders in a fire department to rotate roles. This helps broaden their knowledge and capability as they grow in the organization." Allan revealed a copy of the system map on the desk and explained, "I use the system map to onboard leaders rotating to a new role. We start by refreshing the department's purpose and their position's role in helping the department achieve our mission. Seeing processes they own or contribute to makes our conversation easy. Planning for their first ninety days is much smoother."

Allan used to be anxious about these moves because of the learning curve to learning the role and the work, but the system map and the definition of the processes within it made it so much easier.

USING THE SYSTEM MAP

System maps are a conceptual leap to better understand an organization. It is not uncommon for people to take time to grasp moving from concept to practice. Seeing examples of system maps from various organizations can help that transition. There is no single right way to do a system map; each example is similar but unique to the organization that created it. *The QOS Field Guide* includes examples of system maps, including:

- Hospice Viewed as a System: Importance of understanding the leverage in the "links."
- Health Care Integrated Payer and Provider System: Understanding key partners and including their processes in the organization viewed as a system.
- Fabrication Viewed as a System: Sharing a system map between multiple organizations to ensure shared learning.
- Conrad Company: Using a system map to onboard employees.
- Conrad Company: Using a system map to translate a vision into an ideal design.
- Viewing a Clinical Physiology Department as a system, within Jönköping County Council in Sweden: This subsystem was determined to be a key leverage system to ensure patients had timely access to healthcare.
- Ottawa Intensive Care Unit: Using a systems view to implement improvements.

SUMMARY

The following key ideas were discussed in this chapter focused on understanding the organization viewed as a system:

- A **system** is an **interdependent** group of components (items, people, or processes) working together toward a common **purpose**.
- A key assumption in defining and developing the organization viewed as a system is understanding that **all work can be described as a process.**
- The concept of systems can be applied at different levels of detail in an organization.
    o   Whole organization: low level of detail
    o   Business group, department, or location level: more detail
    o   Department or units: high level of detail
- The system map was defined as a method used to visually depict how components within an organization fit and link together as a system to plan, support, and provide services and products to our customers.
- The differences between system maps and process flow diagrams were discussed. Process thinking provides the building blocks for development of the organization viewed as a system.
- Development of the system map was discussed, moving from a conceptual view of the system to providing the detail necessary to make the system map useful with

the other activities of QOS. The system map acts as a hub for the other activities and is a key differentiator of QOS from other approaches to leading organizations.

- Development of the system map was discussed using three categories of processes: Driver, Mainstay, and Support processes.
- Steps to develop the system map were covered in detail.
- Operational definitions with corresponding ratings were provided to assess the condition of processes in the system map. These ratings provide guidance on gaps that may exist and where improvement may be needed.

Chief Allan initially hesitated to develop a system map of the department. She knew it was a novel idea in her industry. She hoped having a systems view would help her team expand on their adoption of the Science of Improvement and further their development as they adopted QOS.

"These are practical people," she said. "They don't respond well to anything they see as theoretical or not practically useful in the field. Trusting the process and leaning into the learning at every step was critical. The struggle of unpacking and visualizing our work and then having a way to see the current condition of our processes was not simple. I have never seen the team so engaged and in agreement about the department. Understanding our work as a process, seeing how they are linked together, and recognizing all the opportunities to improve has been transformational, and I expect it will serve us well as we continually improve the department."

NOTES

1. Langley et al., *The Improvement Guide*, 2009, 37. Definition adapted from the source: "A system is an interdependent group of items, people, or processes working together toward a common purpose."

2. Chapter 2 defined "systems thinking" as "a way of making sense of the complexity of the world by looking at it in terms of wholes and relationships rather than by splitting it down into its parts. It has been used as a way of exploring and developing effective action in complex contexts, enabling systems change. Systems thinking draws on and contributes to systems theory and the system sciences."

3. "What Is System Dynamics?," *System Dynamics Society* (blog), accessed September 17, 2023, https://systemdynamics.org/what-is-system-dynamics/. "System Dynamics complements systems thinking by quantifying interactions and develops a time-dependent view of how the system behaves. The approach focuses on building computer models that represent and simulate complex problems in which behavior changes. These models bring to light less visible relationships, dynamic complexity, delays, and unintended consequences of interactions."

4. In Chapter 1, Table 1.5 is a tool for leaders to assess the organization's progress in making quality an organizational strategy. This paragraph is the operational definition for the top score for "Viewing the organization as a system." *The QOS Field Guide* contains a more comprehensive version of the assessment tool.

5. Ludwig von Bertalanffy, *General System Theory: Foundations, Development, Applications*, 1st ed. (New York: George Braziller, 1968).

6. Adapted from Russell L. Ackoff and Jamshid Gharajedaghi, "Reflections on Systems and Their Models," *Systems Research* 13, no. 1 (1996): 13–23. Originally four types of systems were defined.

7. Jay Forester, *Principles of Systems* (Cambridge: Productivity Press, 1986).

8. Ackoff, *Ackoff's Best*.

9. Senge, *The Fifth Discipline*, 170–71.

10. Peter F. Drucker, "The Emerging Theory of Manufacturing," *Harvard Business Review*, May 1, 1990, https://hbr.org/1990/05/the-emerging-theory-of-manufacturing.

11. Russell L. Ackoff, "The Future of Operational Research Is Past," *Journal of the Operational Research Society* 30, no. 2 (February 1979): 93–94.

12. Deming, *The New Economics*, 1994, 50.

13. Picture reprinted with permission courtesy of the MIT Press and the W. Edwards Deming Institute. W. Edwards Deming, *The New Economics*, 3rd ed. (Cambridge, MA: The MIT Press, 2018). This chart is adapted from a version first used in August 1950 at a conference with top management at the Hotel de Yama on Mount Hakone in Japan. See Fig,1, "Production viewed as a system," in Deming, *Out of Crisis*, 4.

14. For Deming's rationale for the introduction of "Production Viewed as a System," see Deming, *Out of Crisis*, 4–5.

15. Joseph M. Juran made a similar point with his famous "Spiral of Progress in Quality." See figure 1.1, in Joseph M. Juran and Frank M. Gryna, *Quality Planning and Analysis*, 2nd ed. (New York: McGraw-Hill, 1988), 5.

16. Ackoff, *Ackoff's Best*, 17–19.

17. Russell L. Ackoff, "Beyond Continual Improvement." YouTube video, https://youtu.be/OqEeIG8aPPk.

18. Daniel Gross, "Do They Know Jack?," *Slate*, March 4, 2003, https://slate.com/business/2003/03/why-jack-welch-s-proteges-are-failing.html. Slate describes several executives hired from GE to lead other companies. A few were able to replicate the results of GE. Others struggled to create results or failed.

19. Peter F. Drucker, *The Essential Drucker* (New York: Harper-Collins Publishers, 2001), 11.

20. Deming, *The New Economics*, 1994, 50.

21. Based on Deming's description of "interdependence" in Chapter 4, "A System of Profound Knowledge," Deming, 96–97.

22. See Chapter 3, page 90, for Kohlberg's description of shared identity as a Level 3 focus of his three levels of ethical and moral reasoning; Leadership should keep their focus on the overall system (Level 3).

23. Adapted from figure 11.2, "Concept of a process in Associates in Process Improvement, *The Improvement Handbook: Model, Methods, and Tools for Improvement*, IHI Improvement Advisor Development Program (Austin: Associates in Process Improvement, 2007), 11–12.

24. Mike Veseth, "No Wine Before Its Time," *The Wine Economist* (blog), February 11, 2009, https://wineeconomist.com/2009/02/10/no-wine-before-its-time/. "We will sell no wine before its time" was the slogan of a famous Paul Masson winery advertising campaign.

25. Associates in Process Improvement, *The Improvement Handbook: Model, Methods, and Tools for Improvement*, 11–15.

26. Bryon Murray observed that there was no problem in having people identify driver, mainstay, and support processes. It was having them show the connections that ended up being difficult and sometimes would lose the team.

27. Figure adapted from Deming's "Production Viewed as a System," figure 1 in Deming, *Out of Crisis*, 4.

28. Used in this context from *Oxford Dictionary*: a person or thing that is the most important part of something and enables it to exist or be successful. "Mainstay," Oxford Learner's Dictionaries, accessed July 19, 2023, https://www.oxfordlearnersdictionaries.com/definition/english/mainstay.

29. PlanSource, Inc, "6 Unit Apartment Plan (J0418-11-6)," N.D., https://plansourceinc.com/J0418-11-6.htm.

30. The complete "Hospice Viewed as a Systems Map" follows in figure 5.19, "Hospice Viewed as a System."

31. On the system map, we **do not** show decisions or the steps that the process box represents. Some users hyperlink the individual boxes on the system map to the actual flow chart, procedures, and protocol for that process. Training videos can also allow people to view a three- to five-minute overview of the process, rather than read the flow chart.

32. Numbering should follow some logical sequence. Sometimes it is useful to depict D# for Drivers, M# for Mainstay, and S# for Support processes. Numbering of driver processes starts with "stakeholder feedback" and moves right to left. Numbering Mainstay and Support processes begins from left to right. For example, the key groups or boxes of Mainstay processes may be numbered a M100, M200, M300. For processes within M100 group or box, each individual process may be M110, M120, M130, etc.

33. CEO Joe Balthazor introduced Hallmark in the "Reflections," earlier in this book. He discussed the advantage of using QOS to get results: "Our knowledge of QBS has been directly responsible for our growth as a company. We went from approximately $10 million in annual revenue with warehouses in Wisconsin and Minnesota to nearly $130 million with six warehouses serving 20 states. All six warehouses use the same processes for all functional areas of our system, regardless of the location." This last line describes the advantage to understanding the organization as a system in terms of results.

34. See "Planning" in Chapter 8, figure 8.7 for an example of the application of identifying process condition.

35. Chapter 5 in *The QOS Field Guide* contains additional tests of the system map including reviewing the leadership agenda, current issues, or improvement efforts against the map.

36. Adapted from "Exercise 11.15: Utilize the system map to consider system contributions to problem," in Maccoby et al., *Transforming Health Care Leadership*, 287–88.

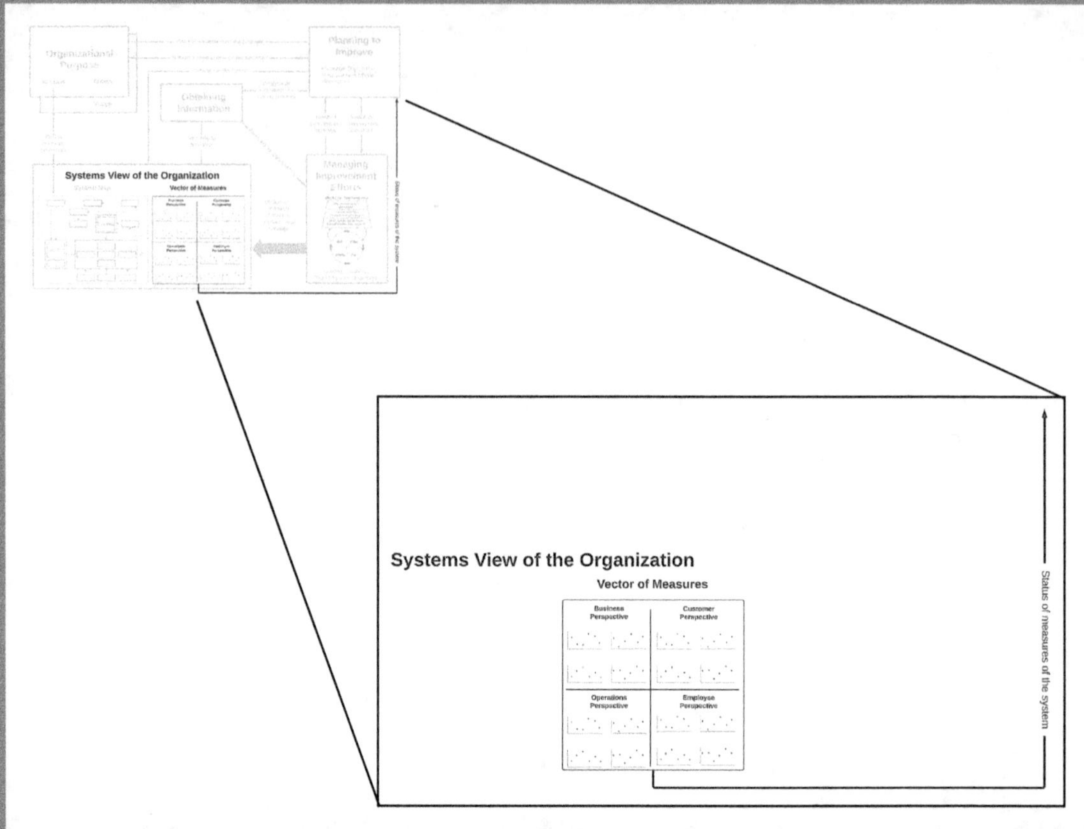

ACTIONS FOR LEADERSHIP TEAM

- Create a vector of measures to understand the performance of the system.
- Visually display these measures as a set of Shewhart charts to see the system's performance.
- Use these documents to understand the impact of improvement on the organization and to learn how the organization functions as a system.

CHAPTER 6

MEASUREMENT OF A SYSTEM

Janice was pleased to receive praise from the Board of Education about her school's performance in the state standardized test program. "Since I became principal four years ago," she reflected, "I have focused on getting our school's scores above the average in the district, and we have finally accomplished this goal in the latest round of tests. It was nice to get the recognition for this result."

Something was bothering Janice, however: "As I received all this positive feedback, I knew not everything in the school was going as well as I would like. In a recent teacher meeting, for example, someone expressed concern about increasing student absenteeism, especially among some of the high-achieving students. And, in this past year, there were multiple complaints from some teachers about not expanding the advanced placement classes. We also exceeded our school budget for the past six months."

"How well is our school actually performing?" Janice wondered. And how could she better appreciate the performance of her school?

A feedback system is required to decide how well an organization is accomplishing its purpose, and the use of measures is one of the most common feedback methods. But a common force for suboptimizing a system is the attempt to define its performance by a single measure (or a few measures concentrated in one area). In many organizations today, the accounting function still defines all system measures.[1] Systems for creating measures in non-accounting areas are often informal or nonexistent.

But using multiple measures to understand a system is not new to most of us. Our primary care doctor usually requires a blood test when we have an annual physical. This test produces a page of data on measures of our physical system. The doctor then discusses the relationship of the various measures and any changes, if needed.

The same thinking can be employed as we understand the organization viewed as a system. Figure 6.1 contrasts the human system with the organization viewed as a system and corresponding "vital signs."

Standard Measures During Physical
- Weight
- Height
- Temperature
- Blood pressure
- Heart rate

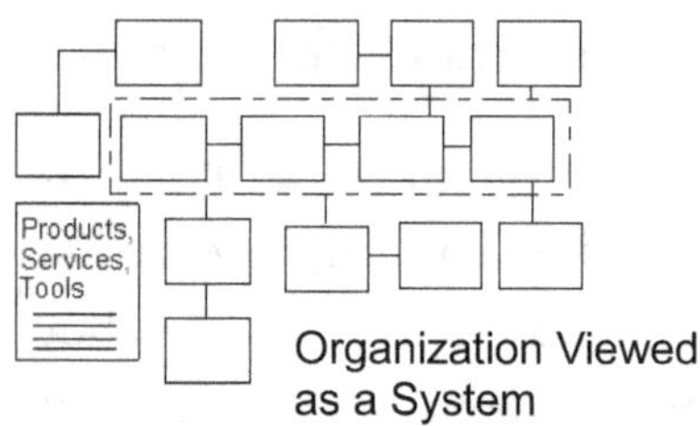

Standard Measures for an Organization
- Financial performance
- Customer experience
- Production
- Safety
- Growth

Figure 6.1. Using measures to understand a system.

Just as we use multiple measures to understand the health of the human system, we can also use multiple measures to understand the health and performance of an organization. Examples of such measures are stock price, return on investment, throughput, percentage of legal cases won, scores on standardized tests, and sales volume. Given one measure of success, almost any organization can be successful in the short term by improving that measure at the expense of other organizational performance measures. Any business, for example, can easily increase short-term profits by decreasing investment in research and development activities.

Typically, the only measures routinely monitored at the system level are financial measures from the accounting system. If there are additional measures, they are often measures of judgment dictated by accrediting or quality assurance systems outside the organization. Sometimes easy to measure items (e.g., number of hits on a website) are included because they are available.

Another analogy to the use of multiple measures to understand a system is the use of our five senses (sight, hearing, smell, taste, touch) to understand the world we live in. None of us would ever choose to only focus on just one of these senses to appreciate our life experience.[2]

Improvement of a system results in the improvement in a set of measures to understand the system. This chapter introduces the name **vector of measures (VOM)** for this concept of multiple measures for an organization. Figure 6.2 illustrates this concept. On the left is the conceptual diagram of an organization viewed as a system from Chapter 5. On the right is a conceptual view of a vector of measures that provides feedback on the system's performance. The vector of measures should serve as both an indicator of present performance and a predictor of how the system will perform in the future. **These measures in the VOM should reflect the organization's purpose (Chapter 4) and relate to all stakeholders, including customers, employees, investors, and the community.** After some initial background, we discuss the development of the vector, learning from the measures using Shewhart charts,[3] and using the vector of measures.

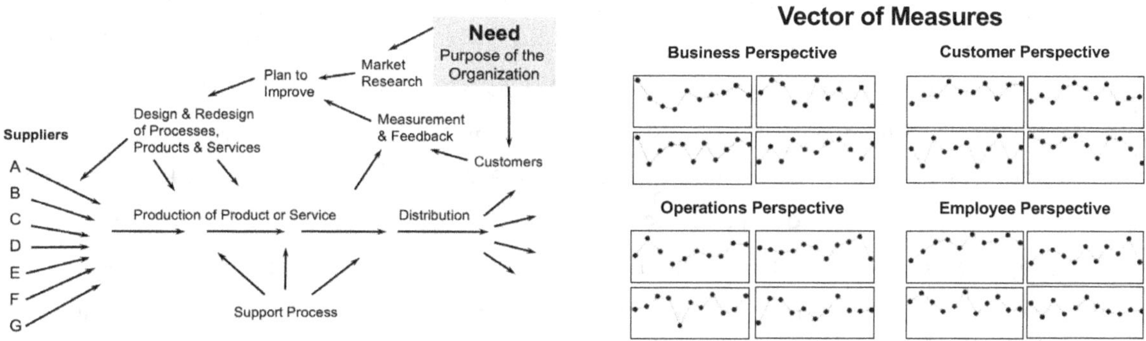

Figure 6.2. Concept of a vector of measures.

In a mature organization focusing on QOS, the vector of measures is an integral part of the organization's management and leadership framework. The leadership team studies the VOM to understand how well they run the organization. Any incentive system that exists is aligned with components of the VOM. Improvement teams use the measures from the VOM to evaluate their progress. During the planning process, the measures help set priorities and predictions for each key measure. The VOM is evaluated and improved regularly as learning occurs in the organization. Finally, the set of measures is analyzed to study relationships and to give insight into how the organization functions as a system.[4]

While the VOM is constructed from quantitative data, it should be used with qualitative data from the organization. Relevant stories from customers, employees, and suppliers that add context to key signals in the VOM should be included whenever the VOM is presented, studied, or published.

The VOM method begins at the organizational system level and can be applied to parts (business groups, regions, divisions, departments, units, etc.) of an organization. Often it is useful to create some measures that can be collected in parts of the organization and then rolled up to describe the whole organization. But the parts of the organization may also have some measures that are unique to their function.

THE CONCEPT OF A VECTOR OF MEASURES

The idea of using a vector of measures to understand the performance of an organization is a departure from how people traditionally think about measurement for an organization. At the top of many companies, leaders typically focus on financial measures, using the language of "money." But within the organization, frontline managers and workers use the language of "things" related to the products and services of the organization to communicate. In that sense, mid-level managers need to be bilingual. When leaders begin to think of their organization as a system, it becomes necessary for them to understand the language of "things" in some instances and for the people who work for them to understand financial performance, the language of "money." Understanding the interdependence of measures of the system also becomes essential. Figure 6.3[5] describes this transformation in using measurement to understand the performance of an organization.

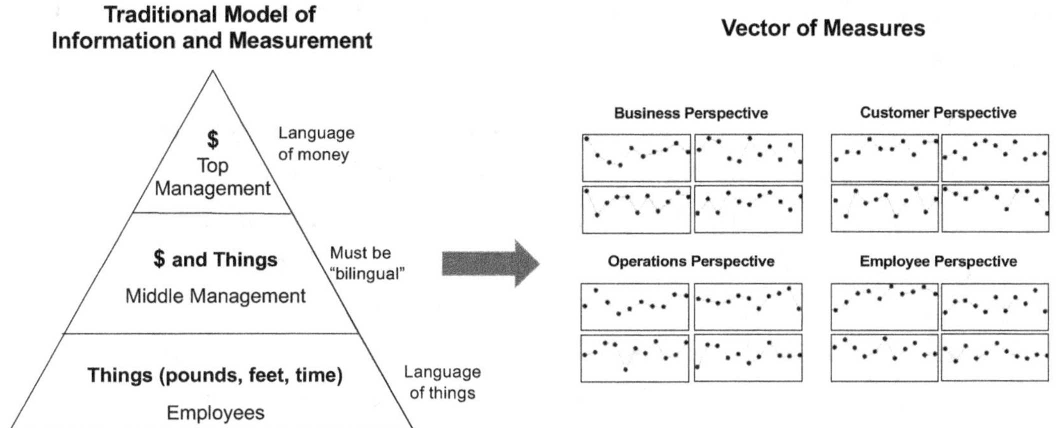

Figure 6.3. The language of measures.

A variety of names have been used to describe a set of multiple measures for a system:

- A family of measures
- A balanced scorecard
- A scorecard
- A report card
- A dashboard
- An instrument panel
- A clinical value compass[6]
- A vector of measures

Some authors emphasize "dashboard," "report card," and "scorecard" as measures related to the local environment where the expectation is for managers to take immediate action if the data indicates a slip in desired performance. The "clinical value compass" is designed for medical microsystems,[7] frontline clinics, and other care centers to view status, patient outcomes, experience, and cost. The other names tend to be for the presentation of more strategic measures and focused on learning.

The concept of a vector provides an excellent analogy to the purpose of this set of measures. The word **vector** has multiple meanings.[8] We combine the linear algebra and engineering definitions to describe a list of numbers (from individual measures) that can be calculated to describe both **magnitude** and **direction**. The individual components of the vector may not communicate useful information about the system performance by themselves, but combining the components yields useful information. Like the various dials on an automobile display, some measures describe the past (e.g., odometer reading), some describe the present (e.g., speedometer), some are there to indicate problems (e.g., oil pressure light), and some describe the future (e.g., gas gauge). We will use "vector" in describing the collection of measures in the QOS framework:

> **The vector of measures (VOM) is a collection of system-wide measures presented in a way to understand the performance of an organization. The VOM serves as both an indicator of present performance and predictor of how the system will perform in the future. The components of the VOM reflect the purpose of the organization and relate to all stakeholders including customers, employees, investors, and the community in a balanced way.**

The vector of measures brings together information from all parts and perspectives of the organization. It thus provides a tool for the leaders to focus planning and decisions on the whole system. Leaders can assess the effect of changes to parts of the organization against the whole. The VOM serves as an indicator of the present performance of the system and a predictor of how the system will act in the future. A holistic analysis of the vector of measures should help predict the organization's future direction. It is the responsibility of the leaders of the organization to plan and manage improvement efforts and operate the system to improve the entire vector of measures.

The measures selected for an organization's vector should reflect the organization's purpose. There should be a direct relationship between the key ideas in the purpose statement and the measures in the vector. The measures selected should also relate to the organization from the perspectives of all parties interested in its success, such as:

- Customers
- Employees
- Owners or stockholders
- Operations (including suppliers)
- Outside environment (including the community)

After the accolades for achieving the goal on test scores had quieted down, Janice spent some time thinking about measuring her school's performance. She reflected on her progress:

I did some research and came across the concept called a vector of measures. This concept emphasized the use of multiple, balanced measures to appreciate the performance of a complex system like a school. I liked the idea of being able to access current performance from the perspective of multiple stakeholders of our school and to also reflect on where we are heading in the future. I currently see data reports for a lot of different measures, but the data are not organized in any way convenient for learning.

Janice decided to spend some time to develop an initial vector of measures for her school.

DEVELOPING AN INITIAL VECTOR OF MEASURES

Organizations have found three approaches useful when initially developing their vector of measures. Leaders should integrate all three methods to create the initial version of the VOM. This section will discuss the three approaches:

- Connect measures to purpose (Chapter 4)
- Develop measures that reflect the interests of each group of stakeholders
- Select measures that represent the organization's direct connection to a larger system (such as a school in a school district)[9]

Connect Measures to the Purpose Statement

One way to develop a vector of measures for an organization is to use its **purpose** as a guide and ask how leaders could measure each of the key statements in the purpose. We can use any or all the components of a purpose: mission, tenets, or vision.

Table 6.1 shows an example of measures identified to support Cherokee Nation's Health Service purpose.[10] Cherokee Nation Health Services (CNHS) operates a network of eight health centers and one hospital, encompassing fourteen counties of Northeast Oklahoma. The twenty-two measures in their VOM (they describe it as a balanced scorecard) reflect the key phrases of their purpose statement.

Table 6.1. Translation of the CHNS Purpose to twenty-two system-level measures

CHEROKEE NATIONS HEALTH SERVICES PURPOSE

The Cherokee Nation Health System protects and promotes health and is the provider of choice through its workforce and in the delivery of a quality experience to those we serve while practicing good stewardship resulting in a happy and healthy Cherokee people.

CNHS purpose	Balanced scorecard measure
"The Cherokee Nation Healthcare Services *protects and promotes health…*"	Immunization rates Unadjusted raw mortality Child obesity, ages two through eighteen Morbidity
"and is *the provider of choice…*"	Citizenry satisfaction rates Percentage of third-party, active-user population and visits Percentage of patients empaneled Average panel size per team/provider
"through *its workforce…*"	Percentage of workforce Cherokee Staff turnover rate Productivity index Incidence rate nonfatal occupational injuries and illnesses
"and in the *delivery of a quality experience* to those we serve…"	Number of cancelled appointments Adverse incidents Third next available appointment Equitable: inside fourteen counties versus outside
"while *practicing good stewardship…*"	Health care costs per capita Revenue per visit Cost per visit
"resulting in a *happy and healthy* Cherokee people."	Quality-of-life index Disability associated life years

In our experience facilitating this work with organizations, this measurement activity often caused leaders to go back and modify their organization's purpose.

Connect Measures to Each Group of Stakeholders

Another method to begin developing the VOM is to consider each stakeholder of the organization. Stakeholders include customers, employees, investors, suppliers, the community, and other relevant groups. Ask what measures would indicate their current satisfaction and predict their future satisfaction with the organization. These measures should go beyond simple Likert-style[11] satisfaction scales to rate the level of agreement from "very dissatisfied" to "very satisfied." The potential measures developed from these questions then can be researched for practicality and availability.

The vector of measures for a manufacturing division of a large corporation was composed of fifteen measures from five different stakeholder perspectives. The vector was purposely balanced by selecting three measures for each perspective. Table 6.2 lists these measures. Each of the fifteen measures is reviewed in a monthly meeting. Then the managers of the division write a qualitative assessment of the current performance of the division and develop predictions for the next three months.

Table 6.2. Vector of measures for a manufacturing division

Perspective	Measures
Customer	1. Number of complaints per one hundred shipments 2. Percent favorable responses to questionnaire 3. Number of active customer partnerships
Financial (stockholders)	4. Total sales 5. Operating profit as a percent of sales 6. Net return on investment
Operations (managers)	7. Total cycle time (order to delivery) 8. Number of accidents/injury incidents/200,000 hours 9. Total first pass yield
Employee	10. Percent absenteeism 11. Percent turnover 12. Percent of employees on improvement teams
Environment (community)	13. Total pounds of material disposed of or emitted 14. Number of talks and papers to community groups 15. Total number of employees

Select Measures for Parts of an Organization

This third approach is useful for divisions, departments, or other groups in a larger organization. It begins by studying the vector of measures used for the containing organization (i.e., at the whole organization level; see Chapter 5 for discussion of "parts of a system"), **then choosing measures relevant in each part of the organization, which are then rolled up to obtain the organization measures (or that support those measures).** For example, if the number of safety events is a measure at the organizational level, each department should also incorporate safety events in the VOM for their department.

Table 6.3 shows an example of this approach for a school district. The district developed a recommended vector of fifteen measures to learn about the performance of the high schools in their community. They asked each of the principals to report semesterly and incorporate them in the VOM at each school.

Table 6.3. Vector of measures for high schools in the district

Reporting focus	Description of measure
Academic progress	1. percent of on-track freshmen 2. AP success rates 3. graduation rates
Students	4. attendance rates 5. average score on climate survey 6. AP enrollment
Faculty and staff	7. student to faculty ratio 8. average class size 9. average score on climate survey
Community	10. total enrollment 11. average score on parent climate survey 12. percent of students passing state standardized tests
Financial	13. total costs versus budget 14. total costs per student 15. faculty costs as percent of budget

Connecting measures to the purpose, reflecting the interests of stakeholders, and representing each part of the organization's system are all useful approaches to develop a VOM. Each approach will give a list of measures that can be consolidated and reconciled to form the initial vector of measures for an organization.

AVOIDING TYPICAL TRAPS WHILE DEVELOPING A VECTOR OF MEASURES

In selecting the measures for the vector, remember that each measure by itself does not need to be an insightful measure of the entire system. When evaluated in isolation from the rest of the vector, any individual measure can be criticized as incomplete, misleading, biased, etc. However, it is only when all the measures are presented and studied—as a whole and at the same time—that they become more useful to learn about the organization as a system. **So, in the beginning, rather than critique individual measures, focus on what aspects of the organization are missing in the measures currently proposed.**

Also, as the vector of measures is developed, do not forget Deming's comments that, "One cannot be successful on visible figures alone. The most important figures that one needs for management are unknown or unknowable, but successful management must nevertheless take account of them."[12] For example, the impact of poor service posted on social media and viewed by present and future customers is difficult to measure. Still, it is vital to the success of a service organization. So, we are not expecting our vector to "tell us everything." The VOM should be supported with qualitative data including stories from patients, students, and other stakeholders of the organization.

The development and use of a VOM should be separated from "goal setting." It is not necessary to have goals for the measures in the vector.[13] Some of the measures are in the vector for learning and perspective. Goal-setting processes, often done as part of a planning process, can use the measures in the vector as appropriate.[14] For example, each year, selected measures could be targeted for improvement, and goals can be established for these measures.

Measures selected for the vector should not serve as the only measures used to learn about the organization. When questions are raised from the study of the vector, additional measures and levels of detail are often required for diagnostic purposes. (Why is the backlog going down? Which parts of the organization are having problems satisfying their customers?) Specific data will often need to be developed to answer these questions, but these additional measures should not be added to the vector every time a question is raised. Often a measure (e.g., safety events) is already an aggregation of events in all parts of the organization and so drilling down into departments is straightforward.

Because of the holistic nature of the measures of the system, no one person, department, or other groups should be responsible for the performance of an individual measure. Instead, the organization's leadership team should all bear responsibility and accept some credit for all the measures in the vector. In addition, it is the responsibility of the leadership team to provide the will and resources for improvement so that the entire vector of measures is improved. Planning for improvement (see Chapter 8) plays a significant role in accomplishing this objective.

It is essential to understand that the relationships and trade-offs among the different measures in the vector are defined by the system of interest (Chapter 5). Any procedure (e.g., financial incentive systems based on one measure) that breaks up the vector of measures into independent measurements without understanding the relationship structure between the vector and the processes in the system, will lead to suboptimization. Likewise, any approach to maximizing or minimizing a single vector measure will suboptimize the system relative to the entire vector. As the vector of measures is being developed, an effort should begin to understand the interrelationships among the measures.

To summarize the key ideas about the VOM in this section:

- Measures for the vector can be identified using the organization's purpose, by evaluating the organization from the perspective of each of the stakeholders, or, for parts of the organization, by selecting measures to support existing ones at the whole-organization level.
- Any measure used in isolation should not be expected to provide useful insights into the organization viewed as a system. Unfortunately, when developing a VOM, there is a tendency to reject measures before appreciating the relationship to other measures.
- It is not possible, or even useful, to measure all concepts important to an organization's success.
- Separate measurement from goal setting.
- The VOM will not contain all the measures useful to the organization. On an as-needed basis, additional diagnostic measures are required to answer specific questions and understand issues raised.
- The VOM should be studied and used as a whole by the leadership team in appropriate organizational meetings.

REFINING THE INITIAL VECTOR OF MEASURES

Developing a vector of measures that focuses on the purpose, incorporates the view of all organizational stakeholders, and is compatible with the VOM of a larger containing system is a significant undertaking. After the initial VOM is completed there are still a number of areas that need to be addressed to turn the initial list of measures (from the previous section) into a useful vector of measures:[15]

- What information should be in the vector of measures? What important aspects of the organization are we missing in our initial VOM?
- How can outside resources help this effort? Sometimes industry groups can provide guidance for a VOM.
- How will the measures be generated? Can we leverage the accounting system, or do we need new systems?
- What technology is needed to support the new measurement system? Both hardware and software should be considered.
- Do the organization's incentives need modification to support the system?
- Who will lead the effort to develop the vector of measures?
- Who should do the work of collecting and reporting the measures?

Table 6.4 has been useful in helping a leadership team organize and prioritize their efforts to further develop the initial set of measures for their VOM.

Janice had worked for the past three months on assembling an initial vector of measures for her school and reflected on her journey of learning:

Based on my reading about a VOM, I started with listing measures related to each of the primary stakeholders. I also scheduled a meeting with the school analyst to put together a database on the measures that we already report: budget, test results, attendance, dropouts, student progression, advanced placement classes, graduation rates. I felt that a comparison of the current reports to the interest of the stakeholders would help me to see how far we progressed to create a vector for our school.

Table 6.4. Worksheet to develop the initial vector of measures, including examples

Proposed measure	Why measure?	Category (perspective)	Units of measure	Source of data	Currently available	Effort to develop measure	Priority (H, M, L)
Customer satisfaction average score	Key measure to learn how customers are feeling	Customer	Average monthly rating received	Marketing CSI system	Yes	Minimal	H
Cycle time on closing new contracts	Key performance measure	Activity measure	Average days for deals closed	Business development	At department level	Create a roll-up database	M

Note: Measure priority: H = High priority, M = Medium priority, L = Low priority. Objective definitions can be developed that are appropriate for the organization.

REPORTING THE VECTOR OF MEASURES

From work described in the previous section, creating a vector of measures is a substantial investment for the organization. The return on that investment is earned when the vector is properly displayed and regularly used for learning, making decisions, and making predictions. How a vector is displayed affects our ability to make predictions and learn about the impact of deliberate changes and other key interactions in the system.

How frequently should measures be reported in the vector? Traditionally, vital financial measures are updated monthly and summarized for board reports quarterly. So monthly reporting of the new measures in the vector seems natural. But school systems have important measures that naturally occur at the end of each semester. While a more frequent study of measures (e.g., daily, or weekly) could improve the learning rate, the resources required to develop these reports may be prohibitive. Subject matter experts should decide the frequency of reporting.

Systems of measures used in many organizations today are not effectively displayed for learning.[16, 17] It's common to see a VOM displayed as a list of measures with the goal and the most recent value of the measure noted. Some organizations add to this tabular display by including a comparison to the value from one year earlier or possibly a progress rating toward the goal associated with the measure. Red, yellow, and green color coding is often used to summarize the status of a measure. This tabular display of measures, with the evaluation of each measure compared to a goal, can lead to erroneous conclusions, and missed opportunities for learning. Figure 6.4 is an example of such a measures dashboard for a hospital.[18]

An effective alternative is to display the measures using Shewhart charts formatted on a single page. Chapter 2 described the Shewhart chart as a method based on Walter Shewhart's theory of variation to learn from variation in data. Figure 6.5 shows an example of a Shewhart chart for monthly revenue for an organization. The chart has a center line of $16.6 million calculated from the 2019–2020 data points. On the chart, the variation of the monthly data points is all within the limits of 12.5 to 20.7, and there are no unusual patterns. Since the process is stable, the extended limits into 2021 provide a prediction of monthly values. (See Chapter 2 to review the ideas of common and special causes, the mistakes often made in reacting to variation in a measure, and the construction of a Shewhart chart.)

FY 2020 HOSPITAL SYSTEM LEVEL MEASURES

Legend for Status of Goals (Based on Annual Goal)
- Goal Met (GREEN)
- Goal 75% Met (YELLOW)
- Goal Not Met (RED)

Contact S. Khamali, 512-555-1974

Measure	Good	Goals		FY 2018	FY 2019	FY 2020 Q1	FY 2029 Q2	FY 2020 Q3
		FY 2020 Goal	Long Term Goal					
Patient Perspective								
1. Overall Satisfaction Rating: Percent Who Would Recommend (Includes inpatient, outpatient, ED, and Home Health)	↑	60%	80%	37.98%	48.98%	57.19%	56.25%	51.69%
2. Wait for 3rd Next Available Appointment: Percent of Areas with appointment available in less than or equal to 7 business days (n=43)	↑	65%	100%	53.5%	51.2%	54.30%	61.20%	65.10%
Patient Safety								
3. Safety Events per 10,000 Adjusted Patient Days	↓	0.28	0.20	0.35	0.31	31.00%	29.50%	0.28
4. Percent Mortality	↓	3.50	3.00	4.00	4.00	3.48	3.50	3.42
5. Total Infections per 1000 Patient Days	↓	2	0	3.37	4.33	4.39	2.56	1.95
Clinical								
6. Percent Unplanned Readmissions	↓	3.5%	1.5%	6.1%	4.8%	4.60%	4.10%	3.50%
7. Percent of Eligible Patients Receiving Perfect Care--Evidence Based Care (Inpatient and ED)	↑	95%	100%	46%	74.1%	88.00%	91.70%	88.70%
Employee Perspective								
8. Percent Voluntary Employee Turnover	↓	5.80%	5.20%	5.20%	6.38%	6.10%	6.33%	6.30%
9. Employee Satisfaction: Average Rating Using 1-5 Scale (5 Best Possible)	↑	4.00	4.25	3.90	3.80	3.96	3.95	3.95
Operational Performance								
10. Percent Occupancy	↑	88.0%	90.0%	81.3%	84.0%	91.30%	85.60%	87.20%
11. Average Length of Stay	↓	4.30	3.80	5.20	4.90	4.60	4.70	4.30
12. Physician Satisfaction: Average Rating Using 1-5 Scale (5 Best Possible)	↑	4.00	4.25	3.80	3.84	3.96	3.80	3.87
Community Perspective								
13. Percent of Budget Allocated to Non-recompensed Care	↔	7.00%	7.00%	5.91	7.00%	6.90%	6.93%	7.00%
14. Percent of Budget Spent on Community Health Promotion Programs	↔	0.30%	0.30%	0.32%	0.29%	0.28%	0.31%	0.29%
Financial Perspective								
15. Operating Margin-Percent	↑	1.2%	1.5%	-0.5%	0.7%	0.90%	0.4%	0.7%
16. Monthly Revenue (Million)	↑	20.0	20.6	17.6	16.9	17.50	18.30	19.20

Figure 6.4. Common display of measures for a hospital.

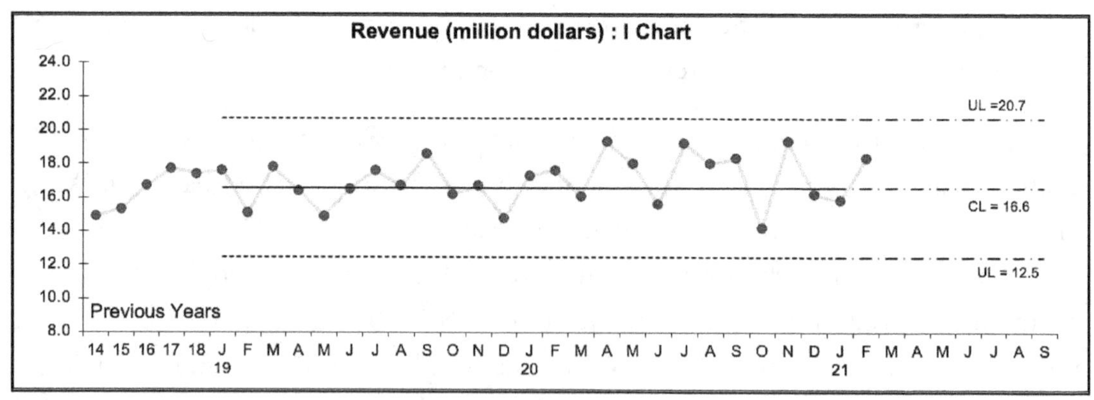

Figure 6.5. Example of a Shewhart chart (an I Chart for monthly revenue).

Figure 6.6 describes the role a Shewhart chart plays in learning and improving a measure.[19] After the appropriate chart is developed for the measure, it is analyzed to detect the presence of special cause (see figure 2.5 in Chapter 2 for special cause patterns). If special causes are present (the right side of figure 6.6), learning should focus on identifying the specific causes that created this signal. These causes can usually be identified by those working in the processes that created the signal for this measure.

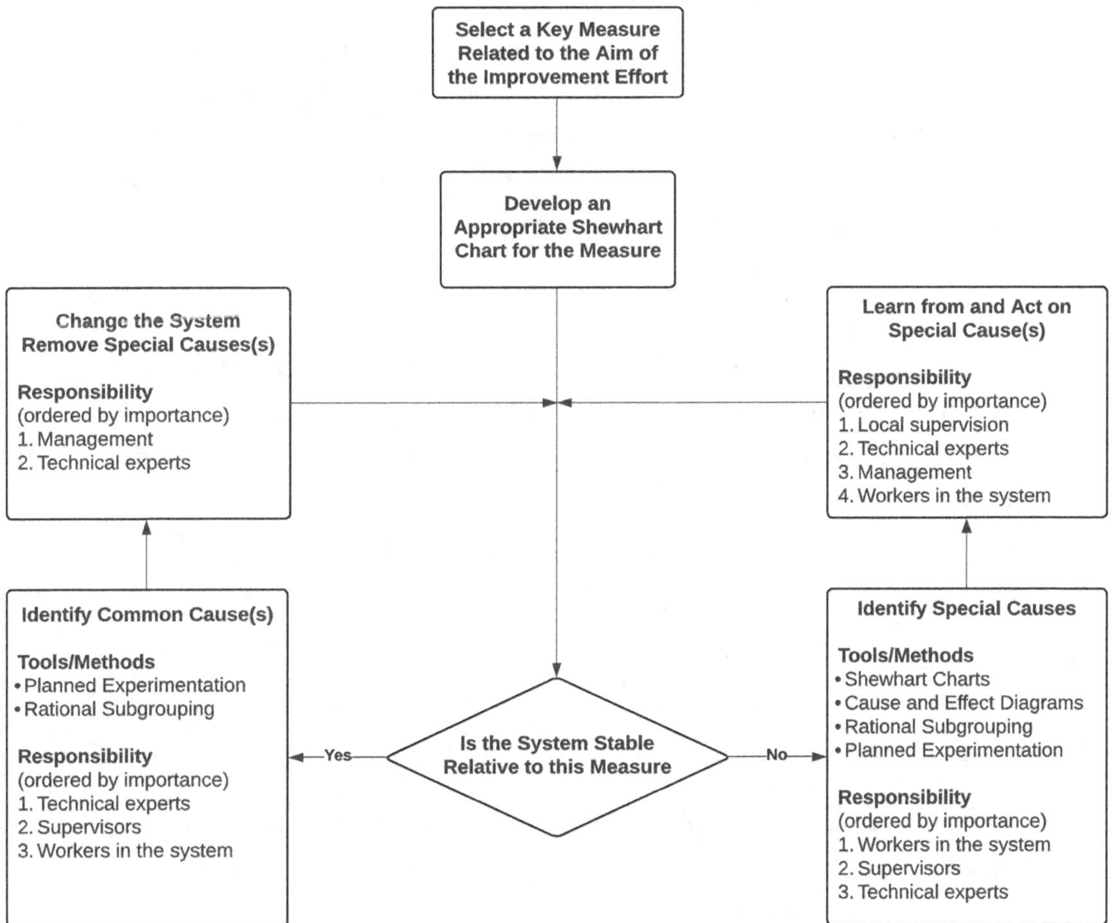

Figure 6.6. Use of Shewhart chart to set a strategy for improvement of a measure.

On the left side of figure 6.6, the measure is affected by only common causes of variation and is thus considered a stable process. Figure 6.5 was an example of a stable measure. None of the individual data points will provide insight into improving the process(es) generating the measure. Instead, improvement comes from changing the common causes in the process by making changes to the system that produces these results. Internal experts, such as engineers, usually lead the work, and the fundamental changes require the approval of management; typically, resources are necessary for such changes.

The vector of measures is designed to measure how an organization is performing as a system today and to indicate its future direction. To obtain this information, it is essential to study the entire vector at one time rather than analyze each component of the vector separately. The idea is to develop a holistic view of the system rather than an analytical study of each component or each individual period's set of measures. Therefore, the most important guidance in displaying the measures is to make sure they are **all presented graphically in one report at one time**. Graphical displays[20] of the measure focus learning on both the dynamic complexity in the organization and the detail complexity represented by the different measures.

There are several advantages to using visual displays of data for the vector of measures:

- Most of the potential learning from data is available through graphical displays.
- The graphical displays are usually easy and quick to prepare.
- Everyone can participate in the learning (analysis); a technical education is not necessary to understand visual displays.
- Interpretation of graphical displays fully utilizes existing knowledge of the measure.
- Graphs tend to lead to a more systemic view of problems and opportunities.

Graphs can identify minute but important details that might be missed in summary statistics or analysis. A good graph is a well-designed presentation of interesting data. Good graphic presentations will have these characteristics:

- Complex ideas are communicated with clarity, precision, and efficiency.
- A lot of information, with the least amount of ink, in the smallest space.
- Multivariate (information about multiple measures in one graph).
- Graphical integrity (does not mislead the reader).

When developing a visual display for the vector of measures, consider the following principles to get graphs that are useful for learning and communication:

- Show complete vector of measures at one time (have detail such as back-up or drill-down).
- Label each axis and other elements to allow for self-interpretation.
- Add annotations of key events related to the measure on the graph.
- Focus the reader on learning, not on the graph itself; keep the graphs simple enough for quick learning.

The vector of measures should be presented for each time period by updating the Shewhart charts and comparing the current value of the measure to the values for past time periods. Presenting multiple Shewhart charts on one page extends this view to the entire system. For example, figure 6.7 shows this format for a vector of measures for a hospital.[21] Earlier, figure 6.4 depicted these sixteen measures as a list of measures with raw data reported comparing intervals like quarters and the same period last year.

A set of Shewhart charts with special causes noted (circled in figure 6.7) provides more information than the color-coded dashboard. Shewhart charts encourage focus on the interesting events in the vector of measures and discourage distraction to the unimportant details. The charts provide consistent signals of special causes that do not require debate. Communication concerning the VOM becomes objective and rapid. Consensus on the status and future actions becomes easier.

The format of all charts on one page allows leaders to see both the **detailed complexity** (the multiple dimensions of the system) and the **dynamic complexity** (the interrelationships among the measures over time). Insights and theories about these interrelationships can be first seen on the VOM report and later verified with a more detailed analysis. For example, in the VOM in figure 6.7, there is clear improvement in the "average length of stay" (Chart 11). This may be the result of improvement teams working to reduce this measure. Has this improvement affected any of the other measures in the system? For example, "percentage unplanned readmissions" (Chart 6) shows a significant increase (the wrong direction) in the last month, and "average employee satisfaction" (Chart 9) shows a special cause on the low side (also the wrong direction). Could these negative results be related to the length-of-stay reduction? Questions like this generated from the study of the VOM will lead to learning and insights about the system.

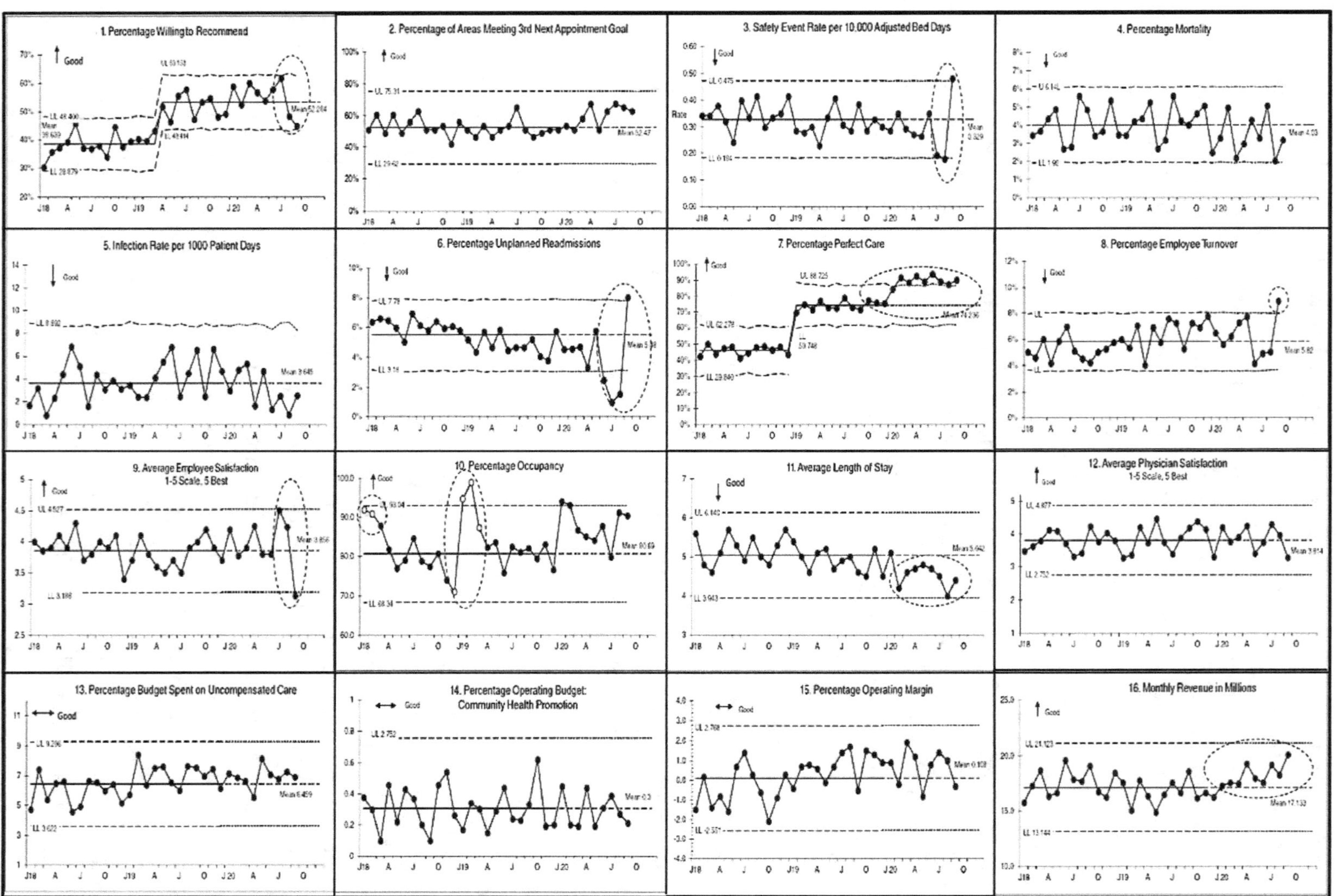

Figure 6.7. Vector of sixteen measures for a hospital (special causes are circled).

Some resistance to displaying the data on Shewhart charts can be expected, especially with financial data. When the data is displayed on charts, people will sometimes begin questioning the validity of the data. "Is it good enough to be on these charts?" Of course, data that contain a tremendous amount of variation can benefit most from analysis on a Shewhart chart. Some on the leadership team may be upset to see patterns and insights they have missed by looking at just the monthly numbers in table form. A good first step in developing the vector is to begin reporting the current financial measures in the organization on Shewhart charts. These measures already have established operational definitions, and baseline data is available from previous years. This will bring out many issues that leaders and managers have with the data and how it is reported.

Janice experimented with using Shewhart charts to display and learn from the data used to create a couple of her measures. She shared her learning with a group of teachers at lunch, saying "I was surprised to learn that the improvement in our test scores was not a special cause signal. But even more surprising was how big our budget deficit had increased over the past three years. I think that getting all our measures on Shewhart charts for the past three years and annotating the key interventions we have initiated will give tremendous insights into how our school is performing as a system and where we are heading in the future. I am excited about getting our VOM together and reported on charts."

USING THE VECTOR OF MEASURES

After developing the VOM, the organization's leaders must begin to use the set of measures regularly. One primary use will be for assessment of the performance of the organization by the leadership team, answering questions such as:

- What are we learning from the special causes on the charts?
- Where are the center lines relative to our predictions?[22]
- What important relationships in the Shewhart charts are we beginning to appreciate?
- What new learning is emerging from our use of the VOM?

Figure 6.8 shows a display of the VOM for an ambulance service[23] organization after a meeting to review the latest data. The markings on the VOM by the executive director summarize the discussion that took place in the meeting as the leadership team explored the interrelationships of the measures.

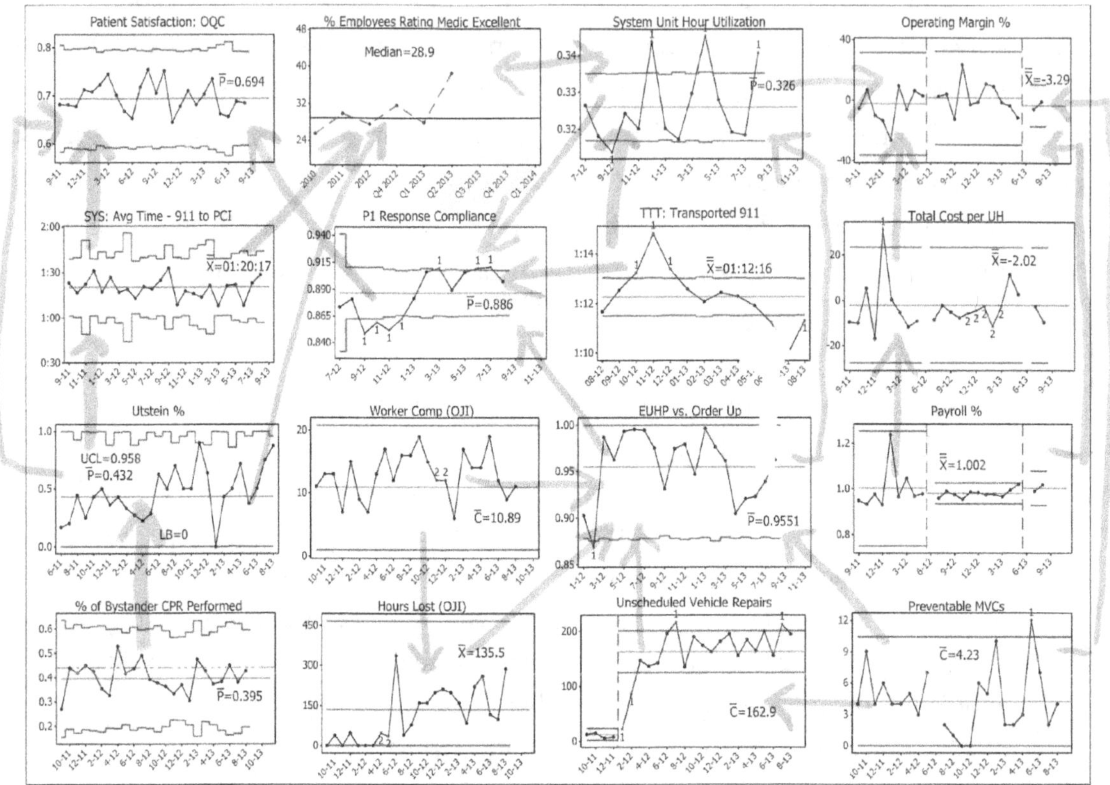

Figure 6.8. Vector of measures for an ambulance service depicting interdependence of measures.

An important use of the VOM in quality as an organizational strategy is to evaluate the results of the major initiatives undertaken to improve the organization. Some other aspects and uses of the VOM include:

- The measures of the system should be available at weekly and monthly staff meetings when the planning and reviews of operations are being done.

- Management reports to employees, customers, owners, and other stakeholders that communicate the organization's status should include the appropriate measures selected from the vector. For example, board reports[24] should be based on the VOM.

- The vector of measures is a crucial input to the planning processes (Chapter 8).

- When developing briefs for improvement efforts ("Planning," Chapter 8), managers should consider the measures in the vector to determine expected results for the effort. Improvement teams should use measures selected from the vector to answer the fundamental question, "How will we know if a change is an improvement?" (See "Managing Improvement Efforts" in Chapter 9.)
- After data is available for three years or more, there will be enough data to do more complex statistical analysis of the vector to learn about relationships and interdependencies between the various measures. Some organizations develop multivariate statistical models to understand better how the measures interrelate and how the key processes in the organization affect the measures.

SOME CAUTIONS ABOUT THE VECTOR OF MEASURES IN AN ORGANIZATION

As with any attempt to measure things, there can be problems associated with developing and using a vector of measures for an organization:

- There is an appropriate tendency for the initial vector to include what is easily measurable rather than what is important to the organization. This is okay for getting started, but it is important to work to move all measures to ones that define the organization's performance and contribute to learning.[25]
- Some of the measures selected will be dictated by outside agencies or auditors and used for judgment or comparison purposes. Usually, these are not useful measures from which to learn about the system's performance.
- A potential measure not selected to be in the vector may be viewed as unimportant to the organization's managers. However, the vector can only contain the vital few measures, so the appropriate time and place to study other measures should be communicated.
- Managers begin to focus only on the measures and lose sight of the key processes in the organization (e.g., coaching a basketball team and only watching the scoreboard).
- When first reported, new measures may be discredited because of their lack of sophistication relative to traditional financial measures.
- Individuals could be financially affected as organizational incentive systems convert to the new vector.

- Some managers will suggest that we wait until "we get our new computer system or the new software" before starting the new measurement system.
- People will expect the measures to satisfy all their needs, not just serve as a system learning tool for the organization. "They don't tell us what to do," "We don't improve anything by making these measurements," etc., are the types of comments that can be expected.
- The vector may lead to a "shoot the messenger" syndrome. When some new measures are first reported, the organization's performance in some areas may be questioned. Individuals may be challenged to immediately correct what has been the typical (but not reported) performance of the organization.
- Managers may drag their feet in developing the new measures if financial measures have traditionally been used to judge their performance. They are not eager to add more to the "blame game." The reactions of top management to the initial data reported will be watched closely.
- When the Shewhart charts are examined, and variation understood, some managers and others may be guilt-ridden for previously celebrating the "ups and downs" of the measures when nothing has changed or reacting inappropriately to special causes. Deming highlighted this issue for leadership: "Help people to pull away from their current practice and beliefs and move into the new philosophy without a feeling of guilt about the past."[26]
- The VOM could be created and updated each month by those responsible, but then not actually used by the leadership team for learning. As a result, special causes on the charts are not investigated, and the charts are not incorporated into other management processes.

Developing an expanded VOM will contribute to a significant transformation of the organization. Leaders should be prepared to address these problems and barriers as they occur.

PREPARING TO USE THE VOM IN THE QOS PLANNING PROCESS

An important use of the organization's vector of measures is in the QOS planning process. The VOM provides a powerful, quantitative focus for priority setting and decision-making, leading to select improvement projects that move the measures to desired goals. Early in the planning process, leaders set priorities for the measures in the vector that should be targeted for improvement. The form in table 6.5 provides a format to review each measure, predict future performance, and make some initial decisions on priorities for improvement. (Chapter 8 describes the use of this information in planning.)

Table 6.5. Analysis of vector of measures for the planning process, with examples and key

Measures of the system	Current level of measure (most recent centerline) value (units)	Stable during last period?	Desired level (target, higher, lower)	Prediction with no changes to current plan (-2, -1, 0, 1, 2)		Priority to improve (H,M,L)
				Next planning period	Future planning period	
1. Customer satisfaction	70%	no	higher	0	1	M
2. Productivity index	83 units	yes	higher	+1	+1	L
Measure 3						
Measure 4						
,,,,,,,,,,,						
Measure K						

Priority for improvement of measure	**Predicted direction in measure (specify time frame for prediction)**

H **Critical** to make improvements in this measure
M Improvements **desirable** in this measure
L **Not important** to make improvements in this measure
	- 2 **very undesirable** impact on measure
	- 1 **undesirable** impact on the measure
	  0 **no change** in this measure
	  1 **some improvement** in this measure
	  2 **significant improvement** in this measure

SUMMARY

Optimizing an organization toward its purpose requires consideration from various perspectives: customers, employees, investors or owners, suppliers, and communities. The concept of a vector of measures provides the mechanism to view the organization from these different perspectives. The VOM provides an assessment of the current performance of the organization as well as a prediction of the organization's future success. While the system map shows how the key processes in the organization interact with each other, the VOM shows how these interactions come together to create the outcomes of the system.

The vector of measures draws together measurements of the organization from the different perspectives of the organization's various stakeholders. The VOM reinforces the system map (from Chapter 5) as a method to see the organization working as a system. Using the vector helps an organization avoid shortsighted focus on single measures of success in favor of a more holistic understanding of the performance of the entire organization. As a result, the impact of changes to the organization can be concurrently studied from the point of view of all stakeholders.

The following are important points for developing the vector of measures for an organization:

- Developing and using the vector of measures can result in a major shift in an organization's focus from treating financial figures as the foundation for measurement to treating them as one of a broader set of measures.
- Investment may be required as an organization learns to measure the nonfinancial dimensions of its system.
- Planning focused on the entire system is necessary to improve the entire vector of measures (for more detail, see Chapter 8).
- The importance of variation in measurements from period to period must be considered in reporting and interpreting the vector of measures. In addition, the use of Shewhart charts for presenting the measures minimizes the costs of overreaction and underreaction.

As the leadership team develops a useful VOM, it should remember important aspects of the organization that are not yet being measured. Deming's admonitions (previously mentioned) of running an organization on visible figures alone should be heeded. As William Bruce Cameron once observed, "Not everything that counts can be counted, and not everything that can be counted, counts."[27] Successful leaders also must consider aspects of the organization that they have not yet learned to measure.

Janice was excited to share her progress in developing a vector of measures for her school. The monthly teachers' meeting provided the opportunity. Janice began, "My intuition told me that I should be learning from multiple measures related to the school's performance. My meetings with the analyst have resulted in a database that includes test results, absenteeism, dropouts, student progression, advanced placement classes, graduation rates, career readiness, teacher satisfaction, and equity for the past three years."

Currently Janice is trying to get all these measures on Shewhart charts that are annotated with the interventions that the school has initiated in the past. She described her expectations to the teachers, saying, "I think this will give us tremendous insights into how the school is performing as a system and where we are heading in the future. I am very curious about the additional insights our leadership team will get from studying this vector of measures, and what new improvement initiatives this learning will lead us to create.

NOTES

1. Accounting and double-entry bookkeeping was invented in 1458 by Benedetto Cotrugli. Today, accounting systems are mandated by law, especially for public corporations. Because of these financial requirements, most organizations have a very sophisticated system to report these mandated measures. For the most part, the same structure does not exist for other measures that are required to manage and operate the system.

2. Chapter 6 of *The QOS Field Guide* includes a summary of the history of the development of the concept of the vector of measures.

3. Shewhart charts and understanding variation were introduced in Chapter 2 as part of the four theories that are the foundation of the Science of Improvement.

4. In Chapter 1, Table 1.5 is a tool for leaders to assess the organization's progress in making quality an organizational strategy. This paragraph is the operational definition for the top score for "Measurement of the system." *The QOS Field Guide* contains a more comprehensive version of the assessment tool.

5. Adapted from figure 3.1 in Joseph M. Juran, *Quality Control Handbook*, 3rd ed. (New York: McGraw-Hill, 1979), 3–11.

6. E.C. Nelson et al., "Improving Health Care, Part 1: The Clinical Value Compass," *Joint Commission Journal on Quality Improvement* 22, no. 4 (1996): 243–58.

7. Eugene C. Nelson et al., "Microsystems in Health Care: Part 1. Learning from High-Performing Front-Line Clinical Units," *The Joint Commission Journal on Quality Improvement* 28, no. 9 (September 2002): 472–93, https://doi.org/10.1016/s1070-3241(02)28051-7.

8. In linear algebra, a vector is a list of number of any length. In aviation, a vector is a course or compass direction for an airplane. As a verb, "vector" can be defined as to guide an object in flight by means of a radio vector. In engineering, vectors represent quantities that have both a magnitude and direction. In public health, a vector is a living organism that transmits infectious diseases between humans or from animal to human.

9. Each of these approaches is described here and illustrated with an example. Additional examples of each approach can be found in Chapter 6 of *The QOS Field Guide*.

10. See table 4.2 "Translation of the CNHS Purpose to System Level Measures," in Maccoby et al., *Transforming Health Care Leadership*, 53.

11. R. Likert, "A Technique for the Measurement of Attitudes," *Archives of Psychology* 22, no. 140 (1932): 55.

12. Deming, *Out of Crisis*, 121.

13. Marilyn Strathern, "'Improving Ratings': Audit in the British University System," *European Review* 5, no. 3 (1997): 305–21. "Goodhart's Law" has been attributed to Charles Goodhart, but others actually interpreted his writings to state the "law": "When a measure becomes a target, it ceases to be a good measure." Our experience is that when a goal or target is connected to a measure, people tend to focus on achieving the goal, potentially causing unintended consequences in the system.

14. See Chapter 8 on planning for more on goal setting.

15. Each of these areas are discussed in detail in Chapter 6 of *The QOS Field Guide*.

16. James Mountford and Doug Wakefield, "From Stoplight Reports to Time Series: Equipping Boards and Leadership Teams to Drive Better Decisions," *BMJ Quality & Safety* 26, no. 1 (January 1, 2017): 9–11, https://doi.org/10.1136/bmjqs-2016-005303.

17. Kelly Ann Schmidtke et al., "Considering Chance in Quality and Safety Performance Measures: An Analysis of Performance Reports by Boards in English NHS Trusts," *BMJ Quality & Safety* 26, no. 1 (January 1, 2017): 61–69, https://doi.org/10.1136/bmjqs-2015-004967.

18. Adapted from figure 13.1, "Tabular VOM Using Green, Yellow, and Red Formatting," in Provost and Murray, *The Health Care Data Guide*, 456.

19. Adapted from figure 4.1 "Using Shewhart Charts to Give Direction to an Improvement Effort," in Provost and Murray, 128.

20. Edward R. Tufte, *The Visual Display of Quantitative Information* (Cheshire, CT: Graphics Press, 1983). For many years, Edward Tufte has led the effort to use visual methods for learning. The ideas here on visual display come from studying Tufte's work.

21. Adapted from figure 13.7 "Appropriate Display of a VOM," in Provost and Murray, *The Health Care Data Guide*, 462.

22. See the section in Chapter 8, "Predict the Impact of Strategic Objectives on the VOM."

23. Vector of measures for Mecklenburg EMS Agency, Charlotte, NC. Former Executive Director Josef Penner (led from 1997–2022) described the relationship and inter-tendencies of processes in the system map through the measures reflected in the organization's vector of measures. Abbreviations are used in the titles of the graphs in this figure; understanding the specific measures is not important in understanding the concept of interdependence of the measures.

24. Jennifer Martin et al., "Board Level 'Picture-Understanding-Action': A New Way of Looking at Quality," *International Journal of Health Governance* 27, no. 1 (January 1, 2021): 105–17, https://doi.org/10.1108/IJHG-05-2021-0047.

25. Roger Quayle (see Foreword) reported that quick wins in the engineering and construction business were financial and safety measures where data was plentiful.

26. Deming, *The New Economics*, 1994, 92–93.

27. William B. Cameron, *Informational Sociology: A Casual Introduction to Sociological Thinking* (New York: Random House, 1967), 13.

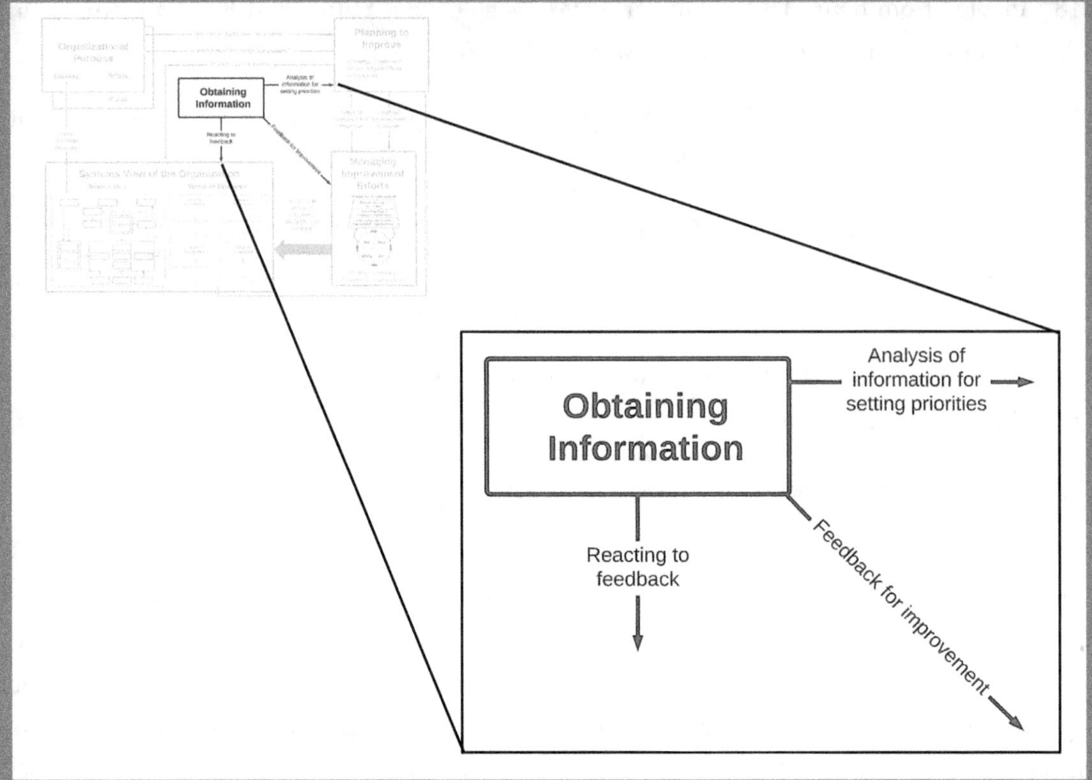

ACTIONS FOR LEADERSHIP TEAM

- Identify the present and future customers of the organization.
- Develop a system to gather information about matching the Need.
- Develop systems to obtain other information relevant to the Need.
- Communicate this information to all parts of the organization.
- Analyze this information to guide planning and improvement efforts.

CHAPTER 7
A SYSTEM FOR OBTAINING INFORMATION

"Craft nonalcoholic beer is fast-growing segment of the beer industry," Kwan explained. "People focused on their health are reducing or eliminating alcohol, but they still enjoy the taste and the socialization associated with get-togethers and bars."

Kwan is the Director of Market Research at a brewing company specializing in craft-brewed nonalcoholic beer. As a startup, the brewery launched with traditional craft beer types and focused on the signature product: Cecelia's NA IPA. There is much competition.

"The founders are starting up the business and concentrating on testing early-stage products.[1] Outside of that, we don't have other ways to learn about the market and customers. Most of our market research comes from the staff's knowledge and passively collected feedback from customers. We mainly react to customers and the market rather than lead it."

Kwan is always trying to learn how the company can differentiate itself from other craft breweries. He knows the organization needs a robust approach for gathering information across varied sources, using the information to redesign existing products, fix problems, improve the system, and inform future planning to continue to be competitive in fulfilling the expectations of its existing and prospective customers.

THE ROLE OF MARKET RESEARCH

Peter Drucker[2] argued that the primary purpose of a business was to create customers. After gaining clarity on the Need they intend to fulfill, organizations required two essential functions to accomplish this:

1. methods to learn the qualities and value that customers want, and
2. improvement and innovation to provide products and services that match the Need.

These methods should not be limited to the marketing function; the whole organization should see through customers' eyes. Management must understand current and potential customers, discover quality relative to the Need the organization intends to fulfill,[3] and innovate to develop products and services that match that Need. When done effectively, sales will happen naturally.

Deming's diagram of "production viewed as a system"[4] includes the Need and purpose of the organization as linked to processes for market research and gathering and using feedback from the organization and its customers. **Market research is a systematic information-gathering process that provides insight into an organization. This research allows leaders to make informed decisions for matching products and services to the need(s) the organization intends to fulfill.**

The system to obtain information from all organization stakeholders provides methods to improve existing products and services and to develop the products and services needed in the future. Deming often referred to this as "constancy of purpose" to stay in business.[5] This information is mapped to the organization's processes, products, and services, creating a system whereby the information can be retrieved and knowledge produced that can be used to react to problems, guide improvement efforts, and support the system for planning.

In a mature organization, the system to gather information is used by leaders to proactively manage customer information. Information is integrated and used to define quality and position products and services in the marketplace. Active processes to obtain strategic information coordinate with the organization's planning processes. The system for obtaining information is fully deployed, integrates information from all stakeholders, and is regularly improved and enhanced.[6] This chapter describes a method for leaders to develop a system to obtain information.

THE OBJECTIVE OF THE SYSTEM TO OBTAIN INFORMATION

One of the most strategic uses of information is to define quality relative to the Need the organization wishes to fulfill. This "need" provides the focus for developing and improving products or services today and in the future. Customer feedback can help define the characteristics of products and services that better match the need. More often, people with knowledge of the product and service are in a better position to learn and improve while observing how and why the customer uses the product or service. For example, Toyota encourages engineers and managers to spend time in Toyota dealerships observing and listening to customers to help improve future car design and development.[7]

In a competitive market, sources of information and knowledge are required to continuously improve through the five essential ways described in Chapter 1:

1. Design a new product or service.
2. Redesign an existing product or service.
3. Design a new process.
4. Redesign an existing process.
5. Improve the system as a whole.

These efforts are essential to earn new customers and maintain existing customers. Someone is always trying to provide a better match to the Need that drives customers to your organization. All products and services, even those viewed as "commodities," can be differentiated. For example, bottled water has been differentiated, and customers now pay more for bottled water than gasoline.

An organization's success and sustainability depend on attracting and keeping customers. Thus, marketing functions play a crucial role. Theodore Levitt frames this view as a "customer-satisfying process":

> Not a goods-producing process…an industry begins with the customer and his or her needs…Given the customer [expectations],[8] the industry develops backward, first concerning itself with the physical *delivery* of customer satisfaction. Then it moves back further to *creating* the things by which these satisfactions are in part achieved…[9] the entire organization must be viewed as a customer-creating and customer-satisfying organism.

LEARNING CUSTOMER DEFINITIONS OF QUALITY

Defining quality for different customer groups requires developing a list of quality characteristics that relate to each of the applicable dimensions of quality.[10] A list can be applied for a current product or service or one to design in the future. The dimensions of quality should serve as a benchmark for developing a list of key quality characteristics to compare how an organization competes in the marketplace.

What does it mean to segment the market? Segmentation involves considering your products and service through factors such as geographic location, the type of industry, and price sensitivity. For example, does your organization only serve a metropolitan area, state, nationwide, or worldwide? Is it dedicated to a targeted industry like education, or construction, or does it serve many sectors? Is it serving individuals or the business-to-business (B2B) market? How does this influence the pricing strategy? One useful segmentation is existing customers versus customers that buy from competitor organizations. The marketing function should take the lead in developing these segments.

With clarity on the segments in the market, the dimensions of quality offer a method to learn how different customers define quality. Figuring out the dimensions that matter most to key segments of the desired market aids in focusing on doing the important things well. The dimensions of quality provide a framework to focus improvement efforts and direct the advertising and selling processes.[11]

For example, imagine a grocery store company surveys its customers who were members of their shoppers' club for input on what mattered, the quality characteristics they think are most important. Table 7.1 shows the responses ranked by what was most important. Also noted is the quality dimension for which each customer response is associated.

Table 7.1. Shopper quality characteristics and dimension of quality

Customer's quality characteristics	Dimension of quality (#)
"Store is clean"	Aesthetics (9)
"Clearly labeled prices," "freshness dates"	Features (2)
"Friendly clerks"	Personal interface (10)
"Accurate checkout"	Consistency (7)
"Wait at Deli and Seafood"	Time (3)
"Have products I want"	Performance (1)

This list is a good starting point for the grocery company to target improvement efforts in current stores and to use them in innovating new products and services to meet the Need to buy groceries and other supplies. How do we collect this type of information? One method a store used was at checkout. The clerks at the checkout register invited customers to complete a feedback form on a tablet while waiting for their groceries to be scanned and bagged. The feedback form asked for open feedback about their shopping experience. Figure 7.1 includes two Pareto charts with the comments sorted as positive or negative and coded using the dimensions of quality.

The "personal interface" with staff is the most important dimension of quality for current customers at the grocery store. They value that staff make them feel welcome in the store and talk with them in a friendly and familiar manner when asking for help with finding an item. "Consistency," "serviceability," and "reliability" are dimensions to focus the improvement and innovation efforts. Customers perceive that sometimes they can get through checkout smoothly and other times there are lines of carts waiting. "Durability" is not a dimension for customers of the grocery store.

While the marketing functions in an organization will lead the efforts to understand the different customer segments and definitions of quality, all staff can be involved in information gathering through their various interactions with customers.

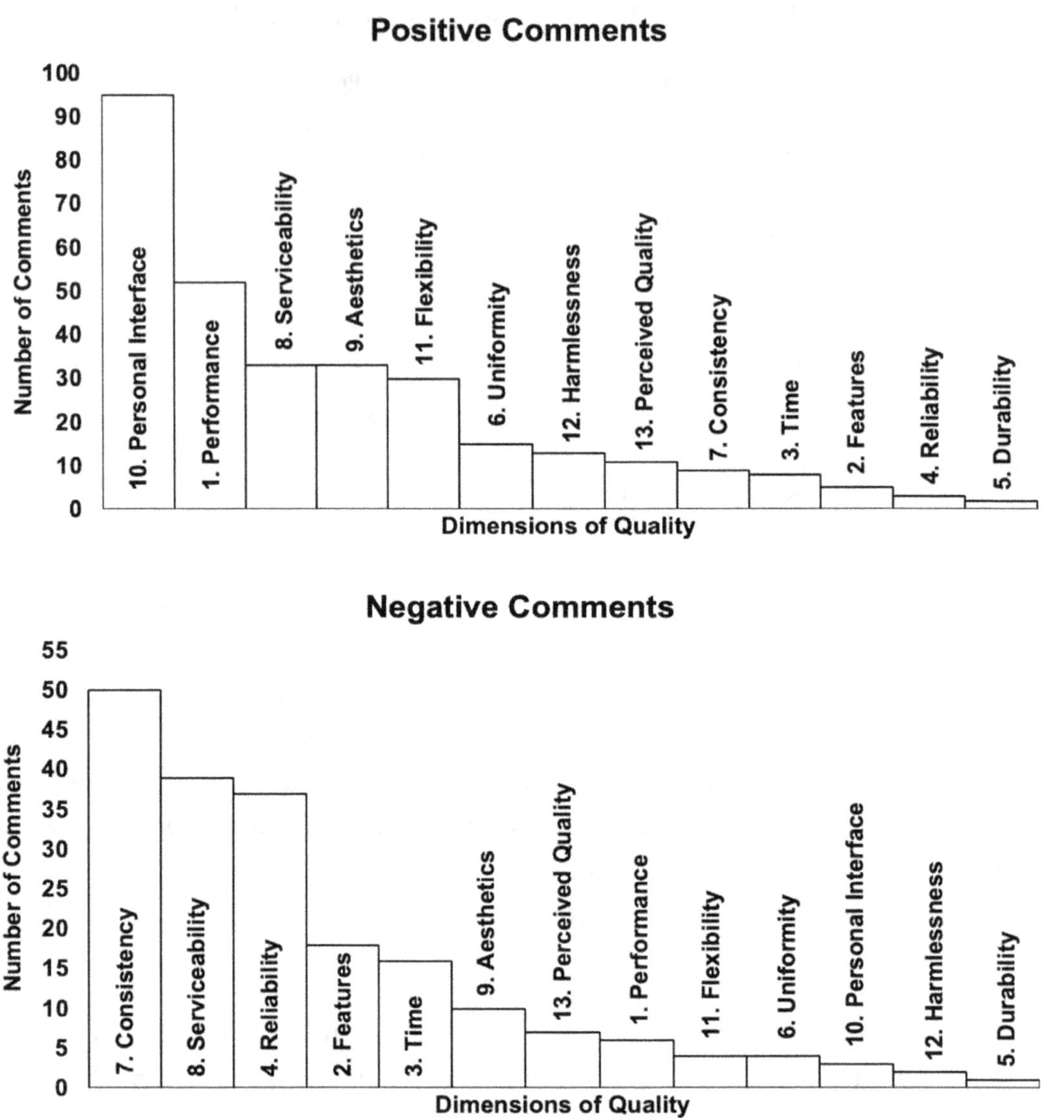

Figure 7.1. Pareto charts summarizing customer feedback coded using dimensions of quality.

LEADING AND LISTENING TO THE CUSTOMER

Pause for a minute and think about organizations which provide exceptional products and services. What organizations consistently meet your expectations and deliver services with reliability? When traveling, perhaps you remembered Southwest Airlines for its ability to board a plane and leave on time with 15-minute turnaround times. Or perhaps you thought of Amazon for delivering the next bestseller to your doorstep in twenty-four hours, or of the Starbucks barista preparing your unique coffee drink.

The examples we choose frequently reflect key quality characteristics like on-time delivery, error-free performance, and the experience that exceeded our expectations. How these organizations provide service is creative, innovative, and novel. These companies do more than deliver what customers ask for; they offer superior service and creative innovations. They continually learn and improve, and so we return as customers and remain loyal.

Organizations pursuing quality as an organizational strategy are clear on the Need they fulfill and continuously pursue learning about how the market and their customers expect to match that Need. Companies strive to deeply understand what is known to support matching the need. Deming observed:

> A good question for anybody in business to ask is "What business are we in? To do well, what we are doing, i.e., to turn out a good product, or good service, whatever it be? Yes, of course, but this is not enough. We must keep asking "What product or service would help our customers more?" We must think about the future. What will we be making five years from now? Ten years from now?[12]

What happens if a company focuses on the current products and services rather than making improvements and innovations relative to the Need in society for the future? In 1967, the K&E Slide Rule[13] company developed a forecast of the future to the year 2067. The report predicted modern domed cities, 3-D television, and computer-aided traffic lanes. What did K&E not predict? Texas Instruments' invention of the handheld electronic calculator in 1967, the replacement for their product.[14] Perhaps if K&E had defined their business in terms of the Need they were satisfying (i.e., handheld calculation), they might have been researching emerging technologies that could replace their current offering.

Need-driven organizations look to the future to provide a better match relative to the existing products and services in the marketplace. Handscombe and Norman[15] describe the knowledge relevant to matching the Need in the context of the available knowledge, what is known by the provider of product or service, and what is known by the customer. How organizations position themselves in relation to the available knowledge and customers has implications. Figure 7.2 presents two potential scenarios to consider:[16]

- **Scenario 1**: The customer is most knowledgeable.
- **Scenario 2**: Provider of product or service (i.e., the organization) is most knowledgeable.

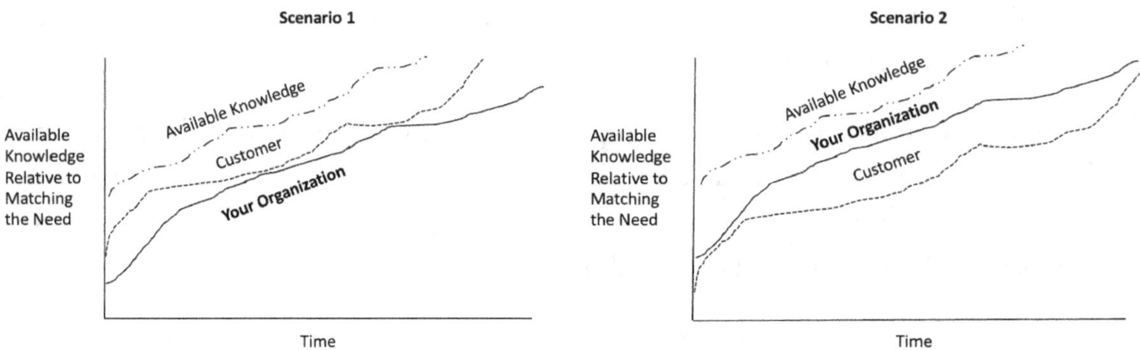

Figure 7.2. Knowledge relevant to matching the need.

Available knowledge, for any particular need, is information that exists in the world about that need: in industry think tanks, university research, on a factory floor in Singapore, or advances in research and development in a business area or industry. Production of new knowledge is growing or evolving all the time. However, technology frequently lags behind the knowledge of what is possible. For example, widespread high-speed internet access is known to be possible, but the actual ability to deliver lags behind the knowledge that it is possible.

There is "available knowledge" for new ways to match the Need in both scenarios. Where does your organization sit in relation to the knowledge relevant to matching the need?

Some organizations operate in **Scenario 1,** where the customer is more knowledgeable than or equally knowledgeable about the Need than those providing products or services. In this scenario, the customer does not look to the organization to lead them; instead, the organization is a service provider or "contract labor." For example, a hospital knows it wants staff to learn about patient safety and hires a company to train and implement the approach. The hospital's patient safety officer knows the current literature and standard approaches and contracts with a service provider to deliver training on this content. The service provider, then, must pay attention to the customer's ask and match the services offered to the customer's request.

In organizations where quality is the strategy, **Scenario 2** is more usual. The organizations providing service are experts in the field and deeply aware of the current state of the available knowledge and how to match the Need. For example, a community wishes to reduce the number of people experiencing homelessness. Leaders have tried several strategies locally, but they are not aware of success in other communities. The community engages a consulting group experienced in helping communities lower their homelessness rate. The group has studied methods, tested strategies, and achieved results in varied settings. In this case, customers look to the service provider to help them match the need. They are looking to the supplier for both the products and services and their subject matter expertise.[17] This goes beyond just meeting customer demand or requirements and is the responsibility of the supplier interested in matching the future expectations of the customer.

Organizations may operate in either scenario depending on the product they buy, or the services customers hire it to provide. An organization with quality as their strategy continually gathers information to appreciate the Need they are trying to fulfill, and use that information effectively to serve their customers, by redesigning products and services to better match the Need.

Kwan and his team all came from craft brewing backgrounds and consider themselves experts:

> We knew what we were doing in making the product, but we noticed our customers were telling us about new brewers and products in the market. They were looking for us in local places they frequented, and they were asking for products and services other breweries had rolled out. One brewer offered a mail order subscription to their pilot program, and another was developing relationships with fitness organizations to position their product at the finish line for local 5Ks and half marathons.

Kwan wanted to understand the market at a deeper level and have an approach that put his company in a position to better understand the Need for nonalcoholic craft beer and to develop products and services that were the best at matching that Need.

THREE LEVELS OF INFORMATION GATHERING

Figure 7.3 presents three levels of information gathering[18] that can be described in organizations:

1. **Problem-solving**: learning from "fires"
2. **Current matching**: operational intelligence
3. **Future matching**: strategic intelligence

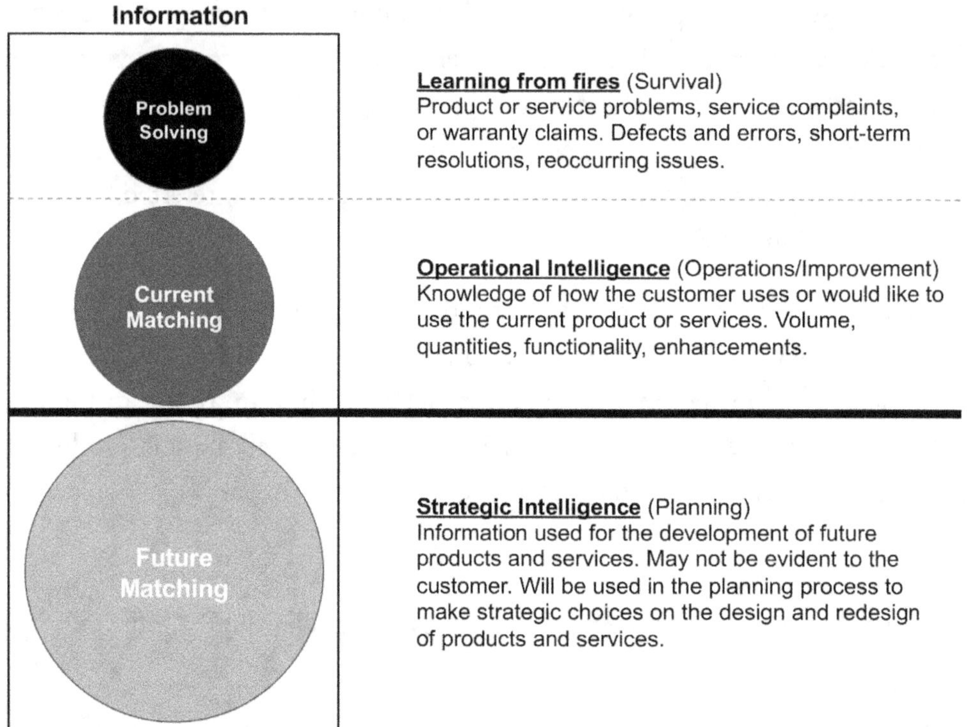

Figure 7.3. Three levels of information.

The first level, **problem-solving**, is familiar to organizations that depend on customer feedback from product problems, online reviews, service complaints, or warranty claims. The prerequisite for this type of information is often an unhappy customer. For example, a customer is trying to assemble a new piece of furniture but discovers a missing piece. They call the customer service line to complain and request the part replacement. This information is critical to allow immediate mitigation (service recovery) to resolve the issue in real-time. But the information is also helpful to a specific process in the organizational system to support making fixes that reduce or eliminate this type of mistake.

Both current and future matching require knowledge of how the customer uses or wants to use the current product or service. This information is sometimes called customer research. **Current matching** is information that supports understanding the current system and the related products and services. It provides feedback on the performance of existing processes or provides meaningful learning to improvement teams working on redesigning processes to enhance performance. For example, customer surveys completed at the end of a service experience give insight into the customer's satisfaction and their reflections on attributes that contributed to or hindered their rating. Whether this information is positive or negative, it provides feedback on the current matching of products and services to the Need.

Future matching is the strategic level of information gathered from research, observation, and listening to customers. It is a proactive approach as opposed to passively waiting for complaints. This information is used to develop future products or services, the match for which may not yet be evident to the customer. For example, a university professor's research published in a management journal notes that organizations increasingly depend on distributed teams that blend internal staff with contractors and partners collaborating virtually. Future matching information is used in planning to determine strategic choices of products and services for future development.

The three levels of information support fixing problems, confirming present quality, and planning for design and redesign into the future. Many organizations collect information at the problems-solving level and information supporting current matching. Handscombe and Norman[19] argue that tomorrow's organizations require "deeper insights" through strategic intelligence gathering to continually improve to match the Need the organization intends to fulfill.

A SYSTEM FOR GATHERING INFORMATION

Organizations collect information in varied ways, in active and passive modes. Organizing the current sources of information, assessing gaps, and creating the needed sources to complete a more holistic system are basic elements of making any Quality Organizational Strategy (QOS). Unfortunately, information sources required to learn about current matching and future matching may not be readily available. Therefore, we must seek out these sources.

Figure 7.4 shows a linkage of sources that form a system of information to support a quest to learn about customers and better match the Need an organization aims to fulfill. A system of gathering information is a core method of QOS. A system must proactively search out, collect, process, and use diverse knowledge to improve. Identifying the sources and methods aids in actively gathering the information that matters and supports acting appropriately, whether that is reacting to service failures, identifying improvement projects, or serving as an input into planning.

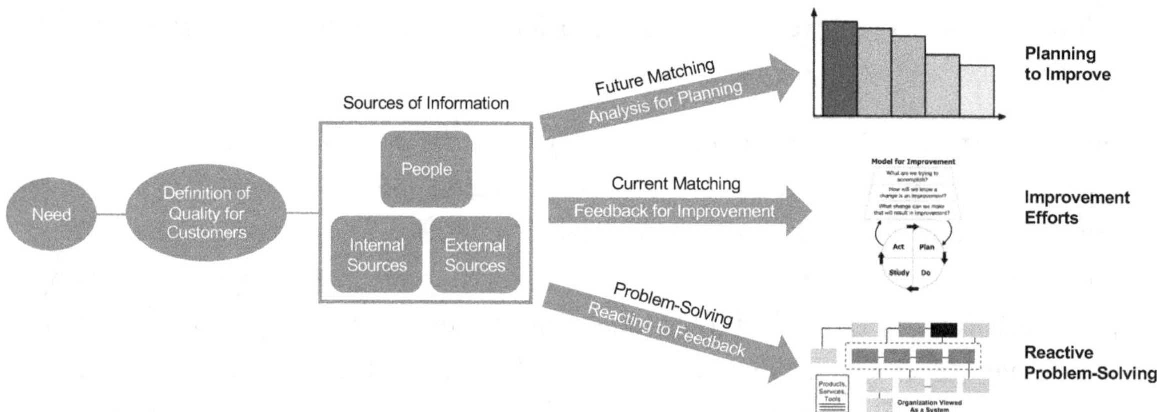

Figure 7.4. System for gathering information.

SOURCES OF INFORMATION

Sources of information include people, internal sources, and external sources. **People sources** include customers, suppliers, and staff. Each stakeholder has some working knowledge of the organization and its products and services. Through people, we can listen and learn and further develop relationships in the process. Inquiry is often an active process. **Internal sources** include customer relationship management data, feedback rating systems, and error or defect reporting. These systems capture data about usage, interaction, reporting, and evaluation of existing operations. **External sources** include scanning the environment for research and opinion reports, trade and peer-reviewed publications, and emerging technology. It also can involve benchmarking best practices within or outside one sector or industry. These sources of information and the methods for gathering information are discussed below.

Data from all sources are collected, captured, and stored to support action. Acting on the information can be immediate, such as reacting to process problems that must be fixed right now, or more long-term, such as information that will help annual planning for improvement. The system must describe the information to capture, document, and relate it to the organization. The remainder of this chapter describes the sources of information and how to convert this information into actionable data.

Obtaining Information from People and Maintaining Relationships

Whenever we are actively obtaining information from people, we need to consider both gathering the information we need and maintaining a relationship with the person(s) providing the information.

The **primary purpose** of obtaining information is to build the **knowledge** of those wishing to gather and use the information. How can we learn about our customers and see if what we are doing or thinking adds value? For example, a food delivery service knows recycling is essential to customers and wants to change its packaging to something easier to stack in the delivery trucks and create less waste. It intends to gauge the appeal of the new packaging from customers. A school system knows proper sleep is vital for teenagers to learn and wishes to change start times for its high schools. Administrators want to learn how this change will affect parents who drop their kids off on their way to work.

The **second purpose** is to create and maintain a valuable **relationship** between the organization benefiting from gathering and learning from the information and the customers or users providing the information from their experience. This effect may extend to the stakeholder groups represented by the people participating in exchanging information.

For example, a designer from an education software company shadows a teacher for a day to learn how he uses the product to teach a class of tenth-grade math students, observing the teacher using the product, asking questions, and seeing how features work in practice creates instant real-world learning. In addition, being present in the classroom, watching the teacher working, and being curious to understand his experience and feedback builds respect and confidence in the product.

Types of People Who Supply Information

Several types of people (stakeholders) serve as crucial sources of information: customers, suppliers, partners, and staff. Each engages with the organizational system from a different perspective and has unique experience and knowledge. What can they tell us that can improve quality? What types of information can they uniquely provide? What is the impact on the relationship that results when we obtain this information?

INFORMATION FROM CUSTOMERS

Customers are an obvious source of information. These are the people the organization exists to serve and include both people currently using your products and service and potential or future customers. Understanding our customers and what matters to them is essential information for improvement.

Customers (both existing and those buying from competitors) can provide details about specific requirements that make products and services fit for their use. For example, a nonprofit philanthropic organization wishes to upgrade its information technology and evaluates your products. Their employees are based at multiple locations working on different operating systems and require all software solutions to be Cloud-based.

Customers may also share a missing element to help better match the need. For example, patients will describe the multiple patient portal accounts they navigate to interact with their primary care doctor, neighborhood pharmacy, the lab, and a handful of specialists. Still, these patients cannot access all their health information through one source.

Customers can tell us their future challenges and requirements relative to the current matching products and services. For example, a corporate training company sees a shift from in-person training to a mixed-method or all-virtual approach and wants help to deliver similar or better results and experiences.

When considering a product or service change, customers can help to gauge the impact of the change. For example, a government client shares that changing a pricing approach from a single fixed cost to a user license approach would greatly reduce the number of teachers in the school system who use the product.

Customers using a competing product or service may explain how a new or redesigned offering could entice them to switch. For example, an internet service provider learns customers like to use their personal Wi-Fi equipment and to avoid paying extra fees. This insight leads to redesigning that service to support customers in integrating their preferred equipment.

And finally, customers are vital sources of learning about potential improvements. They can share when something did not work as intended or is misaligned with how work gets done. For example, a teacher shares a recurring problem with students getting overwhelmed with homework because their teachers have no method to see if other teachers have assigned similar due dates.

When organizations engage with their customers and learn from them, there are many positive effects. First, they build a partnership that says, "We are in this together." Second, providers build trust that can foster loyalty and increase customers' willingness to use a product or service in the future. Finally, sincere efforts to gather information from customers and act on it can positively affect the relationship with a provider. Leaders should use caution as well. Asking for feedback from every customer encounter can feel like a burden or as though the collection is not purposeful.

INFORMATION FROM SUPPLIERS

Suppliers are critical partners in fulfilling customer requirements. Deming advocated building a long-term relationship with suppliers based on loyalty and trust.[20] Suppliers may provide materials (such as a lumber company serving a home builder), software (such as a project management platform), or a consulting or training service. Suppliers hold unique information about the products and services they provide, how a company is or is not using them to the fullest, and how other organizations may be using those services.

Suppliers can also share what their key characteristics are for quality. Suppliers are technical experts in their areas, so they can advise customers on use of their products and services. For example, a software company that draws on data from many sources may know the ins and outs of linking and using data from different systems or tips for alternative ways to get the desired results.

Suppliers may see improvement opportunities to better match customers' needs. For example, a third-party cable installer sees an opportunity to be flexible when conditions change (e.g., working from home or adding a television to the guest room). Suppliers can also be valuable contributors when designing or redesigning a product or service and show opportunities for growing the business. Finally, they can suggest how to create a long-term partnership that evolves from the typical transactional relationship at the procurement stage.

When engaging with suppliers, work toward building a partnership. This engagement can be the foundation for developing a single, long-term source for the products and services they supply. It also might formally motivate them to adopt quality as their strategy.

INFORMATION FROM WORKERS

Employees throughout an organization have a deep understanding of how current processes work. In addition, workers at the point of service have a unique position to observe customers using the existing products and services. For example, the school college counselor knows what it is like for twelfth graders to schedule their college tests, gather academic data, and ask for teacher recommendations. She knows what it takes to guide a student through the process.

Staff experience when and how processes work well, or not, or what it takes to work around issues. For example, a call center worker regularly serves customers unable to order online because the address field rules don't recognize special characters that can occur in mailing addresses. Staff may see processes with varied performance and have specific ideas for what needs to be improved. For example, staff at a self-service restaurant noticed new customers took longer to serve and created a process for a more positive first experience. Quickly identifying a new customer, making team members aware, and redirecting returning customers to another line helped create a good experience for all.[21]

Finally, there is nothing worse than having barriers to doing great work. Staff can share what barriers hinder their work and take the joy out of it. Workers are the subject matter experts in doing the work and serving customers. Actively looking for and listening to their experience and ideas shows their input is valued. When surfacing improvement opportunities becomes the norm, fear of making a mistake or not delivering the best product or service is nothing to worry about, because the culture shifts to learning and building trust. With a focus on creating and continually improving the system, workers move toward a "we"[22] orientation and work together as a team. Finally, creating a culture and processes to learn from and act on worker knowledge demonstrates an openness to change and a relentless focus on improvement for customers.

Customers, suppliers, and workers are vital sources of information. They provide unique insights that support improvement, and learning with them creates a relationship and a positive effect. Organizations need a system to collect and learn from this information.

Kwan reflected on his learning about gathering information. "We considered ourselves customer-centered, so it made sense that they are a key source of information on our products and services. When I started assessing how we learned with them, it was an eye-opener to see we were undervaluing the learning, and the strong relationship that emerges when they see that their input matters. You're not just firing off a survey because it's easy. You actually use their input."

Kwan gained a new appreciation of the importance of the brewery's staff and suppliers as critical sources. "The head of our shipping and distribution learned from stores that packaging was causing issues on store shelves. Customers liked companies that matched the look of traditional craft beer cans. They also needed labeling that clearly showed it was a nonalcoholic product without it being overly distinguishable."

Insights were captured and became inputs to planning for redesigning existing branding and influenced all future labeling.

METHODS FOR GATHERING INFORMATION

There are many methods for gathering information from people and other internal and external sources. Table 7.2 lists the methods by source discussed here.

Table 7.2. Methods for gathering information by source

People sources	Surveys Personal interviews Focus groups Observations Trading places
Internal sources	Customer relationship management Purchasing and Accounts Receivable Compliments, complaints, and feedback Web analytics Defect and bug tracking
External sources	Papers, publications, and conferences Internet Technology Benchmarking Consultant and external assessments

Methods for Learning from People

There are a variety of methods to gather information from people. **An informal conversation** where people discuss how they can better contribute is a common approach and is very important. The important thing is to have a system to easily document the learning and insights from these conversations. There are also more formal methods that gather information in a structured way, including surveys, personal interviews, group interviews, observing, and trading places.

SURVEYS

Surveys are questionnaires using crafted questions and asking for responses through different approaches like Likert scales,[23] multiple-choice, and open-ended questions. Surveying is easier than ever to use with Web-based platforms and email distribution. With surveys, one can efficiently reach a broad group of customers.

Today, nearly every purchase is followed by a brief survey by email or text message asking customers to rate their experience. It includes a few targeted questions or offers an open space for sharing any feedback specific to the service encounter. These surveys are a frequent source of data to help identify real-time issues and provide an ongoing channel for obtaining just-in-time feedback.

Surveys benefit respondents who prefer a written communication style. Software services can track respondents or maintain anonymity. Surveys can be a low-cost method for reaching many people across your service area if you have an established distribution list.

Surveys are not without issue. Frequent pitfalls include poor question design, sampling issues, biased data collection, inadequate analysis, and inappropriate report formats.[24] People receive many requests for input via surveys, which may dampen response rates. (Eventually they realize who is doing all the work in this interaction.) Surveys do not allow for easy follow-up to clarify or learn more about the information. Resources are available to support good survey design.[25]

PERSONAL INTERVIEWS

Individual or personal interviews are a powerful method for learning deeply together. The conversation is guided by a predefined set of questions about a topic and structured or semi-structured to allow more fluid dialogue. Personal interviews offer a deeper conversation, and follow-up questions can aid in understanding and clarifying meaning. Personal interviews may occur in person, over the telephone, or via video conference. Seeing someone enables the interviewer to note the person's body language as added feedback. Empathy interviews are a strategy using open-ended questions to elicit stories and feelings about specific experiences that help to uncover unacknowledged needs. In-person interviews require more logistical consideration and can feel more personal or intimate.

FOCUS GROUPS

Focus groups share many attributes of individual interviews but add more people to the conversation. Focus groups are common in political campaigns and marketing projections to learn from a sample of people about their impressions or opinions. The group dynamic can add learning as people are stimulated by each other and may build on others' thoughts or think about their own experiences differently. When one person shares, others might agree or not and then explore variations in their experience. While a focus group may add to the learning across participants, it may also reduce sharing or create groupthink. Individuals may not feel as open to sharing their personal feelings or experience in the same way they would alone, especially if they perceive they hold a minority view in the group. Focus groups can be in-person or virtual. Like individual interviews, being in person may offer more unspoken feedback and intimacy. Focus groups require a more skilled facilitator.

OBSERVATIONS

A key method grounded in anthropology is direct observation, watching people, and seeing what happens. How do they act, what do they focus on, what order do they do things, what do they have trouble doing, and what are they working around? This information is often best learned by seeing people use actual products and services. Observation can occur in planned simulations or the real world. Watching real-world behavior is a more accurate reflection of the authentic experience (see "Web analytics" in the following section). Through direct observation, one may discover ideas for innovation and improvement not found by asking the customer or analyzing data. For example, no customer ever asked for a microwave oven. This innovation came from people with subject matter knowledge to reduce the time for people to cook food.

TRADING PLACES

This is another method that, like observation, puts us into the process itself. Here we trade places with a customer, supplier, or a worker to have a firsthand experience. Want to see what it is like to be a patient? Serve as a test patient or "secret shopper"[26] and go through the process. Want to learn what a registration clerk's work process is like? Try to register a new patient and do the process yourself. Again, being in someone else's shoes and trying the process can generate practical learning and make the issues in the current approach evident and real.

Each of these methods for obtaining information from people has some advantages and disadvantages. No one way is best for all applications. First, make sure you are learning from the information from internal systems (as presented in the following section). Then consider several proactive methods together to gain the most learning and information. For example, a group interview may confirm the results of a study based on observations or trading places. The most important strategy for obtaining customer information is an active, mixed-method approach. Carefully review the purpose of gathering the information before selecting the method in any circumstance. And finally, remember to be aware of how the method affects the respondent.

Methods for Learning from Internal Systems

Organizations track information internally via many sources. Internal sources are often created for specific purposes and together may provide input to mitigate problems and to plan for improvement. Internal sources include customer relations management, purchasing or accounts receivables, post-service feedback, compliments and complaints, web analytics, and issue tracking.

CUSTOMER RELATIONSHIP MANAGEMENT (CRM)

Customer relationship management (CRM) systems are robust platforms to capture and track customers and the sales pipeline and process. For example, a customer makes an online purchase and creates a unique login. The process collects particulars to support segmenting the customer into categories like age, occupation, or education. In addition, CRM platforms collect customer information, help qualify their match to your products and services, and track customers' behavior over time. These data can be invaluable for segmenting customers, understanding the sources of how customers found your company, and providing data to learn purchasing patterns.

PURCHASING AND ACCOUNTS RECEIVABLE

Information from accounts receivable on customer purchasing provides insight into patterns, including what was purchased, how frequently, the volume, and the relationships between products and services. These details may help companies understand the demand for a product or service, and it can raise questions about how they are fulfilling the need. For example, a lawn maintenance company notes customers with mowing services may also purchase the seeding and treatment services. In addition, these data may lead to learning more about segments of customers or lead to focused communication to highlight bundled services.

SYSTEM FOR DOCUMENTING COMPLIMENTS, COMPLAINTS, OBSERVATION, AND FEEDBACK

All compliments, complaints, observations, and feedback should be captured and stored for analysis and use. Figure 7.5 is an example of a form and structure for capturing this information.[27]

What was said, **feedback (F)**, or what was **observed (O)**.	**Comments by staff receiving** to add further detail	**Immediate feedback:** (action to take **now**) By whom?	**Long-term feedback:** (Potential new design or redesign) Use process and product numbers from systems map.
1. (F or O) Observation—*Customers are having problems installing the new software packages.*	1. *This is a design flaw. The customers believes they can fix it by training.*	1. *We need to gather up the various observations and feedback and share with software development.*	Process(es): 18 Product(s): *Software package* System:
2. (F or O) Feedback—*Customer was very pleased with the prompt delivery!*	1. *Improvements to process #21 appear to be working.*	1. *Give feedback to the team working to develop process #21.*	Process(es): 21 Product(s): System:

Figure 7.5. Customer feedback, observation, and research form.

WEB ANALYTICS

An organization's website is a virtual presence and strongest business card. Websites can track powerful analytics on the locations of people who visit the site, the places they viewed, how much time they spent on a content page, and where they were just before submitting a contact form or purchase. These data are essential in learning about the traffic to a website, how people interact with the content, and the pathway to engagement. Web analytics is an electronic version of observation.

DEFECT OR BUG TRACKING SYSTEM

Many organizations have a tracking system to capture defects or bugs. For example, Apple uses an in-house bug tracking system known as Radar.[28] Developers and engineers document bugs or issues upon discovery and capture the details. These data support improvements that we see in periodic software updates or hardware upgrades. The organization's internal tech support uses a help ticket system to process employee IT issues. These data drive reacting to a problem requiring intervention or serve future planning decisions to shift to another hardware or software.

These are a few sources of information gathering in organizations that regularly collect valuable information about product and service quality and how the organization is fulfilling the need. What are additional sources that exist in your organization?

Methods for Gathering Information from External Sources

Many sources of learning in the world can complement what we learn from people directly involved with an organization or from the systems within the walls of a workplace. These may be within the industry, similar industries, or other areas. Therefore, organizations must consider what additional external sources are valuable to learn from and create processes to gather this information.

Collection of this information may be the responsibility of delegated groups such as research and development or marketing, or leaders with subject matter expertise within the organization might share the role. Many organizations are laissez-faire in their approach to collecting and organizing these data. Organizations pursuing QOS are active collectors who proactively identify sources, decide on collection methods, and have an approach to collecting and organizing the findings to inform planning. The foresight of leaders often comes from paying attention to these sources of information.[29] Like the vector of measures, where multiple measures tell a story, multiple sources of information when studied together enable foresight.

PAPERS, PUBLICATIONS, AND CONFERENCES

Scholars and practitioners share new learning and research in blog posts, trade publications, peer-reviewed journals, and annual conference presentations. This new knowledge may be specific to an industry or generalized across industries, including opinions, summaries of field learning, or the result of more structured research projects. They may add knowledge to existing ideas and practices, offer insight on adaptations, or introduce innovative new ideas. Unfortunately, the volume of new knowledge[30] can be overwhelming, and staying up-to-date on all of what is known is practically impossible.

Identifying a sample of key sources to monitor regularly can help narrow the focus to a manageable level. Sources may include core industry journals, leading thinkers, or organization publications that curate knowledge for their users. Scanning trusted sources helps keep a finger on the pulse of current thinking. An included Web link or a referenced source can serve as a path to additional learning and expanding one's circle of exposure. Information gleaned from these efforts must also be organized and analyzed for future planning.

INTERNET

The amount of information on the internet can be overwhelming. As a result, many companies focus on the following approaches:

- Regularly search your own company, products and services, and key staff using search engines. Search engines are how many organizations learn about you and can make first impressions. Using varied search terms and going several pages deep in the search results will show what other searchers see.
- Social media sites are prevalent forms of communication and connection. People regularly share their experiences and opinions on these platforms, which many existing or potential customers can view. Organizations must have a method to monitor mentions and be ready to respond if an issue requires mitigation.
- External feedback and reviews occur in a variety of venues. For example, many publications review products and services, and individual customers also can share their experiences and ratings on organizations or service providers through independent websites. These can be glowing endorsements or stories about unfortunate failures.
- An organization can appear in news articles, blog posts, and press releases. In addition, services exist to look for mentions of your organization and its products and services, and key terms and summaries are aggregated and delivered to your inbox.

The internet is often the first stop to learn about an organization. A website is the company's opportunity to frame the organization for the customer, and data from analytics can help to understand how customers interact with that content. Information also exists on how others mention, review, or give feedback on the organization. Again, these data cannot be controlled but offer an opportunity to learn and engage to mitigate if needed. Again, as well as reacting to timely insights, some type of system is needed to capture learning and analyze it for decision-making and future planning.

TECHNOLOGY

In the 1970s, Gordon Moore predicted that the capacity of transistors on a computer chip would double every two years.[31] What became known as "Moore's Law" has meant unbelievable technological progress and is expected to continue. Technology in today's global economy advances rapidly with the aid of innovations in information technology and sharing. Artificial intelligence (AI) is currently a technology creating lots of interest in all industries. Organizations must be aware of the various processes that are vital to information inputs concerning emerging technology. These processes are both internal and external to most organizations. Some of these processes already exist, and some require development.

BENCHMARKING

Benchmarking is one method for learning from others. Lateral and best practice benchmarking are two common forms used by organizations. Lateral benchmarking may be a "blind" or a transparent process. A standard scorecard of measures and data aggregated to a quarterly or annual average compares organizations. Lateral benchmarking may help identify organizations performing at a higher level. Once the comparison is made, attention shifts to either best practice benchmarking of an organization with desirable results or focusing on planning for design or redesign.

Best practice benchmarking is a process of structured learning. It is more than simply studying a best practice and attempting to copy it. When organizations benchmark best practices, they identify a process to learn more about and use a method to learn. For example, a food bank wants to learn how to improve its drive-up distribution process flow. They may look to an airline's boarding process or a restaurant's drive-through for inspiration and learning. Organizations can use the Model for Improvement to use a structured approach for benchmarking that increases learning.[32]

CONSULTANTS AND EXTERNAL ASSESSMENTS

Organizations engage external consultants to access information or expert services that it does not possess internally or to assesses specific practices or the organization as a whole.[33] This includes site visits from accreditation bodies and quality award examiners. The external consultant or reviewers summarize the findings in a written report with observations, analysis, and recommendations.

ANALYZING RESEARCH AND FEEDBACK INFORMATION

Most organizations gather information throughout the year, share the information with responsible staff, and act based on problems or opportunities identified. But then what happens to the information? Often data is discarded or filed away with no method to use it later to learn from and improve the system. To retrieve this information when needed requires a way to gather, store, retrieve, analyze, and summarize the information for use.

Figure 7.6 is an overview of a system to capture information for use from customer feedback, research, observations, or informal conversations. The process begins with a formal method, using mechanisms such as dedicated email, a Web-based form, or an app on a mobile device. Staff must include clear and specific details on what they learned; examples can be helpful.[34] Next, the information is tagged with the process or product number from the organizational system's linkage of processes and stored for use.

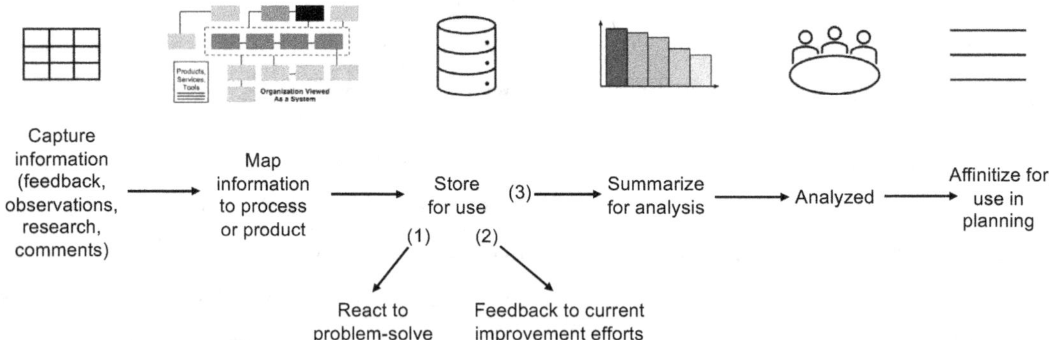

Figure 7.6. System for processing customer feedback and resources.

The tagged information supports one of three actions:[35]

1. **React to problem solve.** Every organization has customer experiences that do not go as designed. Staff will see process issues requiring attention. When receiving information requiring immediate attention, the team responsible for the product or process needs to know. The recorded details aid in investigating and fixing the problem to reduce the issue affecting others in the future. This action is often called service recovery or mitigation.

2. **Feedback to current improvement efforts.** QOS organizations will have a portfolio of chartered improvement projects in progress. When projects are strategically selected, it is common for information to be relevant to the process or product of focus in the improvement teams. As information is gathered from sources, tagged to the appropriate product or process, and stored in the system, it is forwarded to the team leading the improvement efforts.

3. Summarize for analysis for future planning.[36] Stored data is periodically reviewed, categorized, and displayed in Pareto charts (see an example in figure 7.7). The Pareto chart and supporting data are further analyzed by appropriate staff and summarized in an affinity diagram for use as an input into the planning process.

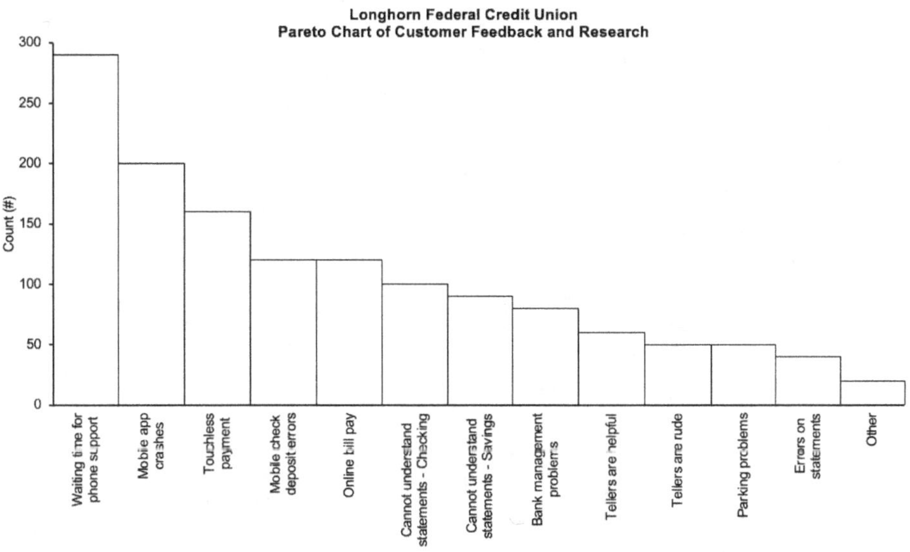

Figure 7.7. Pareto chart of customer feedback and research prepared as input to planning.

Hallmark Building Supplies Inc. is a building supply distributor based in Wisconsin. Leaders at Hallmark prioritized the collection of customer feedback and operations into routine practice and developed an electronic knowledge management system to collect and code qualitative data in real time (figure 7.8).[37] When any staff member observes an opportunity for improvement or receives feedback from a customer, she completes an electronic form. The form allows for capturing the details and connecting the information to the related numbered process and the designated process owner.

The leader responsible for the process reviews these reports as part of the routine standard leader work. That leader determines how the information supports one of the three actions:

1. If she and colleagues can mitigate an issue and correct performance, they will do so.
2. If the information is relevant to existing improvement efforts in progress, she will navigate the information to the appropriate improvement team, or
3. The information will serve as an input for the planning process.

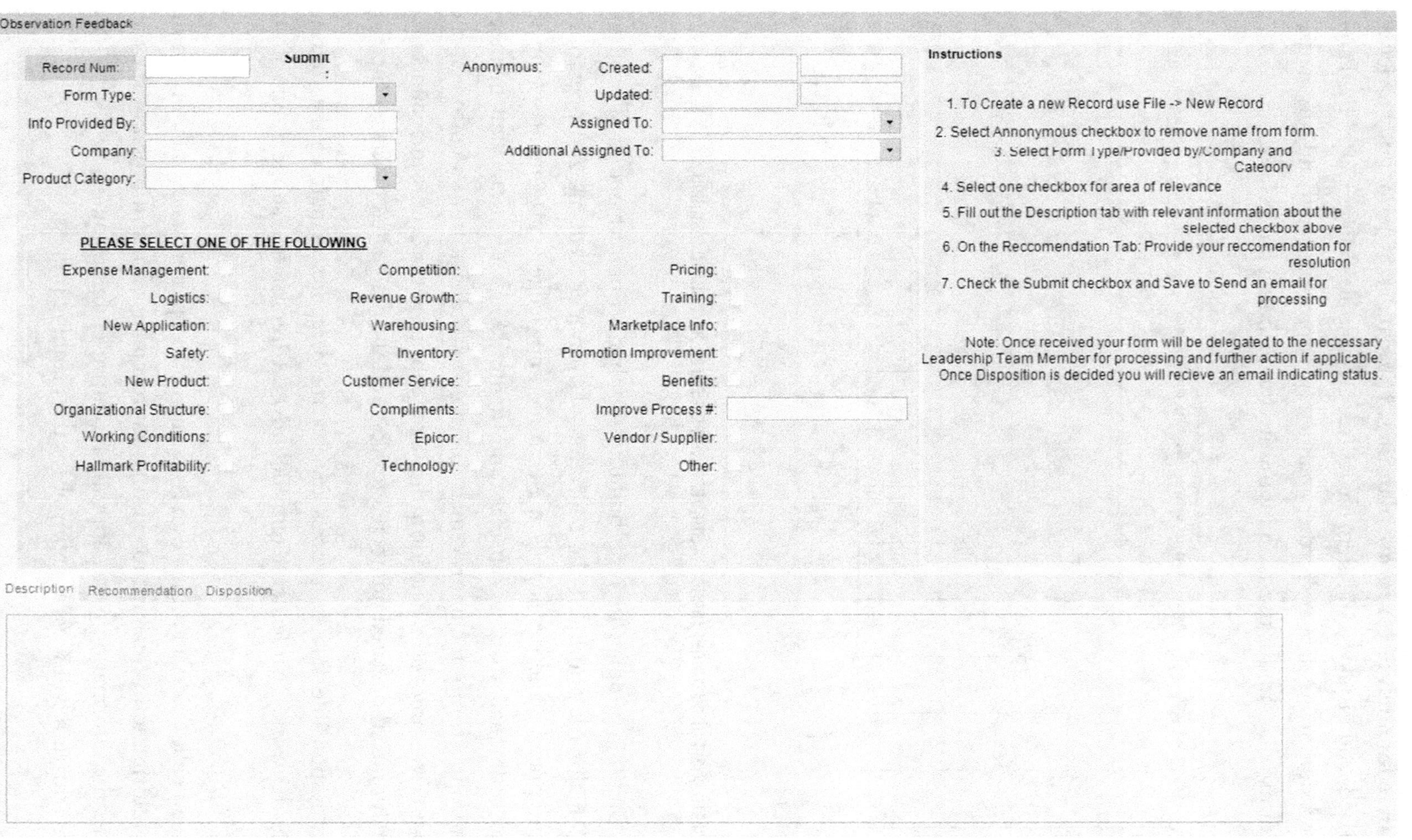

Figure 7.8. Information collection form at Hallmark Building Supplies, Inc.

PREPARING INFORMATION FOR PLANNING

Capturing and learning from research and feedback need not be complicated. Many organizations are bogged down with complex knowledge management systems. Ideally, these systems should allow for easy capture, mapping, summarizing, and analyzing. A system map (see Chapter 5) allows a method to connect this information to specific processes in the organization. This process enables information to come in (yet is often unavailable in most organizations) to become a rich source of information to guide the planning process. It expands the learning beyond negative feedback such as complaints or warranty claims.

The information from the various sources of research and feedback is assimilated, analyzed, and further summarized. The summaries are reviewed, and common themes are noted. Key areas that improve matching products and services to the Need are also identified. This information is beneficial in the planning process.[38]

SUMMARY

Obtaining information from customers, suppliers, staff, and other stakeholders provides the energy to drive an organization with quality as its organizational strategy. Proactive approaches to gathering and using information aid problem-solving and serve as inputs that inform planning. Leaders gain key insight that supports developing products and services to better match the Need of clients.

"When we started testing the smartphone app, and staff started capturing observations and feedback, we were flooded with information. It was overwhelming initially but sorting it into real issues we need to act on now versus input to our improvement efforts or future planning helped us get organized."

As their initial approach settled in, Kwan's team developed a system of mixed methods to gather information from the market and people connected to the brewery, including customers, suppliers, and its staff.

"We found ourselves bringing new insights to the team, and there was a noticeable shift as we were in a better place to solve problems and also to have information that helped us improve into the future."

Kwan's team identified that customers had lots of variety in popular styles like IPAs, darks, and sours, but few breweries were developing and offering pilsners, ESBs, and pale ales. This information would be a key insight included in the planning process to prioritize new products in the upcoming season.

NOTES

1. Eric Ries, *The Lean Startup: How Today's Entrepreneurs Use Continuous Innovation to Create Radically Successful Businesses.* (New York: Crown Publishing Group, 2011

2. Drucker, *The Essential Drucker*, 20–21.

3. See Chapter 1, "Understanding the Need."

4. See Chapter 1, figure 1.1, "An organization viewed as a system."

5. Deming, *Out of Crisis*, 23. This is the first of the 14 Points for Management articulated by Deming: create constancy of purpose toward improvement of product and service, with the aim to become competitive and to stay in business, and to provide jobs.

6. In Chapter 1, Table 1.5 is a tool for leaders to assess the organization's progress in making quality an organizational strategy. This paragraph is the operational definition for the top score for "System to obtain information" *The QOS Field Guide* contains a more comprehensive version of the assessment tool.

7. Hirotaka Takeuchi, Emi Osono, and Norihiko Shimizu, "The Contradictions That Drive Toyota's Success," *Harvard Business Review*, June 2008, https://hbr.org/2008/06/the-contradictions-that-drive-toyotas-success; Deming, *The New Economics*, 1994, 58.

8. Adapted from Theodore Levitt, *Thinking About Management* (New York: Free Press, 1991).

9. Theodore Levitt, "Marketing Myopia," *Harvard Business Review*, July 1, 2004, https://hbr.org/2004/07/marketing-myopia. The authors changed the original quote's use of the word

"need" to "expectations" to remain consistent with the operational definition of "need" used throughout this text.

10. See Chapter 1, "Defining Quality" for the introduction to the source of the dimensions of quality dimensions. The dimensions of quality support developing specific quality characteristics which then can be measures.

11. Yoji Akao, *Quality Function Deployment: Integrating Customer Requirements into Product Design* (New York: Productivity Press, 1990). A method called Quality Function Deployment (QFD) provides a set of tools for developing a definition of quality for a particular group of customers.

12. Deming, *The New Economics*, 1994, 10.

13. William Franklin, ed., "Partners in Creating: The First Century of K+E (1867/1967)" (Keuffel and Esser Co., 1967), accessed August 3, 2024, https://www.sphere.bc.ca/oldsite/download/ke-100-yearbook.pdf.

14. "History of the Hand-Held Calculator," in Guy Ball, "Texas Instruments Cal-Tech: World's First Prototype Pocket Electronic Calculator," *The International Calculator Collector*, Fall 1997, http://www.vintagecalculators.com/html/ti_cal-tech1.html.

15. Richard S. Handscombe and Philip A. Norman, *Strategic Leadership: The Missing Links.* (London: McGraw-Hill, 1989), 79–85.

16. The run charts presented in figure 7.2 are conceptual and not supported by real data. They are based on the experience of the authors.

17. Deming, *Out of Crisis*, 31. Vendors or suppliers should be experts in their products and service and be continuously improving their products and services to match the Need they seek to fulfill. Customers are purchasing their products and services plus their knowledge and their partnership. Point 4 of Deming's 14 Points proposed, "End the practice of awarding business on the basis of price tag alone."

18. Figure 7.3 is adapted from Handscombe and Norman, *Strategic Leadership,* 53. The authors frame the levels of information as an "intelligence iceberg." Problem-solving intelligence is above the water's surface. What reoccurring problems need to be addressed? Operational intelligence is just below the surface. How do leaders need to adjust the organization to continue to meet demand? Strategic intelligence is deeper down. What do customer aspire into the future? What does that mean for the organization's ability to fulfill the need?

19. Handscombe and Norman, 53. Organizations devote a lot of time and attention to problem-solving information and mitigation. Operational information follows by looking at the experience of recent quarters or years to predict the upcoming operational needs. Strategic information gathering is limited. In figure 7.3, the size of the circles reflects the recommended proportions of the levels of information a QOS system for gathering information is designed to collect.

20. Deming, *Out of Crisis*, 28. Point 4 of Deming's 14 Points: End the practice of awarding business on the basis of price tag. Instead, minimize total cost. Move toward a single supplier for any one item, on a long-term relationship of loyalty and trust.

21. K&N Management operates several restaurant franchises in metro area of Austin, Texas. They are a 2010 recipient of the Malcolm Baldrige National Quality Award. One of the authors participated in a site visit at a Ruby's Barbecue where leaders described how they identified the opportunity to create satisfied first-time customers and developed a process to identify them in line, notify the team, and create a service experience aimed at creating a positive first encounter.

22. Kevin Cahill, "Teamwork Reimagined" (TEDxSunValley, Ketchum, Idaho, September 2017), https://www.ted.com/talks/kevin_cahill_teamwork_reimagined.

23. Likert, "A Technique for the Measurement of Attitudes."

24. Arlene G. Fink, *How to Conduct Surveys: A Step-by-Step Guide*, 6th ed. (Thousand Oaks, CA: Sage Publications, 2016).

25. Charles M. Judd, Eliot R. Smith, and Louise H. Kidder, *Research Methods in Social Relations*, 6th ed. (Orlando: Holt, Rinehart, and Winston, 1991), 7–39; Bob E. Hayes, *Measuring Customer Satisfaction and Loyalty: Survey Design, Use, and Statistical Analysis Methods*, 3rd Edition (Milwaukee: ASQ Quality Press, 2008).

26. Secret or mystery shoppers are part of a marketing research technique where a person pretends to be a customer to experience real-world services firsthand. Leaders may also don a uniform and shadow a worker to learn what it is like to be on staff, doing the work. Some leaders go "undercover" and fill a position without the knowledge of coworkers. Ethical protections should always be considered when customers or staff are not informed.

27. "Customer Feedback, Observation, and Research Form" is depicted here in figure 7.5. Figure 7.8 follows with an example from Hallmark Building Supplies Inc.

28. Ken Kocienda, *Creative Selection: Onside Apple's Design Process during the Golden Age of Steve Jobs*. (New York: St. Martin's Press, 2018), 210–11.

29. See Chapter 3, "Leading with QOS" on the importance of leaders with foresight.

30. Rob Johnson, Anthony Watkinson, and Michael Mabe, "The STM Report. An Overview of Scientific and Scholarly Publishing" (Netherlands: International Association of Scientific, Technical and Medical Publishers, October 2018), https://www.stm-assoc.org/2018_10_04_STM_Report_2018.pdf. One report estimates there are about 33,100 active scholarly peer-reviewed English-language journals and 9,400 non-English-language journals publishing more than 3 million articles per year. The number of articles published each year grows by about 3%.

31. David Rotman, "We're Not Prepared for the End of Moore's Law," *MIT Technology Review* (blog), February 24, 2020, https://www.technologyreview.com/2020/02/24/905789/were-not-prepared-for-the-end-of-moores-law/.

32. Chapter 7 of *The QOS Field Guide* has a method for using the Model for Improvement to conduct benchmarking.

33. Edgar H. Schein, *Process Consultation Revisited. Building the Helping Relationship.* Addison-Wesley Series on Organization Development (Reading, MA: Addison-Wesley Publishing Company, 1999), 7–17.

34. In our experience, there are limits to the voice of the customer. Customers may not be knowledgeable or capable of sharing insights beyond what is working or not working. For example, if a customer is struggling with using a software product, they may not appreciate what should be different to ease their issues. A designer observing the customer using the product may uncover opportunities for redesign of the interface or workflow that address their frustrations.

35. The figure of the five activities of quality as an organizational strategy (see Chapter 1, figure 1.8) depicts three arrows from the System of Obtaining Information reflecting these three actions and their connection to three other activities. Action 1, reacting to problems, directs information back to the system for process owners to address. Action 2, feedback to current improvement efforts, directs information to the individuals and teams who are actively working on these chartered improvement efforts. Action 3, summarize for analysis for future planning, prepares the information to be an input into the planning activity.

36. For each product and service in the organization, compile all available qualitative feedback and observations in the past year and code as positive or negative. Next, organize these data by the dimensions of quality (see table 1.4) and display in a Pareto chart. These charts are used to set priorities for improvement and research. Each month, update the Pareto charts with any new information using a stacked Pareto chart. Use the Pareto charts to monitor changes in

customer definitions of quality over time. The Pareto charts may be reset each year after use in the planning process.

37. Figure 7.5 was an example of a customer feedback and research form. Figure 7.8 is an example of the form that is part of software that runs in a Web browser or an application that directly captures the information in Cloud-based storage.

38. Chapter 8 discusses the planning activity. The information gathered through the system, as described in Chapter 7, is a crucial input to planning to improve.

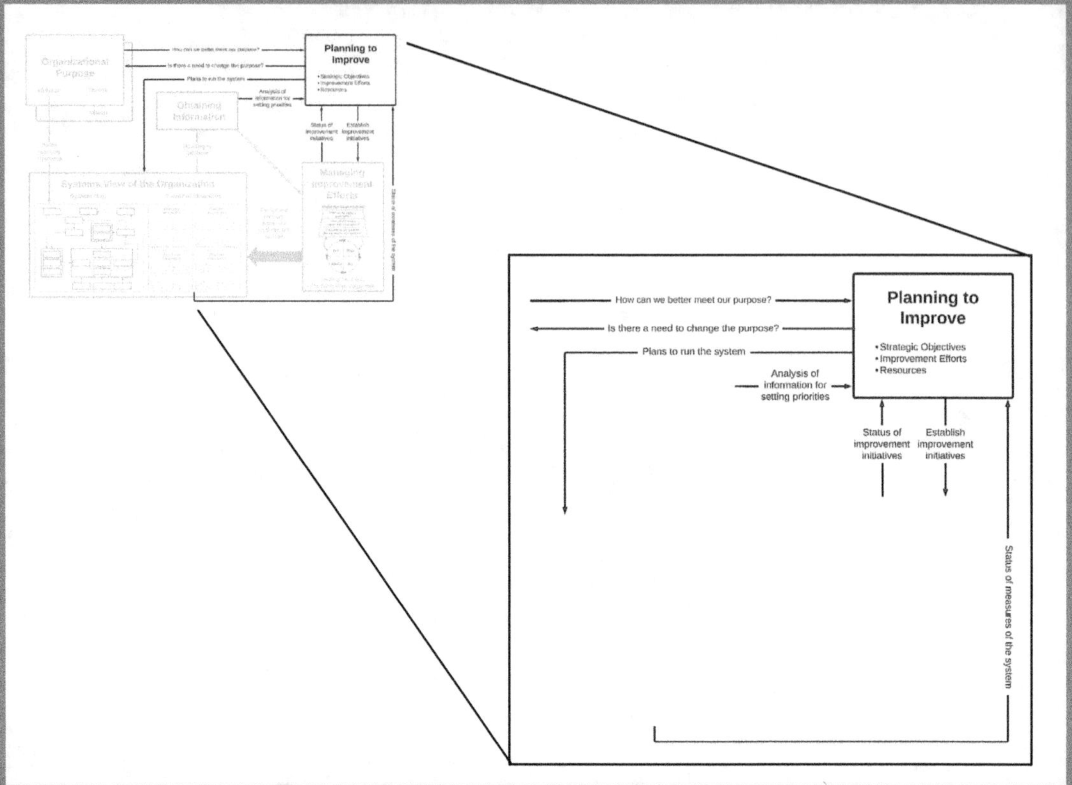

ACTIONS FOR THE LEADERSHIP TEAM

- Summarize the information from customer research and from employees, suppliers, and the relevant external environment.
- Based on these inputs, develop (or update) strategic objectives that could best accelerate the performance of the organization.
- Develop a list, in order of priority, of the processes, products, and services to design or redesign.
- Coordinate this plan with the organization's strategic and business planning and budgeting activities.
- Establish briefs for improvement projects that can be resourced and managed.

CHAPTER 8
PLANNING TO IMPROVE

Jada is the chief operating officer at a highway data collection company. Strategic thinking and continuous improvement are important to leadership, but the various planning events they have done over the years have not proven very useful to the organization:

> The leadership team has always had a planning event at the end of the year. We each take stock of the year, look at data reports, and bring our thoughts on operations and improvement. Most years, we plan and facilitate the meeting internally. Every few years, an expert facilitator is engaged to help us use different approaches—to get us to think more strategically. Our sense of focus and learning during the annual planning exercise is short-lived. The new year starts, and day-to-day work quickly brushes aside the best intentions.

This year is the first planning cycle following the organization's yearlong effort to develop quality as an organizational strategy. Jada is excited to build on their work with QOS this year and run a new method of planning for improvement.

WHAT IS PLANNING IN QOS?

Planning is an opportunity to learn, be proactive, and make choices about the organization's future. It provides a structured approach to collecting diverse inputs about customers, employees, the market, emerging changes from research, best practices, and insights into the current state of the organization's performance.

An effective planning activity yields strategic objectives, a selection of products, services, and processes that, if designed, redesigned, or given additional resource are predicted to achieve those objectives, and allocation of resources.

A mature organization studies and improves its planning process on a formal basis. Leaders keep plans current as new ideas emerge or directions change. The planning documents are used and reviewed throughout the year. The planning process is understood and integrated throughout the organization. All employees understand the strategic objectives of the organization. The organization's leaders view planning as a critical learning opportunity.[1] The focus of planning is to improve the organization from the viewpoint of the external client or customer. This chapter describes a method for leaders to do this level of planning.

Planning to Improve and Operate

How does the organization pursue the accomplishment of quality as its strategy? Where should we focus resources to move the organization in the right direction? Planning can be considered in two basic categories based on their purpose (figure 8.1).

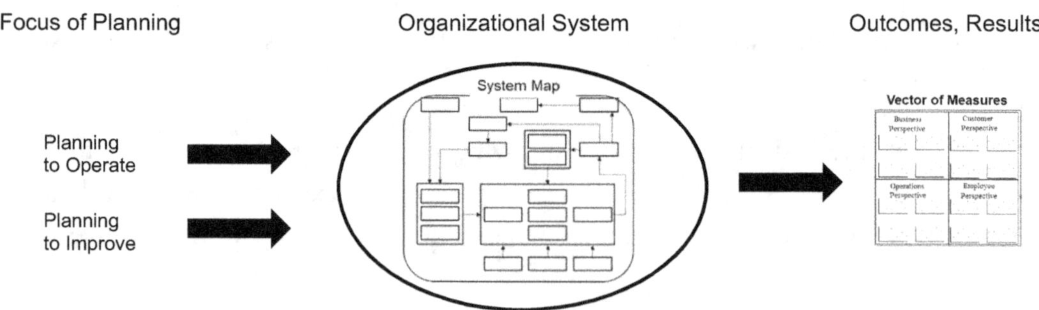

Figure 8.1. Two purposes of planning.

PLANNING TO IMPROVE

Planning to improve includes identifying the processes, products, and services in the organization where design or redesign is predicted to impact the strategic objectives. For example, redesigning the workflow in an insurance office could help a strategic objective of "reducing cycle time in handling claims." Changes can also be directed at improving the total organization. For example, reorganizing the structure of teams in the organization to reduce siloes and increase collaboration.

PLANNING TO OPERATE

Planning to operate addresses all the planning activities that are done to run the existing organization (system). These activities include market planning, financial forecasting, budgeting, production staffing, staffing planning, and training schedules. The activities are informed by the planning system.

An organization can accomplish some of its strategic objectives just by strategic operation of its current system. For example, the action of investing more time or capital to budget for research activities over the next three years could help accomplish a strategic objective of "developing products that better match the Need of our customers." Assigning additional staff to the market development group could help a strategic objective of "expanding the organization into the European market." These actions expand the organization but do not change its structure or processes.

DIFFERENCE BETWEEN PLANS TO IMPROVE AND PLANS TO OPERATE

Sometimes distinguishing between these two purposes is difficult. Table 8.1 includes two examples to illustrate the difference.

Table 8.1. Examples of planning to improve and planning to operate

Example	Plan to improve	Plan to operate
Advertising	Redesign the process of preparing advertising materials.	Create and carry out an advertising campaign.
Product	Redesign of an existing product or develop a new design for an innovative product to replace the current product	Increase the production of an existing product for the upcoming year.

Regardless of the focus of planning, the aim is to improve the vector of measures of the organizational system (outcomes, results, satisfaction, return on investment, lower costs, etc.).

PLANNING AS A SYSTEM

Most managers and leaders are involved in various types of planning, affecting different areas across the organization. As we develop a process of planning for improvement, it is critical to appreciate planning as a system (see figure 8.2).[2]

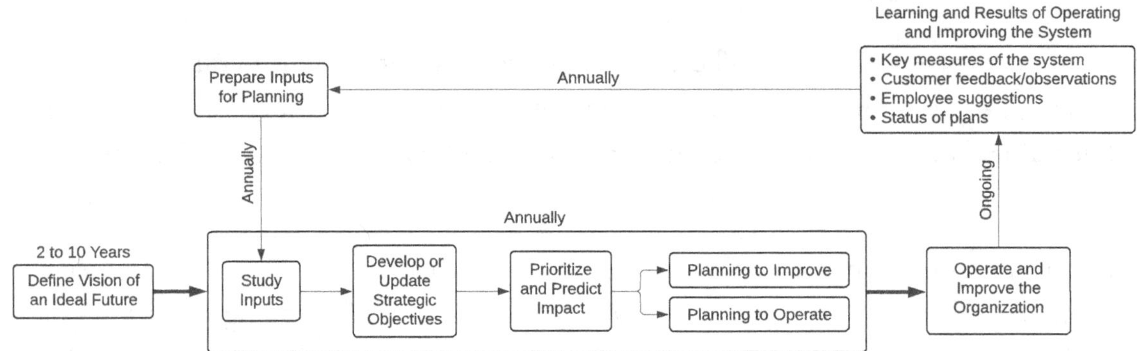

Figure 8.2. Planning as a system.

Planning Systems that Incorporate Planning for Improvement

Does your current planning system incorporate planning for improvement? Here are five criteria to assess whether an organization's existing planning system includes a focus on improvement:

1. Includes strategic objectives to improve the organization from the viewpoint of the external customer
2. Balances short-term and long-term needs of all the stakeholders of the organization
3. Identifies what part of the organizational structure (processes, produces, services, etc.) will be designed or redesigned
4. Provides sufficient information to guide the development of new products and services
5. Includes allocating resources (i.e., budget, personnel assignments, etc.) to improve the organization

The annual planning process is how the organization takes the plans to operate and the plans to improve and operationalizes them into budgets, timelines, resourcing, prioritization, etc. It supports everyone in knowing who is doing what, how, when, and where across the organizational system. The annual planning process serves as an execution strategy for deploying the plans to improve and operate across the organization.

The outcomes of the planning system include:

1. Strategic objectives
2. Improvement briefs for the design and redesign of processes, products, and services
3. Resource allocation

This chapter outlines a method to learn from diverse inputs to develop or update strategic objectives, map them to the organizational system and vector of measures, and to support identifying the impact and prioritization to plan for improvement and operations.

The approach described is structured and includes a process orientation that is more than what most leaders experience in common planning approaches. As we describe each component, the figures and tables support following the journey of the process and build to the final output.

Jada met with the leadership team to assess their current system of planning. The team worked together to answer the five assessment criteria. Jada summarized their responses (see the previous list). She reported:

1. We did create strategic objectives, but they tended to be internally focused.

2. Most of our specific plans focused on short-term operational needs. We never got around to creating actions to deal with the long-term focus.

3. Our actions were focused on doing new actions without a reflection on our existing organizational system.

4. We did a reasonable job of planning for new products, but not much on services.

5. We did not differentiate improvement versus operations in our budgeting and personnel plans.

Based on this reflection, we were all excited about the possibilities of planning for improvement.

THE QOS PLANNING PROCESS

Figure 8.2 displayed a general view of planning as a system. Central to the figure is the annual planning process. Figure 8.3 is a flow diagram of a method to achieve planning. Each step is described, and examples are included to support learning the approach.

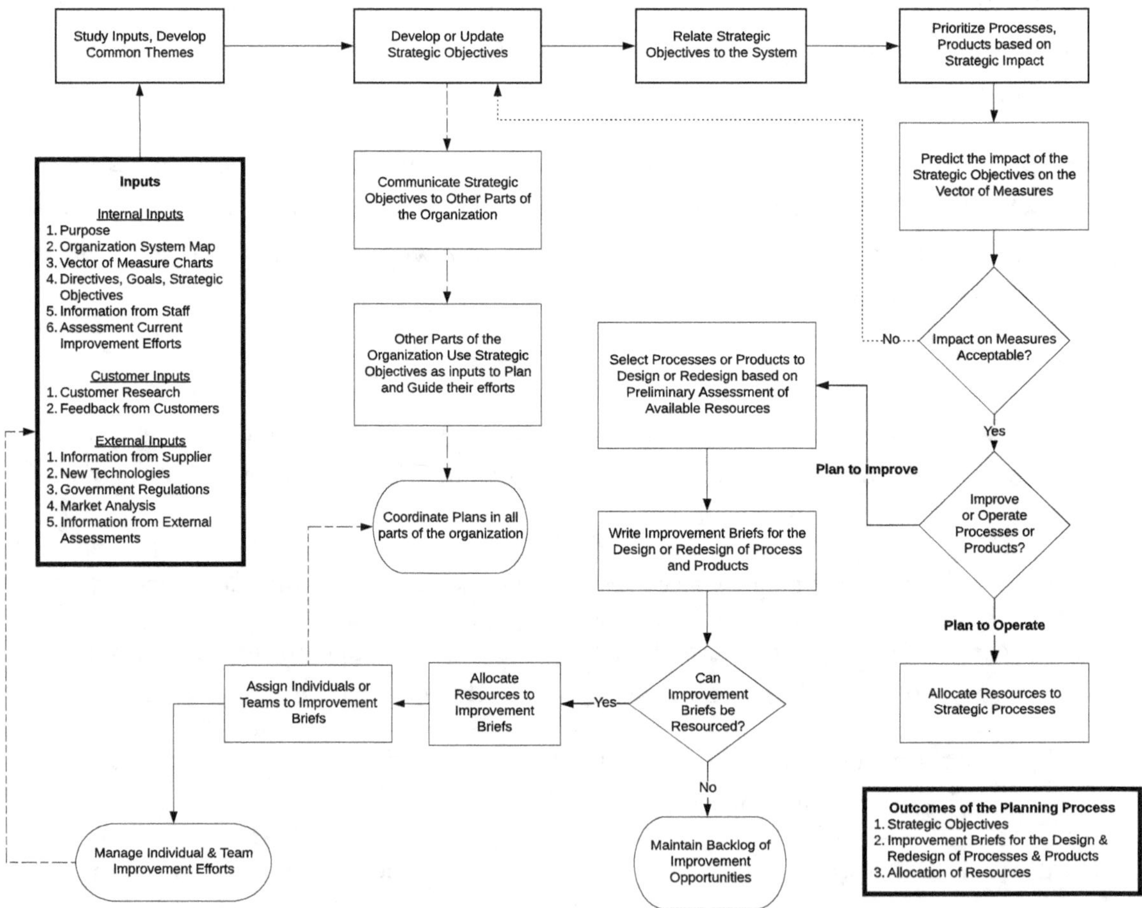

Figure 8.3. The process of planning to improve.

Inputs to the Planning Process

Efforts to gather information[3] enable leadership to learn how the current system is performing and how improvement efforts are working. The information aids learning and developing foresight[4] for the future. The information-gathering activity also provides summaries and analysis of the input for the organization's planning system. Information comes from diverse sources[5] outside and inside the organization and aids learning and building confidence. The following are common components prepared for planning. Inputs include internal, customer, and external perspectives.

INTERNAL INPUTS

Two foundational internal inputs to viewing the organization as a system during the planning process are listed first: the purpose and the organization's system map of linked processes.

- **Information on the organization's purpose** includes the organization's mission and tenets and a vision of the organization's ideal future.
- **The organization is viewed as a system of linked processes (system map).** Also included is a list of current products and services. The current condition of the processes should be rated for their current state of performance.[6]
- The organization's vector of measures: Shewhart charts visually display data for key measures of the system.
- Internal directives, goals, and strategic objectives are developed in other areas of the organization.
- Feedback, suggestions, and ideas are collected from staff.
- Current improvement efforts are assessed.

CUSTOMER INPUTS

Customer inputs are key perspectives in planning and result from active processes to learn about customers and understand their feedback. They include:

- Information from customer research.
- Information from customer feedback.

EXTERNAL INPUTS

Other information relevant to the identified Need and business of the organization informs planners with information external to the organization. This information includes:

- Information from suppliers.
- New technologies.
- Government regulations.
- Marketplace analysis (including information on competitors).
- Information from frameworks, accreditations, or evaluations (e.g., Baldrige Framework, consultant reports, benchmarking).

Preparation requires information sources to be identified, collected, and organized in order to study the details and draw conclusions that support action. Qualitative and quantitative data will require transformation into graphical displays to summarize and enable rapid visual analysis. Developing the inputs to QOS planning requires leaders to plan for the gathering and summary of the information and time to execute the plan and produce the inputs.[7]

Studying Inputs and Developing Themes

Identifying, collecting, and organizing these inputs in preparing the annual planning effort supports learning during the process. Leaders study each input, and themes emerge that guide developing and updating the strategic objectives. In the following paragraphs, a brief description of each input is provided, including what may be included and questions to guide reflection.[8]

INTERNAL INPUTS

Purpose. Leaders should study the purpose of the organization. Does it remain relevant and guiding for the organization? Is it informative to share a story of how the purpose was utilized in practice in the past year? Where was it effectively used, and where was it not? Was it challenged? Are there predicted scenarios in the coming year where the purpose will be important to guide decisions? Does the vision represent the ideal future of the organization?

Organization viewed as a system of linked processes. The organization's current system map will play a fundamental role in the planning process. The most recent version of the map should be visible during all planning meetings. Each process on the map should be numbered and a recent update of the process condition rating noted.[9]

Key measures of the system. The vector of measures with data updated for at least the most recent twenty-four months is displayed in Shewhart charts. Each measure is reviewed to determine its current level, if it is stable (in control), the desired level (goal or target if relevant), a prediction for the measure in the next year if no action is taken, and if it is a priority to improve the measure.[10]

Internal directives developed by other areas of the organization. Strategic objectives, goals, strategies, or directives may exist when planning at a sublevel within a broader organization, such as within a department, region, or business unit. These require study and incorporation in the annual planning process.

Information from staff. Feedback, suggestions, and ideas from the staff closest to the process and to customers are especially important. Their experience and ideas about processes that, if improved, would significantly affect external customers should be sought. They also have vital insights into the organizational environment and culture. These observations and ideas should be summarized from data captured throughout the year from sources like rounding, direct suggestion systems, focused meetings, and surveying. The results can be summarized in Pareto charts around key questions, specific themes or processes, and descriptions of cases.

Assessment of improvement efforts. Summaries of improvement projects chartered in the previous year include the status of each project and its success in achieving its aims. An organization focused on value reflects whether the portfolio of improvement efforts included activities that eliminated problems, reduced costs, or created innovation. This supports evaluating progress in achieving the strategic objectives and shows the effectiveness of the organization's capacity and ability to execute improvement work and produce results. The backlog of improvement efforts held in queue for when the organization has proper capacity and resourcing is also reviewed. This input aids in selecting parts in the system to be improved, understanding the organization's capacity to add new improvement projects, determining resource allocations, and evaluating your improvement methods for what is working or not.

CUSTOMER INPUTS

Customer research and feedback. Customer input should carry a lot of weight during planning. Input can include high-impact areas for improvement and insights on better matching the Need for different segments. Customer segmentation is essential to learning the various definitions of matching the Need from different customers. Useful information from past customer studies and observations, and feedback from daily work with customers should all be summarized and studied. Summarized data is displayed in Pareto charts, and graphical methods help leaders quickly learn from the feedback and quickly grasp the key themes.

EXTERNAL INPUTS

Information from suppliers. Organizations rely on various suppliers for materials, hardware, software, and services. Suppliers are partners in supporting the organization to operate and improve, and regular mechanisms to learn with them are helpful. Suppliers can offer insights on better integrating their products and services, suggesting adaptations to internal processes to improve workflow, sharing best practices from other peer organizations, and considering synergies across vendors.

New technologies. Technology here refers to science or knowledge put into practical use to address problems or develop tools. Methods, hardware, and software are evolving and improving at a dizzying pace. Organizations must be knowledgeable of the effectiveness of current technology and regularly scan for new technologies of potential benefit to the organization. Technology that could replace or alter products and services should also be considered. For example, how will new applications of artificial intelligence (AI) affect those products and services? This information comes from the direct inquiry of suppliers and research of studies, trade publications, conference sessions, and other reports.

Government regulations. Many organizations are affected by changes in local, state, and federal regulations; these can be opportunities or constraints. For example, rules on alcohol distribution and sales can affect microbreweries' packaging and sales channels. Summarize existing or proposed regulations that may impact the organization within the planning period.

Market analysis and future business environment. Planners need an accurate sense of the market. What are competitor organizations' activities? Scanning direct and indirect competitor services and products, coverage in the media, publications and presentations from key leaders, and external market reports may offer helpful insights. Information should be collected and summarized. The aim is not to copy other organizations but to continue to better understand the Need and to focus on how our own organization can add value.

Use of assessment guides, other evaluation frameworks, and benchmarking. Many organizations choose to participate in quality award assessment processes. Quality awards exist in over a dozen countries worldwide, including the U.S., and within many U.S. states. Notable quality awards include the Deming Prize, the Baldrige Performance Excellence Award, and the European Federation of Quality Management (EFQM) Excellence Award. The results of participation in a quality award evaluation may be useful information for the planning process. Many service organizations in healthcare, education, and public safety are required to participate in third-party accreditation processes. Accreditation requirements and current assessments may also serve as inputs to planning. Organizations also use methods to benchmark[11] other organizations. The summary of learning may serve as input to planning.

Summary of Inputs

The planning process begins with the presentation and study of inputs. The inputs are the foundation from which strategic objectives are developed and keep the planners focused on the Need the organization is trying to fulfill. These suggested inputs are typical, but additional sources of information may be helpful to some organizations. Collection, preparation, and proper display in charts, graphs, and interactive displays enhance their usefulness and the ability of participants to study and learn from the inputs.

Organizations beginning the journey of adopting quality as a strategy may not have all the inputs described. Planners should identify what is present and what is not. What does exist may not be ideal, and planners should consider how to adapt for this planning period and enhance it for future planning sessions. Missing inputs will be included in your plan for developing processes in the year to support future planning processes.

Jada and her colleagues reviewed the typical list of inputs for planning. Some of the internal inputs were available. Many were created as the leaders developed QOS during the last year. They now had a workable purpose, a useable system map, and a vector of measures. In building their system for gathering information, new methods were created for collecting input from customers and suppliers, and better approaches were tested to capture input from staff.

"Each leader on the team was actively involved in gathering the inputs. One surprise came from the new sources of information. We had more than a dozen key suppliers, and no method had been in place to learn from them. The feedback they shared this year on how we could improve our relationship with them and doing our work was so useful, and we were unaware of it."

Many inputs, such as information from staff and customer feedback, were significantly upgraded, and the methods used to summarize the themes and match the dimensions of quality (identified previously in this chapter) gave the qualitative data meaning that was not clear before. What was once a loose process of sharing papers or learning from conferences became an organized harvesting method resulting in actionable themes.

"Everyone reviewed the same packet of inputs before the planning process began. We were reading the same quotes, looking at the same Shewhart charts, watching the same technology videos, and seeing the same themes from a system of inputs. We walked into the room in the same starting position and with the same context. It was the first time in my experience that I was entering a planning process where all the leaders were positioned to think strategically and make an actionable plan."

STRATEGIC OBJECTIVES

Strategic objectives are statements of what must be achieved by an organization to move toward its purpose and to make progress on achieving the vision. Other names include strategic goals, strategic initiatives, and strategic imperatives. Strategic objectives are strategic in nature (long-term focused) and not tactical (short-term focused). They are **not** the specific actions required for improvement.

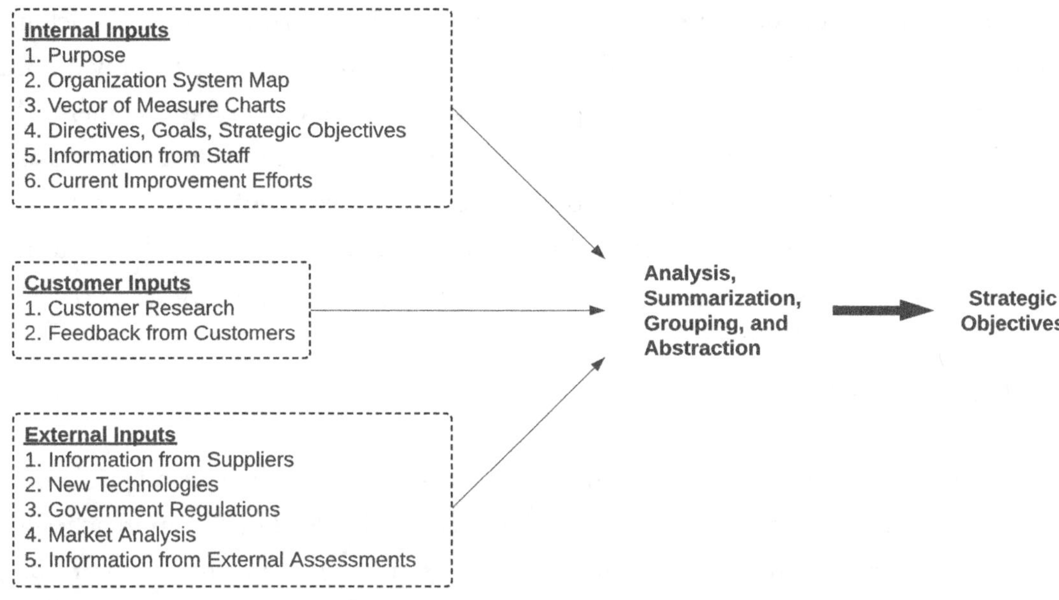

Figure 8.4. Developing strategic objectives.

A strategic objective of an organization might be "to accelerate the introduction of new products to the market." "Increasing the budget of Research and Development in 2024" is not a strategic objective but a tactical action. Strategic objectives should reflect the information learned from the inputs to the strategic planning process (see figure 8.4) as well as the insights of the organization's leaders.

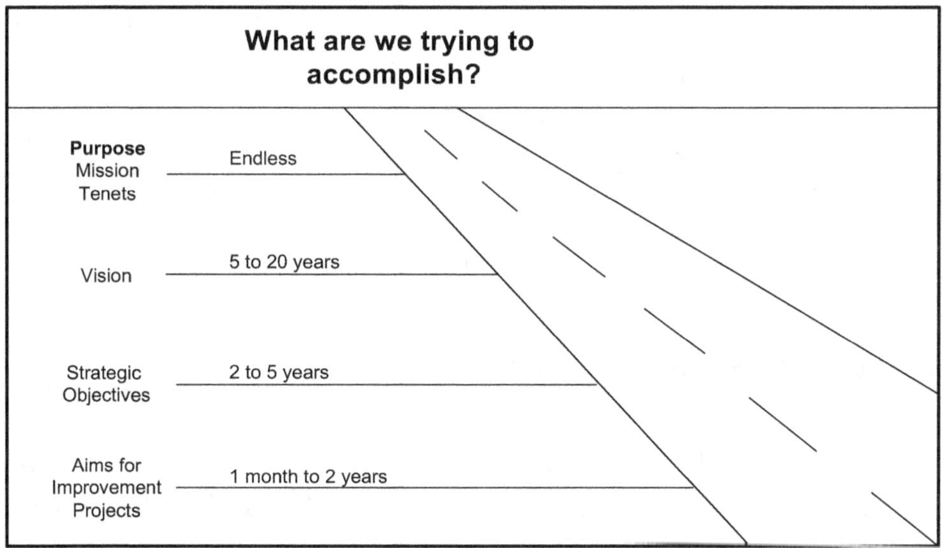

Figure 8.5. Time frame for direction.

The organization's **purpose** provides long-term direction (figure 8.5) and includes the organization's mission, vision, and tenets. The **mission** is endless and provides the organization's focus and the Need the organization is trying to match for customers. The **vision** for an ideal future offers long-term direction for the next five to twenty years and may adapt as stakeholders or the environment shift. **Strategic objectives** direct near-term focus for two to five years. Finally, **aims** for improvement projects developed during planning, taken together, define a specific focus in the coming months to two years.

Developing Strategic Objectives

Information collected from research and feedback is analyzed, combined, and prioritized. Common themes emerge and are used to identify key issues. Finally, approaches are selected to address each issue and are described as strategic objectives[12] (figure 8.6) for the next two to five years. The leadership team reviews each strategic objective individually and then collectively and weights their importance.

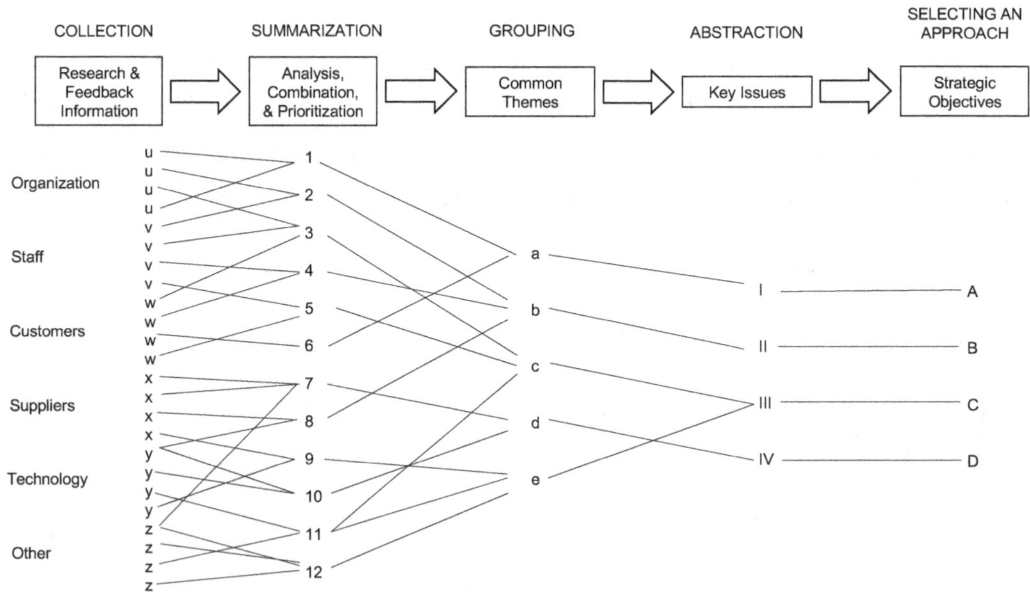

Figure 8.6. Process to develop strategic objectives.

Strategic objectives should focus primarily on the Need and the external customers of the organization, rather than limited to internal issues or financial results. The objectives are focused on causes rather than outcomes (e.g., increasing revenue). Strategic objectives based on improving processes, products, and services will have meaning for large portions of the organization and help enable its commitment. Table 8.2 includes examples of both useful and not useful strategic objectives.

Table 8.2. Examples of strategic objectives

Useful	Not Useful
Increase students on track to graduate with their class	Build a new office wing
Improve access and reduce inequity in the health system	Increase profits
Reduce residential fires from cooking	Increase our market share
Increase on-time grocery deliveries	Recruit more customers
Cut the cost of warranty claims	Decentralize the organization
Convert fleet to being emission neutral	Increase the quality of care
Increase the focus on prevention and early intervention throughout the clinic	Add staff

The organization's leadership must reach a consensus on the strategic objectives to ensure commitment to the improvement efforts and allocation of resources that will follow. **Test the acceptance of the strategic objectives with others in the organization.** Can they understand them? Do they think they are important? If accomplished, do they see how the organization will be closer to achieving its purpose and vision? Can they appreciate their role and responsibilities in the stated objectives?

Include space in this part of the planning process for setting ambitious "moonshots."[13] A moonshot is an ambitious or innovative strategic objective. It may not emerge from the inputs, or be currently possible, but reflects an ambitious stretch to match the organization's target Need in a novel new way.

The strategic objectives are used in the planning process to select the aspects of the system that require design or redesign. Considering that the portfolio of improvement efforts should be kept to a manageable number, **identify three to eight strategic objectives**. Strategic objectives do not have to cover everything the organization is involved in but rather provide focus on the areas of the organization that will be targeted for improvement during the next two to five years. Strategic objectives do not require specific goals or targets, although sometimes these can be useful to communicate the pace or degree of change expected.

When the strategic objectives are communicated to the organization, the planning team could also develop a vision of what the organization will be like after accomplishing the strategic objectives or reflect on the current vision relative to the strategic objectives.

Leaders develop strategic objectives when an organization first undertakes a planning process. In subsequent planning sessions, the strategic objectives are reviewed, updated to reflect new information, and then added to or removed as they are accomplished or abandoned. Strategic objectives should have some permanence and be projected at least two years into the future.

Jada and the team studied the inputs prepared for the planning process. Key points were captured on individual stickie notes and placed on the wall. An affinity diagram method was used to group the stickies into common themes.

"We had five common themes that emerged. We talked about each theme and considered the opportunity we had to address these themes and the organization closer to our purpose."

After a few iterations and some wordsmithing, the team settled on five strategic objectives and listed them on a whiteboard in the room. They listed them from A through E:

Common themes	Strategic objectives
Group 1: Management development issues	A) Improve the way in which we select, educate, and develop our leaders.
Group 2: Problems with introduction of new products	B) Reduce the cycle time we use to develop and introduce products by 30%.
Group 3: Problems due to variation with software products	C) Improve consistency of software products to our customers.
Group 4: Delivery issues	D) Reduce delivery time to our customers.
Group 5: Turnover of engineers	E) Improve our ability to attract and retain engineers.

"After some discussion on the wording, I remember us all sitting back in our chairs and just reflecting on them. I could see heads nodding in my periphery. There were a few clarifying questions. Clarifying a definition or asking if a quantifiable number (like a goal) made sense here or there. That was the gist. Our level of collective agreement was new for us. For the first time, we had strategic objectives we could work with. Together."

Communicate Strategic Objectives to Other Parts of the Organization

New or updated strategic objectives are central to the QOS planning process. Strategic objectives are also useful in other parts of the organization and must be communicated to these groups. Other parts of the organization use the strategic objectives as inputs to plan and guide their efforts (figure 8.8). At the end of the QOS planning process, the plans to improve will require coordination with plans in all parts of the organization.

Method to Prioritize and Predict Impact

Studying the inputs provides a holistic view of how we can better match the Need and the current state of the organization viewed as a system. To continually improve the system, the planning activity supports identifying where innovation, improvement, or more emphasis on execution is predicted to bring the organization closer to achieving the strategic objectives.

The steps to follow progress through a series of actions that build on each other and provide a step-by-step method for planning to improve:

1. Relating strategic objectives to the system: using the organization's system map, map the strategic objectives to all the processes they relate to and weight for the strength of their relationship.
2. Prioritize the strategic impact of processes, products, and services to strategic objectives: Weight the strategic impact of processes, products, and services on the strategic objectives. Display the predicted impact on the strategic objectives and the assessment of the process condition in a scatter plot to show the opportunity for design or redesign.

3. Predict the impact on the vector of measures.

4. Select strategic processes, products, and services.

5. Asses strategic processes, products, and services for resource allocation.

6. Weight priority processes, products, and services for the potential for improvement.

7. Draft improvement briefs for a portfolio of improvement efforts.

8. Allocate resources and assign teams.

Jada's highway data collection company (from this chapter's vignettes) serves as an example of applying this process. Figure 8.7 is the system map for the organization. A box reflects each key process in the organization. The current condition of each process was assessed using the rating scale from table 5.2 in Chapter 5 and noted in the bottom right corner of each process.

In the bottom right corner of figure 8.7 is a legend of the coding used. It has elements introduced in figure 5.14: process name, process number, and process condition rating. Adding an assessment of the strategic weight of a process follows.

Relating the Strategic Objectives to the System and Prioritizing Strategic Impact

What is required to accomplish the strategic objectives developed for the organization? Since strategic objectives are statements of what needs to be achieved by an organization to move it toward its purpose, some actions are required to "start the movement." When organizations develop strategic objectives, there can be a tendency to immediately list action steps, develop schedules, and make assignments to accomplish each objective. Sometimes, a particular manager is put in charge of each objective. All these actions ignore that the organization is a system of interdependent processes, products, departments, and people and that the strategic objectives are only a mechanism to help improve the system. An appreciation of systems by the leadership of an organization is an important prerequisite to effective planning for improvement.

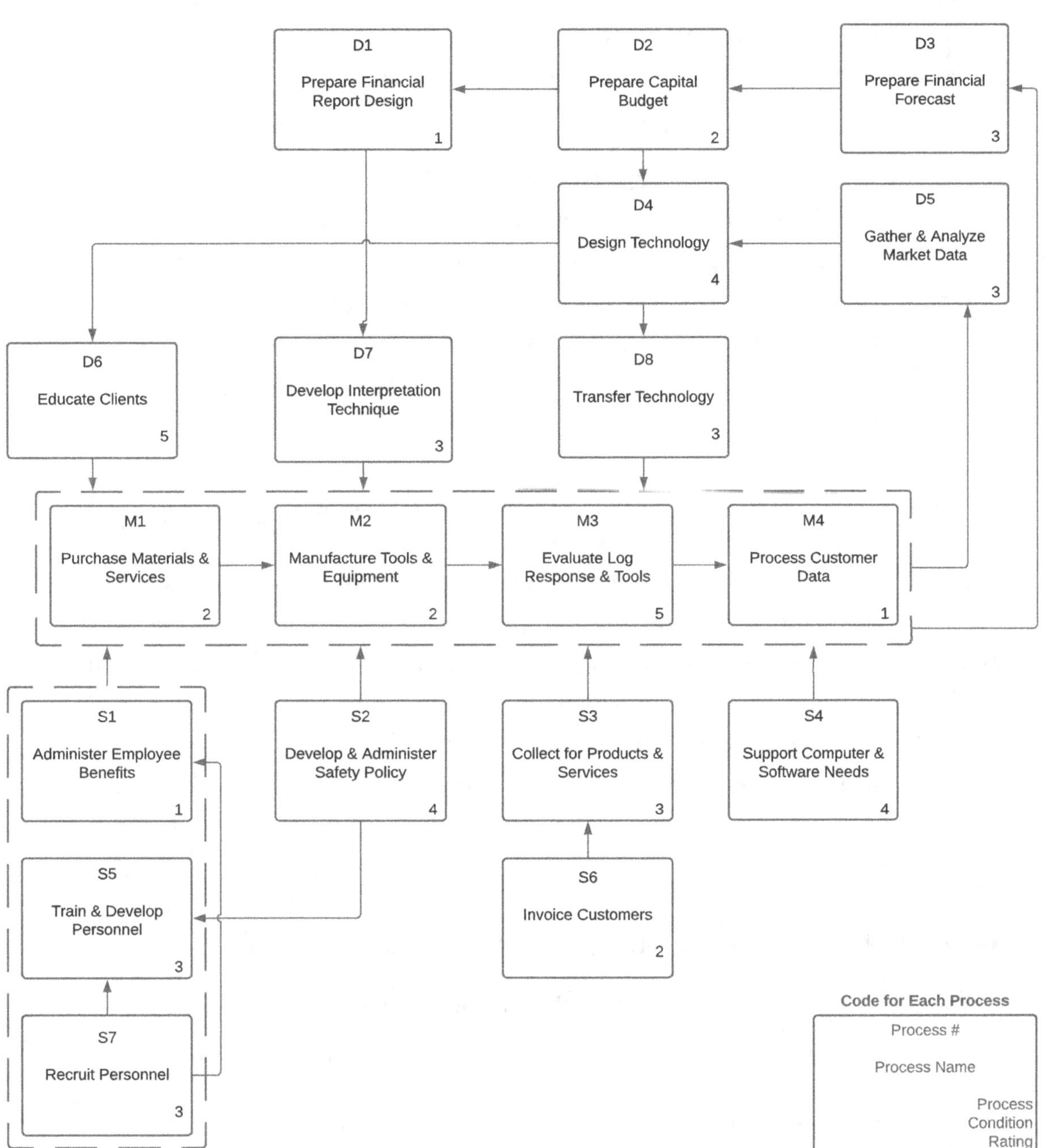

Figure 8.7. System map for a highway data collection company.

Planning to improve and **planning to operate** must be considered in developing actions to accomplish the strategic objectives. In planning to improve, processes, products, and services are weighted for strategic impact, and the process condition is included to identify opportunities to design or redesign to achieve the strategic objectives. In planning to operate, consider where more emphasis or resources to processes, products, or services would aid in achieving the strategic objectives.

To identify the highest leverage of potential areas of impact within the organization, the strategic objectives must not be **approached independently**. The selection of ways to improve and allocate resources should be made only after all strategic objectives have been related to the structure of the system and weighted for strategic impact. The system map, including the important products and services for the organization, provides a method to enable a holistic approach to strategic planning as well as the necessary actions.

WEIGHTS FOR RELATIONSHIP OF PROCESS, PRODUCT, OR SERVICE TO STRATEGIC OBJECTIVES

Leaders know that not every change has an equal effect on the desired outcomes or results. A method is needed to predict each process, product, or service's impact on the strategic objectives to learn where to focus change. Table 8.3 shows weights that can be used to predict impact. For example, a process with no expected impact on the strategic objectives is rated "0," whereas a process essential to accomplishing the objective is rated "5" on the scale. If there is no agreement on a weight assessment, use a weight in between. For example, if the leadership is divided on whether to weight a process "3" or "5," compromise by weighting the process "4."

Table 8.3. Weights for relationship of process, product, or service to strategic objectives

Weight	Operational definition of weight
5	**Must** focus on this process, product, or service to accomplish the strategic objective.
3	Focusing on this process, product, or service will have a **direct impact** on the strategic objective.
1	Focusing on this process, product, or service will have an **indirect impact** on the strategic objective.
-	**No impact** on the strategic objective is expected from focusing on this process, product, or service.

Figure 8.8 shows process M3, "Evaluate Log Response and Tools," as an example of how coding[14] each process looks by the end. Noted in the lower left corner, this process is predicted to impact three of the strategic objectives. Process M3 is weighted a "5" and **must** be worked on to achieve Strategic Objective C.

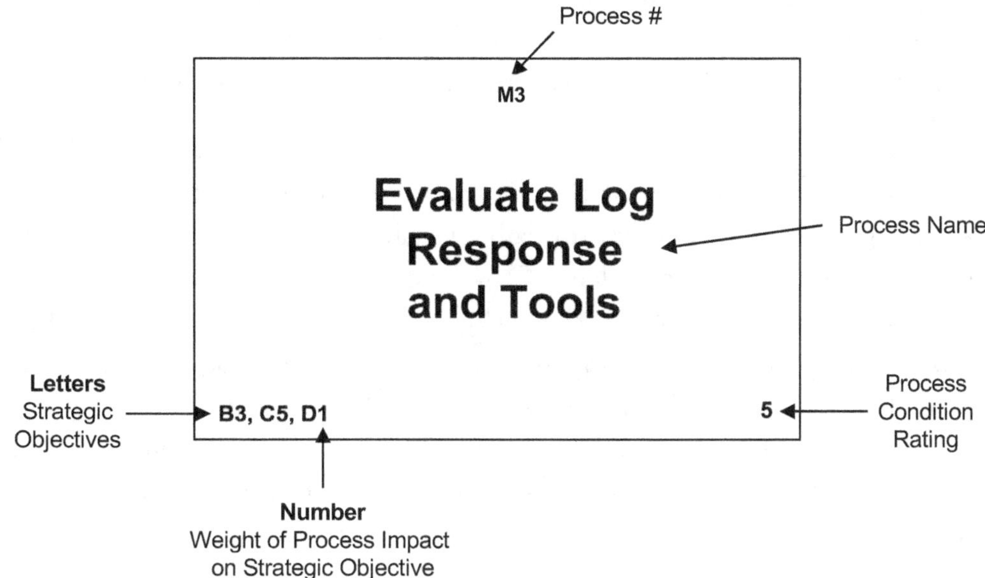

Figure 8.8. Process coding.

Leaders should also ask what, if anything, is missing in the current system to accomplish the strategic objectives. This can reveal potential new processes, products, and services to consider for design.

During the initial QOS planning process, leaders assess the weights of every process, product, and service. In planning processes in the following years, these weights are expected to change, and leaders must repeat the assessment. For example, process M2 was selected as an improvement effort in the initial QOS planning process. An improvement team redesigned the process and sustained the results. In this year's planning, therefore, leaders no longer weight the process as essential to achieving the strategic objective.

For Jada's project, an executive assistant printed a large version of the company's system map and displayed it across the meeting room wall. Starting with Strategic Objective A, the leaders discussed the processes, products, and services that must be focused on to achieve the objective. They continued this process until each strategic objective was related to the system map and weighted for impact. New processes, products, or services were also considered (see figure 8.9).

"This was the first time our planning process connected our objectives back to the organization's work. Historically, we moved from objectives straight to action planning," reflected Jada. "It was new for us to consider a strategic objective and relate it back to our current system as described by the key processes and products in the organization. We started with our products first and then went through the mainstay processes. The discussion was rich, and it was interesting to learn from others about why they had different opinions than mine. Once we reached an agreement, we considered the driver and support processes."

The results were captured and displayed on the organization's system map, which included a new process and product considered important to achieving the objectives.

TOTAL STRATEGIC WEIGHT

After leaders reach consensus on the system's aspects that impact each strategic objective, the next step is to calculate the **total strategic impact** of the product, services, or processes. The total strategic impact is calculated by summing the individual weights: $3 + 5 + 1 = 9$. Process M3, for example, has a total strategic weight of "9." Repeat the calculation for each process, product, or service with a weight noted. Figure 8.10 shows the system map with the total strategic impact recorded in the bottom left corner.

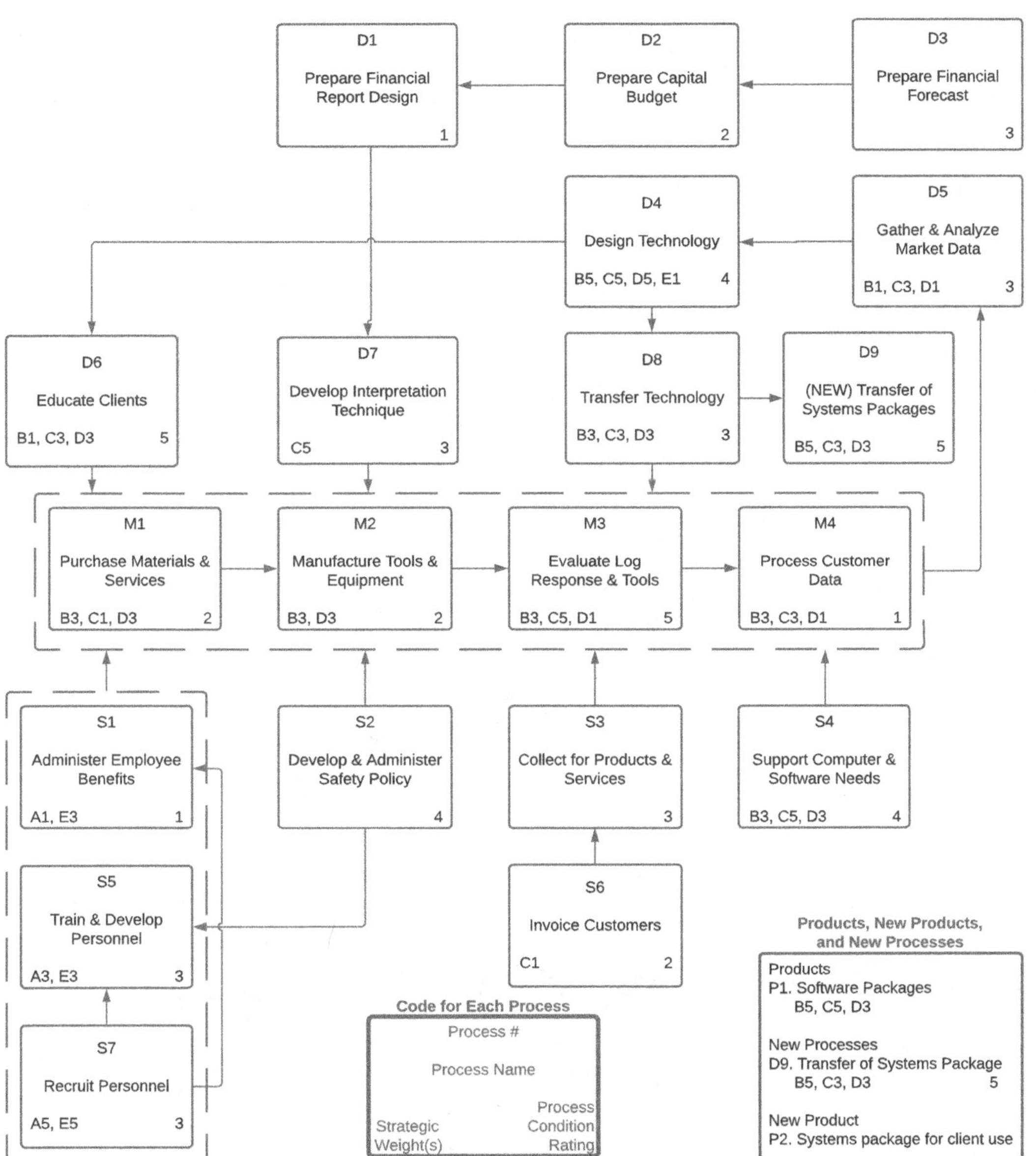

Figure 8.9. Strategic objectives related to the system map and weighted for impact.

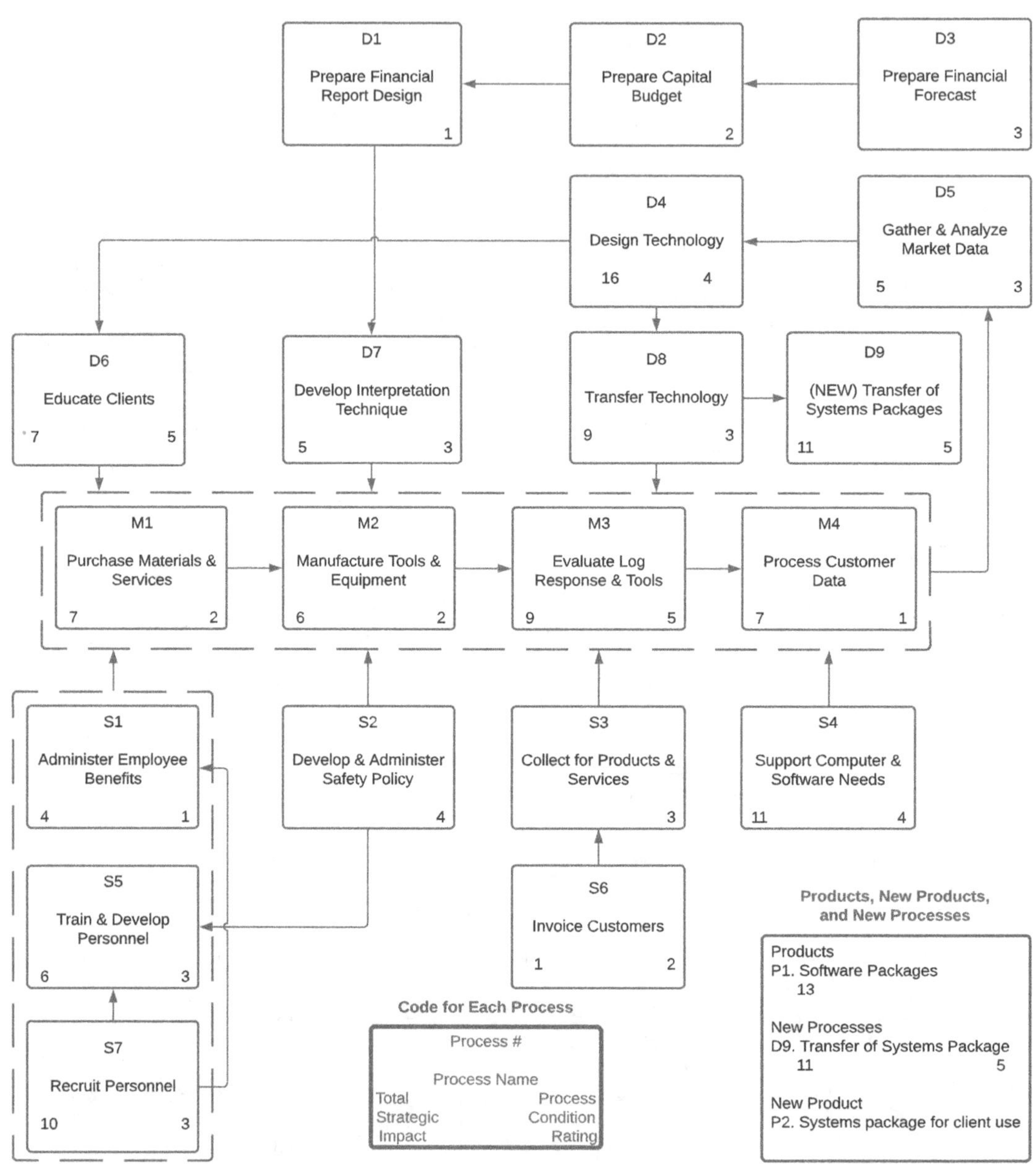

Figure 8.10. System map with total strategic weight for each process, product, and service.

RELATING RESOURCE ALLOCATION TO PROCESSES

An organization can accomplish some of its strategic objectives by focused operation of its current system. After identifying processes, products, and products for design or redesign (planning to improve), where should processes be emphasized to help the organization accomplish the strategic objective? Where could allocating more resources to a process help (planning to operate)? Leaders can use a weighting system (see table 8.4) to rate resource allocation to processes using a similar approach to that described for strategic weighting for impact.

Table 8.4. Weighing system for relating resource allocation (planning to operate)

Weight	Operational definition of weight
5	Allocating resources to this process is **essential** to accomplishing the strategic objectives.
3	Allocating resources to this process will have a **direct impact** on the strategic objectives.
1	Allocating resources to this process will have an **indirect impact** on the strategic objectives.
-	No impact on the strategic objective is expected from operating this process.

Create a list of strategic processes for inclusion in the organization's plan to operate. For example, two processes were weighted as essential to accomplishing Strategic Objective C: Improve the consistency of software products to our companies. Adding resources to (1) Training and Developing Personnel (support process S5) would increase staffing and more staff can increase the output of (2) Manufacture Tools and Equipment (mainstay process M2). Later, this list will be included in the activities to allocate resources.

Using Strategic Impact to Set Priorities

When the selections of the parts of the system are made, priority should go to the processes, products, and services that will have the greatest impact on the strategic objectives. Here are a few considerations:

1. Pareto Analysis: Figure 8.9 related the strategic objectives to the processes, products, and services. Each relationship was weighted for impact. A Pareto chart (figure 8.11) displaying the processes, products, and services in order by the number of strategic objectives it relates to can be useful in identifying high-leverage aspects.

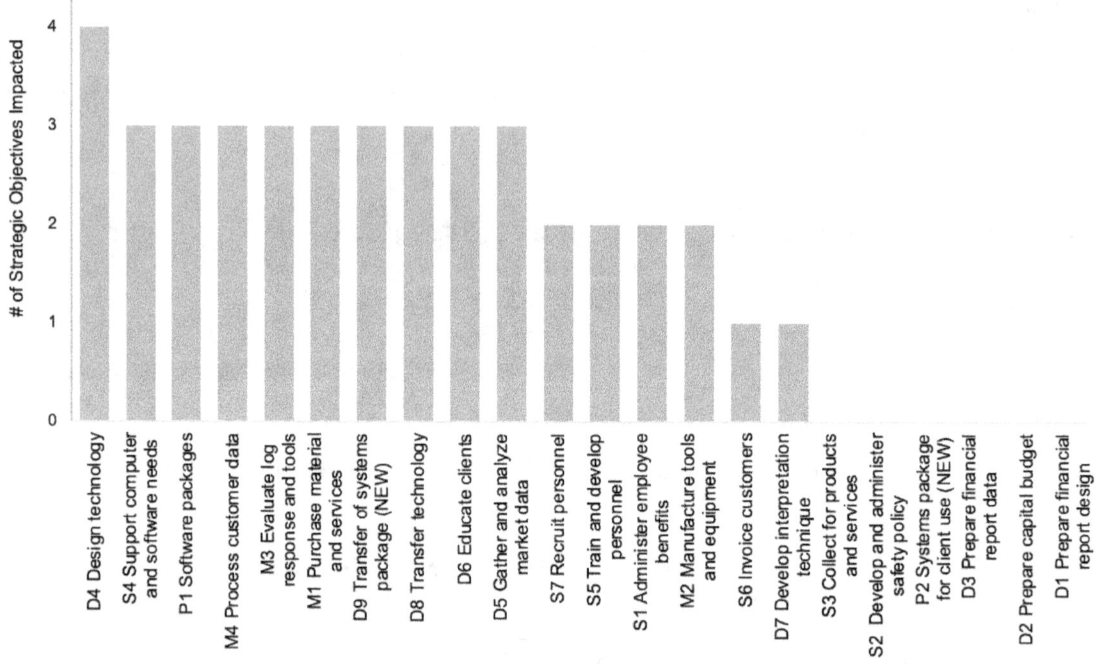

Figure 8.11. Pareto chart of processes, products, and services and the number of strategic objectives each impacts.

2. Coverage of all strategic objectives: Accomplishing the strategic objectives is important for the organization to meet its purpose. Prioritizing processes, products, and services must include a confirmation that all the strategic objectives are covered.

3. Understanding high-leverage links: Prioritizing processes may depend on preceding processes. Existing and new products and services selected for design or redesign may require the support of other processes. Consider linked processes during the prioritization.

4. Holistic view: Consider all the strategic objectives and the organization together. Review the processes, products, and services selected together relative to the strategic objectives. Will focus on these processes, products, and services move the organization toward its purpose?

Including Process Conditions in the Selection

The assessment of the current **process condition**[15] and the predicted **total strategic impact** on the strategic objectives can be combined to support selecting priority processes. Table 8.5 lists each process from the system map and includes the total strategic impact and the process condition rating.

Table 8.5. Matrix of process with total strategic impact and process condition rating for highway data collection company

Processes	Total strategic impact	Process condition rating
D1 Prepare financial report design	0	1
D2 Prepare capital budget	0	2
D3 Prepare financial report data	0	3
D4 Design technology	16	4
D5 Gather and analyze market data	5	3
D6 Educate clients	7	5
D7 Develop interpretation technique	5	3
D8 Transfer technology	9	3
D9 Transfer of systems package (NEW)	11	5
M1 Purchase material and services	7	2
M2 Manufacture tools and equipment	6	2
M3 Evaluate log response and tools	9	5
M4 Process customer data	7	1
S1 Administer employee benefits	4	1
S2 Develop and administer safety policy	0	4
S3 Collect for products and services	0	3
S4 Support computer and software needs	11	4
S5 Train and develop personnel	6	3
S6 Invoice customers	1	2
S7 Recruit personnel	10	3

The data on strategic impact and process conditions can be converted into a scatter diagram to display the data visually (figure 8.12).[16] Processes in the upper right corner of the graph are processes with both an opportunity for improvement and high leverage in accomplishing the organization's strategic objectives. These processes are strong candidates for improvement projects. However, consider other processes that may require improvement before processes in the circle can be addressed.

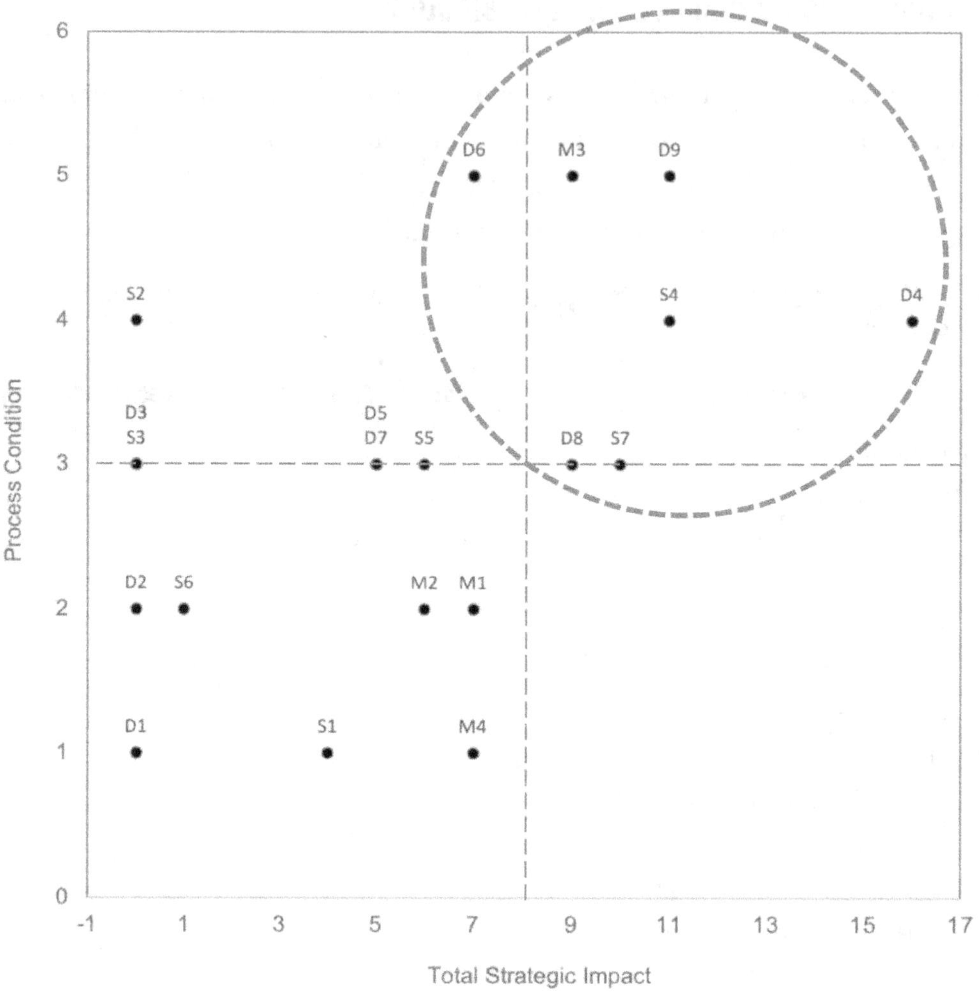

Figure 8.12. Scatter diagram process condition and total strategic impact.

KEY PRODUCTS OR SERVICES IN THE ORGANIZATION

Criteria for key products or services will vary for different organizations. Specific definitions for scoring the status of key products or services should be developed depending on how these products or services support the organization's strategies.

Predict the Impact of Strategic Objectives on the Vector of Measures

An organization's vector of measures provides a way to evaluate progress in performance related to its purpose. The impact on the organization of improving high-leverage processes to achieve organizational strategic objectives should become visible in the vector of measures. Planning for improvement should ideally positively affect the overall vector of measures.[17] For example, would the measure worsen, stay the same, or improve? Is it important if improvement happens? Is it desirable? Or is it critical? These assessments were identified as a key input to the planning process.

Using the strategic objectives, an assessment is added to predict the impact successfully working on each strategic objective will have on each measure. Finally, an overall prediction for the measure from focusing on the strategic objectives is assigned. Table 8.6 adds the predicted impact to the analysis of the VOM prepared earlier in table 6.5.[18]

Table 8.6. Predicted impact of the plan on the vector of measures after a new plan is developed

Prior to developing plan			After new plan is developed					
Measures of the system	Prediction for next planning period with no changes to current plan (-2, 1,0,1,2)	Priority to	Predicted impact from focus on each strategic objective (-2, -1, 0, 1, 2)					Overall prediction for next planning period (-2, -1, 0, 1, 2)
			A	B	C	D	E	
% Uptime	0	M	0	1	1	0	0	1
%	-1	H	1	2	1	2	1	2
Market Share	0	H	0	1	1	1	1	1

Priority for improvement of the measure	Predicted impact on measure
H Critical to make improvement in this measure M Improvements desirable in this measure L Not important to make improvements in this measure	-2 Very desirable impact on measure -1 Undesirable impact on measure 0 No change in this measure 1 Some improvements in this measure 2 Significant improvement in this measure

This process supports deep understanding by helping the planning team develop a shared understanding of the strategic objectives and the expected impact. This analysis is an important "sanity check" to confirm the planning process has not veered off track. If pursuing a strategic objective is not predicted to have an acceptable impact on the vector of measures, updating or replacing the strategic objective must be considered.

Jada's previous planning process generated a list of potential improvement efforts. The facilitator asked the leaders to rank the projects on a scale: "1" was a high priority, and "5" was low. Each leader had projects on the list. If the effort fell in their area of responsibility, they leaned toward rating its value higher. The end tally of the rankings showed that most of the projects were considered important, and it was little help in sorting and prioritizing. All the projects ended up into the queue for the year's plan. Many projects shared the same team members.

"That process was frustrating. We didn't have a method to help us decide what would make an impact or move the dots we wanted to move."

The new planning process mapped the strategic objectives to the system map and considered the effect on the vector of measures. Plotting their assessments on the scatter plot converted their rankings into a visual display that made it easier to agree on where to focus.

As Jada shared, "I had to trust the process a little at the start. I didn't see at first how each step would get us to the endpoint. Starting with the process conditions on a useable draft system map and adding the total strategic impact shifted the discussions. Reviewing the vector or measures and predicting what would happen in each chart was a big aha for me as we reflected on the organization. Building on that learning by connecting it to the strategic objectives brought it all together. When I saw the process numbers floating in that top right quadrant, I was pleasantly surprised. That's where we need to focus. We did that."

The team reviewed the processes identified with an early-stage process condition and a high impact on the strategic objectives and quickly agreed that those were the places to start. The combination of the organized prework and method for working through the data led them efficiently to agreement and clarity. Now they knew what needed to be done.

Selection of Strategic Processes, Products, and Services

Developing strategic objectives and gathering and learning from diverse inputs provides insights and data to identify the strategic work to select and resource. Early in the chapter, planning was framed as including two outcomes: planning to operate and planning to improve. Both must be considered in developing actions to accomplish the strategic objectives:

> **Planning to operate.** This phase involves allocating resources to emphasize an existing process, product, or service in the organization to further a strategic objective. Processes are not changed, or new ones added. For example, adding an additional CT scan may improve the flow of patients requiring imaging for physicians to diagnose in the hospital Emergency Department. The organization's managers will be responsible for appropriately staffing the resources in these strategic processes.

> **Planning to improve.** This phase identifies processes, products, and services to design or redesign, for example, the workflow in a primary care clinic to help the strategic objective of "reducing cycle time to see patients." Improvement projects will be selected to improve these targeted processes, products, or services. Determining an appropriate number of projects will require reflection on the organization's capacity. An organization focused on value has activity in one of three categories: eliminating problems, cost reduction, or innovation. Planning for improvement helps determine the categories in which to focus the organization's resources.

Developing separate lists for improvement, operation, and emphasis can reduce confusion between operating and improving in the planning process. In this step in the planning process, processes, products, and services are selected for improvement (plan to improve) or to consider resource allocation (plan to operate) to achieve the strategic objectives. When developing the list, leaders should consider the resources required to improve or operate and the availability of those resources.

Improvement Project Briefs

How many improvement projects need to be planned? Table 8.7 summarizes the priority processes, products, and services identified for the example company used throughout this chapter.

Table 8.7. Priority processes, products, and services relationship to strategic objectives

Method to accomplish strategic objectives[a]	Strategic objectives[b] (impact weight[c])				
	A	B	C	D	E
Processes (#)					
Design technology (D4)		5	5	5	
Evaluate log and response tools (M3)		3	5	1	
Recruit personnel (S7)	5				5
Support computer/software needs (S4)		3	5	3	
Transfer of systems package (D9 - new)		3	3	3	
Products					
Systems package for client use (P2 - new)	Relationship to high leverage processes				

Note:

a. See Figure 8.9. Strategic objectives related to the system map and weighted for impact.

b. See vignette, page 256–257, for strategic objectives A to E.

c. See Table 8.3. Weights for relationship of process, product, or service to strategic objectives.

The projects, processes, and services selected for design and redesign will each require a draft improvement brief (figure 8.13). Improvement briefs are high-level proposals for the improvement efforts selected. Included is a brief description of the aim of the improvement effort, expected results, and any boundaries. Improvement efforts can involve more than one linked process.

Also included are the sponsor and improvement team leader. The sponsor is the leader responsible for the processes, products, and services selected for design or redesign. The team leader is typically the manager or supervisor responsible for operating the processes, products, and services.

General Description:
Improve the organization's process for supporting computer and software needs (Process # S4). Emphasis should be placed on improving software response time and responding to customers' requests.

Expected Results:
1. Documented process for support of hardware and software needs.
2. Faster response time to requests for software support.
3. Faster response time to requests for new software.
4. Improve response time to customers for software needs.

Boundaries:
1. Existing and new software should be addressed.
2. The process should accommodate different hardware configurations of existing and new customers.
3. Initial focus should be on the software supporting the organization's primary products.

Executive Sponsor: Jada   **Improvement Team Lead**: Arthur

Figure 8.13. Improvement brief for a high-priority process.

Improvement briefs do not replace improvement charters. Once an improvement effort is selected and resources are allocated, the sponsor and team lead assign a team. The sponsor, team lead, and staff team will develop an improvement charter using the Model for Improvement and manage the improvement effort.[19]

Allocating Resources

Selecting strategic work for improvement efforts increases the potential impact of the improvements, but it is also essential to properly allocate the time and resources to do this work. The same applies to parts of the organization identified where emphasis may help achieve strategic objectives. Resources considered include people, staff time, materials, supplies, space, technology, and capital expenditures.

In planning to improve, the members of an improvement team are a combination of key stakeholders with subject matter expertise and improvement personnel with an understanding of the Science of Improvement and the tools and methods for problem-solving, measurement, and testing. Making the improvement efforts add-on-work and failing to allocate people, time, and other resources will stifle or curtail any improvement effort. Improvement work requires dedicated time; staff must have that time be part of the scope of work and commit their attention. **Involvement in a strategic improvement project can require up to 20% of a person's time throughout the duration of the project.**[20] Access to meeting space, materials like flip chart paper and whiteboards, and software for data management and analysis (like Shewhart charts) are also required. In some organizations, project management support personnel are assigned to strategic improvement teams.

In planning to improve, strategic processes are identified where adding additional resources is predicted to affect the achievement of strategic objectives positively. Identification and allocation of resources are critical for business planning.

The system map can be helpful to identify where the work will happen, the staff with responsibilities in these areas, and what other areas are linked. The planning team should make the initial assignments for each selected improvement project. For example, if a process selected for design and redesign is an area of the system where a leader has responsibility, they will likely serve in the role of sponsor and be responsible for the results of the project. Chapter 9 discusses the management of improvement efforts. The sponsor leads resourcing, assigning the improvement team, and managing the improvement efforts.

An **energy grid**[21] (table 8.8) visualizes the selected projects and responsible staff. Proper allocation of time and resources and the timing of projects have implications for the pace of system-level improvement efforts.[22] Insights into the necessary resourcing support business planning and prioritizing the sequence of improvement efforts and the ability to properly resource at this time.

RECONCILING THE BACKLOG OF IMPROVEMENT BRIEFS

If an improvement effort cannot be resourced, it should be placed in a backlog queue. Reviewing the backlog of improvement briefs is part of studying the inputs to planning. Planning teams return to the backlog in the closing steps of planning to improve process. Improvement efforts in progress, new efforts identified in the planning process, and what remains in the backlog are reconciled. Improvement briefs are prioritized and assessed against available resources. Select improvement briefs are placed on the backlog list, which serves as the pipeline for future resourcing as higher-priority projects are completed, and resource capacity becomes available.

Table 8.8. Energy grid of staff by selected priorities for design or redesign

	Design technology (D4)	Evaluate log and response tools (M3)	Recruit personnel (S7)	Support computer/ software needs (S4)	Transfer of systems package (D9 - new)	Systems package for client use (P2 -new)
Jada	●				●	●
Michael		●				
Jessica			●			
Christopher	●			●		
Ashley			●			
Matthew						
Amanda		●		●	●	●
Joshua				●	●	●

Planning at Multiple Organizational Levels

In larger organizations, planning occurs in different areas of the organization. For example, a healthcare organization may do strategic planning for the entire health system, business planning at each facility, and operational planning in each department within those facilities. The planning method can be used for any group in the organization. The inputs and the specificity and scope of the outcomes may be different.

Figure 8.14 illustrates how strategic objectives developed in the organization's planning process are communicated to other parts of the organization providing a formal link to the planning activities. Leaders must ask, "How can our group help accomplish the organization's strategic objectives?" Other parts of the organization use the global strategic objectives as inputs to their plans to guide their efforts. The organization's strategic objectives may be accepted as is or adapted to be more specific to the part of the organization. Additional local strategic objectives may be added that are relevant to the part of the organization.

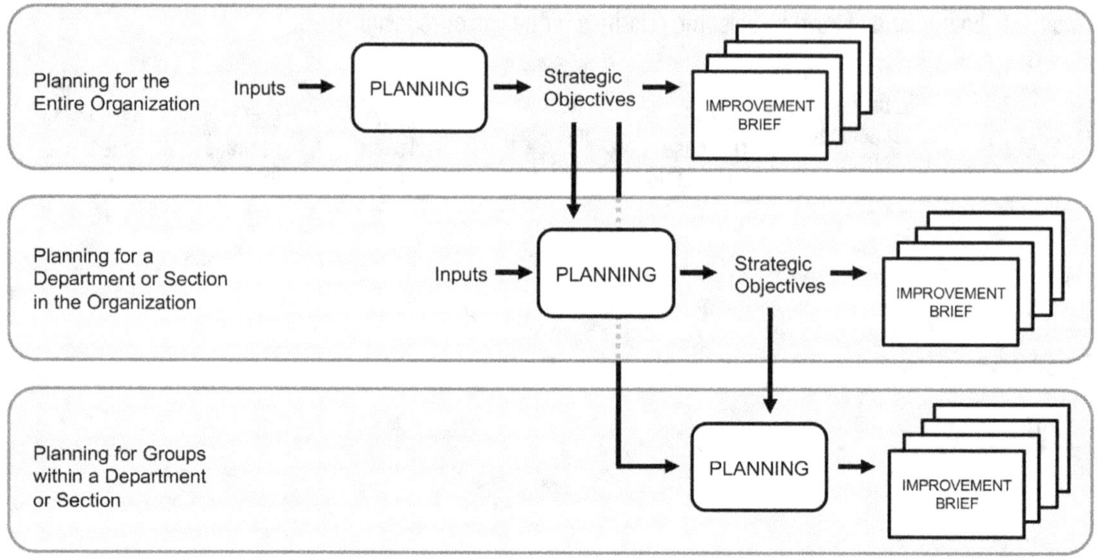

Figure 8.14. Planning throughout the organization.

Planning In Future Years

The process outlined in this chapter describes each of the steps in the first QOS planning process. This process is typically repeated annually. When repeated each year, the process remains the same, but there are a few modifications:

- **Inputs**: An updated system map with current process condition ratings and a current evaluation of the vector of measures are included. The progress or results from previous improvements are included. The backlog of improvement briefs is added.
- **Strategic objectives**: After studying the updated inputs, the strategic objectives are reviewed. Update language and add or subtract strategic objectives as appropriate. The weights of each strategic objective usually change.
- **Redo the relating of strategic objectives to the system and weighting the strategic impact**.
- **Capacity for improvement**: As the organization becomes more skilled at executing results-driven improvement efforts, consider increasing the number of system-level improvement projects.

With each year, the planning process will become more familiar, and facilitating the process will feel more natural. Leadership is often energized by the process to zero in on the strategic priorities and the ease that comes from having a method to learn about the organizational system and to focus improvements and operations.

SUMMARY

When pursuing QOS, the various planning activities are viewed as a system. Leaders clearly understand the organization's purpose and have defined a vision of a desired future. An interactive planning process supports strategic thinking to develop strategic objectives and to follow a method to identify products, services, and processes requiring design or redesign to achieve the intended outcomes. Improvement efforts are sponsored and resourced.

The next chapter builds on the planning activity and describes how the improvement projects identified in the planning process are managed to get the desired results.

Jada reflected on the planning process they had just completed:

> What used to take many days and much wrangling now followed a methodical flow. In the past, the process was draining, and most of the effort centered on building will and commitment and reaching a consensus on the projects individual leaders were championing. Now it was still hard work, but the preparation of the proper inputs combined with a method for summarizing and analyzing the information ended with clear plans to operate and improve.
>
> This time, we left the room tired and energized at the same time. The process made me feel like we were in control. The approach allowed us to have an ideal but practical vision, learn from a system of different inputs, and follow a process that freed us up to be very tactical in selecting where to focus our attention. The portfolio of improvement efforts is clearly the right place for us to work this year, and we identified the right people and created the space for them to do the improvement work. For the first time, I believe the plans we made will be the plans we execute over the next year. I'm pretty sure we will successfully achieve what we prioritized. I couldn't say that confidently in years past. How exciting!

NOTES

1. In Chapter 1, Table 1.5 is a tool for leaders to assess the organization's progress in making quality an organizational strategy. This paragraph is the operational definition for the top score for "Planning for improvement." *The QOS Field Guide* contains a more comprehensive version of the assessment tool.

2. Plans to improve and plans to operate become inputs into the organization's global business planning process. These plans inform other planning including financial, human resources, operations, training, marketing, etc. *The QOS Field Guide* includes an expanded display of the system of planning to incorporate these other planning processes in Chapter 8, "Planning to Improve."

3. The work to draft a purpose (Chapter 4), develop a system map (Chapter 5), and establish a vector of measures (Chapter 6) come together with the sources information from the system to obtain information (Chapter 7) to serve as the inputs for the planning activity.

4. Chapter 3 defined foresight as follows: "Predict the future direction of the organization based on internal and external subject matter expertise, experience, research, dynamic trends, threats, and opportunities. This may be reflected in the Need for new or revised products/services or other changes to ensure the organization's future."

5. The figure of the five activities of QOS at the beginning of this chapter depicts four arrows to the planning activity, one from each of the other activities. The Purpose Activity provides a written statement of purpose of the organization for leaders to use as an input to the planning activity to continually ask "How can we better fulfill our purpose?" The vector of measures provides input on the stability and performance of key results. The Information Activity produces analysis from the customer and the market to guide design and redesign, and the status of improvement efforts informs leaders of the capacity for additional improvement efforts.

6. See Chapter 5, table 5.2 for the operational definitions of a scale to rate current process condition on the Systems Map.

7. In the authors' experience, leaders frequently underestimate the level of effort required to develop the inputs. Preparation should start in the months leading into the planning process and time and resources must be allocated to complete the inputs. Often, each member of the leadership team is given responsibility for specific inputs.

8. *The QOS Field Guide*, Chapter 8 "Planning to Improve," includes more detail about inputs including methods for developing them, along with examples.

9. Chapter 5 included a method for developing a system map and visually displaying the process of the organization. Table 5.2, "Rating definitions of process conditions" is a rating scale for assessing each process's current condition and recording it on the system map (see figure 5.15, "Code for each process"). This rating is used in the planning process to help select projects. The method is further described in Chapter 5 of *The QOS Field Guide*, "Viewing the Organization as a System."

10. Chapter 6, table 6.5 "Analysis of vector of measures for the planning process," is a method to assess the status of the organization's vector of measures. The form is in *The QOS Field Guide*, Chapter 6, "Measurement of the System."

11. See *The QOS Field Guide*, Chapter 7, "A System for Obtaining Information" for the description of a method for benchmarking using the Model for Improvement framework.

12. The *QOS Field Guide, Chapter 8*, "Planning to Improve" includes alternative methods for developing strategic objectives.

13. "A New Meaning of 'Moonshot,'" Merriam-Webster, accessed June 12, 2023, https://www.merriam-webster.com/words-at-play/moonshot-words-were-watching.

14. Regarding process coding, Chapter 5 described naming and numbering each process when developing the organizational Systems Map. Table 5.2 presents the operational definitions of the scale to rate current process condition on the Systems Map. Chapter 8 adds predicting the "strategic weight(s)" for each process in relationship to the strategic objectives in table 8.3, "Weights for Relationships of Process/Product to Strategic Objectives."

15. The process condition rating was captured in each process on the system map in the bottom right corner (see figure 8.10).

16. Each process includes two values: process condition and total strategic weight. The x-axis is the strategic impact (sum of the weights), and the vertical y-axis is the process condition.

17. See table 6.5, "Analysis of vectors of measures for the planning process" for a method to predict what would happen in the next planning period if no changes occurred.

18. Table 8.6 is a sample of the predictions for the total vector of measures from table 6.5 and adds the predicted impact of the strategic objectives from the planning process. The full table is in *The QOS Field Guide*, Chapter 8, "Planning to Improve."

19. See Chapter 9, "Managing Improvement Efforts."

20. Langley et al., *The Improvement Guide*, 2009, 325–26, 341. In our experience, leaders initially feel this level of staffing may be excessive or unaffordable, but organizations that follow

this approach recognize the selected improvement efforts are large, and that strategic projects demanding lots of time are expected to pay a financial or strategic return. When projects are viewed as extra assignments or in addition to daily work, the improvements are typically delayed or never completed.

21. Peter J. Knox, former Executive Vice President at Bellin Health and Senior Fellow at the Institute for Healthcare Improvement introduced the "organizational energy grid" as a tool to visualize priorities and staff allocation to understand potential bottlenecks and overload.

22. See Langley et al., *The Improvement Guide*, 2009, 325–26. An organization can choose to increase the pace without increasing the resources significantly by focusing the team leader's efforts.

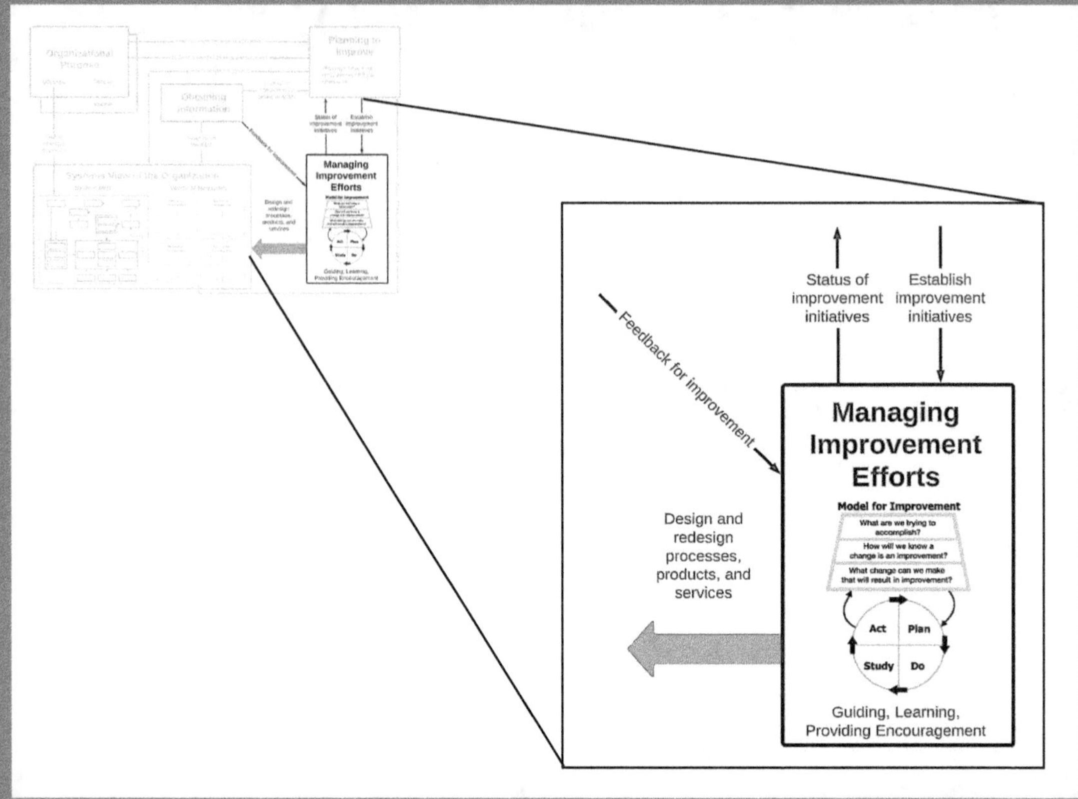

ACTIONS FOR LEADERSHIP TEAM

- Prepare the organization to focus on improvement.
- Define the leadership team's role in managing improvement efforts.
- Execute improvement projects identified in the planning process.
  - o Provide a standard methodology to guide improvement efforts.
  - o Provide training and other necessary resources required for the improvement efforts.
- Provide sponsors and ensure that guidance is provided for improvement efforts.
  - o Remove obstacles and provide recognition.
  - o Redirect and redeploy resources as improvements are made.
- Leadership team studies the improvement results and contributions of improvement efforts of the team to learn about the organization viewed as system and the key forces driving the system.

CHAPTER 9

MANAGING IMPROVEMENT EFFORTS

As the leadership team adopts *QOS*, Mid Tech CEO Herman Haupt is learning that making improvements can result in cost savings and improvement of quality and service to customers. More important, these improvement projects have now connected to the strategic plan for the business. Herman opened the weekly leadership team meeting:

Good morning! Now that we have completed the planning process, it is essential that we execute the improvement projects identified. The opportunities discussed in the planning process have identified several improvement projects necessary to achieve the updated strategic objectives for Mid Tech. Learning from the planning process has made it clear that enhancing performance requires change in the organization, change we all must embrace and lead. We all must develop our capability by actively engaging in and leading these improvement efforts. We each have a role as sponsors for several projects that will keep us on the front line of achieving these improvements and our strategy. In addition to the efforts that have been identified, each of you should identify improvement efforts in your area of responsibility to improve an essential process. The managers in each department should be responsible for identifying and executing a local improvement project at least quarterly.

Leadership teams spend much of their time in meetings to handle and react to problems. When leaders begin acting proactively and making improvements driven by the organization's strategic objectives, a new journey begins—learning from **execution** and getting results. This chapter describes several ways leadership supports the implementation of the plan to improve:

- Preparing the organization to focus on improvement
- The leadership team's role in managing improvement efforts
- Executing improvement efforts identified in the planning process
- Providing a standard methodology to guide improvement efforts
- Sponsoring and guiding improvement efforts
- Leadership team's role in learning about the system

For a mature organization in QOS, improvement initiatives are begun in the formal planning processes using project briefs for selected projects. The leaders provide guidance and sponsorship of the improvement activities, including removing obstacles and giving recognition. A system is used to report the status of improvement efforts. The organization's leaders view the improvement efforts as critical to achieving the strategic and business plans of the organization. All types of improvement efforts to eliminate problems, reduce cost, or create innovation are considered part of an overall strategy for developing and growing the organization. The leaders study the activities of improvement efforts to learn about the key processes in the organization and the key forces that drive behavior in the organization and create the environment for establishing the habit of improvement.[1]

PREPARING THE ORGANIZATION TO FOCUS ON IMPROVEMENT

How do we organize to make quality improvement a fundamental focus of our daily work?[2] What sort of additional structure is needed to support proper execution? Do we need additional people? A separate department? An improvement manager? These questions[3] usually come up early in an organization's effort to improve. The right answers are important and depend on the current management style and the complexity of the organization. There is no one correct answer for all organizations.

Moving from Accountability to Improving the System

The preferred organization for improvement is the **current management structure, focused on the organization viewed as a system.** Quality becomes an organizational strategy when we build on the current organizational structure, develop internal capability, and combine it with the methods discussed in Chapters 4 through 8.

Figure 9.1 depicts the shift from accountability to improving the system. The leadership team breaks the paradigm of thinking about the organization through the lens of reporting and accountability (represented by the organizational chart). Now, leadership connects the organization's plans to improve to its system map. This view more accurately reflects how work and improvement (PDSA icons represent improvement projects) are accomplished and enables the people who work in the system to understand how their work supports the organization's purpose.[4]

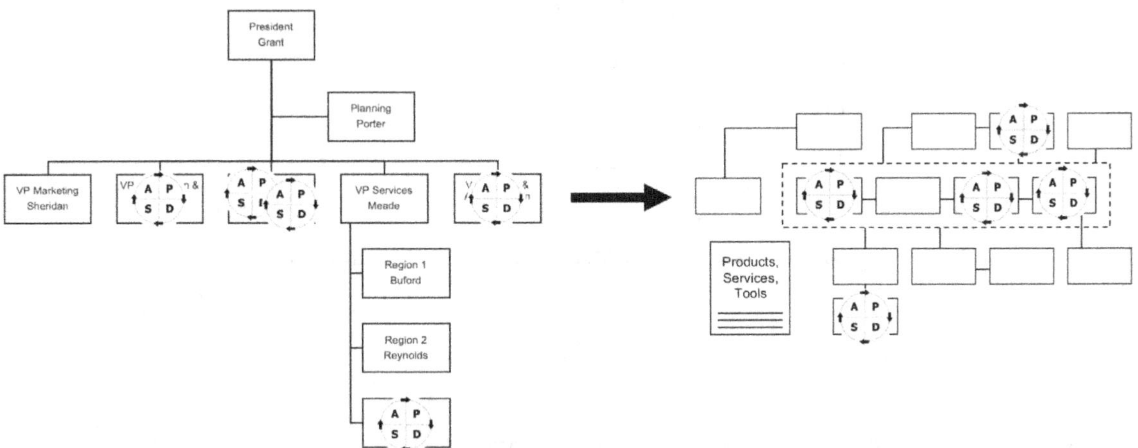

Figure 9.1. Shifting improvement accountability to improving the system.

Quality is now viewed as an organizational strategy led by the **leadership team**. The amount of structure required to make this shift depends on the leadership's strength, the organization's complexity (geographic, business groups, product lines, etc.), and the organization's size.

Need for Additional Structure and Roles

Figure 9.2 depicts this conceptual relationship for adding structure for improvement[5] and represents the general experience of several organizations applying quality improvement as an organizational strategy.

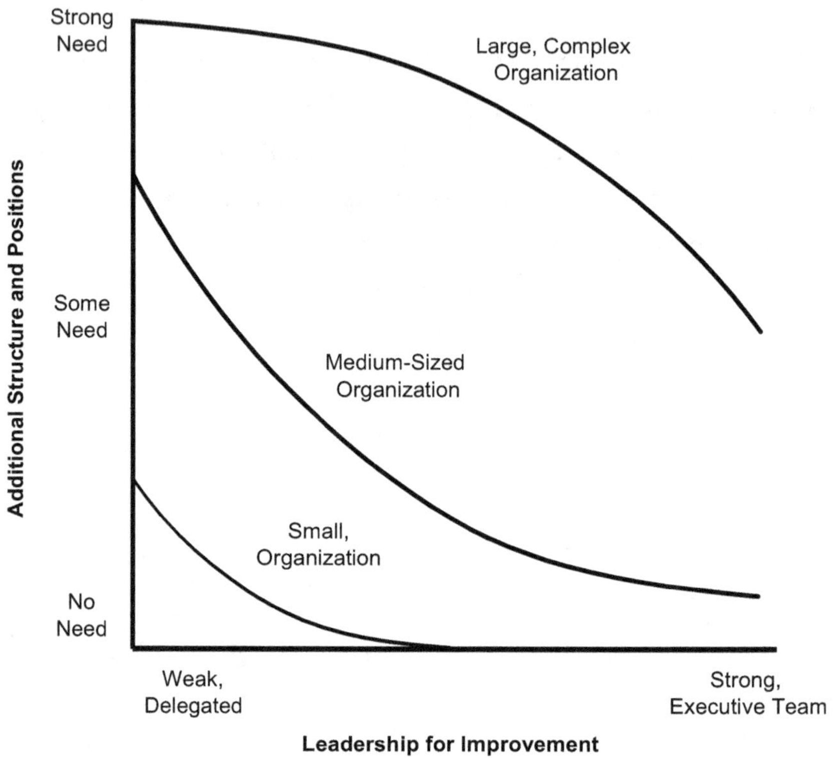

Figure 9.2. Need for additional structure or positions for improvement.

Relying on the current management structure is preferred, but many organizations find the need to create additional structures to organize improvement at the beginning of their improvement journey. Table 9.1 includes examples of additional structures and positions.[6] Larger organizations often require additional structure in the early phases of improvement. As the leadership team integrates the improvement efforts into the organization's daily, routine management practices, additional structure is needed less. Sometimes maintaining "some" structure remains useful for efficiency to coordinate efforts and resources, even with excellent leadership for improvement. Smaller, less complex organizations usually have a minimal need for additional structure. Line management can run the activities early in the journey.

Table 9.1. Additional structure and positions

Structure/Positions	Definition
Quality managers and technology staff	Quality Control and Quality Assurance management and technology positions; typically required for many businesses and organizations.
Improvement advisors/ Quality Improvement (QI) professionals	People who have been educated in the Science of Improvement and trained in improvement theory, methods, and tools.
Quality Council/ Steering Committee	The Quality Council/Steering committee is usually a group of managers who coordinate, guide and review of the progress of improvement efforts. Ensure resources are available.
Facilitator positions	People who are used to managing and coordinating meetings.

The amount of assistance and additional structure varies from organization to organization. Consider the needs and capability of the leadership team and factors unique to that organization when deciding how much structure is sufficient.

Whether an organization is large or small, improvement efforts are conducted by teams as defined projects. The leader accountable for the results of the improvement effort and responsible for the area of the organization where the changes are made is the sponsor and usually the primary author of the improvement brief. The sponsor identifies the team leader who is a person with subject matter expertise, a key manager who controls the resources required, or another person with the knowledge and resource to accomplish the required improvement effort. The sponsor supports the improvement project lead to resource a team. The project lead and team members will build on the improvement brief and develop a formal project charter using the Model for Improvement. More detail about each of these activities follows in this chapter.

Diane, Vice President for Finance, recently visited an organization that has used QOS for several years. She was ready to discuss what she learned about getting started on improvement with the leadership team at Mid Tech.

"I have had an opportunity to spend some time thinking about us getting started on this journey. I believe it is important to get prioritized projects underway immediately. Because this is a small organization, I suggest we don't add a lot of extra positions. We should develop two or three improvement advisors to help guide our project teams. It would be a good idea if these people were team members of our initial project teams. During this initial improvement journey, we can train these people in the Science of Improvement and appropriate tools and methods."

"In the next wave of projects," Diane continued, "we can assign these people to guide the new teams. We should select people we expect to be future leaders in the organization. Let's consider this work a development path for leaders in our organization."

Herman raised his pen in the air and asked, "Diane, how much time should we be prepared to allocate supporting these projects?"

"Be prepared to spend at least ten percent of our time as leaders," suggested Diane.

 Herman quickly said, "That will be about eight hours a week for each of us!" Herman was making it clear to the leadership team that the CEO was expecting improvement work to be a priority.

LEADERSHIP TEAM'S ROLE IN MANAGING IMPROVEMENT EFFORTS

Leadership teams find the journey to become an improvement organization both challenging and rewarding. Rewards come from their profound learning and making contributions that help the organization better meet its purpose. The leadership team also faces challenges, including:

1. Ensuring the execution of planning efforts.
2. Communicating and coordinating groups internally and across organization boundaries.
3. Coordinating education and training in improvement for individuals and teams.
4. Identifying and coordinating the removal of barriers in the organization that inhibit change and improvement.
5. Managing overlapping responsibilities of individuals and teams involved in improvement.[7]
6. Studying the improvement efforts to learn about fundamental causes of problems, opportunities for improvement, and innovation in the organization.

7. Evaluating and publicizing the status of the improvement work in the organization.
8. Redirecting and redeploying resources as improvements are made.

What the authors call "managing improvement efforts" has a crucial connection to the "systems view of an organization"; it is the mechanism by which leaders continually design and redesign processes, products, and services. It is essential for the organization's leaders and managers to clearly understand that improvements do not actually occur until you execute actions in the system.

The four leadership activities of QOS to this point have focused on understanding and aligning the organization. The fifth activity—managing improvement efforts—focuses on executing the defined improvement efforts. **Initiating improvement efforts does not have to be dependent on the other methods of QOS.** If an obvious improvement is necessary, start now and develop the other methods in parallel. The impact of these early improvements may not be strategic to the organization.

Many organizations the authors have worked with developed QOS starting with a three-pronged approach, with each element done concurrently:

1. **Make improvements immediately:** Begin with existing projects currently active in the organization.[8] This helps people experience and understand the approach to improvement and integrates the **habit of improvement**[9] into the organization.
2. **Begin building the system to make Quality an Organizational Strategy (QOS):** This is an ongoing process (see Chapter 11 on "Getting Started").
3. **Build internal capability for improvement:** Identify and develop people who can lead improvement efforts. The potential candidates to build this internal capability should participate as team members in initial improvement teams (see Item 1 in this list). Experience as a team member is invaluable when this person is facilitating or leading other improvement teams.

EXECUTION OF PROJECTS IDENTIFIED IN THE PLANNING PROCESS

Results-driven improvement is at the heart of adopting QOS. The leadership team is responsible for the successful execution of projects identified in the planning process.

To execute these projects, leadership must address the following for the effective execution of improvement efforts:

- Provide a standard method to guide improvement
- Provide training and education in the Science of Improvement, methods, and tools
- Develop internal capability for improvement
- Provide other necessary resources to execute improvement

Standard Methodology to Guide Improvements

Designing or redesigning the organization requires changes that will result in improvement. These changes must be developed, tested, and implemented. People require a method to execute improvement effectively and continually. The Model for Improvement (figure 9.3) is an improvement framework or roadmap[10] that enables people to apply what they learned to ensure that the change is, in itself, an improvement.

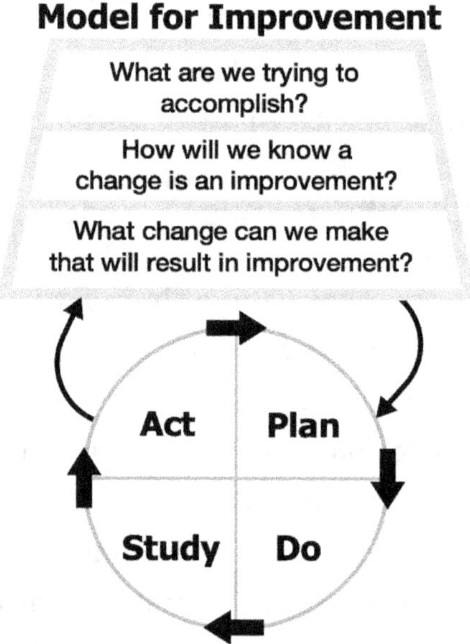

Figure 9.3. Model for Improvement.

It is essential for managers to understand the use of the Model for Improvement and its role in improvement. Using a common road map to guide the efforts to improve throughout the organization provides a shared language for improvement. The Model for Improvement was developed with the Science of Improvement[11] as its foundation and is rooted in a set of three fundamental questions:

1. What are we trying to accomplish?
2. How will we know a change is an improvement?
3. What changes can we make that will result in improvement?

These three questions form the basis of **a trial and learning approach**. The word "trial" suggests we are going to test a change. "Testing" lies at the heart of science. "Learning" implies we have some criteria to study the test (trial). The Plan-Do-Study-Act cycle (PDSA) is our testing and learning mechanism.[12] The focus on the questions accelerates the building of knowledge by emphasizing a framework for learning, using data, and designing effective tests or trials. Science requires prediction before testing. Built into the PDSA cycle is the process of the deductive and inductive learning journey.[13] Learning from testing changes on a small scale is stressed rather than learning from extensive study before attempting any changes.

We can view the basic form of the Model for Improvement as a philosophy and a methodology for improvement:

- **As a philosophy**, the model reflects the rational choice of which actions to take and not to take, based on existing knowledge and in the interest of accomplishing our chosen objectives. As we take planned actions and study effects, our body of useful knowledge grows and matures in a way that continuously enhances the effectiveness of our actions.
- **As a method for improvement**, the Model for Improvement becomes a flexible framework for focused questions and, when appropriate, the use of application-specific tools and methods. It also serves as a guide for building the required knowledge and acting to accomplish the desired results.

In the next leadership meeting, Diane spoke up. "I just finished a book we should look at. It introduced me to a method for executing improvement projects called the Model for Improvement. The chapters walk you through developing, testing, and implementing changes. It felt practical and accessible and could be a common methodology to help us focus our efforts to execute these improvement projects."

Diane knew the Mid Tech leadership team struggled to execute improvement efforts in the past. Everyone was committed, but there was always a lot of bumpiness in working together to try to improve.

"We need to adopt a shared improvement framework as part of a support system to carry out the plan to improve. This would also go a long way in improving communication between departments as we implement improvements and work to hold our gains."

Herman thought Diane's suggestion was very timely. "For this round of new projects, I suggest we adopt the Model for Improvement." Then he turned to Diane and asked her to take the lead in ensuring everyone got a copy of the book. Herman suggested they begin next week to study and share it in their upcoming leadership team meetings.

"I would be happy to make that happen." Diane added, "In addition, I would like to help develop the structure to report the status of projects and share learning." Herman agreed.

The Mid Tech leadership team just learned the importance of having a standard methodology when making multiple organizational improvements. The leadership must put in place the structure to ensure identified projects will get the support and resources required to properly execute identified projects.

Execution of Improvement Projects from Planning

Execution of chartered improvement efforts requires managers ensure the proper provision of resources, remove barriers, and monitor reported project progress. They also must provide the necessary leadership and support during this critical stage of executing the organization's strategy.

Execution begins in the planning process when improvement efforts were defined with the **improvement brief**. Improvement briefs are key outcomes of the planning for improvement process and guide the creation of a project charter and the forming of an improvement team.[14] Project charters guide the execution of projects essential to achieving the strategic objectives identified in the planning process. All the planning in the world is useless unless followed by action; in other words, "nothing happens until something moves."[15] The leadership team must provide guidance and resources to ensure that improvement projects are **moved** to a successful conclusion.

There are several reasons why improvement projects often take longer than expected. Leaders can avoid these issues in the project setup. Early and Godfrey[16] wrote about research at the Juran Institute exploring why improvement teams take so long to complete projects. They discovered that about one-third of the time was useful, while two-thirds were wasted. The management team owned about fifty percent of the wasted time. Wasted time amounted to about twenty-one weeks on a project, and the following activities contributed to the waste:

1. A loss of nearly **six weeks** due to the inability of team members to dedicate sufficient time to the project.
2. Senior executives added **five and one-half weeks** by failing to confront resistance to changes implied by the solution or resistance in providing data, analysis time, and access to needed information.
3. The lack of preexisting measurement criteria added **five more weeks**. Many teams were forced to develop the needed measures first and then collect the required data. In addition, they often had to "sell" the measurement to the management team.
4. Starting with a vague, debatable aim added an average of **four and one-half weeks**. Teams frequently had to rewrite the aim statement and meet with the senior management team again and again until they had a specific, measurable, and acceptable aim.

Table 9.2 displays the most common reasons for the lack of progress and possible remedies. The four wasteful activities described above are highlighted in the table with their respective number (#). Many of these reasons could be mitigated or eliminated by the engagement of people to be developed as Improvement Advisors or Professionals within the organization. Providing this necessary support will ensure the proper alignment of the various improvement efforts to the plans of the leadership team.

ROLE OF PROJECT CHARTERS

Charters provide the focus of a team and prevent wasting time. Godfrey and Early[17] noted that teams starting with a vague, debatable mission added an average of four and one-half weeks to their project time. Organizations using QOS avoid this waste by using well-defined improvement charters.

Table 9.2. Common reasons given for lack of progress and possible remedies

Common reasons for lack of progress	Possible remedies
Lack of a clear (or useful) roadmap for improvement.	Use a common methodology such as the Model for Improvement.
Weak support and encouragement from managers.	Connect charters to the strategic objectives of the organization. Are these still important?
Vague, drifting, or nonstrategic charters. (#4)	Develop charters that call for actionable results.
Lack of preexisting measures. (#3)	Provide technical support for the team to ensure data access and help gather, display, and interpret data.
Failure to quickly confront resistance to change. (#2)	Resistance is often confused with "reaction to change." If people are not informed about the "Why?" of the change, this vacuum can lead to resistance.
Difficulty in data collection, access to information. (#3)	Provide resources from information technology groups or others to gain access to information.
Team members have other priorities ("real work"). (#1). Critical to select the team members who can contribute and are essential to the success of team.	Connect to the organization's strategy and the importance of the work must be stressed from the start.
Team dynamics issues.	Use of a facilitator to help with team issues.
Lose momentum because of infrequent meetings.	Require weekly meetings.
Slow implementation, replication in the organization.	Require the use of the implementation PDSA cycle and checklist; essential for holding the gains.
Reorganization and mobility of management	Has the strategy changed?

Note: Common reasons for lack of progress adapted from John F Early and A. Blanton Godfrey (1995).

The planning for improvement process produces improvement project briefs as a critical outcome. These briefs are aimed at the design or redesign of processes, products, and services to make progress on the defined strategic objectives. Sponsors from the leadership team, who participated in the planning session and developed the strategic objectives, typically write these briefs. They define the necessary improvement efforts to move the organization to the execution of the strategy.

Figure 9.4 is an example of a charter developed by a team to reduce waiting time in a physician's office. The **charter**[18] is a tool that builds on the improvement brief and communicates the purpose for a team or individual involved in an improvement effort.

Project Name: Reduction of Waiting Time   **Number:** 01-0045
Sponsor: Dr. Joe Smith

<table>
<tr>
<td rowspan="2">WHAT ARE WE TRYING TO ACCOMPLISH?</td>
<td colspan="3">DESCRIPTION OF PROCESS, PRODUCT OR SERVICE TO BE IMPROVED:
Suggest and implement improvement to our system to reduce the amount of time that patients spend in the lobby waiting to be treated by a dentist or one of our staff.
LINK TO EXTERNAL CUSTOMER:
Directly affects patients.
IMPROVEMENT OBJECTIVES:
Reduce patient complaints.</td>
</tr>
<tr>
<td colspan="2">BUSINESS IMPACT: Patients waiting for a long period of time influence the other patients in the waiting room. Sometimes they leave and never come back.</td>
<td>ESTIMATED FINANCIAL IMPACT: unknown</td>
</tr>
<tr>
<td rowspan="2">HOW WILL WE KNOW A CHANGE IS AN IMPROVEMENT?</td>
<td>MEASURES: (define)
1. Waiting time will be defined as the difference between the scheduled time of appointment and the time the patient begins the scheduled procedure.

2. Overtime hours will be defined as the total non-planned hours any staff member must stay at the office after the designated quitting time each week.

3. Number of patients late for appointments as compared to scheduled time.

4. Number of patients who forget appointments and reschedule on the date of appointment or later.

Time that patient arrives late for appointment</td>
<td>CURRENT PERFORMANCE:
1. Average waiting time is 15 to 60 minutes estimated. Manual check-in logs have data, if compared to appointment schedule in computer. These have been thrown away daily but can be saved.

2. Approximately 20 hours per week.

3. Available from log if log saved. Estimated at 50%

4. Estimated 10 "forgotten" appointments per week.

5. Available form log if compared to scheduled time.</td>
<td colspan="2">GOALS:
1. 0-5 minutes

2. 0 hours overtime

3. 10% late for appointments.

4. 0 forgotten. 0 reschedules on the date of appointment.

5. Less than 15 minutes.</td>
</tr>
<tr>
<td colspan="3">NOTE: Measures should be directly related to project description and objectives</td>
</tr>
<tr>
<td rowspan="2">WHAT CHANGE CAN WE MAKE THAT WILL RESULT IN IMPROVEMENT?</td>
<td colspan="3">GUIDANCE: (Recommended approaches, initial cycles, documentation requirements, boundaries, etc.)
1. It is desired that appointments for the dentists, as well as the hygienists, be included in the project, but the team may choose to limit the scope to one or the other.
2. Interview and observe dentists, hygienists, and support staff
3. Interview patients concerning changing appointments, reminders and timing of reminders.
4. Change log immediately to include time of appointment, time patient arrived and time patient begins scheduled procedure.
5. Determine the main factors causing the wait time: unnecessary busy work for dentists and hygienists, scheduling appointments too closely, understaffing, paperwork, patients forgetting appointment times,
6. Up to 30 hours a week of a part-time personnel for one month to collect data, make additional reminder calls, etc. Sponsor must approve additional hours
7. Consider internet service which allows reminders via phone and/or e-mail as an alternative to adding personnel.
8. All changes must be tested first before implementation.
9. Use Project Progress form to record all learning cycles instead of minutes. Copy for everyone at reviews.</td>
</tr>
<tr>
<td colspan="2">MEETING DURATION/FREQUENCY: 1 hour - 2x per week
REVIEW SCHEDULE: Noon every Wednesday</td>
<td>ESTIMATED COMPLETION:
2 months</td>
</tr>
</table>

TEAM LEADER: Helen   **TEAM COACH:**
TEAM MEMBERS: Mary, Jean Ann

APPROVALS

SPONSOR/ TEAM LEADER: *Joe*   DATE: *7/15/01*

TEAM COACH: DATE:

Figure 9.4. Charter form example.

The team lead and the team members develop project charters with guidance from the leadership sponsor. The Model for Improvement includes three questions used to organize the charter. Without a clear charter, it is easy to get sidetracked and work in areas of minor relevance to the organization's strategic objectives. People will continually struggle with the appropriate scope of the work. The project charter helps teams and individuals manage their efforts and reduce unwanted variations from the original aim.

Before starting efforts to improve, the team members of the project and the sponsor of the improvement activity should agree on the charter. The sponsor "owns" the charter. The charter provides a contract to do work for the sponsor and leadership team. The sponsor empowers the team and provides resources, time, and support for the team to be successful. Too often, the sponsor is at arm's length from the team. The chartering process is a two-way street between the team members and the sponsor. Agreement on the charter means the team agrees on the expected outcomes, how they will know they successfully achieved the defined outcomes, and a possible path forward on early PDSA cycles. This helps the team with alignment and focus.

If the sponsor cannot commit sufficient resources to begin work on the projects with charters, then the scope of the projects might need to be reduced. The leadership team should review this decision's impact within the scope of planning.[19] When making this assessment, remember that the strategic objectives are meant to be long-term.

Provide Training and Education in the Science of Improvement and Methods

Adults learn when there is a need to know. The improvement project becomes the primary reason to learn about improvement methods and tools when conducting workshops to support improvement efforts. Offering training on tools and methods for improvement without a focused improvement project is not as effective for learning.

Many of us learn by doing. Applying the training or education to an improvement project offers an immediate application of what we just learned. This is important to the adult learner, whether we are discussing education or training.[20]

Education concerning the ideas of variation or systems thinking could commence without expecting immediate results. However, education is far more effective when accomplished with an application. Education is conducted so that a more proficient manager or employee will emerge in the future. Conduct training with improvement team members when required to perform a task to meet a need for results.[21] For example, when assigned to an improvement team, the individual is motivated to learn any tools or methodology that helps to accomplish the results defined by the chartered project.

In addition to the industry-specific training and ongoing education in particular subject matter, organizations focused on QOS require various types of education and training,[22] including:

- Ongoing education in the Science of Improvement.
- Training in using a methodology to guide the improvement effort (Model for Improvement).
- Just-in-time training in using improvement tools and methods required for the improvement project that supports progress on the project.
- Training in group dynamics, interpersonal skills, and change management.
- Training on how to conduct effective meetings, including roles and responsibilities of the team participants.

We suggest the following guidelines to effectively manage and use the limited resources an organization dedicates to development and improvement:

- Integrate workshops into a change strategy for the organization, with participants working on a chartered project.
- Weigh workshops in favor of participants applying what they learn to projects to increase understanding of the concepts.
- Minimize emphasis on lectures.
- Conduct workshops in small segments with follow-up and consultation to help apply the concepts.
- Use virtual learning[23] to allow people to participate in improvement workshops while minimizing travel disruptions to staff's other duties.

Developing Internal Capability for Improvement

Organizations must identify people we call **improvement advisors**,[24] who can advise and facilitate individuals and project teams to execute improvement efforts to achieve results. To be effective, a potential improvement advisor has experience as an improvement team lead or has participated as a member on teams. They require education on the Science of Improvement, the organization's improvement approach (e.g., Model for Improvement), and advanced training with the tools and methods necessary for teams to develop, test, and implement changes.

The organization's plan for the development of improvement capability should answer these questions:

1. Who are the organization's people, line management, or workforce capable of reliably producing results from improvement efforts?
2. What are our resources to further develop their capabilities?
3. How can we combine the actual job assignment with opportunities for improvement, so development happens during regular work assignments? (Otherwise, the improvement effort will be viewed as "extra work.")
4. What body of knowledge, improvement tools, and methods are a proper match for the improvement advisor? The depth of knowledge and skill will change relative to the respective roles of people in context with the complexity of the job.

When selecting people to be improvement advisors, consider who will be future leaders of the organization and benefit from this experience as a development step. Future leaders must understand the Science of Improvement and how improvement projects are created in the planning process and scheduled for execution. The skills necessary for managing an improvement project are essential for effective managers to run their operations.[25]

Other Necessary Resources to Execute Improvement

Providing resources to execute improvement efforts is one of the key responsibilities of sponsors of improvement projects. People and time are the primary resources required for improvement. Other resources include information technology, capital funding, and administrative expenses. More and more, teams need information technology support to access data necessary for improvement projects. Information security is a common barrier, and sponsors frequently must approve for staff to install necessary software and permissions (e.g., Shewhart chart software).

Expenditures, including funding for travel, training, or assistance from outside specialists should be considered part of the improvement effort's resourcing during the planning process. Information gained after starting the work may reveal issues that require additional attention later. Sponsors must address these concerns. Lack of resources is the cause of many failed improvement efforts. Sponsors, team leaders, and Improvement Advisors should express the need for additional resources as required. Some projects may be urgent and time-bound, and sponsors should ensure resources are available to help the team succeed.

Improvement efforts sometimes start with team members reminding management that these efforts will require time and money. They usually express these warnings for two reasons, one **stated** and the other **unstated**. The stated reason is, "We need help in terms of time to do what you are asking us to do." The unstated reason could be, "Let's see if management is serious enough to put their money where their mouth is." A test of leadership **commitment**. When managers are involved with leading the team or as active sponsors, such concerns are usually mitigated. After some success, and once people understand management is genuinely interested in improvement, concern for time and money will diminish. After the initial improvements, evidence of Deming's **chain reaction** should become apparent: improved quality improves financial measures. Following some initial success, people are usually anxious to work on teams to improve and contribute during future years.

SPONSORS AND GUIDING IMPROVEMENT EFFORTS

Leadership provides project improvement briefs and identifies the responsible sponsors during the planning process. In smaller organizations, leadership team members may fulfill the sponsor role. In larger organizations, leadership selects managers with responsibility for the service, product, or processes to be improved.

Three considerations when assigning sponsors to improvement efforts include:

1. Evaluate the amount of complexity and formality of the improvement effort. The more required, the more likely a sponsor will be helpful.

2. Assess the degree of delegated authority the team has to act independently of others. For complex teams whose actions affect different parts of the system, sponsors may be required to help a team be successful.

3. Appreciate the level of established structure in place. In larger organizations, sponsors can simplify communication and ensure management stays in touch with the improvement efforts.

Role of the Sponsor

Sponsors require direct knowledge of why the leaders in the planning process chose the project relative to the organization's strategic objectives. They are usually leadership team members or high-level managers. The sponsor has several responsibilities to ensure the success of the improvement effort:

- Ensure team membership includes subject matter experts to make changes. In addition, membership in the team consists of people with the authority to carry out changes. Sponsors may need to assist the team leader in getting these essential people.

- Sponsors must communicate how this improvement effort supports the organization's strategy and why their time on the project is essential to accomplishing the improvement effort. Team members should understand their role and why their participation is vital.

- Sponsors support the team in translating the improvement brief into a chartered improvement project.

- Sponsors are essential to ensure the allocation of resources to the improvement effort.

- The sponsor must address barriers if the team needs assistance during the improvement journey.

- Sponsors are communication links from the leadership team that developed the strategy and identified the projects to ensure the projects are executed. They also represent the individual and team as they communicate the status of the improvement effort.

The sponsor should know the improvement brief's intent from the planning session. Sponsors require knowledge concerning the work of the improvement effort; experience leading or participating in improvement is preferred. Typically, a sponsor will have an initial meeting with the project lead and team members to communicate why the project is important to the strategic objective, why their time is essential, and what each person's role is in the project. Once the team begins working, the sponsor's primary responsibility is to work closely with the team leader.

Sponsors should be aware of the status of teams regularly. Awareness comes from attending meetings or reviewing regular project progress reporting with the team lead for the improvement effort. Sponsors should note:

- Degrees of success for each chartered improvement project.
- Other departments or individuals who are not on the team but who are providing support.
- Outside resources required for support or knowledge.
- Teams that are learning but have not yet made improvements.

Working with Improvement Teams and Supporting Progress to Results

Sponsors play a key role in working with improvement teams and supporting progress. Sponsors enable improvement project leads to resource teams and define roles, regularly understand and aid project progress, and document learning from improvement.

DEFINING TEAM RESPONSIBILITIES AND ROLES

Experience in developing, testing, and implementing change shows that teams are an effective way to obtain improvement. Getting team representation from the point in the system to be impacted builds support for testing changes. There are several roles associated with teams that sponsors must ensure are filled. These roles have specific responsibilities.[26]

Teams are not the answer to all the needs for improvement. An individual with the specific subject matter expertise, a key manager who controls the resources required, or any other individual with the knowledge and authority (or resources) to accomplish the required improvement effort is often appropriate to execute an improvement effort.

There are common mistakes leadership teams make when forming improvement teams that should be avoided:

- Leaving first-line supervisors and middle managers out of team activities. Organizations transforming from accountability cultures may worry about the free flow of information about what is working and not working. Collaborating on improving the system can aid in changing the culture.
- Calling any group of people who work together an improvement team. Improvement teams have a purpose and roles. Creating effective improvement teams takes some work to build team skills and trust.
- Leaving teams alone. Regular routines where sponsors meet with the improvement teams usually helps progress and provide opportunities to review the aim, discuss the results, guide testing, and remove barriers. Regular check-ins enable the sponsor to keep the leadership team in the loop about progress and learning about the organization.
- Expecting quick results with the establishment of an improvement team. Forming an improvement team and developing a project charter are important steps to realizing results, but problems assigned to teams commonly require unknown solutions. Time is necessary for improvement teams to study the issues, develop effective changes, and test changes before results occur.

SUPPORTING PROGRESS TO RESULTS

Project sponsors receive updates from improvement teams through different routines including informal conversations or emails and more formal structured reviews of project progress.

A **weekly sponsor update** helps maintain the improvement effort's tempo. Updates are brief and typically structured, but less than one page. The purpose of the update should include:

- Provide encouragement and recognition of the improvement effort.
- Learn if the project is on track to a successful conclusion.
- If needed, develop action plans to get improvement efforts back to successful execution.
- Decide whether the project should be modified in some way or stopped based on new learning.

More formal **project review meetings**[27] with the sponsor[28] and improvement team occur regularly (monthly or quarterly, depending on the expected time duration of the project). The intent of the meeting is to learn if the project is making progress or not. If the project is on track, the meeting is an opportunity to learn, plan the next steps, and celebrate the team's efforts. If the project is not achieving results, the meeting is focused on understanding the causes and developing a plan to mitigate them. Sometimes, it may be time to recommend stopping a project.

> Diane finished an article on barriers for improvement teams. She reflected on the experience on the improvement journey so far at Mid Tech, "I see that we are already experiencing two or three of these barriers. I need to share this at our next leadership team meeting."
>
> Diane knew her team required a central way to support managing their improvement. She researched options online and learned about various ways, including using existing office document software and Web-based programs. As Diane gathered the features and pros and cons of each, she decided, "I need to share these options with the leadership team. This should help guide us in how to define a project, provide PDSA cycles, sponsor reports, and the necessary tools and methods to support a typical improvement effort."

STAYING INFORMED ABOUT THE STATUS OF A PORTFOLIO OF IMPROVEMENT EFFORTS

Several tools help leaders manage the portfolio of improvement efforts. Examples include:

1. Method to evaluate project progress, and
2. Display of charts showing progress over time.

Evaluating project progress. Using a project rating scheme provides a method to evaluate and track individual project progress and monitor progress across a portfolio of diverse improvement efforts. Table 9.3 provides criteria to apply to all active improvement projects to evaluate current progress. Select the definition that best describes the progress to date.

Table 9.3. Definitions of project progress ratings

Score	Definition of progress rating
0	Not started. Project has been identified, but the charter has not been completed or assigned.
2	Charter established. A charter has been completed and reviewed. Individuals or teams have been assigned, but no work has been accomplished.
4	Activity, but no changes. Initial cycles for learning and testing have begun (measurement, data collection, study of processes, surveys, etc.).
6	Modest improvement. Successful tests of changes have been completed. Some small-scale implementation has been done. Anecdotal evidence of improvement exists. Expected results and goals are 25% complete.
8	Significant Progress. Expected results achieved for major subsystems. Implementation (training, communication, etc.) has begun for the large system impacted by the project. Project goals are more than 50% complete.
10	Outstanding Success. Implementation cycles have been completed and all project goals and expected results have been accomplished. Organizational changes have been made to accommodate improvements and to make the project changes permanent.

Display of charts showing progress over time. Project progress is assessed monthly when the improvement team prepares the sponsor report. The score is plotted in a run chart and displayed over time. Figure 9.5 is an example of multiple projects in an organization displayed on run charts. Each run chart depicts the status rating of an improvement over time and together, leaders can monitor the portfolio of work in progress. Run chart displays to document their teams' improvement journeys can be created using spreadsheet applications are commonly used by organizations.

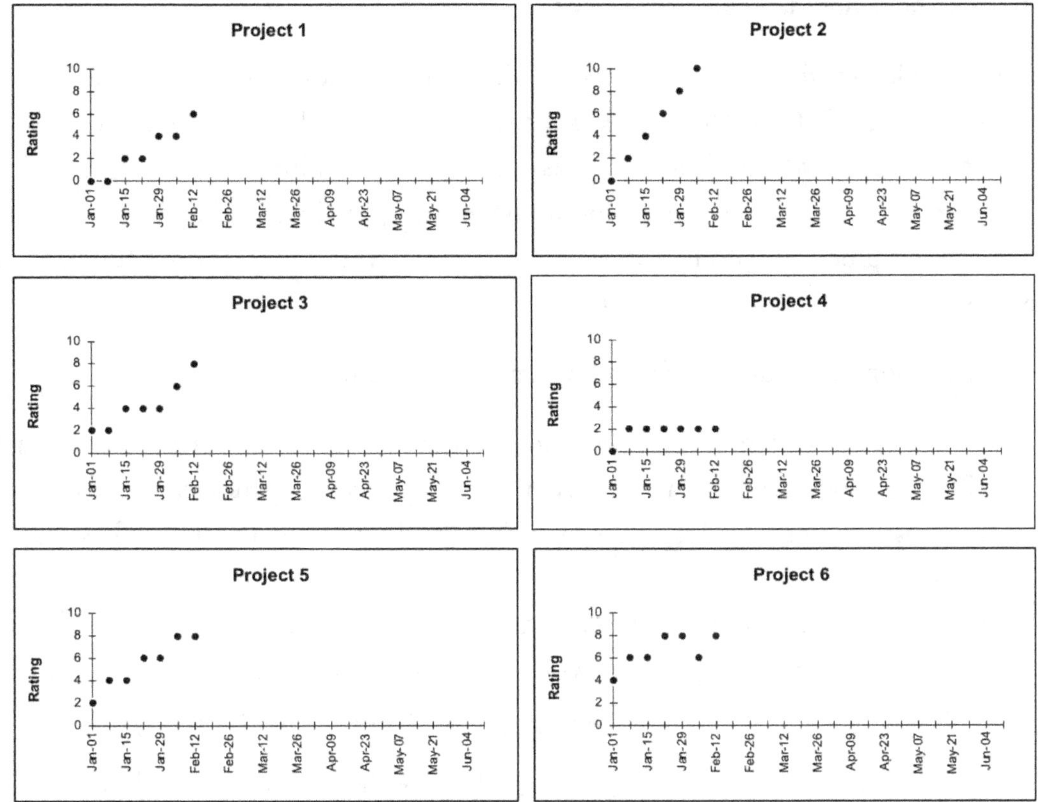

Figure 9.5. Projects tracked with rating scale plotted on run charts.

Mid Tech started tracking the progress of the portfolio of projects in a spreadsheet each sponsor could access from a shared drive in the Cloud. Improvement teams saved their sponsor reports to the drive as an office presentation file. This worked for a while, but it wasn't long before they researched a commercial solution.

"I shared a few Web-based options we could use to standardize reporting and capturing project data. We could continue with a homegrown method, but I made the business case that adopting a Web-based option would both meet the needs of our improvement teams and help leadership monitor progress while reducing the friction to getting important information for learning."

After some brief discussion and a few clarifying questions, the leadership team asked Diane to recommend the solution the organization should purchase a subscription to and agreed to move forward with her choice.

DOCUMENTING LEARNING FROM IMPROVEMENT

"If only HP knew what HP knows, we would be three times more productive." [29] Lew Platt, the former CEO of Hewlett-Packard, was lamenting the lack of documentation to preserve the knowledge gained in past generations. Unfortunately, few of us like documentation. However, there is a lot of knowledge gained from improvement efforts about specific processes, products, and services and how the organization functions as a system.

Documentation of the improvement journey serves two purposes:

1. Provides essential communication and coordination for the teams or individuals making improvements today. For example, people can misunderstand inter-team verbal instructions. Writing it down makes the required work straightforward for everyone.
2. The documentation also leaves "notes to the future." Documentation enables the people in the future to pick up where the prior improvement efforts ended. It eliminates redundant work and makes an organization more productive.

Traditionally, documentation was paper-based, but now it can be captured electronically. Technology continues to offer options that can reduce the burden of capturing important information and make it easier to access. The documentation can be far less strenuous. Leaders wishing to spread improvements from prior improvement efforts can readily follow the improvement journey of past efforts without having to reinvent the wheel and re-document their efforts. People can save time by building on the foundation of learning and improvement established by prior improvement efforts.

Remove Obstacles

Most improvement efforts encounter obstacles as a team or individual attempts to accomplish the expectation described in the charter. We have discussed the downside in terms of wasted time and effort in table 9.2, which displays the most common reasons for the lack of progress and possible remedies. In this section we will be discussing obstacles from a change management view. From a leadership perspective, how do we deal with the typical challenges on our improvement journey? These barriers and obstacles can appear as technical problems, bureaucracy, regulations (both real and imagined), and people. Technical problems are the easiest obstacles to address and understand when we cannot achieve success. The other obstacles create frustration for individuals and teams. ("Why are we having this difficulty? We are just trying to improve our company! Why are these barriers in our way?")

Many barriers are those naturally associated with **change**. Change is a challenge to all of us when we cannot control it. The natural defense is to **react** to change. People need to understand why the change is being made and more importantly the impact on them and their work. For every technical change, there are social and economic changes.[30] When leaders can explain the change in terms of the technical, social, and economic implications, resistance will be reduced. These changes must be developed, tested, and managed to implementation if we are to gain the predicted benefits of the change. Creating structure such that **we make it easy for people to do the right thing and hard to the do the wrong thing** is a key in helping people adopt change.

Provide Recognition

Everyone appreciates recognition for their contributions made in improvement efforts. However, if ignored or if others take credit for their contributions, it can be very demotivating. There are three basic reasons for providing recognition to those contributing to improvement:

1. **Improvement is hard work!** It places a burden of time away from regular duties on those causing the improvement and sometimes creates stress. Leadership shoud recognize this extra effort and contribution.
2. **Recognition is a good vehicle for education.** Staff should create examples inside the organization so others can study and learn. Sponsors should communicate these examples to the rest of the organization.
3. **Recognition of a contribution stimulates self-esteem.**[31] Staff are proud their contributions to the improvement are seen and it fosters intrinsic motivation and increases engagement in their work.

When recognizing improvement efforts, use the recognition systems already in place in the organization. There is no need to treat recognition for improvement differently from recognition for other organizational initiatives. **An invitation to formally present an improvement project to the organization's leadership team is usually the most effective recognition method.** A team's explanation of their improvement journey becomes self-recognition. The presentation should include both the quantitative and qualitative results, summarize lessons learned from successes and failures, and present insights that might be useful to understand the organization.

What other ways can we recognize teams and individuals who have contributed to significant improvement efforts? Organizations have employed the following ideas successfully:

1. Recognize people in everyday company events or other occasions where leaders recognize teams and individuals.
2. Make use of company newsletters, magazines, and other communication tools.
3. Send personal letters signed by a member of top management thanking the individual for their contributions to the organization.
4. Contribute to charities or scholarships in the name of the team or individual.
5. Give visible tokens of appreciation for real contributions (books, caps, key chains, etc.).

The organization's culture should be the predominant consideration when contemplating these approaches to recognition. Also, appreciate that different people and different generations[32] may appreciate recognition methods in different ways. Where one person may really value a plaque handed out at a meeting, another may equally value a personal interaction with a senior leader.

Redirect and Redeploy Resources as Improvements Are Made

When an improvement team completes its project, the system has undergone changes. These changes may cause displacement of people, redesigned work processes, or the need to train people with new or redesigned jobs. The leadership team should reflect on the impact of the improvement project as identified in the planning process; did the project outcomes match predictions? How will the impact of this effort affect the plan to operate, plan to improve, or the financial plan (i.e., the budget)?

Managers should be as aware of the social and economic changes as they are of the technical changes. This is critical if the change is to be accepted and sustained. As the teams perform their work, consider some principles of work design and redesign:[33]

1. Do not expect people to "improve" themselves out of work. Management must take care of the social and economic consequences of job displacement. If people

lose their jobs because of improvement, resistance to change may flourish. A policy of attrition often is adopted to solve the expected short-term displacements. Sometimes the change is not acceptable to the person doing the job. This leads to the second principle.

2. Give people choices. Allow them to explore other opportunities in the workplace. Management should be aware of the impact of displacement and be prepared to explore alternatives for people impacted by the change.

3. Offer people displaced by a technical or economic change influence over their futures. Management should be careful not to take unilateral action in determining the future of displaced people. People tend to support a change if they are involved and have some influence over the change.

As individuals or teams complete the improvement efforts, the leadership team must explore how the results will affect the organization, including:[34]

- What actions are needed by management to reap the benefits of the improvement effort?
- What resources (budgets, positions, equipment and supplies, organization structures, etc.) should be modified due to the improvement effort?
- What permanent changes in the system are required to "hold the gains?"[35] Examples include rewriting job descriptions, changing policies, updating procedure manuals, and reorganizing departments and staff. In addition, The Model for Improvement includes a checklist for PDSA implementation checklist (figure 9.6). Leaders should ensure the team completes Implementation Checklists for each key change they are making to the system.

If the team sponsor does not effectively deal with these issues, the organization may not realize the gains from the improvement efforts. Resources freed up by the improvement efforts should be invested in further improvements. For an organization increasing its market share, the organization may need these resources to run the business.

IMPLEMENTATION AND HOLDING THE GAINS

An improvement effort is successful when the project's measures show achievement of the desired results, and the improvement gains hold. Figure 1.3 provided an operational definition for what we mean by improvement:

> **A change that alters how work is done, or the makeup of a product, that produces visible, positive differences (relative to historical norms) in relevant measures, sustained into the future.**

Now it is time to transition holding the gains and implementing the changes. When an improvement team has begun the implementation of changes using PDSA cycles, those changes must be embedded in the organizational system and structure. Implementation PDSA cycles will generally address these components:

- Description of the change(s)
- Predicted impact of the changes on key measures
- Processes or products affected by the change(s)
- Documentation of the change(s)
- Impact on training

Figure 9.6 is an example of an implementation PDSA cycle checklist to ensure structures were changed to hold the gains for an improvement project. The project focused on reducing referral cycle time for patients, asking:

What are we trying to accomplish?

Reduce referral time for patients that results in patient and staff satisfaction with the referral process.

How will we know it is an improvement?

- Maintain or increase customer satisfaction
- Decrease the time for the referral notification patient (cycle time)
- Increase completion rates for referrals
- Decrease duplication referrals
- Decrease patient barriers to completing referral service (refusals/denials)

The improvement team conducted several PDSA cycles as changes were developed and tested. As part of the PDSA implementation cycle, the team ensured changes were sustained using the implementation checklist. The checklist guides the team to ensure the completion of the elements necessary to hold the gains. Sponsors should ensure completion of the checklist for any projects they are accountable for.

Description of change(s): Weekly list of Priority 1 referrals for each provider printed by team.					

Implementation date(s): 02/12/2018

Predicted impact of change on key measures:

	Measure	Original Level of Performance	Level at Implementation
1	Cycle Time	24 days	15 days
2	Patient satisfaction rating	Neutral to High	High
3	Completion Rates	30 days	9.8 days
4	Staff satisfaction rating	Neutral	High
5			

Processes or Products affected by the change:

	Processes or Products Affected	Process or Product Owner	Number of People Affected	Change in Standard? Yes/No	Measured Acceptance High/Med/Low
1	Referral tracking	Case managers	4	Yes	High
2	Referral reporting	CAC	1	Yes	High
3					
4					
5					

Documentation of change:

Date	Documentation Description	Document Location	Defined By	Approved By	Update Responsibility
11/20/17	Materials/forms defined, available with method to update in place	AMI folder	CAC	Team leader	CAC
11/20/17	Procedure defined, available with method to update in place	AMI folder	CAC	Team leader	CAC
11/6/17	Equipment defined available with method to update additions in place	RPMS RCIS package	CAC	Team leader	Area IT
	Equipment layout defined & labeled (use pictures if applicable)	n/a	n/a	n/a	n/a
	Changes in job descriptions or role statements complete.	n/a	n/a	n/a	n/a

Impact on training:

Date	Documentation Description	Document Location	Defined By	Approved By	Training Responsibility
2/12	Training procedure defined for implementation.	AMI folder	CAC	Team leader	Team leader
TBD	Training schedule complete				
TBD	New employee training procedure complete.				
TBD	Procedure defined which ensures Training procedure is kept up to date due to changes in materials, forms, procedures, equipment, layouts or job descriptions				

Figure 9.6. PDSA Implementation Checklist.

Using the PDSA Implementation Checklist

Leaders we have worked with found the PDSA Implementation Checklist (figure 9.6) to be very useful for learning about their system. As an improvement project approaches completion, the last series of PDSA cycles usually use the implementation checklist. Leaders find this one-page document very useful to ensure that the expected results are achieved. This checklist also helps to shorten the final project review. More importantly, this document brings everyone up to speed on what was achieved and the learning journey of the team. When leaders use the document, it helps the leadership team ask more effective questions for their own learning about the improvement effort. Taking the time to understand the contribution delivered by the improvement effort is a very important part of recognition.

LEADERSHIP TEAM AND LEARNING ABOUT THE SYSTEM

The work of improvement teams and other improvement efforts allows the leadership team to become a real learning organization. The leadership team should study the work and progress of these improvement efforts to gain insights into how the organization works as a system, including how the chain reaction works in the organization for specific projects. Learning should include:

- **Key processes in the organization and essential linkages between processes.** Sometimes when changing a process, an unexpected impact occurs in other organizational processes. Use this learning to update the organization's system map.
- **Underlying forces in the organization can cause problems and create barriers.** For example, what management systems (such as accounting, budgeting, appraisal, etc.) seem to drive the organization? A study of improvement teams can uncover these forces. Management should learn how these forces interact and impact the organization's employees in either positive or negative ways.
- **The impact on the system created by team improvements.** Often improvement efforts result in cost savings, productivity improvements, and other efficiencies for processes in the organization. But how do these improvements impact the key measures of the system (the total organization)? Because the processes and products are not additive, do not expect the combined improvements to add up at the system level.

- **The economic impact of improvements in the system.** How does the chain reaction work in the organization for various types of improvement projects? Can the leadership team see the impact of improvements in the vector of measures? Which type of projects are impacting revenue, productivity, fixed and variable costs, or market share?
- **The long-term social consequences of the technical changes.** How do improvement teams' changes impact the organization's social aspects?
- **Understanding of the external customer's definition of quality.** What types of improvements are recognized by the organization's external customers? What seem to be the essential dimensions of quality for the products and services of the organization?

Using the Model for Improvement to Enable Learning

The Model for Improvement can be used to help managers focus their learning from improvement teams. Each time a meeting is scheduled with a team involved in an improvement effort, the managers should plan a learning cycle using PDSA. The most important part of this PDSA plan will be:

- What specific questions do we want the team to answer?
- What other information will we need to understand the impact on the organization?
- What are our predictions about the answers to these questions?
- With these questions addressed, is there a measure in our vector of measures that we would expect to be impacted by this team?

After completing the team meeting or presentation (the "Do" phase of the cycle), the managers can evaluate the answers they obtained ("Study"), and take appropriate actions ("Act") based on what they learned as a leadership team.

SINGLE AND DOUBLE LOOP LEARNING

Argyris and Schön[36] introduced the idea of learning and change in an organization. Recurring problems require some investigation as opposed to just reacting. Argyris gave an example of single and double loop learning with the use of a common thermostat to control temperature:

> Single loop learning can be compared with a thermostat that learns when it is too hot or too cold and then turns the heat on or off. The thermostat is able to perform this task because it can receive information (the temperature of the room) and therefore take corrective action... If the thermostat could question itself about whether it should be set at 68 degrees, it would be capable not only of detecting error but of questioning the underlying policies and goals as well as its own program. That is a second and more comprehensive inquiry; hence it might be called double loop learning.[37]

Figure 9.7 describes single and double loop learning. Consider a leadership team reviewing a successful improvement project that changed suppliers to get the results required. After the team's presentation, one of the executives recalled that this was the third project in the last year that required a change of suppliers. Immediately, a question was raised: what policies do we have in place that result in us selecting nonoptimum suppliers? This learning journey is an example of double loop learning. Merely appreciating the impact of the change and congratulating the team on the improvement is single loop learning.

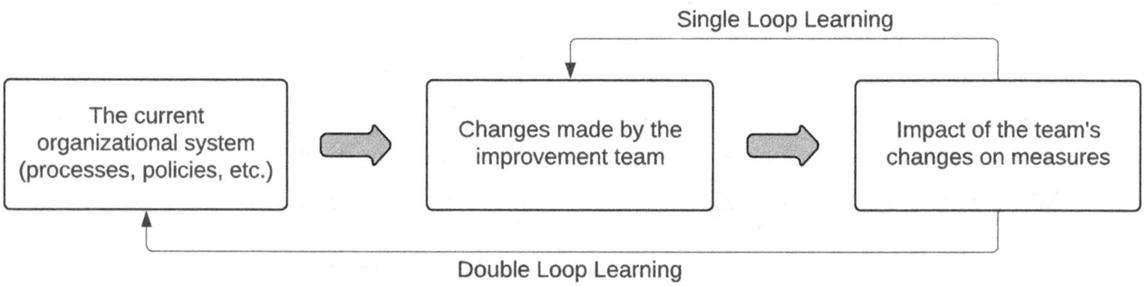

Figure 9.7. Single and double loop learning.

In single loop learning, leaders ask, "What did we do to get results?" If there is a gap in results, we return to another change or improvement effort. This would amount to running another project that would result in changing suppliers in the future. Double loop learning leaders ask, "What policies do we have in place that do not consider the total cost of choosing suppliers?" We are now questioning our assumptions, values, and beliefs that lead us to design the current supplier approval and selection processes.

Within eight months, Mid Tech Company successfully executed five improvement projects. The leadership team enjoyed reviewing the results. Herman addressed the room, "Diane, you did an excellent job of helping people on the leadership team. The use of the software program to help us craft useful charters was a real time-saver. During the last year, we have learned to be more effective sponsors. Monthly reports kept us focused on the projects and helped the leadership team to understand where individuals and teams needed their assistance to remove barriers and challenges to ensure progress. I was concerned about holding the gains, but the implementation checklist ensured that the improvements would be sustained."

Herman reflected on the struggles of one project which discovered that policies in another part of the organization were inhibiting the success of a change they kept testing. "Recall when we learned about the idea of double loop learning and the importance of looking holistically at our system and discovering where well-intentioned policies were inhibiting improvement?"

Diane smiled and said, "That was a huge learning for the project team and more importantly for us as a leadership team."

Herman was pleasantly surprised as the leadership team started to discuss the next round of improvement projects. Mid Tech had established the habit of improvement. Herman reminded the team, "We were only able to execute a portion of the improvement projects identified in last year's planning process. We have several more project improvement briefs that will help us to achieve our strategic objectives. These briefs need to be resourced and turned into actionable charters. I am eager to get started on the next wave of projects!"

SUMMARY

This chapter began with a challenge that many organizations face when presented with a portfolio of projects to be executed to achieve the strategic objectives outlined in the planning process. The structure of the charter details the improvement effort that will provide high leverage by aligning people with a standard methodology to enhance communication and prevent wasted time, false starts, and frustration. The use of sponsors ensures individuals and teams get the support they need to develop, test, and implement changes. The sponsor report is a critical two-way communication method to keep everyone in the communication loop regarding the status and progress on the improvement project.

Gallup reported that only twenty-six percent of people are actively engaged in their work.[38] This chapter provides structure that gives employees an opportunity to make important contributions and take dignity in their work. This approach can contribute significantly to an engaged workforce. Chapter 10 discusses additional leadership guidance to help people become more engaged and make contributions that result in pride and dignity in their work.

NOTES

1. In Chapter 1, Table 1.5 is a tool for leaders to assess an organization's progress in making quality an organizational strategy. This paragraph is the operational definition for the top score for "Managing improvement efforts." *The QOS Field Guide* contains a more comprehensive version of the assessment tool.

2. Associates in Process Improvement (API) first self-published these ideas in 1993 for use with organizational clients. The ideas are the foundation of Part 3 in Gerald J. Langley et al., "Improving Value as a Business Strategy," in *The Improvement Guide*, 2nd ed. (San Francisco: Jossey-Bass, 2009), 307–54.

3. Langley et al., *The Improvement Guide*, 2009, 340–43.

4. The work of people in the organization is given explicit definition in a defined role statement. This was introduced in Chapter 4 and is further emphasized in Chapter 10.

5. Adapted from figure 14.1, "Need for Additional Structure or Positions from Improvement," in Langley et al., *The Improvement Guide*, 2009, 342.

6. Adapted from Gerald J. Langley et al., "Organization to Support the Focus on Improvement," in *The Improvement Guide*, 2nd ed. (San Francisco: Jossey-Bass, 2009), 341–43.

7. Chapter 5 in *The QOS Field Guide* provides an example of using a system map for managing various improvement efforts internally and between partners in the example, "Health Care Integrated Payer and Provider System" and including their processes in the organization viewed as a system (see figure 5.1).

8. In "Getting Started" (Chapter 11), Milestone #1 is "Establish formal improvement efforts with individuals and teams." This is the first step in creating the habit of improvement and in understanding why the methods associated with QOS are essential to ensuring multiple projects are executed.

9. Juran, Joseph M., and Joseph A. De Foe. *Juran's Quality Handbook*. 6th ed. New York: McGraw-Hill, 2010., 296. "The result of completing many improvements creates a habit of improvement in the organization. Each improvement starts to cerate a quality culture."

10. Gerald J. Langley et al., "The Model for Improvement and Other Roadmaps," in *The Improvement Guide*, 2nd ed. (San Francisco: Jossey-Bass, 2009), 453–64. The Model for Improvement is the framework described in QOS. Alternative frameworks are also in use in organizations to provide a consistent and shared language to guide improvement projects.

11. See Chapter 2, "Science of Improvement," figure 2.10 for more details on this important framing of the Model for Improvement. Also, consider the iterative nature of learning using the PDSA cycle.

12. Moen and Norman, "Circling Back"

13. See "Building Knowledge," in Langley et al., *The Improvement Guide*, 2009, 82.

14. Improvement briefs for an identified opportunity to design or redesign can begin within any part of the organization and may or may not be directly guided by the strategic plan.

15. Dean Tipa, "200 Years OF U.S. Army Transportation: Nothing Happens Until Something Moves," *Defense Transportation Journal* 31, no. 5 (1975): 6–16. "Nothing happens until something moves," is the motto of the U.S. Army Transportation Corps.

16. Adapted from A. Blanton Godfrey, "Blitz Teams," *Quality Digest*, October 1996, https://www.qualitydigest.com/oct96/godfrey.html. Dr. Godfrey summarizes research originally conducted by John Early at the Juran Institute; John F Early and A. Blanton Godfrey, "But It Takes Too Long...," *Quality Progress* 28, no. 7 (July 1995): 51–55. The four observations from Godfrey and Early's research are noted in table 9.2, #1, #2, #3, and #4.

17. Early and Godfrey, "But It Takes Too Long...," July 1995.

18. During the planning session, leaders identify what needs to be designed or redesigned in the organization and have input captured in the improvement brief including the aim, expected barriers, boundaries, and initial change ideas. The project lead and team are often better positioned to answer questions like "How will we know a change is an improvement?" or

"What changes we can make that will result in improvement?," which are answered when they convert the improvement brief into a project charter.

19. See "Allocating resources," in Chapter 8, page 273.

20. Clifford L. Norman, "Improving Quality Through Education and Training: A Learner Focused Approach" (American Society for Quality Control: 48th Annual Quality Congress Proceedings, Las Vegas, NV, May 1994).

21. Robert H. Schaffer and Harvey A. Thomson, "Successful Change Programs Begin with Results," *Harvard Business Review*, January 1, 1992, https://hbr.org/1992/01/successful-change-programs-begin-with-results. Many training programs dedicated to quality improvement fall into "activity traps." Often training is conducted but not driven or connected to a need in the organization. Many quality efforts in the 1980s and 1990s equated training to participating in quality improvement. Training and education should be connected to getting results.

22. See "Development of Internal Improvement Advisors: Topical Agenda" for an example in Langley et al., *The Improvement Guide*, 2009, 352–54.

23. Innovation in virtual tools to support live and asynchronous learning expand the opportunity to be creative in developing capability. For example, we observed great success in short bursts of learning (in segments of no more than ninety minutes) spread out over several days. Learners apply what they learn to their improvement efforts in the periods between sessions.

24. These are people who, in addition to having participated in and led improvement efforts, have studied the Science of Improvement. They are prepared to help subject matter experts develop, test, and implement changes based on the principles and methods from the science.

25. Mackenzie, "The Management Process in 3-D." The skills of planning, organizing, staffing, directing, and controlling are essential to the execution of improvement projects.

26. In *The QOS Field Guide*, Chapter 9, "Managing Improvement Efforts," is additional guidance for the essential functions and the responsibilities of the people associated with a team carrying out an improvement project and the responsibilities of those who interface with the team.

27. Adapted from Thomas W. Nolan, "Execution of Strategic Improvement Initiatives to Produce System-Level Results. IHI Innovation Series White Paper." (Institute for Healthcare Improvement, 2007), http://www.ihi.org/resources/Pages/IHIWhitePapers/ExecutionofStrategicImprovementInitiativesWhitePaper.aspx.

28. Chapter 9, "Managing Improvement Efforts," in *The QOS Field Guide*, includes guidelines for sponsors to establish routines for preparing for a project review meeting, facilitating the meeting, and following up with the improvement team. Included is an example of a sponsor report provided by the improvement team or individual carrying out the improvement effort.

29. While consulting with Hewlett-Packard, Lew Platt's quote was used often to make the point that documenting work was essential.

30. Weisbord, *Productive Workplaces*, 75. The important thing to see is that three realities—social, technical, and economic—must be simultaneously worked with if we wish to achieve productive workplaces.

31. The Five Rs are reasons, responsibilities, relationships, recognition, and rewards. See Chapter 2, "Science of Improvement" for more detail.

32. Gallup Inc., "How to Bridge the Generational Gap in Recognition," Gallup, August 29, 2022, https://www.gallup.com/workplace/396470/bridge-generational-gap-recognition.aspx.

33. Adapted from Weisbord, *Productive Workplaces*, 395.

34. "PDSA Implementation Checklist" (figure 9.6) was developed by Jane Norman. The checklist gives an overview of the impact on the organization. This analysis helps to ensure that the changes will be integrated into the system and the gains held.

35. Joseph M. Juran and A. Blanton Godfrey, *Juran's Quality Handbook*, 5th ed. (New York: McGraw-Hill, 1999), 5.39. "Establishing controls to hold the gains" was a phrase that Juran used to describe a step in his remedial journey from cause to remedy. The remedial journey included: developing the remedies, testing, and proving the remedies under operating conditions, dealing with resistance to change, and establishing controls to hold the gains.

36. Chris Argyris and Donald A Schön, *Theory in Practice: Increasing Professional Effectiveness* (San Francisco: Jossey-Bass Publishers, 1974).

37. Chris Argyris, "Double Loop Learning in Organizations," *Harvard Business Review*, September 1, 1977, https://hbr.org/1977/09/double-loop-learning-in-organizations..

38. Jim Harter, "Historic Drop in Employee Engagement Follows Record Rise," Gallup, July 2, 2020, https://www.gallup.com/workplace/313313/historic-drop-employee-engagement-follows-record-rise.aspx.

PART III
PEOPLE

CHAPTER 10

ENGAGING PEOPLE WITH QUALITY AS AN ORGANIZATIONAL STRATEGY

George is the CEO of Heat Exchanger Inc., a company that manufactures and repairs heat exchangers for the chemical industry. A heat exchanger is like a radiator that either heats or cools liquid. During a meeting with his management team, George shared a recent learning.

"This morning, I read an article on a survey from Gallup,"[1] George began. "The results revealed many more people are 'disengaged' in their work instead of being 'engaged.' When the survey started in 2000, it showed a dismal 26% of employees were engaged in their work, and 18% were actively disengaged." George shared a run chart of the data (figure 10.1).

"This chart shows the data on engagement from 2003 to 2021. By 2021, engagement improved to 36%, with 15% actively disengaged. While a 10% increase in twenty years shows some progress, there remains a significant opportunity for improvement."

George and his colleagues discussed the results of the survey. What would the results look like at Heat Exchanger Inc.? How might they be different as the organization continues to pursue QOS? At a natural break in the discussion, he asked the room, "How can we, as leaders, create an environment for employees to contribute and engage at a more substantial rate?"

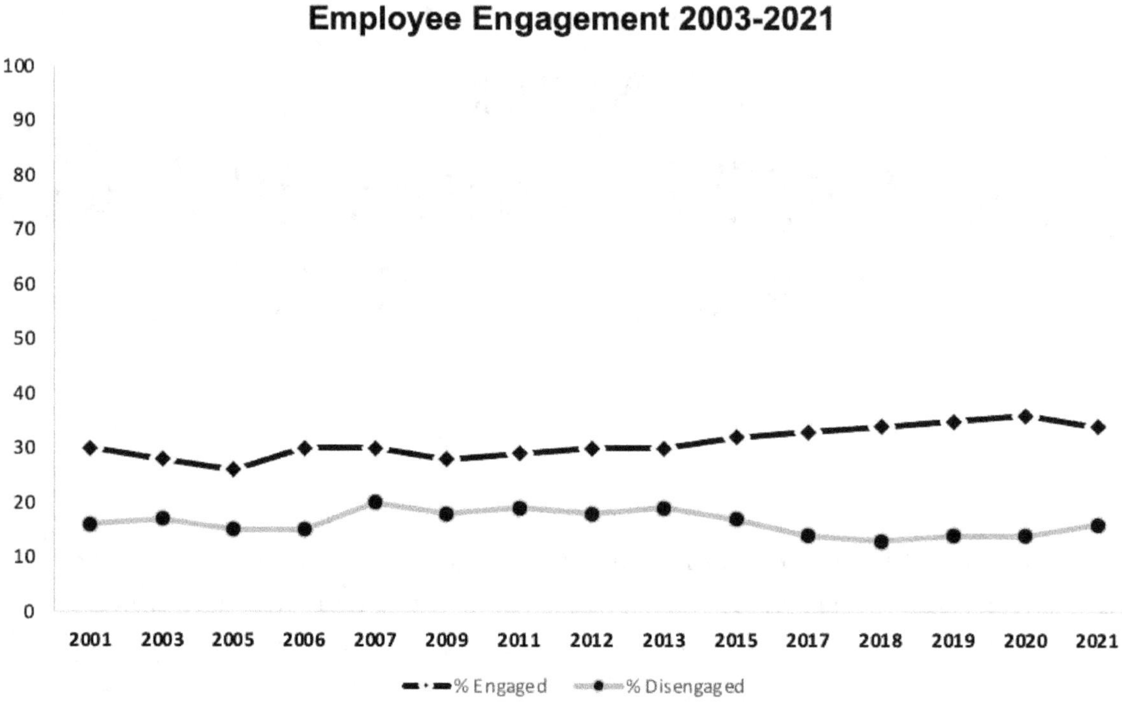

Figure 10.1. Gallup engagement survey results 2003–2021.

The team continued to discuss the issue of engagement at their company. "At first, I found this hard to believe," shared Susan, Vice President of Human Resources. "But when I thought about our turnover rate of employees, engagement may explain why people are leaving. Our absentee rate seems to be another indicator that the findings in the survey mirror our organization."

As an example, Susan told a recent story of asking an employee, who was working on a newly created hybrid workweek, why he was still chronically absent. His schedule allowed him to work two days from home and two days from the office but was chronically absent or missing meetings. The employee curtly replied, "I try hard to do good work, but it feels like my supervisor always wants something else from me or doesn't give the support we need to get it done. Honestly, it leaves me asking, 'Why bother?'" There was some audible frustration among the management team at hearing the employee response. George was not the one who was laughing.

Susan continued, "I was frustrated initially at his response, but then I started to wonder why he has disengaged. Absenteeism, a short tenure, and disengagement are all evidence that management needed to work on improving the staff's pride and joy in work to change the trajectory of engagement. Gallup found three themes related to disengaged," continued Susan, "They were clarity of expectations, having the right resources, and workers being able to do their best work. This might give us a path forward to improve engagement."

Published data such as the Gallup survey results and anecdotal reports from people across sectors paint a picture that people do not feel engaged in their work. People want to contribute and do meaningful work that makes an impact, but traditional organizations inconsistently empower people. The use of QOS provides the structure to address the three issues raised in the survey:

1. clarity of expectations,
2. having the right resources, and
3. workers being able to do their best work.

The inability to contribute and the lack of recognition for contributions are two major factors why people leave or stay and disengage.[2] Managers who do not allow ideas for changes to be tested stifle employee contributions. And in those cases where changes are made which show improvement, recognition to all who contributed is uncommon. When others take credit, what does it do to the individual's pride or willingness to contribute again? Do they feel appreciated for their work?

Some managers consider it their role to do the thinking for their employees and tell them what to do. However, they find working with people challenging, especially when their employees offer new ideas and approaches. So how do we leverage everyone's ideas for improving the system while energizing managers too?

Organizations adopting QOS transform into a workplace that establishes clear expectations and roles, engages staff in problem-solving, fosters deep learning, and celebrates change and improvement. This chapter describes the theory and the practical application of methods to engage staff in the organization. The chapter is divided into five parts:

- Engagement: Create Opportunities to Contribute Improvements
- Engagement Using the Science of the Brain: Neurology
- Engage People Using Structured Role Statement
- Format of the Role Statement
- When Ideas and Beliefs Conflict

ENGAGEMENT: CREATE OPPORTUNITIES TO CONTRIBUTE IMPROVEMENTS

How can we get more people engaged in their work? Leaders often ask us this question. The easiest path is to create opportunities for people to contribute improvements to their work, and in doing so, the benefits of the chain reaction are engaged; quality improvement results in an improvement in financial measures and also "joy in work."[3] The financial changes allow organizations to get more and more of their people involved in improvement.

Working on improving the organization and participating in improvement projects provides many benefits and opportunities to participants:

- People generally like to be involved in decisions that will affect how they work. People also support anything they have a role in planning, developing, and building.
- Improvement work lets employees be a direct part of meeting the Need of their customers.
- Improvement projects allow the individuals involved to develop new life skills that can be applied throughout their careers.
- Participation in a successful project leads to recognition and allows the employee to experience dignity in contributing.
- Improvement efforts often shine a light on the unrecognized skills of employees as they carry out the improvement project. As a result, their leadership potential is recognized, and in some cases, they can be promoted.

Participation in improvement enables autonomy for the individual. **Autonomy[4] is a state of being independent, free, and self-directing and is essential to enabling intrinsic motivation for people.**[5] Additionally, participation in an improvement effort contributes to the skills and education of the people involved, increasing **mastery**[6] of their work. Finally, when employees see their work contribute to the **organization's purpose**, it creates an environment where people can experience dignity in their work.

To enable the power of autonomy, mastery, and purpose, the leadership team must ensure that meaningful improvement projects are selected. When improvements are connected to the organization's strategic plans, the project's importance is typically self-evident.[7] What should be avoided are projects with little significance or value to the organization. People will consider them a waste of time or find the projects compete with the prioritized day-to-day work. When people ask, "How can we motivate people to become more engaged in their work?," the answer is to allow people to contribute to improving their work. It is a short and effective path, creating a win-win solution for the organization and the people making contributions.

Communication within an organization is often cited as a significant problem. When departments that historically operated in competition and conflict shift to participating in projects to improve joint processes, the improvement journey leads to engagement and increases trust and cooperation within the organization.

ENGAGEMENT USING THE SCIENCE OF THE BRAIN: NEUROLOGY

A challenge for leaders is to trigger everyone's intrinsic desire to work, contribute, and engage by creating opportunities to realize the organization's purpose.

Neurology tells us that two parts of the brain—the limbic system and the neocortex—serve key roles in this quest.[8] The **limbic system** or "reptilian brain" was the first to evolve. It deals with emotions, feelings, and intuition which enable us to act quickly to survive (aka, fight or flight). The **neocortex** came later and enables thinking and decision-making; it moves slowly.

Sometimes the two parts of the brain conflict, yet they act together as a system. Consider this example:[9] you are sorting through the daily mail, tossing out junk mail, and suddenly you see a brown envelope from the Internal Revenue Service (IRS)! If you are not expecting anything, you may feel pangs of anxiety and the heart racing as the limbic system engages. The neocortex then engages and causes you to recall something on your tax filing or possibly some other mistake. This is an example of limbic and neocortex systems working together. Notice, too, that the limbic system engaged automatically.

Leaders fortunate enough to be trusted and liked by the people who follow them can use the limbic system to engage staff emotions and feelings by helping them to understand why their work is important and how they, individually and collectively, are contributing to a purpose greater than themselves. This relationship enables the leader to create a message of inspiration that engages "hearts and minds."[10] Note that we do **not** say "minds and hearts." The appeal to emotion and feelings (limbic system) comes before the mind (neocortex).

Engagement requires leaders to provide answers to the "why, how, and what" of our work. The limbic system relates to both the "why" and "how."[11] The neocortex relates to "what." Engagement of hearts and minds requires that begin with "Why?"

Typically, when describing someone's job, managers tend to start with what they do. It is easy to describe. "I make personal computers." Next, some can describe how they do it. "We design the hardware and software." Describing how is more difficult. This traditional path starts with what we do and ends with how we do it, ending before reaching why we do so ("Why do you make personal computers for consumers?").

An alternative path is inspiration, which starts with understanding why the work and contribution is important, then how we conduct ourselves by defined tenets and methods and ending with what we deliver to customers.

Table 10.1[12] is an example of the focus of Apple Inc. using the traditional versus inspirational path. The traditional path begins with what and ends with asking for the sale. Apple does not use this approach. Apple uses the path of inspiration to place emphasis on why it exists as a company that differentiates itself from others in its business—the explanation of how taps into a basic value that guides the development of the products they produce.

Table 10.1. Using why, how, and what: two paths

Traditional path	Path of inspiration
What: We make great computers.	**Why**: In everything we do, we believe in challenging the status quo. We believe in thinking differently.
How: They're beautifully designed, simple to use and user-friendly.	**How**: The way we challenge the status quo is by making our products beautifully designed, simple to use, and user-friendly.
Why: Wanna buy one?	**What**: And we happen to make great computers. Wanna buy one?

Understanding **why** an organization exists and the contribution it makes is not always obvious even to the people who are working in the organization. Deming, in discussing the "Deadly Disease" called "Lack of Constancy of Purpose," said, "People have not decided what it is that they're in business for…they really don't know."[13] This statement is rather stunning.

One of the authors had the experience of seeing this firsthand when working on a partnership between a chemical company and their supplier, who manufacture flat bottom tanks for storage. During the exercise of understanding the Need,[14] when answering the question "Why are these products and services vital to your customers?" the engineer for the manufacturer said to the customer, "Well, you just need flat bottom tanks!" The customer replied, "No, we don't. We have an inventory problem! We don't like the tanks; they get us into trouble with the EPA. If your company could figure out how to run a water park through the chemical plant to deliver product just-in-time, we would be happy to get rid of the tanks." The engineer reflected, "I have been going to bed for the last fifteen years thinking you needed flat-bottom tanks." A happy ending to this story: the manufacturer began offering a service to ensure the tanks were safe and compliant with the EPA. The customer then readily bought the product.

The methods of QOS provide structure to help the leadership team articulate the **why, how, and what**. For example, an essential part of **how** should be the organization's beliefs and values detailed in the tenets of the purpose statement: How will we conduct ourselves in carrying out our purpose? Table 10.2 describes relationships between the QOS activities for the leadership team and the Five Rs of motivation.[15] The crossroads of working these ideas create a holistic strategy for the engagement of people.

Effective engagement of people to support needed change is typically more effective when reasons for the change show how the change will support the organization's purpose. People are motivated when they are supporting work that allows them to contribute to work that is larger than themselves. For example, a plant manager within a chemical plant was very effective when introducing change. Routinely, the plant manager explicitly defined the connection to their value of safety to increase the adoption and support of the change and to minimize resistance.

Table 10.2. Five Rs of motivation and five activities for leaders

Five Rs of motivation	FIVE ACTIVITIES FOR LEADERS				
	Purpose, tenets, and vision	System and Vector of Measures	Information system	Planning	Managing individual and team efforts
Reasons	Reasons that people can embrace and become engaged in the vision. Answers the question of why we exist, our contribution, beliefs, and values, detailed as tenets.	System aligns people with the processes they own and run. Corresponding measures enhance engagement in the system.	Provides both strategic and tactical information needed to achieve the purpose and role within the organization.	Provides strategic objectives, identified improvement efforts, and resources that offer reasons for people to be engaged.	Charters improvements as the means to achieve strategic objectives and realize the vision, providing opportunities for engagement.
Responsibilities	Aligns role of individuals and departments to contribute to the purpose and vision contributing to engagement.	Identifies processes owned/managed and improved to monitor progress toward success. Defined in role statement.	Defines key information sources for foresight, planning, and measurement reporting. Defined in role statement.	Uses system maps to strategically identify and target change responsibilities for achievement and engagement.	Defines role for individuals and departments to effectively run, improve and hold gains.
Relationships	Links role descriptions to purpose with internal and external relationships defined for collaboration and engagement.	Identifies important relationships for engagement between processes, external partners, and measures.	Coordinates internal and external documentation, measures, and sharing to increase collaboration and engagement.	Defines internal and external collaboration and partners that are essential to strategy and success.	Includes SMEs as core team members for improvement efforts for engagement.
Recognition	Appreciates contributions toward the achievement of purpose.	Understands key system interactions impacting improvement.	Values reporting and measurement analysis.	Acknowledges planned improvement contributions.	Coordinates formal recognition of improvement contributions.
Rewards	More customers and aligned partners.	Effective and high-capacity processes.		Organized and communicated priorities.	Engaged employees.

ENGAGE PEOPLE USING A STRUCTURED ROLE STATEMENT

Managers play a crucial role in helping people understand their work in supporting the overall mission defined by the leadership team. Working with people to understand how their work relates to the organization's mission and connecting the specifics of their role to the system map of the organization takes both insight and time.

Typically, there is one mission statement for an organization.[16] In support of the mission, role statements for organizational units and individuals are defined. The use of the word "mission" should be reserved for the organization. Utilizing the term "role" for individuals and groups ensures there is no confusion that the mission is the focus for all in the organization, and role statements are an agreement that defines the specific contribution of people or groups in the organization and how each is connected.

The role statement gives permission to individuals to carry out their roles, communicate with others in the system, and take the initiative in operating and improving their related processes. Clearly defined roles reduce or eliminate the typical time wasted by managers who must be involved in decisions solvable at the local level by the people responsible for the work. Fundamentally, investing time to define roles upfront will pay dividends in savings many times over in the future.

What must the manager do to properly integrate the individual and their corresponding role into carrying out their everyday work? Table 10.3 describes the leadership team's role in creating the structure and the manager's role to ensure people are engaged by understanding their responsibilities relative to their role.

FORMAT OF A ROLE STATEMENT

A **role statement** helps to define relationships between people, organizations, and their respective tasks relative to and in support of the overall organization's purpose. A standard format for role statements is useful when engaging people in understanding how their job is connected to the mission and work of the organization and how it enhances communication throughout the organization. The role statement breaks traditional boundaries of organizational hierarchy and focus on communication and actions necessary to meet the organization's mission. In addition, the standardized format helps people understand and cooperate with others as they work to carry out the organization's mission while executing their role.

Table 10.3. Leadership team role in developing and executing the structure of QOS and the manager's role in integrating the individual into the system

Leadership activities	Leadership team role in developing the structure of QOS	Manager's role in integrating the individual into the system
Establish purpose (Creating will)	Creates a mission, tenets, and vision statement.	Works with their individual employees to create and use role statement that supports the overall purpose of the organization.
Systems view	Creates **a conceptual view** and **detailed view** using a system map of the organization.	Uses the system map to show linkages relevant to each individual employee's role. Identifies what processes, products, services, and links owned. Run or possess expertise for the specific job.
System measurement	Establish vector of measures (VOM) for system that is connected to the purpose of the organization.	Links the measures in the VOM to the role. Shewhart charts and the role family of measures are used for specific measures in the role statement.
Gathering information to develop **ideas** and changes	Defines and creates a system to gather key learning from the system. A balance of information that provides foresight and research for learning and improvement.	Helps to define those processes with opportunities for gathering and communicating information and ideas. Role statement defines these responsibilities.
Planning to set priorities (Prioritize key ideas)	Studies the inputs to the planning process, develops strategic objectives, identifies what part of the system will be designed or redesigned and allocates resources to operate and improve the system.	Communicates strategic plan and which parts of the system the role impacts to support the overall plans. Managers helps to make choices for local improvement projects to support overall strategic objectives for the organization.
Managing individual and team efforts (Execution)	Manages the execution of the improvement projects defined in the planning process. Final responsibility for the successful execution of chartered efforts rests with the leadership team.	Defines responsibilities for daily maintenance and improvement of the processes related to the role. Improvement efforts related to the role are carried out using the Model for Improvement.

Figure 10.2 summarizes how the five leadership activities of QOS inform the components of the role and engage employees in the overall strategy of the organization and its execution. A role statement is not the same as a traditional employment job description[17] which is a written description of a job that includes information regarding the general nature of the work to be performed, specific responsibilities and duties, and

the employee characteristics required to perform the job, usually without reference to the organizational system.

Role Statement
XYZ Company

How this role supports the purpose
Primary Responsibilities:

Process	Measures

Conduct:

Responsibilities for Improving the System:

Organization Relationships:

External Relationships:

Personal Improvement:

Qualifications/Abilities:

1. Purpose
- Role is defined in context of support for the organization's Purpose.

2. Organization Viewed as a System
- Processes connected to Role
- Measures related to processes

3. Information System
- Defined under:
  - Responsibilities for Improving the System
  - Organization Relationships
  - External Relationships

4. Planning
- Contributes to applicable inputs during the planning process

5. Managing Improvement Efforts
- Participates in chartered improvement efforts and ongoing improvement as defined under Responsibilities for Improving the System.

Figure 10.2. Components of the role statement and quality as an organization strategy (QOS).

Role descriptions include the standard information from the job description but also describe:

- How the role supports the mission of the organization.
- Specific processes and measures that are the responsibility of that role.
- The expected conduct concerning tenets.
- Responsibilities for learning.
- Responsibilities for the system improvement.

Figure 10.3 is a standard template[18] that ensures that all essential elements of the role are developed:

- **How this role supports the mission.** Role statements are specific to how the role supports and helps achieve the organization's purpose. The role includes the processes that relate to the work of the individual and how they nest within the mission. It aligns the organizational system and helps individuals and teams understand their contributions and responsibilities to the organizational purpose. Defining a person's role in key processes, current measures of performance, and in improving the system are key aspects.

ROLE DESCRIPTION
Position Title: **FLSA Code:**
Department Title:
Function:
Supervisor Title:

Company Mission

Role Statement – How this position supports the mission:

Primary Responsibilities (See System Map)
All work is a process. Each role has process responsibilities that are interdependent and impact the overall system. Processes currently defined for this role are listed below. We must be aware to define new processes and eliminate obsolete processes as our role evolves.

Process	Owns (Authority to Make Changes)	Works (Follows Procedures & Policies)	Subject Matter Expert

Backup Responsibilities:

Current Measurements of Performance
. Below are the measures that have been currently defined for this position:

-
-
-

Improving the System

Organizational Relationships/ External Relationships

Qualifications/Ability
-

Personal Improvement

Qualifications/Abilities
-

Figure 10.3. Role statement: standard template.

- **Key processes.** Use the system map to identify key processes (or groups of processes) where the person works. Are they the owner of the process, do they work within it, or do they serve as a subject matter expert? Do not include short-term or temporary tasks in the role statement. This helps avoid developing first drafts that include too many ideas and are too long and complex.

- **Specific processes.** These are also used to define the level of authority the person has with changes and future improvements. For example, if a role owns a process, this person can sponsor an improvement project, giving authority to a team to design or redesign the process.

- **Current measures of performance.** To determine the level of performance for a role, define process measures and include the frequency of data collection and reporting. For example, individuals may use hourly or daily frequency to detect issues quickly, while managers and sponsors may use weekly, monthly, or quarterly measures based on the same data.

- **Improving the system.** Everyone fills a role in improvement. That role may be as a participant in an improvement project to design or redesign a process identified in the planning process, and it can include identifying and reporting defects, recognizing the organization's need for supplies and resources, and looking for opportunities to enhance efficiency.

It is important to work with the individual responsible for fulfilling the role to make the draft concise, with a useful level of detail. Be specific and clear. Figure 10.4 is an example of a completed role statement for a Warehouse Team Member. Note how clearly the document states the warehouse team member's role within the organizational system and includes their specific contribution to processes, what measures are related to the work, and their responsibility to continually improve the organization. Role statements will evolve as the organization adopts QOS.

Role statements are a high-leverage method to create an environment where all employees are engaged and contribute to the organization's purpose. When getting started, here are some guidelines for developing and integrating the role statement into the organization:

1. Suggest a process to develop role statements that managers can use for all their employees.
2. Develop a process to update role statements as learning occurs.
3. Connect role statements and human resource job descriptions, if required.

ROLE DESCRIPTION
Position Title: Warehouse Team Member   **FLSA Code:** Non-exempt
Department Title: Operations
Function: Receiving and Distribution
Supervisor Title: Director of Operations

The Distributor Company Mission
Consumers and businesses need building products and a system of distribution and installation that provides value in the market we serve. The Distributor Company matches this need by influencing the market through innovative marketing programs and the reliable distribution of materials.
Role Statement – How this position supports the mission:
The Warehouse Team Member directly supports the Mission of The Distributor Company through reliable distribution of material by receiving and storing materials, filling orders accurately and coordinating cost effective shipment of materials to customers. The team member contributes to a reliable distribution system by organizing and keeping the warehouse safe and clean.
Primary Responsibilities (See System Map)
All work is a process. Each role has process responsibilities which are interdependent and impact the overall system. Processes currently defined for this role are listed below. We must be alert to defining new processes and eliminating obsolete processes as needs of our role dictate.

Process	Owns (Authority to Make Changes)	Works (Follows Procedures & Policies)	Subject Matter Expert
Receives work order		X	X
Picks, packs, and stages order		X	X
Cuts half sheets/large samples using circular saw and records in half sheet log daily	X	X	X
Receives display orders		X	
Receives and stores material		X	X
Documents damaged material		X	
Inspects and documents returned material		X	
Organizes Warehouse	X	X	
Documents shipping information daily in Order Shipment Record Log		X	
Documents inventory changes and adjusts inventory		X	

Backup Responsibilities: Fills in for other Warehouse Team Members as needed
Current Measurements of Performance
Performance measurement is a dynamic process which assesses processes and the individual together. As new methods are developed; they will be incorporated as appropriate. Data collection forms are used daily to communicate specific information to the Operations Support Team. Additionally, routine warehouse audits will be conducted to assure inventory and warehouse management compliance. Below are the measures that have been currently defined for this position:

- Order Shipment Record Log (Daily)
- Freight Documentation Shipment Log/Daily Receipts
- Half Sheet Log (Daily)
- Number of late shipments (daily)
- Total pickups and shipments per day

- Number of returns per week
- Inventory Audit results (monthly)
- Warehouse organization/housekeeping/safety monthly audit
- Freight claims (damaged) daily
- Number of problems/observations recorded weekly

Improving the System
All Distributor Associates are responsible for documenting and fixing problems in the system. The team member is responsible for documenting, communicating, and suggesting solutions for:
- Equipment that needs repair or replacement
- Things that go wrong and can be prevented
- Things that could be made easier or more efficient
- Equipment or supplies that are needed
- Items that were identified as a problem or observation on an Inventory or Warehouse Audit
- Safety Incidents and/or issues

Organization Relationships
- Reports directly to Director of Operations
- Coordinates routine activities with Customer Service Representatives
- Regular contact with Sales Representatives
- Shares information throughout The Distributor Company

Qualifications/Ability External Relationships
- Daily contact with Distributor Company customers
- Daily contact with Distributor Company freight suppliers

Personal Improvement
The Distributor Company will provide resources and support for education and training. It is the associate's responsibility to seek approval, schedule and participate in education and/or training that will prepare him/her for present and future needs.

Qualifications/Abilities
- High school diploma or general education degree (GED)
- Specialized certification in forklift activities
- Forklift certification required
- Basic understanding of operating a PC
- Basic math, reading and writing skills
- Ability to safely operate swing mast forklift

- Able to safely use circular saw
- Able to accurately complete freight bills
- Ability to distinguish colors
- Demonstrated effective problem-solving skills
- Able to safely lift and carry up to 45 pounds unassisted

Figure 10.4. Role description example.

Susan was excited to share her learning about launch of new role statements at the weekly leadership team meeting. George finished the first two agenda items and then asked, "Susan, can you please bring the team up to date on the use of role statements?"

"Thanks, George," Susan began. "When we started the QOS journey, I wondered what role the HR Department would play. When you asked me to build on traditional job descriptions and develop role statements,[19] I was skeptical. After learning about the intent of role statements, however, I was excited. We now have the ability to help people connect to our purpose and their work. More importantly, they understand their role in making improvements, using measurements, contributing feedback to our system for gathering information and providing information to the strategic planning process. I have participated in several meetings with the leaders around this table, who described the process as far more proactive. The front-end effort is reducing their overall management time and freeing them up to do other priorities like developing new business. And they also feel their people are now more connected to their work and empowered to do what they need to do and fix problems."

The leadership team continued sharing their experiences with the shift to using role statements. When it came time to end the meeting, George closed with, "Thank you. I was expecting great things, and I am pleasantly surprised by the ripple effecton time savings. See you next week."

WHEN IDEAS AND BELIEFS CONFLICT

Continuous improvement of an organization requires change. When people are asked to use a new method or change current practice, it is usually easier to adopt when the change is their idea, or they have contributed to its development. The change should also be consistent with existing attitudes and beliefs in the organization's culture. If this new method or change is inconsistent, then people need time to work out this inconsistency while seeking to adopt the requested change. This internal conflict is called **cognitive dissonance**.[20] Cognitive dissonance is a concept from psychology, referring to the state of having inconsistent thoughts, beliefs, or attitudes, especially as relating to behavioral decisions and attitude change. Individuals generally seek to maintain consistency in their beliefs, attitudes, and behaviors.

While adopting quality as a strategy, what happens when a person is part of an organization with a culture developed over time? Figure 10.5 returns a set of ideas first introduced in Chapter 3, "Leading with Quality as an Organizational Strategy," to describe how change affects behavior, attitudes, and culture. The ideas were revisited in Chapter 4, "Establish and Communicate the Purpose of the Organization" adding how the organization's culture relates to tenets and how the organization's vision can create changes that require new behaviors.

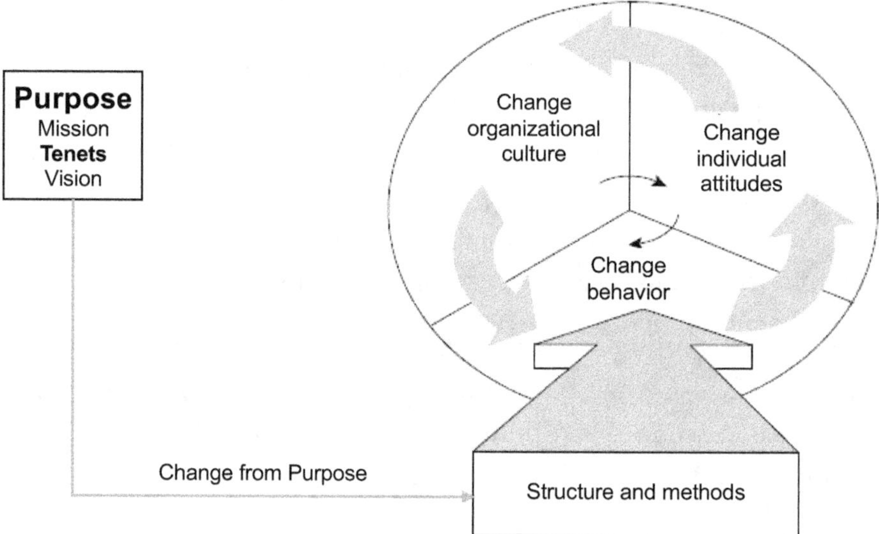

Figure 10.5. Culture can change attitudes in individuals.

The espoused **tenets** of the organization should reflect the culture. But an individual in the organization also holds beliefs and attitudes about a new change proposed in the organization. For example, they may fear not being familiar with the specific change proposed or not knowing what "good" will look like on the other side. They may fear failure, but they know how to work in the way things are today and may be successful in the current situation. The idea of a change is creating a cognitive dissonance.

Change is part of an organization continually pursuing its purpose through improvement. Many changes require individuals to behave differently. To eliminate the dissonance, individual attitudes must change to adapt to the change. The first step is for the leaders of improvement to connect the change to the organization's purpose. The large arrows in the model moving counterclockwise demonstrate the power of a change that first impacts attitudes; **eventually, they can change the culture of the organization.**

For example, using a method like the PDSA cycle, people can design and execute a change and study what happens. Allowing individuals to "test" a change using the PDSA cycle and contribute to modifications gives people the opportunity to create accommodations and redefine their attitudes and behaviors (e.g., resolve cognitive dissonance). This is especially important if the behavior is a deeply held belief by the individual. If the required behavior continues to be in opposition to one's core belief system, the individual may decide to leave the system or organization.

What happens if a person is new to an organization with a culture developed around quality as an organizational strategy? The smaller arrows moving clockwise show the impact of culture on new people coming into the organization. New people learn the importance of the organization's tenets and beliefs (culture) and the corresponding work methods that exist to help them be successful. As people conform to the organization's culture, their attitudes adapt, and their behavior matches the expected behaviors in the organization. For example, when a new employee comes into an organization and observes that others in the culture learn from data over time, they see that jumping to ideas before understanding the stability of the process is not the norm of the organization's culture, and they conform their behavior.

Two factors affect the strength of the dissonance: the number of dissonant beliefs and the importance attached to each belief. How do we reduce dissonance? Here are three ways:

- Reduce the importance of the beliefs. For example, fear of change was a belief previously described. The method of small-scale testing reduces the risk of failure and increases the person's understanding of the system.
- Add more beliefs. Add beliefs that are in line with the beliefs in the culture in order to outweigh the dissonant beliefs. For example, a leader may have a belief he or she needs to be involved in staff decision-making to reduce errors and rework. Methods like system maps, defined processes, useful measures, and defined role statements

increase clarity, reduce errors, and rework, and lessen the leader's feeling that they
need to be so involved in the details.

- Change the dissonant beliefs so that they are no longer inconsistent. For example, a
  belief may exist that a change comes with added cost. If so, then data showing the
  current cost of waste from a process reduces the dissonance.

Dissonance can be prevented. Engage people in the change through planning and
participating in improvement projects. People learn deeply about change when
chartering a project, as they understand a problem and develop ideas and test changes
and ideas using PDSAs. Allowing people time to learn and contribute to the change
reduces resistance and builds success, alignment, and better results, thereby avoiding
dissonance. In addition, the structure of an improvement project allows individuals to
redefine personal beliefs and attitudes toward change and opens their perspective for
potential in the future.

How can leadership resolve the dissonance that can prevent engagement? Applying
QOS methods creates structure and provides methods that are very effective in helping
people to be active participants in understanding the organization and contributing to
designing and redesigning their work. This active role in the change and participation
in the improvement aids staff through typical challenges and barriers and toward
becoming engaged in improvement.

The leadership team at Heat Exchange Inc. met to discuss the journey of
learning about themselves and, more importantly, the theories and methods to
engage people more effectively. George opened the meeting.

"Good afternoon. I was just reflecting on our learning journey. It occurred to
me that Susan's work was to develop the role statements, so that as this idea
was implemented, we took the first steps to ensure that people are connected
to our Purpose. This enables them in their role to make improvements and
other contributions to our company. As managers and supervisors discussed
how each person's role supported the organization's overall mission and tenets,
people could see how they fit, and that their work was important. As I walked
around and asked questions, people understood their role relative to work
processes and measurements defined by viewing our organization as a system.
I have heard from many of you on the leadership team that people were no
longer seeking permission to act. Given the defined roles, people are proactive

and more comfortable about it. I want to thank all of you for your work in achieving this very important objective."

"Communication in the leadership team has significantly improved," observed Roger, VP of Engineering. "We as leaders are asking more questions to achieve shared meaning around topics that deserve our attention. The rush to get something done quickly has been replaced with systems thinking to ensure that problems have not only been resolved, but more effectively addressed relative to the system."

Susan added, "The 'blame game' has disappeared from conversations. Leaders are more interested in helping design systems that allow people to take dignity in work and become more engaged to help make improvements. Employees are routinely offering suggestions and asking to be part of improvement and in the last six months, absenteeism has dropped by more than 30%."

SUMMARY

This chapter began with a discussion of engagement and how the methods of quality as an organizational strategy can help to better engage the workforce. It presented how leaders can use QOS methods to elevate people's engagement and design systems to enable them to do a better job.

NOTES

1. Harter, "U.S. Employee Engagement Data Hold Steady in First Half of 2021"; Harter, "Historic Drop in Employee Engagement Follows Record Rise." The Gallup Survey Data on engagement was first introduced in Chapter 3, "Leading with QOS."

2. Gallup Inc. and Workhuman, "Unleashing the Human Element at Work: Transforming Workplaces through Recognition" (Washington: Gallup, May 11, 2022), https://www. workhuman.com/resources/reports-guides/unleashing-the-human-element-at-work-transforming-workplaces-through-recognition#main-content. Results highlight the importance of recognition. Recognition enables dignity in work.

3. See Chapter 1, figure 1.9 for our enhanced version of Deming's Chain Reaction.

4. "Autonomy," Merriam-Webster, accessed March 25, 2023, https://www.merriam-webster.com/dictionary/autonomy.

5. Daniel H. Pink, *Drive: The Surprising Truth About What Motivates Us* (Edinburgh, U.K.: Cannongate, 2018), 5. Pink's ideas are featured in an excellent TED Talk video titled, "The Puzzle of Motivation." Pink notes activating intrinsic motivation is essential and the traditional use of "carrots and sticks" has failed. The finding is not new and was first discovered by Dr. Harry Harlow, a Professor of Psychology at the University of Wisconsin, who demonstrated in 1949 that rewards can hurt engagement. Harlow's results were verified again in 1969 by Edward Deci, a psychology graduate student at Carnegie Mellon University.

6. Senge, *The Fifth Discipline*, 141. Personal mastery is the discipline of personal growth and learning. People with high levels of personal mastery are continually expanding their ability to create results in life they truly seek. From their quest for continual learning comes the spirit of the learning organization.

7. More on selecting projects is found in Chapter 9, "Managing Improvement Efforts."

8. Simon Sinek, *Start with Why: How Great Leaders Inspire Everyone to Take Action* (New York: Penguin Group, 2009), 56.

9. Adapted from Richard M. Restak, *The Big Questions: Mind, The Big Questions* (London: Quercus Publishing, 2016), 26.

10. Douglas Porch, "Bugeaud, Gallieni, Lyautey: The Development of French Colonial Warfare," in *Makers of Modern Strategy: From Machiavelli to the Nuclear Age*, ed. Peter Paret (Princeton, NJ: Princeton University, 1986), 394. The term "hearts and minds" to refer to an approach to bring a group on side is attributed to French general and colonial administrator Hubert Lyautey in 1985.

11. *Start with Why*, 40–41; Simon Sinek, "How Great Leaders Inspire Action" (TED Talk, TEDxPuget Sound, Newcastle, WA, September 16, 2009), https://www.ted.com/talks/simon_sinek_how_great_leaders_inspire_action. Sinek describes how leaders can use the why, how, and what of our work to engage the limbic and neocortex of our brains.

12. Table 10.1 adapts an example Sinek uses from Apple Inc to show how Steve Jobs connected people through a path of inspiration. Sinek, *Start with Why*, 40–41.

13. *Management's Five Deadly Diseases: A Conversation with Dr. W. Edwards Deming* (Chicago, 1984), https://www.youtube.com/watch?v=ehMAwIHGN0Y. See additional discussion in "Diseases in Obstacles," in Deming, *Out of Crisis*, 97–148.

14. See "Introduction," Chapter 1, table 1.3 for questions to recognize the Need.

15. See "Five Rs of Motivation," in Chapter 2, "The Science of Improvement."

16. Chapter 4 of *The QOS Field Guide* describes the idea of nested mission and role statements for a city school district. Business groups or product lines in an organization may have nested missions or role statements. Here, Chapter 10 describes the development of role statements for individuals.

17. "Job Description," SHRM, July 22, 2021, https://www.shrm.org/resourcesandtools/tools-and-samples/hr-glossary/pages/job-description.aspx. This is the Society for Human Resource Management's (SHRM) operational definition of a job description.

18. The role statement template (figure 10.3) and example (figure 10.4) contributed by Jane Norman.

19. No law requires organizations use traditional job descriptions, but they are typically a standard human resource practice. Role statements can be adapted to include the additional details commonly found in a job description, or the role statement can complement a traditional job description.

20. Leon Festinger, *A Theory of Cognitive Dissonance* (Stanford, CA: Stanford University, 1957). A more up-to-date examination of Festinger's contributions is discussed in Carol Tavris and Elliott Aronson, *Mistakes Were Made (But Not By Me)* (Boston: Houghton Mifflin Harcourt, 2007).

PART IV
APPLICATION

CHAPTER 11

GETTING STARTED: BEGINNING THE QOS JOURNEY

Esther clears airport security and sits on the bench to put her shoes back on and retrieve her phone from her bag. She looks overhead at the signs for directions to the lounge. The entrance is across the way. She takes the stairs and settles into a comfortable chair by the window.

"The conference was equal parts energizing and conflicting," reflected Esther. "I enjoyed seeing old colleagues and meeting new ones. The collective desire to be great leaders and lead great organizations that get results was electric. Hearing speakers share results once believed impossible was energizing. But other presenters described troubling gaps in their industry's performance. Why are there so many places still not sorted…not excelling?"

On the flight in, Esther had reviewed her organization's monthly financial, safety, quality, and human resources reports. By most benchmarks, performance was on average or a little better than peer organizations. This was okay or comfortable to some, but others on the team were frustrated with reoccurring issues and a general sense we could do better.

"On the drive to the airport, I split a ride-share with an old friend," Esther continued. "His organization was recently recognized with a national quality award. His team led a great session sharing their story. Everything sounded like such common sense. What was different was a straightforward method and discipline. The pride and joy they shared from the hard work and learning together was contagious. They grew thirty percent in the first year and reduced operating costs by twenty percent while maintaining the same loyal staff team. When I asked how they did it, how they got started, he recommended a book that inspired their approach and helped them change."

Esther searched for the book online and added it to her tablet to read on the flight home. She skimmed the chapter titles and the opening pages. The ideas and methods resonated with her and built on her experience doing improvement projects. The last chapter was called "Getting Started." She clicked the link to see the concrete steps she could take at her organization to begin adopting QOS.

WHY CHANGE?

What causes a leadership team to decide to embrace change and begin adopting quality as a strategy? Many leaders and organizations do not proactively change. They are satisfied with good people who desire to do good work, put forth their best efforts, and react to changes in their marketplace. The status quo is to work harder, message better, inform, educate, maybe change some policies, and in the end, experience similar results. It is a rare case for an organization to decide to be different, change its leadership methods, sharpen its focus, put its head down, and generate impactful and quantifiable performance improvement.

Ask leaders why they shifted[1] from their previous leadership approach to pursuing quality as their strategy, and they may struggle to put their figure on the specific moment or event. But listen to their story, and some themes emerge.

- **Catastrophic event**: An employee is severely injured, a patient dies unnecessarily, or property is lost due to damage or a fire. An adverse event happens in a high-profile way that reveals flaws in the system or causes public pressure for change.

- **Inadequate methods**: Leaders continuously work hard to improve the organization's results and make little or no progress. Results remain the same. Problems reoccur. The current leadership approach is not getting improved results.
- **Unexpected change**: Many organizations are plugging away as they always have only to discover their products and services are no longer the best match to their customers' requirements; their expectations have shifted.
- **Best practice outside of accepted benchmarks**: Many leaders benchmark performance with peer organizations. Suppose that results are equal to or better than competitors. In that case, we might be complacent. But what happens if we think we could be better, or there are examples of organizations performing outside what is currently believed possible?[2]
- **New idea**: Sometimes, we don't even know that we are looking, yet we discover new ideas that shift our thinking. Maybe it is a presentation at a conference, a story in the media from another industry, or a book like this one. A leader discovers a new way of thinking that changes how they think about your approach and offers a new way to improve.[3]
- **Early success in applying improvement theory**: An organization applies improvement theory to projects and realizes success. Leaders want to expand the potential of methods that achieve results by including more people and addressing more significant organizational issues.
- **Other organizations are doing it**: Leaders learn that competitors or other organizations in the industry are applying improvement theory in their organizations.

There are many appropriate reasons to change and adopt QOS. Whether we see it or not, every organization has pressures from key stakeholders, competition, technology changes, and a need to continue improving value.[4]

Dr. Deming's chain reaction summarizes the intent of adopting QOS.[5] There are Needs in the world. Organizations exist to deliver products and services that best match the Needs of customers or clients. Leaders must understand the Need and their client's definition of the best match to the Need. This knowledge supports the continual improvement of quality by improving the whole system and designing and redesigning products and services. This leads to decreasing costs, increased productivity, and increased value. This results in more pride and joy in work and the potential for increasing market share or increasing profits. Everybody wins.

What triggered Esther to begin to explore QOS? "Some people don't get why we made a choice to change when we were technically doing fine—maybe even better than just fine," she reflected. "But it didn't feel fine to us. I am working with some of the smartest people of my career. Really good human beings. This wasn't just a job for us; we're here together because we believe in the organization's purpose."

She thought, "We all worked hard; tried our best to do what we signed up to do. That was a given. When we hit our goals, it felt great. I tell you, though, it wasn't always easy, or pretty. We were constantly starting and stopping, revising work, making the same errors, and we were about as fluid as trying to do the breaststroke the length of a swimming pool wearing a fully soaked pair of sweats. I just knew we could do so much more."

Esther has the right ingredients of people and expertise, she could see other organizations that were leading in her field, and she wanted to be proud of what the organization was accomplishing and feel joy in doing the work. She just didn't know how.

CONSIDERATIONS BEFORE BEGINNING

Many leaders move cautiously before committing to change and embarking on a new strategy. Experience with false starts or efforts that launched with enthusiasm and then gradually faded back to the status quo encourages them to want to know what they are getting into, the level of effort they can expect to invest, and the resources required to support the change work. They focus on the need to learn and change within the leadership team[6] to make QOS effective and sustainable.

Leadership's Will to Change

Latham[7] describes two primary forces required to shift from the inertia of the current state and resistance to changing it. First, there is dissatisfaction with the current state of the organization. Dissatisfaction can be internal when leaders are dissatisfied with the recent results or how they must work to get the results. It can come from customers and clients who find that the company's products and services do not match their need or see that competitors better match their need. It can also be from regulatory audits surfacing areas needing improvement.

The second is a vision of a preferred or ideal future state. As in Esther's story, cases of organizations achieving organizational excellence and receiving recognition, benchmarking organizations that live their ideals, or even a "fire in the belly" to do better. Dissatisfaction with the current results and a compelling ideal state aid in building leadership's rationale for change and adopting new methods to pursue quality as a strategy.

A Commitment of Time and Energy

A common phenomenon for many leaders—and humans generally—is the desire to find a "silver bullet" or a quick fix to a problem. Miracle diets and flashy exercise programs are great examples of selling a solution to help us secure health quickly. The ingredients to good health (whole foods with lots of fruits and vegetables, adequate sleep, and frequent movement) are well known and documented, but discipline and consistency are not.

Deming[8] famously picked on managers who contacted him to purchase "my formula." Some asked him to come out for a couple of consultations to set them on the right path for quality or send along the practices from Japan that they could adopt and get the results. Pursuing quality as a strategy and continually striving for organizational excellence takes time, ongoing commitment, discipline, and hard work.

A key ingredient to QOS is that the leadership team must lead and do much of the actual work. This doesn't mean the senior leaders do all the work or are involved in every detail. However, it does mean they do much more than approve the strategy and then delegate the effort to others only to be updated at the quarterly meeting.

The time commitment varies by the scale of the organization and the pace the leadership team sets to transform. The more leadership time invested, the quicker they can expect to see results. A starting benchmark is to carve out a minimum commitment of ten percent of work time or about two days per month. Before processing that number, consider that the average knowledge worker spends fifteen hours a week (seven and one-half days per month) on email alone.[9]

Two days a month, therefore, is a very reasonable starting point for working on QOS. These two days should include current time in meetings and other activities that can now focus on QOS. So, it is not all about additions to the commitments already on the calendar. By allocating ten percent of the leadership team's time, an organization can expect to see some meaningful progress within a year.

When starting QOS, carving out the time for the work will take attention and discipline. Working forward, where do we predict to be each quarter? Where will we be by the end of this month? By the end of this week? As mentioned, many leaders block time in their calendars and dedicate portions of existing meetings to integrate the work activity into the current daily schedule. As the work develops and progresses, it quickly becomes high-value time, and leaders often increase their commitment and devote more attention to this exciting new work.

The dedicated time allows space for several actions, including preparation, learning methods, and regular application to daily activities.[10] First, prepare by reviewing materials, studying theories and ideas, and engaging in discussions with colleagues. Next, preparation includes education and training sessions when colleagues come together to learn deeper about the theories and methods, test applying them, and plan how to use the learning in daily work in the weeks ahead. Finally, the practical value becomes strongest when leaders follow through on the plans and test the ideas and methods daily with colleagues and staff.

The leadership team owns the pace of adopting quality as a strategy. When leaders own the work and make progress on the planned activities, ideas, and methods, the practical value grows. Collins called this "The Flywheel Effect,"[11] a continuous accumulation of effort applied in a consistent direction. Researching leaders and organizations who transformed to "great," there was never a single event or action but a cumulative effect:

> The flywheel image captures the overall feel of what it was like inside the companies as they went from good to great. No matter how dramatic the end results, the good-to-great transformations never happened in a fell swoop. There was no single defining action, no grand program, no one killer innovation, no solitary lucky break, no wrenching revolution. Good-to-great comes about by a cumulative process—step by step, action by action, decision by decision, turn by turn of the flywheel— that adds up to sustained and spectacular results.

Leadership actions at every turn push the flywheel. For example, living the tenets when making decisions, using the system map to understand the interdependencies of work in progress, Leaders will also begin to predict the effect of changes, conduct daily problem-solving utilizing the improvement methods, and continually chip away at strategic improvement efforts. All this work will cumulatively lead to adopting QOS.

External Support

Quality as an organizational strategy builds on a foundation of theories and methods developed over the last century. Reading the pages of this book and recognizing ideas like mission, vision, and tenets, systems thinking, Shewhart charts, and the Model for Improvement, QOS can feel familiar. How they are framed together and presented as a system may feel novel. Many leaders will wonder, "Can we do this ourselves, or do we need external support?"

Beginning the journey to transform an organization and leadership approach to QOS requires stepping back and seeing the organization and the work holistically. It also requires having a level of knowledge and ability in the concepts and methods involved. A Chief Executive, Operations Officer, Financial Director, or Quality Leader can drive this work. Internal consultants (such as organizational development or improvement advisors) may also be critical supports. What's essential is understanding the Science of Improvement and the theories and methods of QOS and improvement. Equally important is the ability and discipline to see the organization as a system and to chip away at stepwise progress to develop the organization using the QOS activities.

Many organizations do not already have that expertise or discipline. Or leaders might desire an advisor with experience with QOS adoption in multiple organizational contexts. An external advisor or consultant is frequently a helpful partner in the design, implementation, and learning system required to begin and progress through the journey to develop, use, and sustain QOS. A quality methods practitioner, organization development facilitator, or management consultant will not necessarily have expertise in QOS. The ideal external support has experience in QOS, brings knowledge and expertise from each lens of the Science of Improvement, has experience building capability and coaching teams to achieve results, and is a skilled facilitator and teacher.

Finally, the decision to consider outside support can be driven simply by wanting freedom within the organization and to not have the added responsibility of organizing the work and building the approach simultaneously. For example, an external advisor can provide the framework and discipline to enable leaders to focus on the learning and the work; they can also serve as safety checks to help teams avoid groupthink and other cultural barriers; and they can give feedback on the work to the team to support formative evaluation and planning.[12]

ASSESSING THE ORGANIZATION'S CURRENT STATE

Assessing an organization's current state relative to the QOS framework is a powerful opportunity to reflect on how the work is progressing and whether the leadership team shares similar assessments. Chapter 1 provided an opportunity to complete an assessment of progress in QOS.[13] Reading each chapter and gaining a deeper understanding, readers were encouraged to update that assessment. Table 11.1 includes the activities we learned about and then adds two high-leverage areas to assess: progress on improvement efforts and evaluation of the key business process.

Table 11.1. Assessment of leadership system and key activities

Key Activities
Understanding the purpose of the organization
Viewing the organization as a system
Vector of measures
System of obtaining information
Planning for improvement
Managing improvement efforts
The Model for Improvement
The learning system for improvement
Progress on improvement efforts
Evaluation of key business processes

Each area of the assessment tool includes a scoring scale from zero to ten, and an operational definition accompanies each even number score. Odd values on the scale should be used when all is complete at one level, but everything is not yet complete on the higher level. Zero on the scale means the area is not present or operating at even a basic level in the organization. A ten describes an organization that understands the approach and fully integrates QOS into running and improving the organization. The chapters in Part II - Building a System of Improvement focused on the five activities of QOS. Each chapter described the operational definition for the achievement of the activity (for a score of ten). The total possible score across all areas in the assessment is "100."

The leadership team should ask each member to complete the assessment independently. Each person assesses the organization from their perspective and their position in the organization. Figure 11.1 is an example of a scatter plot diagram used to visually display the compiled individual results to learn from the scoring and this variation in perspective.

Figure 11.1. Scatter plot of leadership team's QOS assessment.[14]

The assessment results are a powerful tool for learning about the organization and QOS. They also guide the work ahead and where to start. For example, looking at the chart, we quickly see that two key learning opportunities are assessment variation and low-average scores:

1. **Assessment variation.** Each leader used the same operational definitions to score the areas, but there is variation in the leadership teams' assessment of the organization's maturity against those operational definitions. This variation is a rich learning opportunity. The variation can surface differences in agreement about the present state of the area, the degree of leadership knowledge and skill in the area's focus, or awareness of the area due to each leader's role in the organization.

2. **Areas with low-average scoring.** Many leaders have never used a framework and assessment tool to evaluate their organization. The assessment tool is a learning tool as the leaders read the definitions for each score level and think about how the organization is currently performing in the area. Scores at the lower end of the scale are not uncommon, and leaders can be humbled by their assessment and inspired to see what could be possible when working on QOS.

These two learnings from the assessment tool are the first tangible use of the assessment results. Reviewing the results, inviting reflections, and discussing the results in each area are great for developing a shared sense of where we are today and where to begin to focus the work. They may also surface any worries and disagreements. As an outcome of the self-assessment and reflection, many teams feel motivated and create the will required to take on this journey.

On Esther's return, she shared her thoughts with the team in talking points. She was not the only one grappling with this struggle to do the right work and get the results they wanted. She confided to one of the other leaders: "I don't know why I was surprised everyone felt as I did, maybe to different degrees. The more we talked, the more validating it was to hear the agreement to commit to what we were doing together. We all felt there must be a better way."

Esther reflected on her experience, "When I showed everyone the book, we considered starting off on our own. We decided instead to find an external partner experienced in advising leaders to adopt quality as their strategy. We figured we needed the time and space to do the change work, and that she would bring the methods to help us do the work and guide us to learn deeply along the way."

The external advisor used an assessment tool with each leader to evaluate the current leadership system and key activities. Results were summarized in a chart of the average rating, to appreciate the variation within our team's impressions. Esther reflected, "We agreed our work in the last year to build improvement capability was progressing. At the same time, our assessments about to what degree we progressed were varied within the standardized rubric for each area. The chart display of our data provoked some rich discussion. These were new types of conversations for us. They were great. We were ready to learn."

WHERE TO START?

Many people want a road map to chart their path when starting a new journey, but leaders often must set their own course. A sense of direction can ease worries and create movement when something feels new or complex. Where do we start? What steps do we need to follow to do this work? In the QOS framework, there is no single answer to these questions. It depends. QOS begins where you are and builds from what matters most to you. However, the framework does provide some direction through the interdependencies of the five essential quality activities. Three common starting points include:

1. building a learning system
2. getting results on the current portfolio of improvement efforts, and
3. reflecting on the organization's purpose.

Many leadership teams begin with their own learning system. In Chapter 1, we introduced Gavin's[15] definition of a learning organization as "an organization skilled at creating, acquiring, and transferring knowledge, and at modifying its behavior to reflect new knowledge and insights." A learning system is a collection of processes, practices, and artifacts that help leaders learn new ideas and concepts and bring them to results-driven improvement work. It supports defining, testing, learning, and adapting as leaders innovate, design, and redesign the work system.

Senge[16] described the idea of learning organizations as places "where people continually expand their capacity to create the results they truly desire, where new and expansive patterns of thinking are nurtured, where collective aspiration is set free, and where people are continually learning how to learn together."

Education of the leadership team on the Science of Improvement and the QOS framework is a helpful place to start bringing in new knowledge, learning together, applying that learning to the organization's work, debriefing about what happened, and adapting based on that learning. The first session often begins with an overview of the QOS activities, reviewing the assessment results and other artifacts helpful to understanding where to begin the journey, including the current strategies driving the organization, active improvement efforts, and pressures affecting the organization. This first session helps unite the leadership on QOS as a theory and method and can create agreement on the next steps and where to start. The learning system begins with leadership education, then grows to include continual formative evaluation,[17] organization-wide will-building and awareness, and application and integration of quality as the method of leading and managing.

It's tempting to approach this work as an educational program or theoretical exercise, but the theories and methods are only worth pursuing if they will support continually improving and getting results that position the organization for sustainable gains. Today, most organizations have some improvement efforts underway at any given time. These won't go away because leaders are starting the QOS journey. It's also common that the existing methods to pursue improvement vary, and current results may be slow or nonexistent. Nevertheless, **improving processes, services, or products in the system is a crucial skill for organizations pursuing QOS.** The work at hand is the right place to start quickly learning about the organizational system.

After reflecting on the improvement efforts, the leadership team understands what is underway in the organization. Asking the staff in each area what improvement efforts exist adds more to the list. Reviewing recent leadership meetings can also lead to finding potential new improvement efforts.

Chapter 9 describes how to charter improvement efforts using the Model for Improvement. If not already in use, the three questions in that chapter are helpful tools to use with existing improvement efforts to frame charters uniformly. Next, leadership should review each charter and current progress and assess what would help the project team achieve its aim. Finally, a leadership team member should begin participating in each improvement effort. Serving as an executive sponsor can accomplish this.

The key is to begin with the work in progress, reduce any friction from moving these projects forward, and focus on using improvement tools and methods to get the desired results. Doing so sets up a system to manage current and future improvement efforts: a method to identify, charter, resource, and track improvement across the organization.

After the initial QOS overview and planning session and documenting formal improvement efforts, leaders find starting with the purpose activity insightful. The "Introduction" (Chapter 1) describes organizations that are designed and operated to deliver products and services that match customers' needs. Customers have wants and requirements—quality dimensions—for their products and services. Understanding the Need and client requirements are essential inputs for an organization's purpose and how it translates its mission, vision, and tenets. Most organizations have elements of a purpose statement (e.g., mission, tenets). Still, many have not looked at them in a while or considered how they serve (or don't serve) to provide direction for the organization's design, redesign, and operation. Reviewing and using the purpose is an essential starting point and is strongly linked to the rest of the QOS framework.

Assessing our organization's current state, developing our learning system with the start of leadership education, then identifying and engaging in formal improvement efforts, and focusing on a purpose are solid foundations to build on. Then, leaders build on the work in progress and set a course for learning, discovery, and improvement.

Last year, Esther participated in a year-long advanced-level improvement program and led a project to improve the organization's process of managing grant work. She learned how to use tools and methods she thought she knew (such as driver diagrams, the PDSA cycle, and run charts) at a level several degrees higher than before. Her colleagues supported her and wanted the staff to learn about improvement. She held several one-day workshops, and QI projects were started across the organization.

"We felt pretty good," reflected Esther. "We were building improvement capability. Staff was engaged when I ordered the iconic Mr. Potato Head toy online and used an exercise to learn about PDSA testing and making run charts.[18] Several people stepped forward to start improvement projects in areas they had a personal interest. Some of those projects are still in progress." The team also used a project evaluation method to understand project progress. They looked at project aims and the measures if they had that data. Then, they learned about the individual or team's activities.

Esther continued, "If you asked us if we should start with focusing on improvement efforts, we would have said 'No.' We felt we delivered great training, and the staff was willing to try what they learned on issues they wanted to fix. After evaluating the projects, however, we found that projects were moving slowly or stalled. I couldn't tell if any changes resulted in improvement. It goes without saying, we were working hard, but not getting the results we wanted."

Organizations adopt improvement tools and methods and train staff to set them up to improve things that matter. Some require project-based, capability-building efforts to enable learners to apply the tools and methods on projects by achieving the desired measurable results. It's not unusual for organizations to train staff but have only episodic examples of results-driven projects, of using the methods with fidelity, and of achieving their aims.

Esther continued her reflection: "I compared the list of active improvement projects against the topics on my weekly staff meeting agenda and on my calendar, and there was little overlap. We were wrestling with work every day and never thought to use improvement there. If we want to build a system of improvement, we need to learn how to do results-driven improvement. We needed to charter the improvement efforts for the issues right before us."

When quality is the strategy and the Science of Improvement is the operating theory, immediate improvement challenges may be the best place to start. Results will never be realized without successfully completing a project. Leaders learn quickly as sponsors or project leads exactly how the organization needs to be set up for success.

QOS IS A SYSTEM OF ACTIVITIES

The activities of QOS described in Part II are visually displayed as five activities and presented in a sequence of chapters. **It would be a mistake to think about the activities as distinct events or actions and miss their interdependent linkages (see the arrows showing the interdependence of the activities in figure 11.2) or to assume the chapter organization is a prescriptive flow or sequence. In practice, leaders will develop the organization in all five areas and the learning system.**

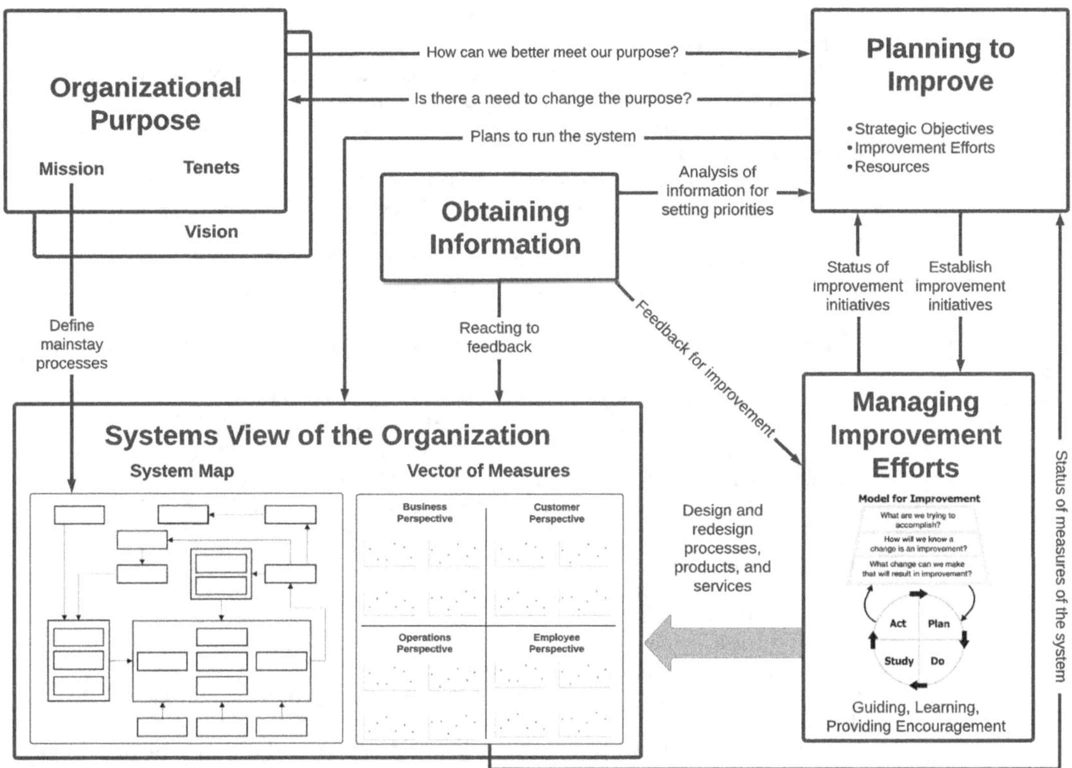

Figure 11.2. Interdependence of the five activities.

The education of the leadership team may follow a progression mirroring the book chapters and support further development of these areas. The flow may also deploy where the leaders' self-assessed areas were less developed, and there is the will or a requirement to start with a specific area of work, such as a system map or vector of measures. QOS is adaptable to what suits the organization. After the purpose lays the foundation and provides constancy of direction, work can start and be active in all the other areas. Table 11.2 summarizes methods for leaders to focus on across the five QOS activities.[19]

Table 11.2. Methods for leaders to focus the organization on improvement

Methods	Description of actions for making quality an organizational strategy
Purpose activity	**Establish and communicate the purpose of the organization** • Develop a written statement of purpose for the organization, including the mission, tenets, and vision. • Communicate this purpose to the organization by relating the work of different parts of the organization to the purpose. • Document connection of purpose with the role statements for departments and all employees. • Use this purpose to guide and focus the organization as it conducts business, makes decisions, and manages improvement.
System activity	**View the organization as a system** • Understand the major processes and products/services in the organization. • Document how these processes link together to form a system. • Use the system map of the organization to understand the work and focus of improvement efforts. • Create a vector of measures to understand the performance of the system. • Visually display these measures as a set of Shewhart charts to see the system's performance. • Use these documents to understand the impact of improvement on the organization and to learn how the organization functions as a system.
Obtaining information activity (customer focus)	**Establish a system to obtain information relevant to the Need the organization is fulfilling** • Identify the present and future customers of the organization. • Develop a system to gather information about matching the Need. • Develop systems to obtain other information relevant to the Need. • Communicate this information to all parts of the organization. • Analyze this information to guide planning and improvement efforts.
Planning activity	**Planning to improve** • Summarize the information from customer research and from employees, suppliers, and the relevant external environment. • Based on these inputs, develop (or update) strategic objectives that could best accelerate the performance of the organization. • Develop a list, in order of priority, of the processes, products, and services to design or redesign. • Coordinate this plan with the organization's strategic and business planning and budgeting activities. • Establish briefs for improvement projects that can be resourced and managed.

Managing improvement activity	**Manage improvement efforts**
	• Prepare the organization to focus on improvement.
	• Define the leadership team's role in managing improvement efforts.
	• Execute improvement projects identified in the planning process.
	  o Provide a standard methodology to guide improvement efforts.
	  o Provide training and other necessary resources required for the improvement efforts.
	• Provide sponsors and ensure that guidance is provided for improvement efforts.
	  o Remove obstacles and provide recognition.
	  o Redirect and redeploy resources as improvements are made.
	• Leadership team studies the improvement results and contributions of improvement efforts of the team to learn about the organization viewed as system and the key forces driving the system.

"When I first saw the QOS figure, I focused on the five activities," Esther said as she reflected on her early experience with QOS. "The arrows and text in between felt busy. I even removed them from the picture I used. I didn't initially appreciate that each method has a role and is dependent on each other—they're linked. Having seen the components of the whole framework more clearly, I then added the linkages back into my picture."

As Esther's team looked at starting work on an activity, they first read the description of the actions for QOS. These were the outputs they would work toward. Esther reflected, "We try to develop our organization to manage individual and team improvement efforts. What will that look like? We need to train people and provide the resources required for improvement efforts. We need a shared method to guide our improvement. The leaders need to guide and sponsor the improvement work, remove barriers that get in their way, and celebrate their work, their curiosity, and learning, and to recognize the team's results."

Leaders also study and learn from the team about key processes and forces driving the organizational system. As improvements are made, leaders redirect and redeploy resources to other areas. Esther continued to reflect, "Being clear about what we were building toward defines what 'good' looks like. Now we understand how the concepts we learned in our study sessions could be merged with our efforts and how to apply the ideas to yield results."

ASSESSMENT OF ACTIVITY PROGRESS AND MATURITY

The QOS assessment provides a tool to gauge the maturity of the organization in each area. The operational definitions in the tool support leaders in seeing what progress might look like as they work on developing each area of their organization. A score of ten reflects a mature organization that has successfully made quality its organizational strategy.

The tool starts as an assessment of the current state, and the content presented in each chapter provides the methods for developing and using each activity. The leadership may reassess annually and continue using the QOS assessment to track progress as the organization matures. The updated assessment, then, is input to reflecting on progress, appreciating the plan's execution, and planning for adjustments that will support movement.

MILESTONES FOR QUALITY AS AN ORGANIZATIONAL STRATEGY

QOS can take several years to mature. Moving from where the organization is today to full maturity in all areas comes over time. The actual time frame depends largely on the leadership's will, momentum, and investment in time. As a leadership group adopts this strategy, it's common for leaders to ask: "How are we doing?" or "How do we know we are making progress in the improvement process?" The vector of measures of the organization provides a quantitative view of how the organization is performing. However, these measures are also influenced by forces such as the economy, market changes, competitors' actions, and a host of factors, making it difficult to evaluate specific progress in making quality the organization's strategy directly.

Once an organization embarks on the QOS journey, there are three expected phases of growth:

1. **Phase 1 – QOS Development**: Getting started to make quality the organization's strategy.
2. **Phase 2 – Using the QOS system**: Full integration of the improvement process in the organization.
3. **Phase 3 – Understanding QOS**: Improvement is a basic component of the organization's structure.

Each phase includes a set of corresponding milestones typical for organizations as they develop. Milestones are qualitative outcomes along the journey. Imagine them like QOS tokens or badges,[20] picked up as you work and reach a noteworthy stage. Milestone progress is another measure and complements the scatter plot of regular assessment results.

The milestones do not have a prescriptive sequence, and some might depend on others. Many of the milestones in Phases 2 and 3 depend on the foundations established in the milestones of Phase 1. The milestones reflect "typical"[21] organizations, but organizations vary. Table 11.3 summarizes the milestones for each of the three phases of development.

Table 11.3. Milestones for Quality as an Organizational Strategy (QOS)

Phase 1 QOS development	Phase 2 Using the QOS system	Phase 3 Understanding QOS
1. Establish formal improvement efforts with individuals and teams. 2. Begin leadership education. 3. Recognize purpose and publish purpose statement. 4. Leaders begin delivering awareness education sessions. 5. Develop a view of the organization as system. 6. Establish key vector of measures of the system. 7. Identify system for customer research. 8. Formal improvement effort is successful. 9. All leaders participate in quality improvement effort.	10. Use the purpose statement in organization. 11. Use the systems map in the organization. 12. Use key measures in reports. 13. Analyze and condense customer feedback and research. 14. Leaders learn from improvement efforts of teams and individuals. 15. Planning drives improvement efforts. 16. Business plan integrates improvement. 17. Improvements are made to a major management system. 18. Involvement of suppliers in improvement. 19. Involvement of customers/partners in improvement. 20. A system is in place for developing capability in the Science of Improvement. 21. Reflect and recognize major improvements in the maturity of QOS. 22. Role statements connect all employees to the system. 23. Improvements are understood in terms of the Chain Reaction.	24. Leaders use Model for Improvement in decisions for learning. 25. Constancy of purpose is understood. 26. Leaders have a systems view. 27. Leaders understand variation. 28. All employees are listening, observing, and reporting what they learn. 29. All business planning processes are fully integrated with planning for improvement. 30. Concepts of improvement are incorporated in the business infrastructure. 31. Everyone is involved in improvement. 32. Improvement philosophy, methods, and tools are used in day-to-day work. 33. Social change is understood as it relates to changes in psychology. 34. The Science of Improvement is used to develop and make changes.

The following sections describe the three phases of the QOS journey and the typical milestones achieved within each stage. At the start of each phase, a chart[22] displays the five activities and learning system along the vertical axis. Milestones for the phase are grouped in the "swim lane" for their related activity. Interdependent milestones are indicated. This "typical" reflection is adapted based on each organization.

PHASE 1: QOS DEVELOPMENT

Phase 1 milestones reflect the "getting started" or development phase of the QOS journey and typically occur in the **first six months to one year**. Figure 11.3 displays key milestones the organization accomplishes in this startup phase across the activities. The first three milestones are interdependent.

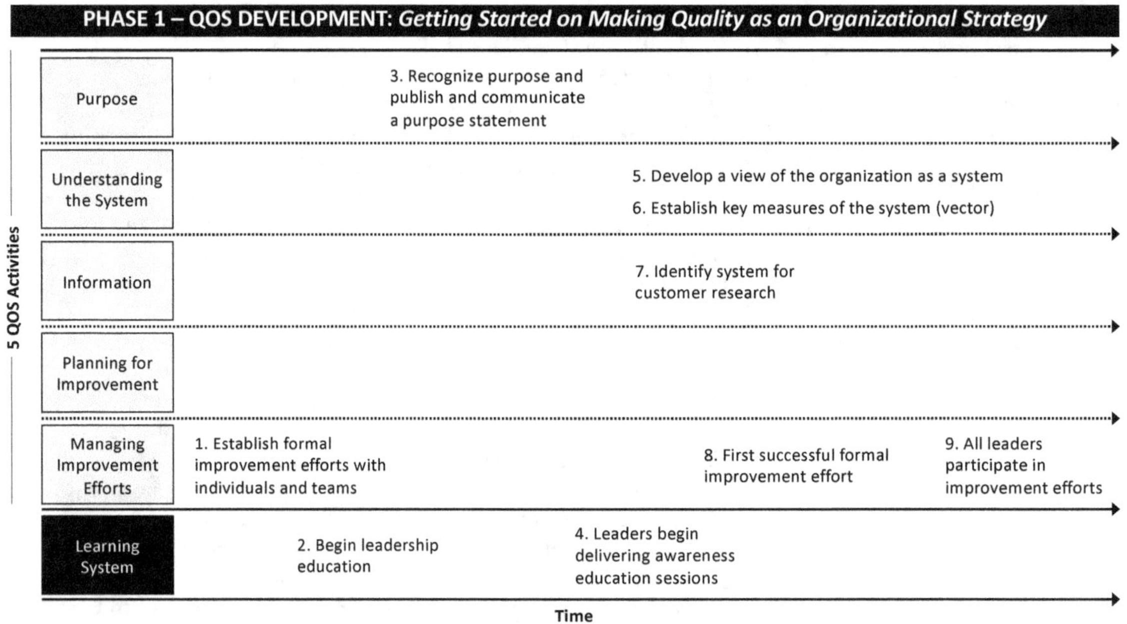

Figure 11.3. Phase 1 milestones for developing the QOS system.

REACHING THE QOS DEVELOPMENTAL MILESTONES OF PHASE 1

Congratulations on reaching these nine milestones! They are the typical achievements an organization will experience as it begins to build its system of improvement, and they will lay a foundation for the five activities when beginning to use QOS to operate and improve the organization.

Esther had heard that the development phase for QOS typically takes six months to a year. It's the start-up phase of the five activities, it begins the deep learning journey, and it builds the capability to get results on improvement efforts in a mainstay process. She reflected six months into her organization's journey, "We started slowly. We were being cautious about this new way of thinking. At the first quarter review, we knew we needed to create space to put the work front and center if we were committed to changing. From then on, QOS work became integrated into our daily work—no risk of it getting pushed off as a special project. We refined our purpose during a Friday workshop, and Monday morning, we discussed it in the staff meeting and modeled our tenets. We can't say we value 'curiosity' if we don't practice it when staff members bring new ideas to the floor, or a team explores why we create inconsistent user experiences."

The development phase engages leadership in deep learning as the activities create a method of understanding the organization. It's hard work, but Esther and her colleagues felt every deep dive was like running a 5K road race. They were worn out from the effort but energized by the experience, and each mile marker felt like progress.

"We'd hit the end of the day, and no one was packing up to leave. The pain points and friction we were experiencing were now visible. We were having these 'aha moments' in real time, together. We appreciated why people weren't clear on what we were doing or where work wasn't defined in a shared way. On the outside, it probably looked daunting to see us doing all this inward-looking work and coming up with lists of stuff we needed to create or fix. To us, though, a new frontier opened up, because we knew where we needed to focus and had enough ideas and a method to get started."

PHASE 2: USING THE QOS SYSTEM

The Phase 2 milestones reflect continuing the development work and entering a stage of the QOS journey where leaders consciously use the system to improve the organization. **Phase 2 typically lasts a year or two.** Figure 11.4 displays key milestones an organization accomplishes in this phase across the activities. Some milestones are interdependent. For example, Milestone 13: Analysis and Condensation of Customer Feedback and Research, produces inputs to the planning activity and precedes Milestones 15 and 16, which both are achieved as a result of the planning process. The other milestones are not as interdependent.

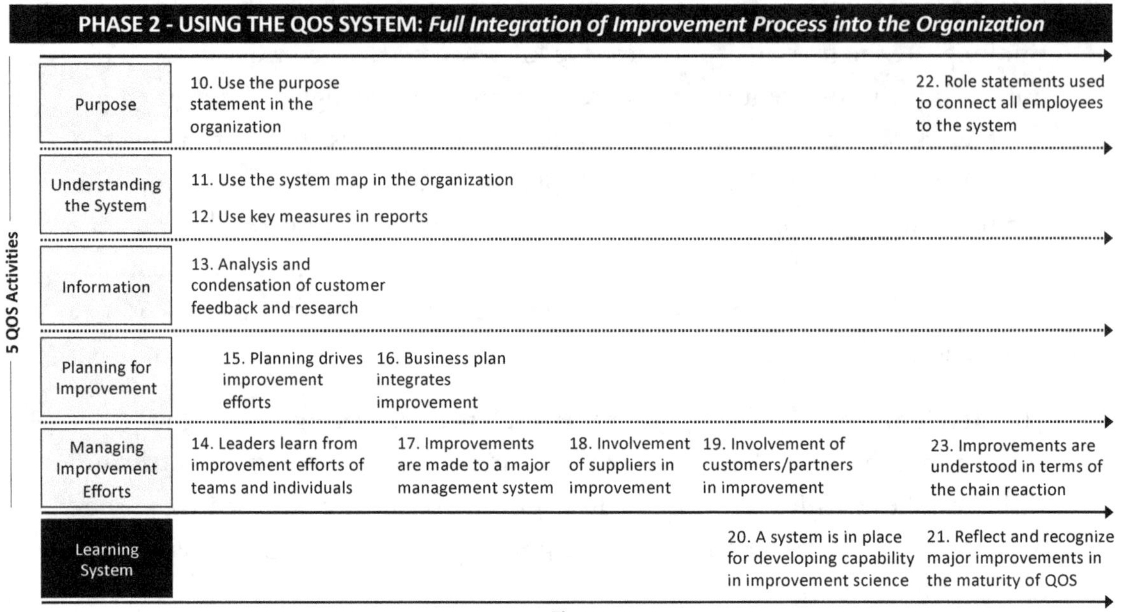

Figure 11.4. Phase 2 milestones for using the QOS system.

REACHING THE MILESTONES OF PHASE 2: USING THE QOS SYSTEM

These fourteen milestones are the typical achievements of the second phase as the organization completes the development of QOS and begins to use the new processes. As leaders work on the five activities and build maturity, these milestones continue to provide an appreciation of progress. The foundation for the five activity areas is completed, and leaders begin to use the system to operate and improve the organization.

Esther returned to the annual conference that started this QOS journey a year before. Her friend from the shared airport ride, from the company using QOS and recognized with the Baldrige award, was there too. They caught up over coffee. Ester shared her experiences. "I have a totally different mindset this year. Our work to develop QOS is so fulfilling. I think I can say that's true for most of us. A couple of colleagues were initially resistant. I sat them down one-on-one and clarified that QOS was our path. One is now very active. The other moved on to another organization with a more traditional leadership approach. Everyone's welcome on our bus, but they must decide to stay on or get off.

"I won't say it was easy, and I can see why leaders often don't follow through with organizational transformation. Professionally, it has changed how I lead. QOS is a different leadership system that enables us to understand our organization profoundly. We can lead at a level I don't think I could have described before we started, and I love it.

"We completed our first full planning event in the last quarter. The external advisor coached us to use the planning process systematically. Clear plans to update existing operations and a set of QI projects were clearly defined at the other end. And we all agreed that this is the work we should be doing.

"I have never felt this focused and clear about my work. We don't just have a plan; we have precise steps for delivering what we care about to our clients. We are going to fix processes and services that are really going to help move the ball down the pitch. And I'm confident we have made the space and resourced our team to do it. This kind of clarity is new to me."

As they enjoyed their break, they continued to share their pride and joy in their work, in being more in control of where the organization was going, and possessing such a deep understanding. Next year, they agreed, would be exciting.

PHASE 3: UNDERSTANDING QOS

The Phase 3 milestones reflect a continuation of the QOS journey, where leaders use the system to improve the organization, and QOS becomes fully integrated into the organization's strategy. **Phase 3 typically takes a year or two.** Figure 11.5 displays the organization's key milestones in this phase across the activities. The milestones in Phase 3 are not strongly interdependent.

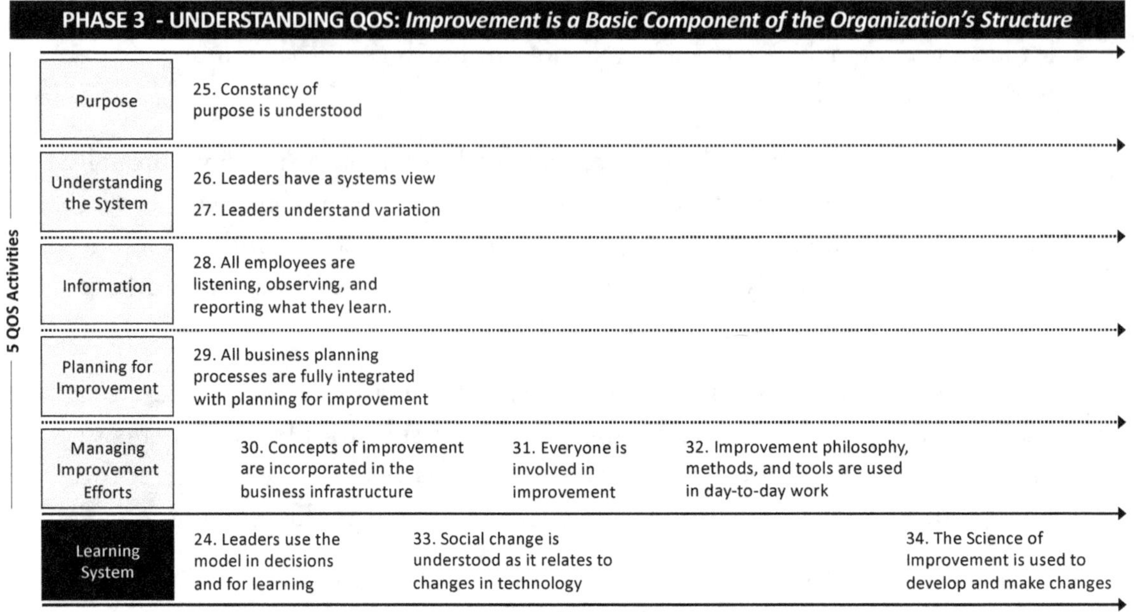

Figure 11.5. Phase 3 milestones for understanding QOS.

REACHING THE MILESTONES OF PHASE 3: UNDERSTANDING QOS

These final eleven milestones are the typical achievements of the third phase, a time when the organization has developed QOS and is now hardwiring improvement into the organization's fiber. It is becoming how leaders lead and manage the organization. The organization has fully adopted quality as an organizational strategy. Understanding QOS never ends; it is a continuous learning journey.

SUMMARY

Leaders desiring to adopt QOS should understand that they are taking the first steps in a long journey. No map makes it simple to see the exact route they will take, and no recipe exists to describe every step they will take. Their actual path will be based on learning. This should not discourage you from starting the journey. Those who have done so describe it as one of the most fulfilling experiences of their professional careers.[23] They learn profoundly about their organizations, their colleagues, and themselves. They build skills and abilities they never learned in university that are transferable to any organization or industry. They appreciated moving from educated guesses, best efforts, hard work, and theoretical tools and methods to practical and tactical approaches to learn, test changes, understand results, and then hold the gains. QOS is not for everyone, but it will be transformational!

Esther and the leadership team worked through building the scaffolding for all the activities of QOS. They learned building a solid first draft, one that was "good enough" to use, was essential. They understood that everything would be improved several times as it was used.

Esther reflected on the journey, "It was hard to break our predisposition to plan and create a nearly perfect product and then wrestle everyone into compliance. We knew that didn't work well, but it was so hardwired into our psyche and work culture. We wanted to be moving. We agreed to experiment with defining the minimum required to move forward. We did this with our purpose statement, our Systems Map, and vector of measures to start. We built a draft good enough to get started, and we learned by using it. This reduced the drag on getting going. We also quickly learned what was right, what needed tweaking, and when to add. It was a hard change at first, but I'm so glad we did. I was learning so quickly, which wasn't true of our usual ways."

Esther's team continued to iterate toward using and improving the QOS methods. Old practices were ended, and new ones were wired in their place. It took planning and work to install the new way to work. As they used it and onboarded new staff, they watched the culture change. They knew what the right work was, and they either had the proper processes in place or had a line of sight on the path to designing or redesigning what was needed.

Esther continued: "We think hard about maintaining the flywheel of momentum,[24] of building what works and then installing it, weaving it into the fabric of the organization. We do this to sustain the gains we've made. It's also important to maintain constancy of purpose as people naturally enter and exit the organization. We all saw examples of similar organizations who did amazing work toward adopting QOS, but found that it didn't stick when a new CEO came in. We will not be one of those organizations. We have decided we always want quality as our strategy."

NOTES

1. We interviewed more than a dozen leaders about why they shifted to using improvement as their leadership method. Most could not concisely describe their reasoning. Dr. A. Blanton Godfrey framed three causes from his experience: disaster, ego (wanting to be the best), and the discovery of a new idea that makes so much sense and is so different than what they do, and they think something is there. He gave the example of when leaders first read Eliyahu M. Goldratt's business novel *The Goal* about the "theory of constraints." Eliyahu M. Goldratt and Jeff Cox, *The Goal: A Process of Ongoing Improvement*, 4th ed. (Great Barrington, MA: North River Press, 2014).

2. Michael Dell, founder of Dell Technologies described in an interview that benchmarking to the competition may not be useful. What if the competition isn't very good? He argued understanding your customers was more valuable. See "Michael Dell, Founder of Dell—Early Failures, Battling Carl Icahn, Learning from the Competition, and How to Play Nice But Win (#534)," *The Tim Ferriss Show Transcripts*, September 29, 2021, https://tim.blog/2021/09/28/michael-dell-transcript/.

3. Many leaders describe Dr. Deming's four-day workshops and books as this type of disrupter. The ideas interrupted the way they thought about organizations, leadership, and improvement and this motivated them to change.

4. Latham, *[Re]Create the Organization You Really Want!*, 1.

5. See figure 1.9, "Why quality as an organizational strategy" for a modified version of Deming's Chain Reaction.

6. It is often assumed that when we assemble a group of people, we have a "team." Becoming a team requires development. This can start by understanding the roles that various leaders will play on the team. "Types of Leaders" that comprise a leadership team was discussed in Chapter 3, "Leading with QOS." Understanding these types and corresponding roles can begin the development process of moving from a group to a team.

7. Latham, *[Re]Create the Organization You Really Want!*, 36.

8. "Hope for Instant Pudding," attributed to James K. Bakken for the Ford Motor Company, in Deming, *Out of Crisis*, 126.

9. Giselle Abramovich, "If You Think Email Is Dead, Think Again," accessed February 2, 2022, https://business.adobe.com/blog/perspectives/if-you-think-email-is-dead-think-again; "How Leaders Spend Their Time," CMOE, August 22, 2014, https://cmoe.com/blog/how-

leaders-spend-their-time/. These are two recent surveys on the time committed to email communications.

10. Two practical examples are using tenets and a systems map. Leaders may add reviewing decisions to confirm they are incorporating practical values like team-based or ethical behavior. The system map can serve as a tool to support recognizing where work is happening and who is linked to it.

11. Jim Collins, *Good to Great* (London: Random House Business Books, 2001). Josef Penner, former Executive Director of the Mecklenburg EMS Agency, Charlotte, NC, described the "flywheel effect" as an essential ingredient of their QOS journey. No single activity or change was as effective as the daily, cumulative discipline of leading with quality as a strategy. The daily repetitive persistence created a momentum that carried the shift to organizational excellence with QOS.

12. Gareth Parry et al., "Practical Recommendations for the Evaluation of Improvement Initiatives," *International Journal for Quality in Health Care: Journal of the International Society for Quality in Health Care* 30, no. suppl_1 (April 20, 2018): 29–36, https://doi.org/10.1093/intqhc/mzy021.

13. Table 1.5 in Chapter 1 is a tool for leaders to evaluate progress in the organization's building of the QOS system of improvement. *The QOS Field Guide* contains a more comprehensive version of the assessment tool.

14. The x-axis of the scatter plots is the average assessment score. The y-axis is the standard deviation or variation in assessment across the leaders The scale of the axes is adjusted to fit the data. These data are from an organization at the start of their QOS work. None of the averaged scores for the leadership team displayed in figure 11.1 are greater than a four out of a possible ten points.

15. David A. Gavin, "Building a Learning Organization," *Harvard Business Review*, July 1, 1993, https://hbr.org/1993/07/building-a-learning-organization.

16. Senge, *The Fifth Discipline*, 1.

17. Laura C. Leviton et al., "Evaluability Assessment to Improve Public Health Policies, Programs, and Practices," *Annual Review of Public Health* 31, no. 1 (2010): 213–33, https://doi.org/10.1146/annurev.publhealth.012809.103625; Parry et al., "Practical Recommendations for the Evaluation of Improvement Initiatives."

18. David M Williams, "Mr. Potato Head PDSA Exercise." (DMW AUSTIN LLC, 2024), https://www.davidmwilliamsphd.com/resources/pdsa/mr-potato-head/. David M. Williams,

PhD, developed an exercise to teach the plan, do, study, act (PDSA) cycle testing, PDSA documentation, and run charts. Mattel's Mr. Potato Head toy is used, and learners take turns developing change ideas, testing changes, and learning as they work to assemble the toy for time and accuracy.

19. Table 11.2 describes key actions leaders work toward developing and using as they pursue quality as their organizational strategy. These are the typical outputs of each activity.

20. Tokens and badges are common symbols of recognition in games and wearable devices when a user achieves a milestone. For example, a wearable personal information device might notify you when you reach 10,000 steps in a day.

21. The adjective "typical" is used here to mean common for most organizations. It's recommended to begin with the assumption that an organization is typical.

22. The charts are an adaptation of a Gantt or PERT (program evaluation and review technique) chart. The swim lanes reflect the related activities and milestones. The placement from left to right is intended to reflect the typical sequence of the milestones when one milestone precedes another.

23. See the "Reflections from Leaders with Quality as an Organizational Strategy" on page xiii.

24. Collins, *Good to Great*.

SELECTED BIBLIOGRAPHY

Throughout the book, notes at the end of each chapter cite references for key concepts to explore further the ideas presented. The following are key sources behind the development of the QOS framework.

Ackoff, R. L. *Creating the Corporate Future.* New York: John Wiley & Sons, 1981.

Associates in Process Improvement. *Quality as a Business Strategy.* Austin: Associates in Process Improvement, 1998.

Deming, W. Edwards. *Out of the Crisis.* Cambridge: Massachusetts Institute of Technology, Center for Advanced Engineering Study, 1986.

————. *The New Economics for Industry, Government, Education.* Cambridge: Massachusetts Institute of Technology, Center for Advanced Engineering Study, 1993.

Langley, Gerald J., Ronald D. Moen, Kevin M. Nolan, Thomas W. Nolan, Clifford L. Norman, and Lloyd P. Provost. *The Improvement Guide: A Practical Approach to Enhancing Organizational Performance*, 2nd ed. San Francisco: Jossey-Bass, 2009.

Maccoby, Michael, Clifford L. Norman, C. Jane Norman, and Richard Margolies. *Transforming Health Care Leadership: A Systems Guide to Improve Patient Care, Decrease Costs, and Improve Population Health.* San Francisco: Jossey-Bass, 2013.

Moen, Ronald D., Thomas W. Nolan, and Lloyd P. Provost. *Quality Improvement Through Planned Experimentation*, 3rd ed. McGraw-Hill Education, 2012.

Provost, Lloyd P., and Sandy K. Murray. *The Health Care Data Guide: Learning from Data for Improvement,* 2nd ed. San Francisco: Jossey-Bass, 2022.

Senge, Peter M. 1990. *The Fifth Discipline.* New York: Doubleday/Currency.

Weisbord, Marvin R. *Productive Workplaces: Dignity, Meaning, and Community in the 21st Century.* 3rd ed. San Francisco: Jossey-Bass, 2012.

Q

AUTHOR PROFILES

CLIFFORD L. NORMAN

Cliff is an author and international consultant with Associates in Process Improvement (API). He held management and quality positions with Norris Industries, McDonnell Douglas, and Halliburton. Since 1986, Cliff has worked internationally in computer, health care, and manufacturing industries using improvement as a business strategy while developing internal consultants for these organizations.

Norman helps organizations build productive relationships while viewing the organization as a system and helps to develop their use and understanding of analytic statistical methods following the Model for Improvement. As an improvement advisor and faculty member with the Institute for Healthcare Improvement (IHI), Cliff was instrumental in developing and supporting the IHI Improvement Advisor course.

Cliff was one of the developers of the Quality as a Business Strategy (QBS) framework in the 1980s. He has used QBS with clients for more than thirty years. He is also the author of several papers on the Science of Improvement and is a coauthor of *The Improvement Guide*, 2nd Edition and *Transforming Healthcare Leadership*.

Cliff holds a BS in Police Science and Business Administration and an MA in Behavioral Science from California State University. He is a senior member of the American Society for Quality and an ASQ Certified Quality Engineer (CQE). In 2023, he was awarded the American Society for Quality's (ASQ) Deming Medal.

Email: cnorman@apiweb.org
Website: apiweb.org

LLOYD P. PROVOST

Lloyd is a statistician, advisor, teacher, and author who helps organizations make improvements and foster continuous learning and improvement. His experience includes consulting in management systems, planned experimentation, planning, measurement, and other methods for improving quality and productivity. He has consulted with clients worldwide in various industries, including automotive, chemical, construction, education, electronics, engineering, food, government, healthcare, manufacturing, professional services, retail, and transportation. Much of his current work is focused on healthcare improvement in developing countries.

Lloyd was one of the developers of the Quality as a Business Strategy (QBS) framework in the 1980s. He has used QBS with clients for more than 30 years. He is also the author of several papers relating to the Science of Improvement and coauthor of *The Improvement Guide*, 2nd ed., *The Health Care Data Guide*, 2nd ed., and *Quality Improvement Through Planned Experimentation*, 3rd ed.

Lloyd holds a B.S. in Statistics from the University of Tennessee and an M.S. in Statistics from the University of Florida. Currently, he is a senior fellow at the Institute for Healthcare Improvement (IHI) and faculty in the IHI Improvement Advisor Professional Development Program. He also is a senior member of the American Society for Quality and was awarded the American Society for Quality's (ASQ) Deming Medal in 2003.

Email: lprovost@apiweb.org.
Website: apiweb.org

DAVID M. WILLIAMS, PHD

Dave is an advisor and teacher who helps leaders and organizations worldwide improve and enhance their organizational systems. He has worked across sectors including business, education, government, healthcare, and public safety. Much of his work is on building results-driven improvement capability and advising leaders to adopt quality as an organizational strategy (QOS).

As a senior leader at the Institute of Healthcare Improvement (IHI), he was responsible for leadership and improvement science and methods. He previously worked as an organizational systems consultant, a chief quality officer, and a health care board member. He is a subject matter expert on ambulance service delivery systems and a former paramedic.

Dave developed the IHI Chief Quality Officer Professional Development Program and has authored papers and contributed to textbooks on the Science of Improvement and ambulance service. Currently, Dave is a lead faculty member for the IHI Improvement Advisor Professional Development Program. He is also a senior member of the American Society of Quality (ASQ).

Dave holds a BS in Emergency Medical Services Management from Springfield College; an MS in Emergency Health Services Management from the University of Maryland, Baltimore County; and a PhD in Organizational Systems from Saybrook University.

Email: dave@dmwaustin.com
Website: davidmwilliamsphd.com